Alex Vatanka is Senior Fellow at the Middle East Institute and Jamestown Foundation in Washington, DC. A specialist in Middle Eastern geopolitics with a focus on Iran, he was previously the Senior Middle East Analyst at Jane's defence and security group in London.

'Excellent. Vatanka offers timely insights into an important geopolitical relationship that is often overlooked but is critical to understanding some of the key elements that have contributed to relations between Iran, Pakistan and America.'

David Patrikarakos, author of *Nuclear Iran: The Birth of an Atomic State*, I.B.Tauris, 2012

'In tracing the course of Iranian–Pakistani taut relations over nearly seven decades, Vatanka's lively, thoroughly researched book threads together those personalities and events that have shaped two of the most challenging countries faced today by Western policy makers. The book provides for a sound understanding of areas of foreign policy and regional and global alliances that once figured so prominently in the Cold War and also now in the fight against global militant extremism. The Shi'i–Sunni rivalry, regional nuclear proliferation and the American dimension are also illuminated by this book's wide-ranging, engrossing narrative.'

Marvin Weinbaum, Director of the Pakistan Center at Middle East Institute, Washington, DC and Professor Emeritus at the University of Illinois at Urbana-Champaign

'A fascinating and enlightening study of the complex and intricate relationship between two key Islamic states, Iran and Pakistan. This much-neglected connection between the Middle East and South Asia will only become more important in the future. This book explains clearly and cogently why that matters.'

Bruce Riedel, Senior Fellow, Brookings Institution

'This book is a supreme example of all the works so far done on the subject. Vatanka's composition, the sources he has consulted and the ease with which he expresses himself make this a unique task of scholarship.'

R.K. (Ruhi) Ramazani, Edward R. Stettinius Professor Emeritus of Government and Foreign Affairs, University of Virginia

IRAN
AND
PAKISTAN

SECURITY, DIPLOMACY
AND
AMERICAN INFLUENCE

ALEX VATANKA

I.B. TAURIS
LONDON · NEW YORK

To Heidi, Martin, Kathrin and my parents

New paperback edition published in 2017 by
I.B.Tauris & Co. Ltd
London • New York
www.ibtauris.com

First published in hardback in 2015 by I.B.Tauris & Co. Ltd

ISBN: 978 1 78453 690 9
eISBN: 978 0 85773 915 5

A full CIP record for this book is available from the British Library
A full CIP record is available from the Library of Congress

Library of Congress Catalog Card Number: available

Typeset in Garamond Three by OKS Prepress Services, Chennai, India
Printed and bound by CPI Group (UK) Ltd, Croydon, CR0 4YY

CONTENTS

Acknowledgements   vi

Preface to the New Paperback Edition   ix

Introduction   1

1. On the Road to India: Iran's and Pakistan's
   Intertwined History   5

2. 1947–1958: Early Hiccups, as Iran and Pakistan
   Both Look to the US for Protection   12

3. 1958–1965: Regional Turbulence and an Unlikely Union   27

4. 1965–1969: The Northern Tier: A Fluid Fault Line   45

5. 1969–71: Iran's Intervention over the Pakistani Defeat
   of 1971   66

6. 1971–77: The Shah and Pakistan's Reluctant Dependence   82

7. 1977–1988: Zia, the Shah and the Coming of
   the Ayatollah   129

8. The Arrival of the Shi'a–Sunni Schism in Relations   171

9. 1988–2001: Geopolitical Foes, Sometime Partners   195

10. 2001-Present: Afghanistan, the Arab Challenge and Iran's
    Soft Power in Pakistan   226

Epilogue   258

Notes   265

Bibliography   291

Index   296

ACKNOWLEDGEMENTS

In Islamabad, I asked a group of retired Pakistani diplomats about access to the archives at the Foreign Ministry. 'Don't bother inquiring,' one of them replied. I took that to mean that the archives were simply off-limits to outsiders. But he continued. 'What you will find about Pakistani policy deliberations [toward Iran] in the archives in Washington or London are probably more complete than what you will find here,' the former Pakistani ambassador insisted.

As implausible as it sounded at that particular moment, with time and after combing through declassified American and British documents relating to Iranian–Pakistani affairs dating back to the late 1940s, I came to appreciate the sentiment the Pakistani diplomat was conveying. The Iranians and the Pakistanis each have, of course, separate accounts of events relating to seven decades of state-to-state relations. That was not the point.

The point is that Iranian–Pakistani ties, in moments of cooperation or rivalry, have over the years been hugely shaped by their respective attitudes and interests vis-à-vis the Western world. And among Western powers, the Americans and the British have beyond question been the most influential players in this part of the world.

It is in American and British archives one finds important clues or even the missing details that can better explain the actions of Tehran and Islamabad toward each other over the years. The United States in particular has since the mid-1960s been the third and undeniable column in Iranian–Pakistani relations. And where Washington opts to stand on relations between these two countries will continue to be crucial as Iranian–Pakistani relations move forward.

Research projects on political history in Iran and Pakistan, as is the case in most of west Asia, are invariably sensitive. Official archives are mostly not available to unsanctioned outsiders. Personal interviews and memoirs, when possible and available, are therefore critical sources. Accordingly, this book project benefitted greatly from the time and insights of many individuals.

Ardeshir Zahedi was most gracious in hosting me in Montreux. His many years of working with the Pakistanis as foreign minister and as a close confidant of the Shah of Iran made him an invaluable authority. In Washington, Assad Homayoun, a former senior Iranian diplomat from the Shah's era, was most helpful in his suggestions given his postings both in Islamabad and later in Washington.

In Rawalpindi, Islamabad and Lahore, Asad Durrani, Shamshad Ahmad, Talat Masood, Khalid Mahmood, Taqi Bagash, Arif Ayub, Rasul Baksh Rais, Javid Hussain, Massarrat Abid and Asma Khawaja were able to open my eyes, and many doors, to leave me deeply appreciative of the making of Pakistani foreign policy. Thanks also to the Institute of Strategic Studies (Islamabad) for generously hosting me.

In Kabul, Haji Mangal, Davood Moradian and Vahid Mojdeh, gave me important first-hand accounts from the days of Soviet occupation and Taliban rule. Combined they provided me with a strong understanding of the nature of Iranian–Pakistani rivalry on Afghan soil. Thanks also to Shahir Ahmad Zahine, Melek Zahine and Rahim Khan for making my stay in Kabul a fruitful and wonderfully memorable one.

Among Iranians with government experience in the Islamic Republic, Abol-hassan Bani-Sadr, Hossein Mousavian, Abbas Maleki and Ali-Akbar Omid-Mehr deserve my special thanks for the time they took out to speak with me on the various aspects of Iran's foreign policy toward Pakistan and Afghanistan in the post-1979 era.

Among former American officials with a wealth of experience in the region, I am particularly indebted to Michael Metrinko, James Dobbins, Bruce Riedel, Zalmay Khalilzad, Charlie Naas and Jim Placke. Vali R. Nasr, F. Gregory Gause III, Ahmad Kamal, Arif Jamal, Toby Dalton, Yousaf Butt, Ann Wilkens, Vinay Chawla, Rahimullah Yusefzai, Shah Jahan, Ahmad Etmad and David Mack each helped me along the way. Meanwhile, the staff at the offices of the American Institute of Pakistan Studies (AIPS) in Islamabad, the Foundation for Iranian Studies in Maryland and the Library of Congress in Washington were always supportive. At the Jamestown Foundation, I depended faithfully on its president, Glen Howard, and senior fellow Michael Ryan to guide me during the various aspects of writing this book. I stand grateful to them both.

At the Middle East Institute, there is a long list of colleagues who provided insights and advice. In particular, Marvin Weinbaum, a leading scholar on Pakistan, gave me generous and indispensable advice throughout the course of the project. I thank also the institute's president, Wendy Chamberlin, and Kate Seelye and Paul Salem for their continuous encouragement. The wonderful support I received from the many research assistants at MEI also needs to be noted. They all have my sincerest thanks but specially Desiree Bryan, Joshua Lee, Tawab Malekzad, Saher Naumaan, Abduallah Khurram, Munazza Khan, Maria Gaetskaya and Nausheen Rajan.

Afshin Molavi and Karim Sadjadpour never failed to make valuable suggestions and introductions. They and other friends, Michael Rubin, Ali Alfoneh, Mehdi Khalaji, Siamak Dehghanpour, Fatemeh Aman, Meir Javedanfar, Miriam Lanskoy, Richard Kramer, and many others each in their way nudged me along to complete this book.

At I.B.Tauris, I am thankful to publisher Iradj Bagherzade and my editor, Azmina Siddique, for seeing promise in the initial idea and guiding me forward each step of the way.

Last but not least, my deepest thanks to my dear wife Heidi and my darlings, Martin and Kathrin, for all the love and support.

PREFACE TO THE NEW PAPERBACK EDITION

The prevailing literature on the history of Iranian-Pakistani relations includes plenty of routine platitudes. There is a tendency to focus on the romanticized period in relations, the years from Pakistan's independence in 1947 until the fall of Mohammad Reza Pahlavi, the Shah of Iran, in 1979. This era is routinely characterized as the period of brotherly ties and close cooperation in various fields.

And yet closer scrutiny shows that even the earliest years were much more complicated than the standard accounts want us to believe. No doubt, there was an initial desire on both sides for friendship and cooperation, which had certain indisputable bedrocks. The shared geography, including a 909 kilometre common border, and close historic ties between Persia and the subcontinent that had spanned many centuries did undeniably offer a strong foundation for partnership. At the same time, these celebrated commonalities should not be exaggerated.

For example, the oft-cited warm cultural, sectarian and economic ties have in fact never been critical factors in keeping Iran and Pakistan close. That was true even in the heyday of relations in the 1950s and 1960s. Instead, it was the vision of one man, the Shah of Iran, and his fervid fears of Soviet expansion into West Asia that advanced a common Iranian-Pakistani understanding around shared security threats confronting both countries.

Much of the joint efforts against the Soviets paid off, but various historical sources illustrate that even in this context the Iranian-

Pakistani partnership was anything but straightforward. In fact, it was a rollercoaster ride behind the scenes, and one that became considerably more complicated with the coming to power of Ayatollah Khomeini and his Shia Islamist rule from 1979. This book identifies the key turns and twists in relations dating back decades.

The toppling of the Shah at the hands of revolutionaries and the rise of a radical Islamist movement around Ayatollah Khomeini had massively alarmed Iran's Sunni Arab neighbours but at first had little impact on Pakistan's bottom line. During the Iran-Iraq War (1980–88), when the Arab states of the Persian Gulf were bankrolling the military efforts of Iraq's Saddam Hussein and imploring Islamabad to abandon Iran, the Pakistanis were undeterred. The Pakistani military dictator, Muhammad Zia-ul-Haq, the architect of Sunnification policies at home, paid lip service to Sunni Arab calls but in practice opened the port of Karachi to Iran so that its international trade traffic was protected from the Iraqi air force, which was targeting Iranian ports. In this period, Pakistani-Iranian trade thrived and yet Islamabad succeeded in calming Arab displeasure. Later on, in the late 1980s and the 1990s, top officials in Islamabad approved and actively assisted Tehran's then-emergent nuclear ambitions. In other words, in its dealings with Tehran, Islamabad struck a sensitive balance, and it paid off.

As of 2016, Iranian and Pakistani relations were again at an important juncture. In June 2013, Hassan Rouhani, a cleric running on a political platform of moderation and compromise, was elected as Iran's president. By July 2015, Tehran and the world powers had negotiated a deal that would significantly curb Iran's controversial nuclear programme in exchange for an end to nuclear-related sanctions that the United Nations had imposed on Tehran from 2006 onwards. Suddenly Iran was about to return to the international mainstream, and hundreds of foreign delegations would soon arrive in Tehran looking for political deals and economic and trade opportunities.

Nawaz Sharif, the Pakistani prime minister, was among them but Pakistan's options vis-à-vis Iran were still hugely complicated by one factor: Saudi Arabia. Riyadh, in its escalated regional competition for influence with Iran since the Arab Revolutions of 2011 broke out, was actively courting Islamabad to join hands with the Saudis to confront Iran and her regional allies. In the eyes of Saudi Arabia, Pakistan, which is home to the world's second-largest Muslim population and is the only nuclear-armed Islamic country, provides much needed critical mass in its efforts against Tehran. Pakistan, however, wavered.

Pakistan has frequently been forced to have to pick between the Iranians and the Arabs. More often than not, Islamabad has managed to come out of it unscathed. In fact, it has repeatedly benefited from being courted by both sides. Today, Pakistan has much closer ties to the Arab countries of the Persian Gulf and particularly Saudi Arabia, home to millions of Pakistani expatriates and a source of subsidized oil and other financial incentives. But Iran is a large immediate neighbour and a nuclear-threshold state looking to surface from years of international isolation. These realities force Islamabad to give Iran another look as it weighs Saudi requests for support.

In the end, Nawaz Sharif opted to pledge neutrality in this Iranian-Saudi competition. Instead, he vowed publicly that Islamabad was prepared to act as a mediator between Tehran and Riyadh. This simple blueprint, tried-and-tested for some 50 years, will guide Pakistani decisions in the foreseeable future in this biggest of regional power clashes.

That Pakistan does not want to become yet another regional victim of a nasty Iranian-Saudi power struggle is entirely fathomable. Today, sectarianism is the foremost scourge on Pakistani society. Given its huge population of around 190 million people, with a roughly 80 to 20 percent Sunni-Shi'a split, Islamabad has to do everything in its power to prevent the country becoming even more of a battleground for sectarian competition fuelled by Iran and Saudi Arabia. As it has done so many times before, Islamabad will seek to mollify the concerns of both Tehran and Riyadh, but without falling victim to their cold war for regional supremacy.

On the other hand, the question of Afghanistan's future has the potential to put Iran and Pakistan on a direct collision course. The 1990s witnessed an intense proxy conflict on Afghan soil with each side supporting rival Afghan factions. This quest for influence in Afghanistan can reemerge with a vengeance particularly if the Western powers decide to pull away from that country.

Still, the greatest impediment is that neither Iran nor Pakistan has the other as part of its top-tier foreign policy agenda. It is almost as if managed tension is the best that can be hoped for in the bilateral relations. Structural roadblocks are an important constraint. It is the two countries' respective security and intelligence agencies – and not the foreign ministries – that are the dominant actors in shaping policy toward each other. This in turn makes security-centric considerations dominate the conversation.

In comparison, trade and economic cooperation are almost entirely absent from the bilateral discourse in any meaningful way despite ample rhetorical pledges. Among its immediate neighbours, Iran today trades least with Pakistan, which happens to be by far its biggest neighbour with a 190 million strong market. What history demonstrates is that it is cold and tactical geopolitical calculations that will fashion Tehran and Islamabad's approach to each other in the foreseeable future. In doing so, the huge potential for much broader and multifaceted relations will be left unexplored. To undo this reality, however, plenty of mistrust that continues to exist first needs to be broken and that above all requires political foresight in Tehran and Islamabad.

Washington D.C.

INTRODUCTION

In October 2014, Iran and Pakistan engaged in yet another round of border skirmishes. In pursuit of anti-Tehran Sunni militants who had carried out attacks inside Iran, Iranian security forces unilaterally crossed the international border, leading to clashes and the death of a Pakistani soldier. The situation rapidly escalated when the Pakistani side returned Iranian mortar fire in kind. Over the last decade, such skirmishes between the two countries have become commonplace; however, this was the first time that the Pakistanis had returned fire. For a moment, it looked as if the two largest countries of west Asia were at a tipping point.

On the face of it, the potential consequences looked dire if Iran and Pakistan did not promptly end the hostilities. Pakistan is, after all, a nuclear-armed state; Iran is a nuclear-threshold state. The sizes of the conventional military forces of each country rank among the top ten globally, with Pakistan and Iran armed with 642,000 and 523,000 men respectively.

And yet, the international community barely registered these Iranian–Pakistani skirmishes. The world has become uncannily accustomed to periodic scuffles between Iran and Pakistan on a border that cuts through the divided Baluchistan – a region that has long been beset by ethnic unrest, smuggling and militancy, and which is a playing field for a host of intelligence services.

In fact, the Iranians and the Pakistanis themselves have largely adapted to these cyclical shoot-outs and fundamental strains in relations. On the one hand, the record of the last decade shows that neither Tehran nor Islamabad likes to see this border violence spiral out of control. And yet, on the other, each side has seemingly accepted limited and localized hostilities as part of their relationship – that is, as long as the violence can be contained, a dangerous and potentially a very costly assumption to make.

To better appreciate this posture, one has to consider the regional context. The truth is that Pakistan is still by and large obsessed with India to its east and, to a lesser degree, with Afghanistan to its north. Islamabad does not want to open a new front to its west against Iran. The Iranians, for their part, are not prioritizing relations with their large and nuclear-armed eastern neighbour. Tehran is still predominantly occupied with handling its interests and relations in the Arab world and with Western countries.

Resigned acceptance of this tormented state of affairs continues to mark Iranian–Pakistani relations. Following the October 2014 border skirmishes, Sartaj Aziz, the top foreign-policy and national security advisor to Pakistani Prime Minister Nawaz Sharif, merely called the incidents 'very unfortunate'. Aziz then suggested that better border control would alleviate problems in relations. This announcement was tantamount to an epic understatement of the complexities and regional competition that, in essence, lies at the heart of relations. Official Iranian statements that downplay the underlying frictions are equally disingenuous. This is a reality that belies the oft-touted notion of Iran's and Pakistan's relations as 'brotherly'.

To find a time when relations were brotherly in a genuine sense, one has to travel decades back in time. In fact, the golden period of Iranian–Pakistani relations lay in the formative years of Pakistan, after it was born following India's partition in 1947. Since then, at least in Iranian eyes, Pakistan has moved from first being considered a close ally to becoming a buffer state, and finally ending up as a rival and a threat that has to be contained. For the Pakistanis, Iran was once an important benefactor and Tehran a key conduit to the West. Iran's 1979 revolution changed all that, and turned it into an erratic player whose often pariah status massively diminished its usefulness as a neighbour and partner.

A friendship that withered with time

In the totality of Iranian–Pakistani relations over the course of their history, the evolution of one man's opinions epitomizes the reasons behind the ups and downs in relations over the years. That man was Mohammad Reza Pahlavi, the Shah of Iran from 1941 to his downfall in 1979.

The Shah set out with a heightened degree of excitement when Pakistan was first born in 1947. For him, Pakistan was Iran's wild eastern frontier, a shaky young nation with multitude of ethnic, religious and social fault lines, and a tantalizing target for Soviet machinations. In fact, preventing Moscow's creeping influence in Pakistan was a primary objective of the fiercely anti-communist Shah. He also happened to believe that instability and political turmoil in the east would inevitably spill over into Iran itself.

For the Shah, Pakistan over the years morphed into a critical buffer zone, a line of defence against not only the Soviets but also the then Soviet-leaning India. And he mostly considered Pakistan as an inevitable partner in keeping their nearby common neighbour, Afghanistan, stable, intact and safe from a Soviet takeover. This was certainly how successive Pakistani governments perceived the Shah's policy towards their country.

The former Pakistani president, Yahya Khan, once said that the Shah had been categorical in declaring: 'Pakistan's security is my [Iran's] security.' But it was the same Yahya Khan who, in the 1960s, inadvertently set in motion a process that would begin the drift in relations. And yet, to blame personalities alone for the ups and downs in relations would be an analytical mistake. Neither country has ever genuinely considered optimum relations as an end in itself. For both Iran and Pakistan, bilateral closeness was always meant to reap something strategically larger.

Rivals in all but name

In the context of the Cold War and his staunch anti-communism, the Shah needed the political backing and military support of the United States to be able to resist the mighty Soviet Union that straddled Iran's northern borders. Only Washington could underwrite anti-Soviet efforts in south-west Asia. But Iran's regional allies – including Pakistan, which was a top-tier partner – also played a critical role in the Shah's mind in rolling back the potential of Soviet expansionism.

Nonetheless, the America–Iran–Pakistan triangle against the Soviets – and, at times, the Indians – was anything but straightforward or continually benevolent. In fact, Iran and Pakistan have, over the years, often found themselves competing to outdo each other in attempting to appeal to Washington. That was certainly the case before Iran's revolution of 1979, but traces of this tendency lingered even after the anti-American Islamists took power in Tehran. Iranian–Pakistani rivalry for influence in Afghanistan since the 1980s best illustrates this nearly forgotten reality.

In the early 1970s, the geopolitical equilibrium in south-west Asia was endangered by a unilateral Pakistani decision to dash for the nuclear bomb. The Shah had nuclear ambitions of his own, but he nonetheless argued that such an overt move by Pakistan would undermine broader regional interests that Tehran and Islamabad shared. However, the Iranian monarch's appeal to the then Pakistani leader, Zulfikar Bhutto, fell on deaf ears. The two men had once had a close friendship, one dating back many years, but it included a jealousy and rivalry between these, the leaders of south-west Asia's two largest countries. Each man wanted his country to be the pre-eminent regional power.

In hindsight, the July 1977 military coup in Islamabad that removed Bhutto from power, combined with the fall of the Shah in Tehran in February 1979, ushered in an entirely new era in Iranian–Pakistani relations. The first two decades of bilateral relations had been rather close, sometimes exemplary in their neighbourly cooperation. Tehran had taken much pride in the fact that it was the first capital to recognize the nascent Pakistani state after it was born, a gratification that endured over the years even as geopolitics ultimately put the two countries on different paths. The coming to power of a Shi'a theocracy in Tehran in 1979 merely added layers of complexity to this already manifold and entangled relationship.

The intimacy that distinguished relations in the early years reflects the many linkages between the two countries. Shamshad Ahmad, a former Pakistani ambassador to Tehran and foreign secretary, highlighted three factors that underpinned relations. 'The Iran-Pakistan relationship,' he says, 'has largely been shaped by geography, history and culture.'[1] There are indeed many who consider Pakistan to sit on a civilizational fault line in south-west Asia, where the Persian and Indian civilizations meet. But rivalry is arguably the fourth, and most undeniable, factor that has shaped Iranian–Pakistani relations, as each country has set out to become the dominant power in this western corner of Asia.[2]

CHAPTER 1

ON THE ROAD TO INDIA: IRAN'S AND PAKISTAN'S INTERTWINED HISTORY

The extent of Iran's once significant standing in Pakistani society is still evident in a multitude of aspects of life in that country, ranging from language and culture to religion and even its basic expression of nationhood. Pakistan's national anthem, 'Qaumi Taranah', is almost entirely written not in Urdu but in the Persian language. The anthem was officially adopted in 1954, at a time when Pakistanis were still busy establishing the basic structures of a nation state following independence from Great Britain in 1947.

In May 1949, Iran became the first United Nations member to recognize Pakistan's independence. In March 1950, the Shah of Iran became the first foreign head of state to visit the new country, and it was for his visit that the Pakistani national anthem had been hurriedly completed. Shortly before, on 18 May 1950, the Iran–Pakistan Friendship Treaty had been signed in Iran.[1]

Over the course of the next 29 years while he was Iran's absolute ruler, the Shah, would devote considerable attention to Pakistan. Within the Pakistani political elite, the Iranian monarch found plenty of admiration for his country but also high hopes for regional collaboration and receptiveness to Tehran's overtures. These included an acceptance of the Shah as a dependable and resourceful mediator when Pakistan faced down challenges from what it saw as two bothersome neighbours, Afghanistan and India.[2]

Iranian diplomatic cables from the late 1940s shed light on the extent to which newborn Pakistan looked to Iran for guidance. One dated 13 September 1947 describes a request by the Pakistani parliament for 'a book or any papers about [the] constitutional laws of Iran'. The Iranian diplomatic transcripts show that the Pakistanis 'wanted to prepare the correct [constitutional] laws', and hence they looked to Tehran for advice and as a model.[3]

Early defining personal ties

In those early days following Pakistan's independence, personal relations between the leaders of the two countries were also a major diplomatic factor. Iskander Ali Mirza, the first president of Pakistan, in many ways epitomized the elite-to-elite friendship that characterized ties.

Born into a prominent Bengali feudal family in then East Pakistan [now Bangladesh], Mirza belonged to the Shi'a branch of Islam, which is the majority religion in Iran. In fact, the founder of Pakistan, Mohammad Ali Jinnah (*Quaid-i-Azam*, or Great Leader), was himself a member of Pakistan's minority Shi'a population – albeit of a 'heterodox' kind.[4] If solely based on the sectarian background of key personalities, then the early post-independence period in Pakistan can be termed the 'heyday' of the country's minority Shi'a elite. But in those days sectarianism in Pakistani society between the majority Sunni and the minority Shi'a Muslims was nowhere near the dividing factor that it is today.

Mirza had other ties to Iran. His second marriage was to an Iranian woman, Nahid Afghamy. Nahid had been the wife of Colonel Mehdi Afghamy, the Iranian defence attaché in Karachi.[5] She was also the daughter of Amir Teymour Kalali, a highly respected Iranian politician who first came to prominence in the 1930s when he was elected to Iran's national parliament.[6] She fell in love with Mirza after meeting him in the early 1950s, and the two subsequently wed in 1954. The beautiful Nahid was the cousin of Nusrat Ispahani, who would herself later marry another future leader of Pakistan, Zulfikar Bhutto.[7]

Nusrat might have followed in the footsteps of her distant cousin by marrying into the Pakistani elite political class, but her political stature in her own right would eventually reach unprecedented heights. With her husband's execution in 1979 at the hands of Zia ul-Haq, Nusrat would become the matriarch of the Bhutto political dynasty, which to this day plays one of the most prominent roles in Pakistani politics through its command of the Pakistan People's Party, one of the country's principal political movements.

The two beautiful cousins were members of an Iranian merchant community with a long history on the Indian subcontinent, including a prominent presence in those regions that later emerged to make up the state of Pakistan. Nusrat's Kurdish–Iranian parents had migrated to Bombay from Persia, as Iran was known then, and she was born in British-controlled India on 23 March 1929. In Bombay, Nusrat's early childhood would be passed in a city where many Iranian Shi'a businessmen had, from the mid-nineteenth century onwards, settled down and produced notable families such as the Shirazi, Namazi, Shustri, Yazdi and Ispahani. They became noted patrons of religious life there, and some scholars consider them pioneers in the growth of Shi'ism in western India.[8]

When Hindu–Muslim communal violence erupted following the departure of the British from India in 1947, Nusrat's father was unnerved by the death of a number of Iranian Muslim friends in Bombay. He opted to give up the family's lucrative soap factory and subsequently resettled in Karachi, the 'City of Lights' and the first capital of the new Muslim-majority state of Pakistan.[9] They thrived in their new homeland, and the Ispahanis rose to become one of Pakistan's leading families.

The legacy of Persian conquests

The flow of ideas, people and trade between Persia and the Indian subcontinent dates back millennia. A considerable amount of this intertwined history is still readily visible in everyday life across the subcontinent. War and Persian conquest also played an important role in shaping perceptions.

Mohammad Reza Pahlavi's own beloved Peacock Throne was war booty from India. In the spring of 1739, the Persian Nader Shah sacked Delhi at the Battle of Karnal and looted a vast part of the treasures of the Mughal Dynasty, including the 'fabled Peacock Throne and the Kuh-I Nur [Mountain of Light] diamond'.[10] For the Iranians, Nader Shah's swift defeat of Muhammad Shah, the Indian Mughal Emperor, became a national legend that still stands. For the peoples of the subcontinent, that momentous battle passed into the popular psyche as a moment of national humiliation.

Persia's infatuation with the Indian subcontinent has an equally long track record. Over two centuries before Mohammad Reza Pahlavi championed the idea of an economic union of Indian Ocean rim countries, with Iran and India at its heart, Nader Shah is said to have forced a marriage between his son and the daughter of Muhammad Shah to sustain a 'treaty of union', which he was pressing on the Indians.[11]

But the 'tyrannies and cruelties of Nader Shah' had greatly upset the Indians, and the idea of a union did not outlast the withdrawal of his army from India.[12] The gate where the Battle of Karnal took place would for centuries be known as *Darvazhi-khun* (Gateway of Blood), and in India the term 'Nader Shah' became synonymous with 'massacre'.

While the swords of the Persian conqueror's army were resented, India could not, over the centuries, resist Persia's soft-power reach. In his fascinating study, Juan Cole points out that at one stage there were perhaps seven times more Persian readers in India than were in Persia itself. Cole notes that:

> the centrality of the Persian language to chancery and bureaucratic practice in South Asia contributed to the creation of a large Persophone population which would transmit Iranian cultural achievements in poetry, philosophy, theology, mysticism, art, travel accounts, technology ethics, statecraft, and many other fields from one area to the other.[13]

Historically, the Persian-speaking heartland in pre-Partition India comprised the coastal regions of Sindh adjacent to the Indian Ocean running north to today's modern Pakistani city of Multan.[14] The rulers of the Mughal Empire had made Persian the official language of their court. Its use at official levels began to decline only after the British colonial power in 1843 made English the official language of its Indian colony.

Persian expatriates

Not only their ideas and influence but Iranians themselves have, through the centuries, emigrated in large numbers to the subcontinent.[15]

According to Cole, 'because of the ways in which [the Muslim Iranians] could rise high in Indian Muslim courts, these Iranian migrants played a significant role in Indian political and economic life'.[16]

Over the last five centuries, Iranians have left Persia for the Indian subcontinent for various reasons. Some did so in order to find economic opportunities, while others sought religious freedom in India. From the early sixteenth century, when the Safavid Dynasty took power in Persia and zealously adopted and enforced Shi'a Islam as the official faith, many Persian Sunni Muslims chose to settle in India.[17]

But not all Persian immigrants to India in this period were Sunnis. One prominent religious leader who settled in India was the Aga Khan, the spiritual leader of the Ismaili Muslims, a small sect of Shi'a Islam. In 1843, after an unsuccessful rebellion against the Qajar rulers, the first Aga Khan moved from Persia to Bombay. His grandchild, Sir Sultan Muhammad Shah, or Aga Khan III, would in 1908 become one of the founders and the first president of the All-India Muslim League, and the movement would by 1947 ultimately establish the independent and Muslim-majority state of Pakistan.[18]

Persian Shi'a immigrants in India in the sixteenth and seventeenth centuries were not only sought after as advisors but 'played a key role, both in founding new [local] dynasties in South Asia and in encouraging the conversion of newly established regional rulers [to Shi'ism]'.[19] From Bengal in the east to Kashmir and Punjab in the west, many landed nobles on the subcontinent converted to Shi'ism – an act emulated in many cases by the peasants who lived on the lands of their overlords.[20] Feudal landed Shi'a families in Pakistan today include those of former President Asif Ali Zardari and of his deceased wife, former Prime Minister Benazir Bhutto.

The legacy of these conversions is evident in the estimates of the size of Shi'a populations in India and Pakistan. In the case of India, the Shi'a population is today estimated at some 24 million from the total Indian Muslim population of some 161 million people.[21] In Pakistan, Shi'as are estimated to make up about 20 per cent of the population (35 million) of some 180 million people. Only in Iran can one find a larger Shi'a population than those in India or Pakistan.[22]

The historical affinities and present-day statistics reflect more than merely the religious legacy of the subcontinent's centuries-long interaction with Persia. The Islamist regime that took over the reins of power in Tehran in 1979 has had a particular political interest in cultivating the Shi'a communities of the subcontinent, and especially those found in Pakistan, as conduits for expanding its influence.

Ties born in the shadow of the Cold War

However, it was during the rule of the Shah of Iran, which spanned the period from 1941 to 1979, that Iran's modern relations with Pakistan took shape. The policy legacy from this era still lives on more than three decades after the fall of the Shah. During his reign, Tehran's top priority was to keep the Soviet threat at bay in south-west Asia. That overriding objective informed the bulk of Iranian calculations involving Pakistan for decades. On the question of Pakistan's future and independence, the Shah was even willing to raise the stakes in the shifting geopolitical environment of his time. He would repeatedly come to Pakistan's rescue, but over the years his doubts about the country built up.

Islamabad's defeat in the 1971 Indian–Pakistani war and the loss of East Pakistan (which emerged as Bangladesh) particularly alarmed the Shah, and made him acutely aware of Pakistan's many predicaments and its colossal needs as Islamabad faced the Soviet-leaning Indians. The Shah would become gravely concerned that Pakistan could simply fall apart as a nation state, and thus weaken the anti-Soviet forces in south-west Asia.

In December 1971, as Pakistan's military defeat at the hands of the Indians had become a certainty, the Shah proclaimed in reference to Pakistan that a 'weak ally often turned out to be a burden'. The British, the former colonial power on the subcontinent, shared his analysis and concerns, which undoubtedly heartened the Iranian ruler who considered Western backing pivotal in keeping the rest of Pakistan from disintegrating.[23] Over the next few years, the Shah often had the fate of Pakistan as a key item on his foreign policy agenda.

In a July 1973 meeting with US Secretary of State Henry Kissinger at Blair House in Washington, DC, the Shah was categorical. He said he had informed the Soviet leadership about Iran's 'commitment to Pakistan's security'. Kissinger was informed that the Shah had told the Indians too that 'that an attack on Pakistan would involve Iran', and that Iran would 'go to Pakistan's aid'.[24]

Iran, the Shah said, 'could not tolerate the [further] disintegration of Pakistan'. Meanwhile, the United States played a prominent role in his thinking on the defence of Pakistan. This led the Shah to tell Kissinger that 'It is in the interest of Pakistan to have US moral support and Iranian physical support', by which he meant military supplies.

As the Pakistani author Hafeez Malik has put it, the Shah had by this time 'developed a paternalistic attitude towards Pakistan'.[25] But this attitude had been long in the making. From the moment that bilateral relations were first established, the two nations had developed disproportionately. Iran's star had risen, overwhelmingly thanks to the influx of petrodollars and what they would enable the country to achieve at home and abroad.

In turn, Pakistan was in a state of trepidation. By the time the Shah spoke to Kissinger in 1973, the Iranian monarch more or less saw himself as the benefactor of Pakistan, the troubled neighbour that needed Tehran's sponsorship for its survival. The Pakistanis were well aware of this sentiment, and deeply resented it. And yet, geography, geopolitics and US influence kept Tehran and Islamabad close to each other. It was only after Iran's 1979 revolution that this basic balance was broken.

CHAPTER 2

1947-1958: EARLY HICCUPS, AS IRAN AND PAKISTAN BOTH LOOK TO THE US FOR PROTECTION

The standard narrative is that Iranian–Pakistani relations were at the outset innocent and brotherly, and that ties became complicated only over time. This, however, is true only to an extent. Declassified records show that the earliest Iranian and Pakistani governmental exchanges were wrought with a combination of official inexperience and caution, and that the presumed innocence in the early years of their relationship is more myth than reality.

Perhaps nothing exemplifies this better than the debacle surrounding the framing and signing of the Iran–Pakistan Friendship Treaty in 1949-50. This agreement was supposed to quickly bring the two countries closer, but it ended up nearly derailing relations before they had even had a chance to develop.

Apprehensive neighbours

In early 1949, the Iranians asked the Pakistanis for a 'friendship treaty', a request which the Pakistanis were 'anxious to comply with' but were unsure about how to proceed.[1] Pakistani Foreign Minister Mohammad Ikramullah turned to the country's former colonial masters, and asked London for an 'educational note' on how to go about drafting such an accord.

If the Pakistanis were unaware of procedure and protocol, the reservations on the Iranian side were even graver. Iran opted to go through London even though it was the Pakistanis it was attempting to befriend.[2] Two years after Pakistan's independence, Tehran evidently still believed that London continued to call the shots. This was a reading that, when they discovered it, hugely upset the Pakistanis.

At the heart of the matter was an Iranian fear of infringing on British sensitivities. The British Embassy in Tehran informed London that the 'Persian government has privately informed us that it is thinking of a friendship treaty with Pakistan' but that the Iranians were 'anxious [that they] might do anything that would be out of keeping with Pakistan's dominion status' in the context of the country's position as a former British colony and a Commonwealth member. The embassy continued: 'The Iranian Foreign Undersecretary feels for some reason that it is preferable to ask us [Britain] rather than the Pakistan Embassy for advice.'

When the authorities in Pakistan found out, they were furious. The angry line from Karachi was that 'Pakistan has already entered treaties [. . .] without the [British] King's authority', that 'no other government has raised this question before' and that 'Pakistan is surprised that of them all, Persia should see fit to stand on a point of trivial technicality'.[3] But for the Iranians, whatever impacted Britain's interests was anything but trivial. Seen from Tehran at the time, the power of the British Empire, even after it had withdrawn from the Indian subcontinent in 1947, still loomed much larger than any hopes for friendship with the nascent Pakistani state.

Indeed, the Iranians were far from irrational in their views. This perception of the British, the 'cunning fox' as Persian lexis would have it, was undeniably fair if British behaviour in the region is considered through a historical lens.

In the period from roughly the 1850s to the 1950s, the British had been intimately involved in Iran's political and economic life, and had profoundly affected the country's political landscape. In southern Iran, the region adjacent to the British-controlled Indian subcontinent, London's political sway had long been unrivalled.[4]

Tehran was not blind to the potential upset that its circuitous approach caused to relations with Pakistan. The Iranian official in charge of drafting the friendship treaty, Deputy Foreign Minister

Ali-Gholi Ardalan, was dealing with the British and repeatedly asked them to 'keep their conversations away from the Pakistanis'.[5] This saga continued for almost a year. Outwardly it appeared to be so much needless fuss, as at stake was merely a diplomatic nicety in the shape of a friendship treaty. But the Pakistanis certainly did not see it that way.

The demand by the Iranian side was in effect calling into question independent Pakistan's status as a sovereign entity. Karachi wanted a 'state-to-state agreement'. Tehran wanted 'an inter-governmental agreement' that would avoid the question of whether the British king was the ultimate head of state of Pakistan since the country was a member of the Commonwealth. The Pakistanis rejected the Iranian proposal out of hand, as it basically called into question the nation's hard-earned sovereignty and its capacity to act on its own. This, the Iranians at the time either did not comprehend or did not respect.

Britain was anything but an impartial party in this debacle, its actions being far from those of an independent arbiter. For London, as diplomatic correspondence shows, there were fears about the broader ramifications of the Iran–Pakistan Friendship Treaty. British cables from London instructed staff in embassies in Tehran and Karachi that 'the point at issue raises delicate questions on which the Commonwealth Relations Office are finding difficulty in forming a considered view'. Elsewhere, it was acknowledged by the British Foreign Office that London 'fully understood why Pakistan would resent having the British King George have to seal the treaty with its Muslim neighbour to the east'. Nonetheless, the point was repeated that only the British King, George VI, could be signatory to such a friendship pact, and that this matter went beyond the mandate of the native Pakistanis.[6]

This was a shining example of how the British were having a difficult time moving on from the role of colonial power. London thought that it 'would be a pity to allow a precedent to become established', given that other former colonies were observing from the sidelines. Instead, the British asked the 'confused' Pakistanis to be careful that their actions 'might not be construed as discourteous to the King', and warned that the treaty 'might not be recognized internationally'.

In all this, the British tone was supremely patronizing. In one of the cables, the Commonwealth Relations Office issued a statement:

If they [Pakistan] were determined to go their own way, and for example have the Governor-General [of Pakistan] make the treaty in his name without reference to the King, we could not stop them, but it should be possible to make it clear that we wished to offer advice not with any desire to restrict Pakistan's freedom of action but merely in order to explain certain aspects of treaty procedures with which the Pakistan authorities are perhaps unfamiliar.[7]

In the end, after much hesitation, wariness and aggravation, a treaty of friendship between Iran and Pakistan was finally signed in May 1950. In retrospect, it is not the treaty itself that is memorable. Instead, it is the uncomfortable process leading to the document's ratification, which tells us that the earliest Iranian–Pakistani official contacts were hugely afflicted by awkward uncertainties about what each side wanted and expected from the other.

However, Iran–Pakistan relations would, shortly thereafter, be streamlined. In 1956, a new Pakistani constitution was adopted that ended the country's status as an independent dominion of the British Empire. Tehran no longer needed to play so deferentially to British sensitivities in regards to its dealings with the Pakistanis.

Pakistan became a parliamentary republic, and was henceforth known as the Islamic Republic of Pakistan. Adopting the designation 'Islamic Republic' turned out to be a symbolic act, aimed at fostering a sense of national identity among Pakistan's myriad ethnic groups, all of whom adhere to some branch of Islam. Islam was thus the 'lowest common denominator', but Islamist policies would not be pursued in the country with any great zeal until the arrival of General Zia ul-Haq in 1977. The period from 1956 until Zia's arrival on the scene would come to be seen as epitomizing the heyday of relations between Iran and Pakistan.

The anti-Soviet platform

Throughout the 1950s, relations grew closer. In March 1956, the two countries signed a cultural agreement and in 1957 an air-travel agreement was penned. But arguably the most important move of the decade came on 6 February 1958 when, after two years of negotiations, Tehran and Islamabad were finally able to agree on their common border.

This rugged, 909-km-long frontier had been defined during the years 1870-2 by the Anglo–Perso–Afghan Commission under the leadership of Sir Frederic J. Goldsmid, the British commissioner given the job of demarking Persia's borders with British-controlled India and Afghanistan. At the signing of the new Iranian–Pakistani border treaty, the British Foreign Office commented that, as in the 1870s, it had taken some two years of negotiations to agree on the border and that despite all this latest efforts the 'Goldsmid frontier had only slightly changed'.[8]

For the Pakistanis, however, the 1958 border deal with Iran was a crucial step. Since the country's inception in 1947, disputed international boundaries had been a critical factor that continuously undermined Pakistan's well-being. To its east lay the dispute with India over Kashmir, over which the two countries first went to war in 1948 and then subsequently in 1965 and 1999. To its north, the Afghans have never accepted the Afghan–Pakistani border as legitimate. To be able to finalize the border with Iran as early as 1958 created breathing room for the young nation of Pakistan. The agreement has never since been called into question by either side.

The American factor

Thanks to such efforts and progress, high-level contacts continued to blossom. But as the Iranian–Pakistani relationship evolved during the Shah's era, it steadily became much more of a friendship guided by the Shah, who, with his geopolitical considerations, acted as the driver, shaping ties between the two nations. The role of the United States also proved to be significant, as events in the 1950s and 1960s soon demonstrated.

At this time in Tehran, geopolitics meant only one thing: fearing Moscow and preparing a line of defence against the Soviet Union. The Shah had good reason to fear the Soviets: his own throne was at stake in the matter, something he was keenly aware of. During World War II, some 60,000 Soviet troops had occupied vast regions in Iran's northwest, some as close as two hours' drive from Tehran itself.

In 1945-6, barely five years into his reign, the Soviets had instigated ethnic rebellions in Iran's northern and western provinces of Azarbaijan and Kurdistan and helped establish local communist puppet states that sought separation from Iran.[9] Joseph Stalin's Soviet troops finally withdraw from Iran in April 1946, but with notable reluctance and only after much prodding by the United States.[10] Fear about the Soviets, however, would remain a continual – albeit fluctuating – feature of the Shah's 37-year reign.

The Shah's zeal to confront the Soviet Union was of course wholeheartedly embraced and nurtured by successive American presidents. Immediately after World War II, US presidents Harry Truman and Dwight Eisenhower lay the foundations for both Iran and Pakistan to become the pro-US pillars that would act as a wall against the spread of Soviet communism.[11] American expressions of political support for the anti-Soviet leaders of Iran and Pakistan would become a fixed feature of Washington's approach to this part of the world even though more often than not US material support – particularly military supplies and financial aid – fell short of the expectations of both the Iranians and the Pakistanis. This would prove highly frustrating over the years, but the Pakistanis felt particularly slighted.

While the US military footprint in Iran dated back to the early 1940s, when the first batch of American military advisors arrived to train the Shah's armed forces, the country was not at the time bound by any formal regional defence or security mechanism.

To its west, Iran's neighbour Turkey had since 1952 been part of NATO. To its east, Pakistan had in September 1954 joined the South East Asia Treaty Organization (SEATO). This was NATO's sister organization – albeit a rather dysfunctional sibling – in east and south Asia. The 'odd one out' was Iran. As one US diplomat deployed to the region at the time recalls: 'If [the US] managed to get Iran involved, we would have a complete containment policy along the borders of the Soviet Union.'[12]

Iran's absence from a regional defence club was soon rectified, and in 1954 Iran, Pakistan and Turkey signed an agreement to increase security cooperation among pro-US states in south-west Asia. The United States had at first preferred to include Israel and the Arab states in such a regional mechanism. That turned out to be an impossible task as the Arab–Israeli conflict proved an insurmountable stumbling block.

Moreover, many of the Arab leaders of this era looked at such pro-Western collective efforts as nothing more than a sly attempt to prolong Western domination of the broader Middle East. The Egyptians and the Saudis were also worried that the emergence of such Western-led treaties would stand in the way of the then-nascent Arab League, which had been established by six Arab countries in 1945. Given these common sentiments found in the broader Middle East, the US press – as early as 1954 – reported that the idea of a Middle Eastern defence organization was 'dead, mainly because of Arab opposition'.[13]

Instead, Washington nudged and was able to convince the authorities in Baghdad, Tehran, Istanbul and Karachi (which was Pakistan's capital until 1958, when the seat of government moved to the newly built Islamabad) to come together.

At a meeting in February 1955 in Baghdad, Turkey and Iraq first signed the charter that would become the foundation for 'mutual cooperation' and the left the door open to other states to join. Within months, Iran, Pakistan and the United Kingdom had signed up. The organization would at first be called the 'Baghdad Pact'. It would later be renamed the Central Treaty Organization (CENTO).

The earliest expectations turned out to be somewhat lofty – and not because this was an unprecedented case of regional security collaboration. Already in July 1937, Iran, Iraq, Turkey and Afghanistan had signed the Saadabad Agreement, a non-aggression treaty that also stipulated security cooperation. The Baghdad Pact was different because it leaped from a mandate of preventing aggression among member states to establishing a collective defence against other parties. That notion of collective defence would prove highly elusive and, in the end, would be the treaty's undoing.

One of the pact's key planners, John Foster Dulles, the US secretary of state from 1953 to 1959, famously dubbed this the 'Northern Tier', a barrier to defend against the Soviets. Dulles, a stern personality of strict Presbyterian upbringing, had emerged as one of his era's most prominent voices in the US foreign-policy community. He had also been one of the chief architects of SEATO. Now, as he saw it, the Baghdad Pact 'was the bridge in the containment policy the United States was following at the time between NATO in the west and SEATO in the east'.[14]

Dulles knew the Shah very well, and some would probably argue that the Iranian king partly owed his throne to the Dulles family from Watertown in upstate New York. In August of 1953, John and his brother Allen Dulles, who was at the time the head of the Central Intelligence Agency (CIA), had provided the critical American backing for Operation Ajax.[15] This was a coup that had returned the Shah to power after he had briefly fled the country following the loss of a political battle against the popular nationalist prime minister, Mohammad Mossadeq.[16]

One could infer from the 1953 US intervention in Iran that the Shah's relationship to Dulles was akin to that of a servant to his master. That assessment, however, was inaccurate in many ways. The Shah would gradually become a much bolder personality in his dealings with Washington, and would often leave John Dulles and other American officials fuming.

The Shah's plea to Dulles in Karachi

On 9 March 1956, barely two years after the coup in Tehran, the 68-year-old John Dulles met the then 35-year-old energetic young Shah in a setting where the two men had a chance to express and share views. Dulles was in Karachi to attend a SEATO summit. The Shah had plenty on his mind to fire off at Dulles, but at least he was on friendly territory. The one-hour morning meeting took place at the governor general's residence in Karachi. The governor general at the time was none other than the Shah's good friend, Iskander Mirza. Two weeks later – after Pakistan had revised its constitution – Mirza took the helm as the country's first president.

The Shah was still on shaky political ground back home, but that was hard to detect if one went by the points he raised with the US Secretary of State. Whereas Dulles posed questions about socio-economic stability in Iran, the Shah was seemingly obsessed with only one issue: the menace of Soviet communism. On the issue of CENTO and Iranian military involvement in US-led efforts, Dulles found the Shah to be set in his mind and tenacious.

Dulles thanked the Shah for his 'courageous action in committing his nation to the Baghdad Pact and doing so entirely on his own responsibility without any prior bargaining with any other countries'.[17] This was Dulles telling the Shah that Washington looked kindly on Iran openly siding with the United States despite the guaranteed Soviet ire that such a move would invite. At first, Dulles interpreted the Shah's remarks as 'his irrevocable commitment to stand against Russia and never give in', but the American knew the Shah well enough to know that was not the end of it.

The good-humoured atmosphere during the meeting stumbled somewhat when the Shah insisted on emphasizing the 'strategic importance of Iran' and on describing his country as the 'most critical spot in the world'. Dulles, knowing full well that this depiction was part of the Shah's appeal to the United States for more arms and financial aid, was prompted to remind the monarch that 'many countries in the world regarded themselves as the most critical spot'.

Dulles told the Shah that in fact their hosts – the Pakistanis – had told him the very same thing, and that all the countries Dulles visited considered themselves to be critical in preventing a 'breakthrough of communism'. According to the US Secretary of State, each of these countries had their own military and financial demands on the United States, the levels of which collectively reached 'astronomical proportions' that the United States could not meet.

After hearing all this, the Shah still requested American military deliveries and aid to the tune of '$75 million per year over three years'. Predictably the plea failed to impress Dulles, who judged the figure to be 'surely excessive' and who felt forced to give the Shah some perspective. Dulles 'hastily sketched the American foreign policy' on a piece of paper, and then told the Shah that the 'American people generally did not appreciate the significance of the Middle East and South Asia'. For the stern but tactful Dulles, this performance amounted to a gentle refusal.

This was a rebuff that the Shah would hear many times from consecutive US administrations, and it would not be until the arrival of the Nixon Presidency in the 1970s that the Iranian ruler felt that Washington was receptive to his pleas for large-scale military exports to Iran. He also felt that Washington prioritized the military needs and demands of Pakistan and Turkey over those desired by Tehran.

The meeting in the Pakistani governor general's office ended with Dulles asking the Shah if he had any impressions of Jawaharlal Nehru, the Indian prime minister whom Dulles was shortly due to meet on the continuation of his trip from Karachi to New Delhi. Undeterred by the American's blunt brushing-off of his requests just a few minutes earlier, the mention of Nehru's name was an opportunity for the Shah to once again return to his status as the anti-communist crusader he considered himself to be.

The Shah agreed with Dulles that 'Nehru's foreign policy almost always coincided with Soviet policy', but moved on to explain that

Tehran had informed the Indian premier to 'keep his nose out of [Iranian] affairs'. Expressing doubt about Indian policies was probably the one topic that the Shah brought up with Dulles that gratified Mirza and the Pakistanis more than anything else.

The transcript of this meeting between the Shah and Dulles is revealing in a number of ways, but two features stand out in regards to the Baghdad Pact and Iranian–Pakistani ties. First, throughout the conversation, the Shah's focus is on trumpeting the evils of Soviet communism in the hope of ratcheting up Washington's appetite to arm and provide funding to Iran. This was, incidentally, the exact same approach that the Pakistanis were taking at the time vis-à-vis the United States.

This brings up the second notable highlight from the meeting: the total absence of any mention of joint Iranian–Pakistani efforts in facing down the Soviet Union. In fact, according to Dulles' notes, the Shah did not mention Pakistan once during their conversation. At this time, the Baghdad Pact had been a reality for nearly a year but clearly the organization faced an uphill battle in nurturing a genuine sense of collectiveness.

As could have been predicted, the launch of the Baghdad Pact angered the Soviets. Soviet leader Nikita Khrushchev told the Shah that the 'pact is aggressive and directed against us [the Soviet Union]'. The Shah told him that it was a defensive pact, to which the Soviet leader replied: 'Don't make me laugh.' In the years that followed, Khrushchev did not ease off on the Iranian ruler. He famously told President John F. Kennedy in 1961 that the Shah's regime would eventually fall 'like a rotten fruit into Soviet hands'. And he even ordered an unsuccessful KGB assassination attempt on the monarch's life in February 1962.[18] Small wonder, then, that the Shah would remain paranoid about the Soviets.

Khrushchev also told the Shah that the Baghdad Pact would 'break up like a soap bubble'. Some 20 years after the Soviet leader uttered those words to him, the Iranian monarch recalled this conversation when he was sitting in his Caribbean exile and writing what would turn out to be his second and last memoir. The Shah described Khrushchev as a man of peasant upbringing who was 'alternately good-natured and cunning', but clearly with a knack to see through all the pomp around Baghdad Pact. In 1980, a year after the collapse of the accord, the Shah admitted that that old, burly Russian leader had called it correctly all along when he dismissed the pact as no more than a paper tiger.[19]

An evasive security pact

The Baghdad Pact, as with SEATO, would from its earliest days struggle for credibility due to an ambiguous mission and lack of commitment on the part of its member states.

On 14 July 1958, the Shah of Iran and Iskander Mirza, the Pakistani leader at the time, were both in Baghdad to attend a meeting of Baghdad Pact leaders when Iraq's bloody revolution broke out. In what must have been an unnerving moment for the visiting foreign dignitaries, Iraq's King Faisal was executed by the pro-Soviet republican Iraqi revolutionaries. The fall of Faisal, and the total powerlessness of the Baghdad Pact states or Washington to do anything about it, was a daunting realization for the other pact leaders. The lesson was clear: this was not a pact that they could rely on to preserve their domestic political rule.

The Shah and the Pakistanis were still willing to give the organization a chance to prove itself. They were fully aware that prospects for the Baghdad Pact would depend heavily, if not entirely, on the willingness of Washington to invest in the enterprise. On 20 July 1958, the Shah met the US ambassador to Iran, Edward Thompson Wailes. The Pakistani president, Iskander Mirza, was also in Tehran at the time. The Shah told Wailes that Iran and Pakistan were both in favor of 'coordinating efforts to swiftly remove' the new, leftist Iraqi revolutionary regime.

The Shah and the Turkish Government, and also the Pakistanis, were all publicly making the argument for an intervention in Iraq to prevent the coup there from having a regional spill-over effect. But quietly, the Shah was also fearful about a unilateral Turkish intervention in Iraq, which in his view would come at Iran's expense.[20] He urged Washington to talk the Turks out of it; he would rather have had the United States take the lead. He asked the Americans to wait until the situation was 'ripe', but urged an intervention in Iraq nonetheless.[21]

This was another example of the implicit competition among the Baghdad Pact members. As a trend, this could have been thoroughly foreseen. A few years earlier, at the conclusion of his visit to Washington in December 1954, the Shah had specifically asked President Eisenhower to commit to upholding the anti-Soviet militaries in the region, but also called on Washington to make sure that there was a 'balance of power between Turkey, Iran and Pakistan'.[22]

Field Marshal Ayub Khan, Pakistan's army chief during Mirza's presidency, also hinted at this rivalry in his memoir. He recalled 'a very informal dinner' in July 1958, also attended by President Mirza, the Shah of Iran and President Celal Bayar of Turkey. According to Khan, during the dinner conversation the CENTO leaders came to openly admit the 'disadvantages and dangers inherent in any political or military alliances of a regional character'.[23]

This was doublespeak on the part of Khan: he was saying that the 'paradoxical advantage of the Baghdad Pact', as he referred to it, was that it reinforced the futility of collective defence – at least in that part of the world. The leaders of each of the region's countries knew that they had to rely on themselves or sign a bilateral security deal with the United States. Anything else was pointless.

The point that the pact was of little use as a political lifeline was again reiterated shortly after the upheaval in Baghdad. Barely three months after the revolution in Iraq, Iskander Mirza himself was removed from power by a coup at the hands of Pakistan's military leaders, led by the very same Field Marshal Ayub Khan.

In 1959, the pro-Soviet revolutionary regime of Abd Al-Karim Qasim in Baghdad officially quit the Baghdad Pact; henceforth, the body would be known as the Central Treaty Organization (CENTO). Despite its renaming and relaunch, the organization would continue to suffer from the same symptoms as before.

Immediately after the fall of King Faisal in Baghdad and Iraq's exit from the Baghdad Pact, the United States had to act swiftly to keep the alliance from falling apart. At a ministerial council meeting of the remaining members, the United States decided to became signatory to a declaration promising that the organization would 'in the interest of world peace' agree to cooperate with the CENTO nations. In such language, this sounded similar to NATO's Article 5 – an attack on a member is an attack on all members – and the notion of 'collective defence'.

The Iranians and the Pakistanis were ecstatic about this turn of events, which was viewed as an American concession. They saw it as a sign that the United States would strengthen its association with CENTO, and hoped that this meant increasing American military and financial aid. Becoming even more entangled with CENTO, however, was not the United States' intention.

Within six months, it became clear that Washington merely wanted to prevent the disbanding of CENTO but had no intention of writing a 'blank cheque' for the remaining CENTO states. A US State Department memorandum to President Eisenhower from 23 February 1959 made it clear that Washington needed to remind Iran, Turkey and Pakistan that the United States would not assume the 'same obligations which they had assumed among themselves in Article 1 of the Baghdad Pact'.[24] This article guaranteed that members 'will cooperate for their security of defense'.[25]

To the great disappointment of the proponents of CENTO, this American posture would in effect remain in place for the 24-year duration of the organization's life.

Iskander Mirza and his Iranian wife

On the bilateral front, despite the regional upheaval around them, the second half of the 1950s was a period in which relations between Iran and Pakistan grew considerably closer. This was the time when General Iskander Mirza, a man of noble Shi'a and Bengali roots, led a country that comprised both West and East Pakistan (the latter to become Bangladesh). Mirza, a Sandhurst-educated officer with a sparkling personality and British mannerisms, first ruled as governor general from August 1955 and then as president from March 1956 to October 1958 when he was overthrown. While in office, he got along famously with the Iranian leadership.

Some Pakistani accounts have attributed Mirza's closeness to the Iranians to his Shi'a Muslim faith, which is the majority branch of Islam practised in Iran and the sect of about 20 per cent of Pakistanis. Some even label Mirza the 'Shi'a president'. A number of Pakistani historians have argued that at the time a movement existed in Pakistan that supported the idea of a 'union between predominately Sunni Pakistan and Shia Iran, in which the Shah of Iran would be the head of the state!' The US Embassy in Karachi had even identified some of the key senior government voices in this movement. US diplomatic cables at the time spoke of the 'growing theme of Shia domination of Pakistan'.[26]

Iranian accounts dispute sectarian empathy as a factor that shaped the growing ties between the two countries. The Shah himself makes no such mention in his memoirs or anywhere else. Ardeshir Zahedi, twice foreign minister of Iran and a close friend of Mirza, called such insinuations far-fetched: 'The Shia-Sunni divide was not important at the time.'[27] If his Shi'a faith was not a driver that led to closer ties with Iran, Mirza's wife – a woman with an impeccable Iranian pedigree – made sure that the country was never far from his thoughts.[28] Throughout his tenure in high government office, Mirza and his wife were frequent visitors to Iran.

As his son wrote, years later in a biography, one of Mirza's chief preoccupations was the need to 'address [Pakistan's] defense problems'.[29] Given the colossal job that it faced in countering India, Pakistan's military means in those early post-independence years were at best patchy. For one, at Partition India had been the overwhelming beneficiary of the military production lines that existed on the subcontinent; Pakistan had received very little of this infrastructure.[30]

The Shah of Iran, too, was notorious for his infatuation with guns and armaments from a young age – father had made him a colonel when he was 11 years old – and later in his life he would regard himself as a great military strategist. As Abbas Milani observed in his biography of the Shah, the Iranian monarch's fixation with martial themes arose because he saw the military as 'key to power'.

It was, then, hardly surprising that Mirza and the Shah bonded over military matters. Photographs that show the men together were mainly taken when they attended military parades or kept each other company on shooting ranges. They also shared a basic political philosophy: both men believed that it was not the time to adopt Western-style democracy in their respective countries. Mirza had openly expressed the thought that 'democracy was unsuited for a country like Pakistan',[31] and the Shah shared this sentiment – a view that he held until almost the end of his rule.[32] The two men's friendship would last until Mirza's death.

General Ayub Khan, the head of the Pakistani military and the man who was ultimately responsible for Mirza's removal in the bloodless coup of October 1958, later – and disingenuously – explained that the takeover had occurred because the 'armed forces and the people demanded a clean break with the past'.[33]

Mirza's family had a different perspective. His son, Humayun, blamed his father's fall from power on one person alone: Nahid Mirza, the Iranian-origin second wife of the toppled president. Humayun did not hold back in his criticism, and has nothing but contempt for his stepmother, calling Nahid a 'crude' and 'power hungry' individual. She is painted as the principal reason for Mirza's low standing among the military cadre, diminished thanks to her 'authoritarian behavior and mistreatment of lesser officers'. Nahid is said to have 'aspired to rival Queen Soraya [the Shah's second wife] of Iran' and kept a 'court of hangers-on around her, most of whom were of Iranian origin; they called her Malika (Queen)'.[34]

Humayun's statements should not be viewed as an expression of anti-Iranianism: if anything, Mirza's Iranian friends would prove at the end to be his most loyal, a fact that Humayun himself acknowledges in the same biography of his father. Instead, Humayun's views on Nahid are most likely a reflection of a son's anger of his father abandoning his mother for another woman. After all, any suggestion that Nahid played a critical role in the lead-up to Pakistan's October 1958 military coup is entirely unsubstantiated.[35]

Humayun quotes Ayub Khan as saying that, 'If it had not been for that woman [Nahid], your father and I would have been able to work things out', a suggestion that the coup of October 1958 was avoidable. But, as Wayne A. Wilcox explained in the early years after the event, the Mirza–Khan relationship and rivalry for power was far deeper than anything Nahid could be accused of having orchestrated. It was probably not coincidental that the coup occurred only three months before Ayub Khan was due to relinquish his post as chief at the Pakistani armed forces on 16 January 1959. In other words, Khan had 'just three months' to strike for power and it 'was then or never'.[36]

Mirza ended up in exile in London, where he relied on an array of sources to support himself and his family. Among those who supported the Mirza family in London were the Shah of Iran and Ardeshir Zahedi, the Shah's foreign minister, son-in-law and confidant.[37] Mirza died in November 1969.

Despite Humayun Mirza's claim that the 'Iranian' Nahid was the primary reason for the falling out between his father and the Pakistani military, it was nonetheless Ayub Khan who, of his own volition, refused to allow a funeral to be held in Pakistan. Instead, the Shah stepped in and arranged for a state funeral to be held for Mirza in Tehran. In the end, Pakistan's first president found his final resting ground in a mausoleum in southern Tehran, not far from the blissful pistachio farms that then dotted the area.

CHAPTER 3

1958-1965: REGIONAL TURBULENCE AND AN UNLIKELY UNION

Ayub Khan, Mirza's successor, continued to look to Iran as one of Pakistan's principal allies. The Iranians never really warmed to Ayub Khan, the striving Pashtun, in the same way that they had to Mirza, but maintaining congenial inter-state relations was the first priority. The self-promoted field marshal, at the time the only Pakistani military officer to have ever held such an elevated rank, made an official visit to Iran on 9–18 November 1959.

This was a grand state visit of the kind rarely seen by Iranians or Pakistanis alike, and included plenty of pomp and ceremony. During his eight-day visit, Ayub Khan travelled across Iran. He attended a sports festival and military drills on the hills outside the capital, and later received an honorary degree from Tehran University. The visit included a trip to the north-eastern city of Mashhad, not far from the Afghan border, where the Sunni Ayub Khan paid his respects at the holy shrine of Imam Reza, the eighth Shi'a imam, and his travels also took him to the ancient cities of Esfahan and Shiraz in central Iran.

Khan seemingly took every opportunity to generously praise his younger host, the Shah, and the latter's country. He told his Iranian hosts: 'we embrace the same faith and have a common cultural heritage. Your language and literature have been the fountainhead of inspiration for us for centuries.' He continued: 'Your literature is our literature, your historic heroes are our heroes, your friends are our friends and your enemies our enemies.' Ayub Khan described Iran and Pakistan as having a 'common heritage, one soul in two bodies'. The relatively young and still impressionable Shah could have not been anything but flattered by such lavish praise of him and his country.[1]

The American and British embassies in Tehran were paying close attention to Khan's every move and statement during his eight days in Iran. The British were particularly delighted to find that the Pakistani leader was 'favourably impressed by His Majesty's [the Shah's] robust attitude towards the Soviet menace and his apparent determination to remain loyal to his [Western] allies and resist Soviet pressure'.[2]

Britain and the United States were anxious to push Iran and Pakistan to forge a closer alliance against the Soviets, an objective that Tehran and Islamabad shared. Nonetheless there were, already in those early days, evident differences about where the most imminent threats would come from.

At the time, the Shah was preoccupied with the fall of the Iraqi monarchy and the emergence of Arab leftist-nationalist revolutionaries. It was this kind of threat that the Shah viewed as being ideally countered by CENTO.

The Shah and the idea of strength in unity

Ayub Khan, who would end up ruling Pakistan from 1958 until 1969, told a story of how panic-stricken the Shah became when the 14 July 1958 revolution in Iraq toppled the monarchy in that country. Fearing that the regional reverberations of the leftist takeover could put his throne in jeopardy, the Shah is said to have asked Ayub Khan about the 'idea of a confederation of Iran and Pakistan with a single army and with the Shah as the head of the state'.[3]

Such a confederation might at first appear bizarre and unworkable. After all, Iran and Pakistan as two nation states do share certain commonalities, but many more factors separate them than bring them together. That was as true in the 1950s as it is today. Still, two distinct realities existed at that time that made such an idea less than outlandish.

First, Iran and Pakistan were already members of the budding new organization CENTO. There was already much talk about political, military and economic integration as part of the structures of CENTO. A confederation would have been a major leap, but it would in effect have been an enlargement of a process that was already under way in practice.

Second, the Shah had not envisioned the idea out of the blue. Right next door in the Arab world, four regional countries were at the time already experimenting with political confederations. In 1958, Egypt and Syria agreed on a union, which became known as the United Arab Republic. This Arab, socialist and pro-Soviet merger frightened the Shah and other monarchs in the region enormously. In reaction to the Egyptian–Syrian pact, the Hashemite kings of Iraq and Jordan, King Faisal II and his cousin King Hussein, had established the pro-West Arab Federation.

Seen from this angle, the Shah turning to the Pakistanis with the idea of a confederation makes sense given that these were the two large non-Arab and anti-communist states of south-west Asia. Turkey was the only other sizeable non-Arab and anti-communist country in the region but it enjoyed an elevated security shield as a member of NATO, which it had joined in 1952. However, the concept of a confederation between Iran and Pakistani would stay on the drawing board from the moment the Shah first raised it with Ayub Khan in 1958 all the way up to the mid-1970s.

Ayub Khan's initial reaction to such suggestions was less than receptive, although with time he too would hint at such an arrangement as a possibility. He remarked during his 1959 Iran visit that CENTO was not 'an instrument of aggression or interference', an obvious reference to the political upheaval in Iraq after the toppling of the pro-Western monarchy in that country.[4]

Instead, Khan sought to turn the spotlight on Afghanistan, which after India represented Islamabad's key foreign challenge – if not an outright threat. During his trip to Iran, he particularly protested against Afghan aircraft overflying Pakistani airspace. However, much more importantly, he also questioned Kabul's close ties to Moscow and the presence of 'many Soviet technicians in Afghanistan'.[5]

In fact, the foreign policies of the Afghan leadership were so disturbing to the Pakistanis that the two countries would often be on a war footing. Khan and his successors in Pakistan all looked to the Shah to act as a mediator, convincing the Afghans to change course. This the Shah did, and he was largely successful when, over the years, he repeatedly stepped forward to arbitrate between his belligerent eastern neighbours. But the Afghan–Pakistani split proved enduring, each of the Shah's numerous peace-making efforts undone by a prevailing scepticism in Kabul–Islamabad ties that lasts to this day.

A confederation of Afghanistan–Iran–Pakistan

One of the foremost paradoxes of this period was the frequent airing of the idea of a regional confederation – to include Afghanistan, Iran and Pakistan. This concept bordered on absurdity, particularly given the outright hostile relations between Afghanistan and Pakistan. In the case of Iran and Pakistan, circumstances for closer ties were more straightforward but certainly not without hurdles either.

As early as the late 1950s, even before Tehran enjoyed the financial windfall of its oil bonanza, there were those in Pakistan who advocated the coordination of governmental policies between Iran and Pakistan. And as time would show, this was hardly a spur-of-the-moment impulse. And as late as the mid-1970s, Zulfikar Bhutto asked the foreign ministry in Islamabad to prepare policy papers on the issue of a potential confederation with Iran. Those documents are said to be still in existence, but safely under lock and key.[6]

The Shah too entertained the idea of Pakistan as an anchor to bolster his own position at home and in the region – at least in the early years of his reign, when his grip on power inside Iran had still to be developed and he feared external subversion.[7] While at the time the idea of a broader confederation between Afghanistan, Iran and Pakistan had some appeal, its larger drawbacks could not be denied. This was true equally from the perspective of all the three capitals involved. On the plus side, there was the appeal of cooperation along economic and military lines, which would chiefly be aimed at keeping out Soviet meddling whilst having such efforts also underwritten by the United States and other Western powers. In terms of obstacles to such a venture, the list was longer and more persuasive, the obvious and primary one being related to the question of compatibility. Of the three states, two (Iran and Afghanistan) were monarchies while one (Pakistan) was a presidential republic.

Iran was ruled by a young and often vacillating king, who was nonetheless in charge of a country with some 2,500 years of imperial history. In comparison, its two eastern neighbours were mere infants as nation states. Afghanistan did not become a nation state in the modern sense of the word until the latter part of the nineteenth century, and declared itself a sovereign state in 1919.[8] Pakistan became an independent state only in 1947, and its national identity was still in its earliest formative stages when this idea of confederation was first floated.

One of America's principal scholars on south-west Asia in that era closely monitored all the talk of a federation in the region, and could not help but find himself puzzled by the prospects for such a political union. His name was Louise Dupree, a US southerner and a World War II veteran who had had studied anthropology at Harvard University and had first visited Afghanistan in 1949. In the next half century until his death in 1989, Dupree would teach generations of American diplomats and analysts from the US State Department, the CIA and other government agencies.[9] He was les than convinced about the viability of a confederation between Afghanistan, Iran and Pakistan.

Dupree noted in the early 1960s that Pakistan had a 'strong presidential system and experimental Basic Democracies Program'. In Afghanistan, there was a 'theoretical constitutional monarchy but actually an oligarchy, with ultimate power in the hands of the army-backed prime minister'. Iran was 'another theoretical constitutional monarchy, with the Shah in tight control and backed by the army'.[10] As he had revealed to Ayub Khan, the Shah of Iran of course envisaged himself head of such a confederation. Whether the Afghan king, Mohammad Zahir Shah, or Pakistani leaders would have agreed to that arrangement is highly doubtful.

Additional obstacles also lay in wait. At that time – unlike today, and certainly among Pakistani and Iranian political elites – one's sectarian background was generally not much of a factor. As Ayub Khan and others after him would state, the focus was on emphasizing similarities and not differences. But even then, the mere thought of Sunni-majority Pakistan being ruled by the Shi'a Shah of Iran was an abomination to many. One observer was quoted as saying that Pashtun Afghans would accept the idea of a federation with Pakistan but not with Iran: 'Pashtun tribesmen would never permit federation with Shiite Iran without bloodshed.'[11]

Despite the fact that the idea of a tripartite confederation would periodically resurface until the mid-1970s, the critics of such pretentions had a point. This was not just about the conflicting political modalities of the three countries, or about religious and cultural differences. Much more everyday conflicts were also in the way.

The idea of a 'confederation' that included Afghanistan and Pakistan was at best a case of misplaced priorities. The two countries had repeatedly broken off diplomatic relations. As one commentator pointed out at the time, it seemed that the leaderships were engaging in 'federation fantasies' when they should focus first on re-establishing diplomatic ties, but that 'the idea that federation will be a panacea is hard to shake in the minds of some Afghans, Pakistanis and Iranians'.[12]

Meanwhile, the other regional countries' experiments along these lines had less than a stellar record to show for them. Egypt's Gamal Abdel Nasser had in 1958 orchestrated the creation of the United Arab Republic, joining Egypt and Syria in a union that lasted only three years. In response, Jordan and Iraq had merged, and this time the union lasted a meagre six months and came to an end with the toppling of the Hashemite Monarchy in Baghdad in July 1958. The challenges facing a confederation between Iran, Pakistan and Afghanistan would have been far greater even than those faced by these short-lived examples.

Pashtunistan

By far the weakest link in the debated idea of an Afghanistan–Iran–Pakistan confederation was the dismal state of affairs between Kabul and Islamabad. Relations had begun very badly, and would remain tense.

At first, the Afghans could not come to terms with the creation of the state of Pakistan. In fact, Afghanistan was the sole vote against Pakistan's admission into the United Nations in 1947. Pakistan's creation was an affront to Afghan nationhood because the new state included regions and peoples that successive regimes in Kabul have considered an integral part of Afghanistan.[13]

Afghanistan, except for brief periods when it was itself an empire, had always been a series of disjointed tribal kingdoms. This was until Russian designs in Central Asia greatly alarmed Queen Victoria and British colonial interests, which then forced the Afghans into a modern state in order to act as a capable buffer against the expansionist Russians.[14] Hence, the coming together of tribal regions that would make up Afghanistan.

For the British, the 'jewel in the crown' of their empire was India, to be defended at all costs. To do this, London went ahead and arranged for a definitive demarcation of the border between Afghanistan and British India. The boundary has since been known as the Durrand Line, named after its British originator, Sir Mortimer Durrand.

The Durrand Line subsequently became the 2,600-km-long Afghan–Pakistani border. The disputed boundary cut through historically Pashtun-populated regions, in effect dividing one 'nation' into two parts.[15] This has since remained one of the unfinished chapters left behind by the 'Great Game' between Imperial Russia and Britain in the nineteenth century. In 1947, when it was born out of British India, Pakistan inherited this border dispute with Afghanistan. To this day, with some 13 million Pashtun in Afghanistan and about 30 million in Pakistan, Kabul does not accept this internationally recognized boundary between the two countries.

Over the decades, successive Afghan governments have raised the issue of the 'fate' of the Pashtun people in their dealings with Pakistan. Each time, the Pakistani authorities have balked, fearing that Kabul's ultimate goal is the annexation of the Pashtun regions of Pakistan and the creation of a 'Greater Afghanistan'.

Unsurprisingly the 'Pashtun Question' has been a constant irritant in relations. One of the first diplomatic crises in Afghanistan–Pakistan ties erupted as early as 1955, when Pakistan incorporated disputed Pashtun tribal areas adjoining the common border. On the announcement of the decision, an angry Afghan mob attacked the Pakistani Embassy in Kabul and relations between the two countries were severed. The situation was only resolved after Iranian, Turkish and Iraqi mediation.[16] It would become the first salvo in the many spats that have since followed.

On 6 September 1961, tensions led to Kabul once more sealing the border. This time, the Afghans also refused to accept any shipments that arrived in Afghanistan via the Pakistani port of Karachi. This was a rather bold move, as the Afghans more than anyone else depended on this route for supplies. In Washington, the US Government acknowledged the gravity of the dispute, and in October that year President John F. Kennedy dispatched a special envoy – Livingstone T. Merchant – to defuse the crisis.[17]

Merchant returned to Washington empty-handed. The Afghan king, Zahir Shah, flattered that the United States should see fit to intervene in such a high-profile fashion, sent a note to Kennedy and thanked him for his 'benevolent endeavors as exemplified by Ambassador Merchant's mission'. Zahir Shah – predictably, although without providing specifics in the letter – blamed the stand-off on Pakistani policies.[18]

Iranian mediation turned out to be more fruitful. The Shah himself engaged in shuttle diplomacy, and on 26 May 1963 brought Afghan and Pakistani delegates to Tehran. The fact that the Iranian monarch's own relations with Afghan King Mohammad Zahir Shah had recently improved helped significantly.[19] The Shah proudly announced that the meeting had resulted in 'an agreement to re-establish diplomatic and economic relations between Islamabad and Kabul'.

The Iranian side was certainly thrilled with the turn of events. The foreign ministry in Tehran later summarized this as 'The Shah's finest moment as a mediator', and called it an 'example of wonderful Iranian diplomacy [that] the world had witnessed'. Ayub Khan sent the Shah a telegraph to express his 'deepest thanks' for the latter's 'glowing mediation'.[20]

However, as with prior third-party mediation efforts, the May 1963 deal proved to be more a case of accord on paper than in substance. Only three days after the agreement was announced, Afghan minister Sayd Rashtyia said the issue of 'Pashtunistan continue to divide Afghanistan and Pakistan', while Zulfikar Bhutto – then merely a 35-year-old delegate who had travelled to Tehran – declared that 'Pashtunistan was a dead issue'.[21]

As far as the 1963 agreement was concerned, two realities were evident.[22] Turning to Iran as an outlet to the world was not a quick fix, and would at best become a solution to Afghanistan's transportation quandary only in the long term. Furthermore, disagreements over the Durrand Line and the question of Pashtunistan would linger for years to come.

Iran was also – albeit unwillingly – becoming a beneficiary of these frequent Afghan–Pakistani rows. Before the Shah's mediation, as the disruption from the border closure increased, the Afghans turned to Iran for relief. In April 1962, Tehran and Kabul signed a five-year transit agreement, providing Afghanistan with an important alternative conduit to the world. However, there is no evidence that Iran's intention was ever to gain more leverage in Afghanistan at the expense of the Pakistanis. Nonetheless, in subsequent decades any innocence in posture about access to Afghanistan would all but disappear in Iran–Pakistan relations.

For the Shah, the primary (and likely only) reason to cater to Kabul was to keep the Soviets out of the impoverished country that sat at the heel of the mighty Soviet Union. In 1960s, besides the transit agreement, Iran also signed new trade deals with the Afghans, including one covering the export of refined Iranian petroleum products. At the time, a 'highly placed Iranian government official' confidentially told the US Embassy in Tehran that the price for Iran's products had been set '5% below the Soviet price'. The United States viewed the agreement as a 'major milestone', although it also foresaw many practical obstacles to its implementation.[23] Nonetheless, the centrality of the Soviet factor in Iranian–Afghan dealings was impossible to ignore.

Iranian fears about fallout from the Afghan–Pakistani dispute

One of the key components of the May 1963 Afghanistan–Pakistan agreement in Tehran was that Kabul would refrain from pandering to the idea of Pashtunistan. The Shah looked on the Pashtunistan dispute not simply as one that kept his two eastern neighbours divided but also as a factor ripe for exploitation by the Soviets. In such a scenario, the Shah believed that the entire anti-Soviet Northern Tier would be in jeopardy.

Again, the Shah was not merely paranoid in fearing a Russian hand at work. In December 1955, the Soviet leader Nikita Khrushchev had visited Kabul and declared that Moscow supported the Afghan stance on the question of Pashtunistan. Moscow's decision was aimed at drawing neutral Afghanistan closer into the Soviet orbit, and it cared little for Pakistan's reaction.[24] The Pakistanis were, after all, firmly in the US camp. Moreover, the Soviets were already courting Pakistan's nemesis, India.

The Shah was extremely fearful about Khrushchev's intentions. He had only a decade earlier seen first-hand the way in which Moscow had supported ethnic separatists in Iranian Azarbaijan and Kurdistan. Aiding separatists was a card that Moscow had played elsewhere, and now they were openly backing the Afghan Government on the question of Pashtunistan. In Shah's mind, left unchallenged this would have meant the dismemberment of Pakistan.

Back in Islamabad, in order to strengthen Pakistan's hand, Ayub Khan more forcefully linked the question of Pashtunistan to the Soviet threat and Western interests in west and south Asia. In referring to the Afghan–Pakistani border, Ayub Khan told CENTO leaders that the Khyber Pass (a mountain pass connecting Afghanistan and Pakistan) had 'seen perhaps more invasions in the course of history than any other area in Asia', and that by defending it Pakistan is defending the entire subcontinent. 'If Pashtunistan should ever come into being,' he warned, then the Soviet Union 'will have succeeded in eroding a peripheral area to its power, weakening Pakistan immeasurably, and shifting [the] world balance of power one step further in favor of the Communists'.[25]

Ayub Khan had American policy makers in mind when he raised the prospect of the Soviet threat to the subcontinent and sought Washington's help to prevent the creation of Pashtunistan. Khan's calculation was correct: the United States too detected that the Soviets had adopted incitement of the Pashtun issue as a ploy to destabilize the pro-American government in Islamabad.

Preserving the Northern Tier

In early-1960s Washington, the idea of an anti-Soviet line of defence along the 'Northern Tier' still had plenty of credibility. Hence, the Americans wanted to look at ways of bringing pro-US states in south-west Asia closer together in order to bridge this geopolitical fault line. It was from this perspective that Washington would come to ponder the idea of a confederation between Iran–Pakistan and Afghanistan.

For the United States, the idea of a confederation was seen as the best tactic in removing the one significant disagreement on the table: the idea of Pashtunistan and the Afghan–Pakistani quarrel. As one American policy paper put it, a 'confederation would tend to eliminate this dispute, or at least greatly reduce its importance'.[26]

US planning took into account practical military needs as much as political considerations. Were a confederation to be achieved, Afghanistan's vast landscape would, it was said, give Pakistan 'additional space in which to maneuver her military forces against a Soviet invasion'. This was indeed the age of tank wars, when one of the greatest Western fears was an onslaught of hordes of tanks unleashed from the nearby Soviet Union. In that sense, US policy-planning papers from the time echoed the sort of alarms that Ayub Khan had been raising. Afghanistan sat on the southern Soviet flank, and was seen by the Americans as the bridge that would make it possible for Soviet forces to reach the shores of the Indian Ocean. This would be a colossal strategic net loss for the United States in those relatively early years of the Cold War.

The same American policy papers would also raise the prospect of a multitude of obstacles in the path of an Afghanistan–Iran–Pakistan confederation. In fact, they would question whether it was at all beneficial to US interests. Afghanistan, for instance, given that it trailed Pakistan as a nation state on so many levels, would become a burden for the young nation.

Islamabad would have had to fill the many gaps, a commitment that US analysts at the time predicted would in the end weaken Pakistan itself. There was also the unknown Soviet reaction to such an American-instigated confederation, given that Afghanistan had long been seen as neutral ground. The Afghans and the Soviets had signed their first friendship treaty as early as 1921.

The Indians too would have fervently objected to the confederation. New Delhi's key objective was to prevent Pakistan becoming the 'landlord' of the Afghans. There was no way of predicting how the confederation would in practice have evolved, and that worried India. With all these questions in the air, Washington then chose to vacate the driving seat on the confederation project. It let it be known that it was happy to leave Afghanistan and Pakistan to work it out. Washington would facilitate if the two governments demonstrated a 'convincing mutual desire'.[27]

This the Pakistanis duly noted. In August 1962, speaking in Quetta, President Ayub Khan publicly broached for the first time his ideas concerning a loose federation of Afghanistan, Iran and Pakistan. In the same speech he managed to cast it as a project for the long term and, with a few pointed remarks about the Afghanistan–Pakistan border dispute, Khan effectively excluded the possibility of serious consultations on the matter of a confederation. However, Washington strategists had already begun to explore paving the way for regional integration among US allies in south-west Asia.

Reviving the 'Empty Triangle'

After some initial consideration, the US perspective on the notion of a 'confederation' in south-west Asia took a different route. Rather than contemplating the question of political amalgamation, the Americans went back to the drawing board and reminded themselves of the key goal they sought to accomplish. Washington principally cared about keeping the Soviets out and minimizing the appeal of the communist narrative that targeted the populations of the three countries of Afghanistan, Iran and Pakistan.

US policy now advocated and sought funding for regional integration along economic lines, aimed at bettering the lives of the ordinary people of the region. Arguments in favour of such an approach were straightforward: there was no better vanguard against the Soviets and their designs than fewer people going hungry and suffering from a sense of economic disillusionment.

CENTO, despite being an entirely untested military alliance, became the first platform around which closer economic integration would be built. The pan-regional development of road, rail and communication infrastructures would be at the heart of American efforts. This idea of economic integration moved closer to realization as the United States agreed to assist Iran in the development of the so-called 'Empty Triangle'.

§

The 'Empty Triangle' is a vast three-cornered zone linking Iran, Afghanistan and Pakistan. In 1963, Louis Dupree called this barren region 'an inhospitable zone of sandy and basaltic pebble dessert, swamp, and eroded badlands, once an alternate route of invasion, once supporting a large population by an intricate irrigation system'.[28]

The zone, twice the size of Iraq, had in effect been in decline since the demise of the Silk Road trade in the fifteenth century, when lucrative Europe–Asia trade increasingly switched to the world's sea lanes. In the half-century since Dupree made those remarks many of the same conditions remain, and the Empty Triangle remains largely desolate – a harsh terrain most suited to the crisscrossing of Afghan opium traffickers with their deadly cargo.

But back in the early 1960s, Washington was optimistic that an economic renaissance in the Empty Triangle would be possible and helpful in advancing US geopolitical interests in south-west Asia. Among key ideas was the development of Iran's port of Bandar Abbas on the Persian Gulf into a major regional hub. The intention was to establish a network of roads from there to the interior of eastern Iran. These highways would then eventually connect with the networks of western Afghanistan and Pakistan.

For land-locked Afghanistan, such projects appeared particularly heady, linking the country to world markets and reducing dependence on its Soviet neighbour to the north. Afghanistan had already lost its transportation options via Pakistan after the two countries broke off ties in September 1961.

US State Department cables from the time also show that Washington was squeezed on the matter. On the one hand, the United States feared that the prolonging of the Afghan–Pakistani spat and unavailability of the port of Karachi for Afghan trade would only force Kabul into 'total dependence on the USSR'. Accordingly, American diplomats in the region urged Washington to 'make every effort to reopen the Karachi route on normal basis'.[29]

The option of Iran as an outlet for Afghanistan was both sound and being pursued, as the US aid package for the Empty Triangle showed. It would take time to come to fruition, a disadvantage highlighted by the Afghans and recognized by the Americans. Meanwhile, the Pakistanis were not necessarily too happy about this new Iranian conduit, as it would only lower Islamabad's leverage over Kabul. With all this in consideration, US diplomats pushed the idea that Afghanistan needed not one, but three principle outlets to the world.

The northern route ran through Soviet space, accepting that this was Afghanistan's only fallback option and a fact of life whether Washington liked it or not. The Pakistan exit route, via the port of Karachi, was kept on the table because it had in recent years carried the bulk of Afghan trade and it was also a way to keep Islamabad engaged despite the 1961 sealing of the Afghanistan–Pakistan border. In the 1950s, the United States had in fact gone as far as seeking to strengthen Afghanistan's economy by championing a 'free port' in Karachi to be made available for Afghan trade. US diplomats concluded that 'while [the] US desires exploring possibilities assisting in improving [Afghan] access through Iran', pressing short-term needs made it necessary to pursue 'sincere effort to open normal transit through Pakistan'.

The new Iran outlet, however, was the one that the United States clearly favoured as an alternative in the long term. The Americans specifically expressed an interest in helping the Afghans build a decent road from Herat in western Afghanistan to the Iranian city of Mashhad, at the time the worst of the border roads connecting Afghanistan with the outside world. A highway from Bandar Abbas to Herat would in turn reduce by 1,100 km the distance between Afghanistan and its nearest major port for exports and imports. The total cost of the development program for the Empty Triangle was estimated at $100 million, of which Iran reportedly would pay 65 per cent.[30]

America, and economic growth to stop communism

Washington's bottom line was clear: it would support Afghanistan as long as its government was not 'unfriendly to the United States and not subservient to the USSR'.[31] US policy was to strengthen Kabul's hand so that it would not need to turn to the Soviets. A key element in this was to broker better ties between Afghanistan and Pakistan. But Afghanistan was clearly identified early on as the weak link. The United States hung a 'carrot' in front of the Afghans, making the promise of weapons – through Pakistan – as a way of bringing Kabul into the fold. At the same time, the United States did not offer the prospect of any regional defence arrangement with Afghanistan until it had proven itself. Afghan–Soviet economic agreements and the rise in the number of Soviet technicians was seen in the United States as a Soviet ploy to draw 'Afghanistan out of its present buffer sIinto the Soviet orbit'.[32]

To deal with the Soviet threat in Afghanistan, Washington identified three measures that it would encourage: a confederation or closer economic and political cooperation with Pakistan; Kabul improving its relations with Iran; and the provision of direct US economic and military aid to Afghanistan.

Some of the projects that the United States helped launch in the region were quite formidable. This included what was then the world's longest line-of-sight microwave telecommunication system, to run from the Turkish capital Ankara through Tehran to Karachi at a distance of some 5,000 km.[33] Scott Behoteguy, a US diplomat who was involved in the planning of the project, recalled it as a very technically challenging enterprise: 'Relay stations had to be built on the top of Turkish mountains, Iranian mountains and Pakistani mountains.'[34] This project would subsequently become the backbone of Iran's telecommunication system.

As early as 1968, a CENTO-inspired railway linked Iran with Turkey, and a number of new highways across the country dramatically transformed the transportation sector in Iran.[35] Roads were built across the three countries, providing much better connection from Europe, via Turkey through Iran and Afghanistan, with the Indian subcontinent. Some of the earliest international travellers who would benefit from the new passageways were North Americans and Europeans, who came mostly in search of Afghan drugs. This movement of people in the late 1960s and 1970s – coined the Hippie Trail – was arguably the least of the intended goals of the CENTO leaders when they signed up to the idea of closer economic integration.[36]

However, economic cooperation and integration remained a secondary priority for the CENTO member states, all of whom had more pressing security concerns. The exception was the United Kingdom, which felt that CENTO's organizational activities were adequate. London particularly did not want to turn CENTO into an anti-Indian front, as Pakistan so desperately desired.[37]

The Pakistanis pushed the argument that the CENTO members in the region – i.e. Iran, Pakistan and Turkey – should press ahead with deepening ties among themselves. But the diplomatic conditions were not right for Islamabad to propose a renunciation of CENTO in favour of an entirely new alliance. The Turks, the Iranians and (to a lesser extent) the Pakistanis did not want to offend US or, particularly, British sensibilities. Instead, Islamabad floated the idea of a complementary organization to CENTO.

This was a compromise that the Turks and the Iranians could sign up to, and considerable effort was invested in assuring the highly sceptical British and Americans that this new planned organization would not sound the death knell of CENTO. The Western powers opted to pay lip service to this idea in the hope of preventing the drift from gaining full force. British officials simply stated that London 'warmly welcomes increased cooperation between the regional members of CENTO', but warned of the 'danger of allowing any organization that is set up to duplicate and consequently weaken CENTO'.[38]

As with the debacle that beleaguered the signing of the 1950 Friendship Treaty, Tehran now made sure that its relations with Islamabad did not infringe on its standing in the eyes of London and Washington.[39]

Accordingly, in tandem with economic integration efforts as part of CENTO, Iran, Pakistan and Turkey in July 1964 launched the Regional Cooperation for Development (RCD). Zulfikar Bhutto, whose political star had risen and who was by now foreign minister, had pressed President Khan about the 'wisdom of establishing closer economic and diplomatic links with Iran and Turkey as a way to nurturing Islamabad's regional Islamic alliance'. The Pakistanis pushed this idea in the hope that the new partnership would have much more 'depth' than CENTO in the realm of defence cooperation. Officials in Islamabad were particularly incensed at the time that Western countries, including the United States and the United Kingdom, were still providing arms to India.[40]

Within the framework of the RCD, there was much discussion about increasing trade between the three countries, the exchange of industrial information and defence cooperation.[41] In July 1964, the Shah and Bhutto would meet at the RCD conference, held in Istanbul. On the eve of the conference, Bhutto wrote in his memoirs that:

> Iran, Pakistan and Turkey constitute a single civilization [. . .] permeated by a common faith [. . .] Unlike the nations of West Europe, no two of us have gone to war against each other, in the relevant past.[42]

Away from the grand political gesturing, real-world obstacles again stood in the way of economic integration. As early as the 1960s, Iran had been keen to export to Pakistan – items such as coal, cement and petroleum products. Pakistan too wanted to export to Iran, but this was not viewed as a high-priority issue for the Iranians.[43] Tariffs remained high, cooperation was not open-ended and economic protectionism seemed to be the overriding factor. Petty squabbles would often shoot down prospects of economic cooperation before a venture had even been given a proper chance to be tested.

On one occasion, in August 1964, a year-old agreement between Tehran and Islamabad that allowed Pakistani fishing fleets into the Persian Gulf came to an end after Pakistan pulled out. The Pakistani firm, Pakistani Ocean Industries, cited 'exorbitant fees' required before it could renew the contract. The Iranians demanded a price tag of $200,000 per year for ten vessels. It soon became clear that this substantial fee hike was part of an Iranian attempt to push the Pakistanis out as Tehran sought to establish its own fishing fleet in the Persian Gulf.[44] In such a competitive environment, Bhutto's call for economic integration never had a chance to take off.

As an organization, the RCD was only partly meant to supplement CENTO's endeavours. One of the other intended objectives of the three countries was to create a degree of distance between themselves and the United States. This was a time when Ankara, Islamabad and Tehran were each on their own toying with the notion of lessening tensions with the Soviets. As one commentator put it, the idea of the RCD was an important 'symbol of their desire for regional political collaboration outside the context of the cold war alliance'.[45]

It was not only in relations with the United States that the CENTO countries were keeping their options open. For example, while the Shah was known to toy with the idea of a confederation with Afghanistan and Pakistan, he was at the same time 'putting out feelers to Arab leaders' as well. His alleged attempts along these lines did not go unnoticed.

On 20 September 1962, the Pakistani newspaper *Dawn* reprinted an article from *Al-Ahram*, the top state-run Egyptian paper at the time, in which it was claimed that the Shah of Iran had reached out to King Hussein of Jordan with a proposal to establish a loose association between the two. The Egyptian newspaper claimed that the Shah's intention was to create a regional counter to President Nasser of Egypt, and stop the spread of pro-Soviet Nasserite influence in the Arab world.

The Pakistanis at the time questioned the authenticity of the alleged letter, given that a government-owned Egyptian newspaper was making the claim. The episode does not seem to have shattered anyone's illusions in Islamabad. One Pakistani reaction was put this way:

But if His Majesty [the Shah] had written the letter, he would be justified, for many of us believe President Ayub is using Iran in order to coerce India into closer relations with Pakistan. What President Ayub really wants is closer India-Pakistan relations, not a federation with Iran and Afghanistan.[46]

§

The rise of the Cold War by the early 1950s had been enough reason for the like-minded anti-Communist governments of Iran and Pakistan to join hands in CENTO, in the RCD and through other regional endeavours. But none of these efforts prove to be wholehearted, and the threat posed by the Soviet Union was insufficient to force CENTO to become a genuine complement to NATO.

The CENTO members each considered different threats as posing a bigger challenge to them than the Soviets. The Turks were focused on Greece and the dispute over Cyprus; the Iranians were above all alarmed by pro-Soviet regimes in the Arab world, such as Egypt; and the Pakistanis were entirely fixated on the balance of power vis-à-vis India.

Charlie Naas, at the time a US diplomat in Ankara working on CENTO affairs in the organization's early years, recalled that each of the member states 'had their own reasons for membership and there was not much agreement about anything' on hard-core security matters. 'There was some minor cooperation on counter-intelligence targeting the Soviets, but that was it.' Naas highlighted an even bigger obstacle: 'CENTO members all wanted to take from the collective pool, but did not want to contribute to it.'[47]

Another critical weakness in CENTO's set-up was the gap between perceptions about US commitment to the organization and Washington's actual willingness to help the members when push came to shove. The first substantial test came during the Indian–Pakistani war of 1965.

CHAPTER 4

1965-1969: THE NORTHERN TIER: A FLUID FAULT LINE

In 1965, a decade after it was founded, CENTO faced its first test. In the spring and summer of that year, Pakistan and India engaged in a series of border skirmishes in Kashmir, the disputed territory in the Himalayan foothills that each claims for itself. These skirmishes ultimately led to a full-scale war in August 1965. On 6 September, Foreign Minister Zulfikar Bhutto used a hurried press conference to announce an ultimatum. A wearied Bhutto told the world that 'the future shape of Pakistan's relationship with all countries of the world' would depend on their attitude toward what he called 'India's naked aggression against Pakistan'. It looked as if Islamabad wanted to cash in its chips.

In the first instance, Pakistan naturally turned to its CENTO allies in this hour of need. As Bhutto put it: 'Is it unfair to expect that they [CENTO members] will come to our assistance?' He contended that CENTO was a 'collective self-defense against aggression', and that his country expected from its allies 'not only moral and diplomatic support but also tangible material support'. Bhutto added that the 'CENTO members have been informed', and that an intervention on the side of Pakistan was expected.[1] But it was not that straightforward.

Ankara and Tehran were both under pressure from the United States to stay out of the India–Pakistan conflict.[2] At the very least, the United States did not want to see American weapons given to the Iranians and Turks end up in the service of Pakistan against India – a country the United States did not want to antagonize, as it was a formidable counterweight to China in Asia. By and large, the Turks and the Iranians caved in to Washington's pressure. Bhutto's hope for a CENTO lifeline – if he ever truly believed it himself, and if it was ever anything more than mere swagger for the Pakistani public – remained unfulfilled. An international condemnation of India never materialized. Neither Turkey nor Iran – nor anyone else, for that matter – broke off relations with India.

When it became clear that CENTO would not save the day for Pakistan, Islamabad backtracked. On 9 September, only two days after Bhutto had given the world an ultimatum, the Pakistani Foreign Ministry declared that Islamabad 'had not invoked the Central Treaty Organization in its conflict with India', and that as far as military assistance was concerned 'no talks were envisaged with Turkey or Iran'.[3] The statement was a huge face-saving exercise; Pakistani hopes for CENTO as a defence backup lay in ruins.

CENTO's collective paralysis should have been foreseen by anyone who had paid attention to the body's performance, and Islamabad should have been the least-astonished capital. The Pakistanis had not only bitterly complained about CENTO's futility throughout the early 1960s but also willfully sought to compensate for it. The world, for example, had noticed with some surprise that President Ayub Khan and his young foreign minister, Zulfikar Bhutto, were absent at the 1965 annual CENTO meeting that took place in April in Tehran. Instead, the Pakistani leaders had travelled to the Soviet Union, ostensibly home of the very same foes that CENTO had been established to counter, to gauge Moscow's position and readiness to work with Islamabad.[4] The trip to Moscow was simply grandstanding, but thus was Pakistan's tempestuous disposition toward her CENTO partners – and it was noticed.

The lessons of the war of 1965

In the early phase of the 1965 war, Pakistan's media raised expectations of an intervention by regional CENTO members, meaning Iran and Turkey. Pakistanis were told that Radio Tehran had announced that the Iranian Government felt itself 'duty-bound' to come to Islamabad's aid, and that Iranians would not 'fail to extend every possible assistance to their Pakistani brothers and sisters'.[5]

The *New York Times* reported that large groups of Iranian youth had gathered outside the Pakistani Embassy in Tehran in an act of solidarity and to volunteer to fight the Indians.[6] There were at the time unsubstantiated Pakistani reports that Turkey was considering severing diplomatic ties with India.[7]

On 8 September, Iranian premier Amir Abbas Hoveida visited Ankara to discuss Pakistan's request for military help from its CENTO allies.[8] On 14 September, Hoveida and Turkish Foreign Minister Hasan Isik travelled to Islamabad. They met President Ayub Khan and Foreign Minister Bhutto, and discussed Pakistan's political and material needs. The key question was how to overcome American objections to a CENTO involvement in the conflict. In the end, a solution to that challenge could not be found.

The British, the only full CENTO member located outside the region, were emphatic. London maintained that the organization was only meant as a line of defence against Soviet communism, not India or any other entity. Washington echoed this sentiment almost verbatim. In fact, both Washington and London laid much of the blame for the 1965 war at Pakistan's door.

When US diplomats told their Pakistani counterparts that Washington's alliance with Islamabad was one only against the Soviets and 'not against the Indians', the bruised Pakistanis would hit back, 'We were your ally; why did you stab us in the back and betray us?'[9] They might have been hurt, but the United States calculated that they still needed Washington and would not do anything drastic such as openly breaking with the United States and pivoting towards Moscow.

Nor was Pakistan's case helped by the fact that its foreign minister, Zulfikar Bhutto, was held in such low esteem in Washington. Dean Rusk, the US secretary of state at the time of the 1965 war, called Bhutto a 'very unreliable man, and we knew him to be an unreliable man who was out to do the United States no good'. As Rusk put it, the Pakistanis could be as upset as they liked but US President Johnson 'wouldn't bow and scrape before people like that' in reference to what both men believed was Bhutto's duplicitous character.[10]

Washington also disliked Bhutto's flirting with the communist Chinese regime of Mao Zedong, at the time a chief US adversary in Asia. If the Pakistanis found Washington to be an unreliable ally, the Americans felt the same way about the behaviour of Islamabad. The Shah of Iran was an anxious spectator on the sidelines, watching this American–Pakistani duel in order to heed its lessons.

There was, furthermore, clearly an American anger at play that regarded the 1965 war as a reckless step on the part of both India and Pakistan. Rusk insisted that the United States had strongly 'urged the two sides to take steps that would avoid the conflict', and that Washington had made it clear that 'if they wanted to ignore [its] advice and go to war with each other [then] the US wouldn't pay for it'. As Rusk put it, the subcontinent had been the principal recipient of US aid and the war was a 'big burden to the United States'.[11] Officials in Washington did not see their stance in the 1965 conflict as a betrayal of Pakistan.

As early as 1961, Washington had expressed dismay at the use of American-supplied weaponry by the Pakistanis in fighting Afghan insurgents who would periodically launch attacks against Pakistan. As one Pakistani editorial put it: 'if American military aid cannot be utilized in warding off attacks on our territory, what is the earthly purpose of receiving it. We might as well dispense with it.' This sentiment was not limited to dissident voices in the Pakistani media. In the spring of 1962, President Ayub Khan himself stated bluntly that he saw little value in CENTO and none in SEATO, and thought that Pakistan would be better off without both of them.

When in 1962, John F. Kennedy's White House decided to provide arms to India – which had panicked when the Chinese attacked it that year – the Pakistanis were more than annoyed. When it came to India and Pakistan, Islamabad saw that the United States wanted it both ways. Secretary Rusk admitted as much a year before the 1965 war, when he acknowledged the steep challenge the United States faced on the subcontinent.

On 26 October 1964, in a morning meeting with the British foreign secretary, Patrick Gordon Walker, Rusk called Pakistani behaviour 'America's primary concern' in the region. The two foreign secretaries agreed that Washington and London could not 'solve the Kashmir problem' and faced the 'basic trouble of trying to keep on friendly relations with two countries which hated each other'. 'Endless patience appeared to be needed', stated the transcript from that meeting.[12]

Lessons for the Shah

Not only the United Kingdom and the United States but also their regional allies, Iran and Turkey, proved reluctant partners in Pakistan's most fraught hours in that autumn of 1965. The Iranians did provide some military back-up to Pakistan in the war of 1965, but the bulk of its material support was limited to small arms and ammunition. When a Turkish defence official was asked about the prospects of Pakistan receiving aid from Turkish troops, he replied, 'We are keeping them for Cyprus.'[13] On the provision of aircraft assets, something desperately sought by the Pakistanis, Ankara basically argued that Turkey could not provide military support to Islamabad because 'her jets were under NATO command'. At least from the perspective of politicians and military leaders in Islamabad, this was a cop-out.[14]

If the Pakistanis detected a lack of solidarity, the Iranians and the Turks viewed their stance as dictated by other overriding priorities, namely placating US anxieties about containing the Indo–Pakistani conflict. The Iranians were more willing than any other CENTO member to help, but Tehran's ability to assist was limited. It feared that acting without US blessing would harm US–Iran relations. When the Shah raised the issue with the US ambassador in Tehran, Armin H. Meyer, he was cautioned against it and told that Washington might then 'have to stop arms aid to Iran'.[15] From his particular vantage point in Tehran, the American Ambassador saw the Shah's persistent push for more military supplies as a 'serious burden on the Iranian economy'.

The Shah could not justify purchasing American arms that he could not in fact afford, only to pass some of his older weaponry to his Pakistani friends. At times, the Shah's military procurement efforts aimed at helping Pakistan came close to creating international scandals. In one instance in 1967, Iran provided about 50 F-86 Sabre jets to Pakistan. Manufactured under licence in Canada, the aircraft had been sold a number of years earlier to Germany, which in turn sold them to Iran, which passed them on to Pakistan. The Indians discovered this and complained bitterly to the Americans, whom they suspected had given the Shah the go-ahead despite Washington's own arms embargo on Pakistan since the 1965 war.[16] Almost until he was toppled, New Delhi would regard the Shah as Islamabad's go-between and guarantor of its basic military requirements.

As late as 1968, Ambassador Meyer sent a secret cable to Washington expressing the view that, if push came to shove, it was 'much [more] preferable' if the Pakistanis received some of the weaponry they needed from Turkey, rather than Iran.[17] The Shah nonetheless continued his military assistance to the extent that he could get away with. At other times, Iranian military support was less tangible. For example, during the 1965 India–Pakistan war, many of Pakistan's aircraft were sent to Iran to escape the superior Indian Air Force's raids inside Pakistan itself.

Meyer's warning to the Shah was not an unexpected American position. It was essentially the same warning that the Turks had received a year earlier when they had turned to Washington during another regional conflict. In 1964, CENTO-member Turkey faced a crisis over its policy towards the Mediterranean nation of Cyprus, after communal violence broke out between the Turkish and Greek populations on the island. Greece, another NATO state, was backing the Greek Cypriots. Ankara began contemplating an invasion of Cyprus, and looked to Washington to determine what a US reaction would look like. The answer the Turks received from the Americans was both clear and revealing for others.

In that 1964 Turkey–Cyprus conflict, President Lyndon Johnson told the Turks they should not expect anything from the United States or NATO. Washington went on to let Ankara know that the United States would not even come to Turkey's aid if the invasion of Cyprus that it was planning led to a Soviet counter-intervention, as Moscow had hinted it would.[18] The message to the Turks was crystal clear: Western powers would not come to its aid in regional conflicts that were not somehow tied to larger US objectives in the setting of the Cold War. The Turks quickly abandoned the idea of an invasion of Cyprus for the time being, and instead began a process of rapprochement with the Soviet Union.[19] Iran and Pakistan too shared the perception that CENTO states could not rely on Washington – or at least not in regard to regional conflicts that did not involve the Soviets.

The Turks, the Pakistanis and the Iranians gave little consideration to the predicament that the United States found itself in, and the near-impossible task for Washington of having to pick sides in a conflict between two NATO allies, Greece and Turkey, or choosing between Pakistan and India. It is argued that the Turks, along with the Iranians and the Pakistanis, had at best improbable expectations about CENTO's mission, namely as a line of defence against the Soviets only. Alternatively, it could be claimed that the CENTO countries of Iran, Pakistan and Turkey were deliberately 'pushing the envelope' and seeking to drag the United States into local conflicts in which its immediate national security interests were not at stake. Either way, it is hard not to acknowledge that Washington performed poorly in managing the expectations of the CENTO states. That was certainly one of the key headlines from the Indo–Pakistani war of 1965.

The other main fallout from the 1965 conflict was its psychological impact on Iranian opinion regarding Pakistan's worth as a strategic ally. For Islamabad, the war of 1965 had at best been inconclusive and Pakistan had certainly failed in its objectives. The Shah recognized this, and from then on India would be regarded differently from Tehran.

§

For now, the Shah retained much sympathy with the Pakistani viewpoint. He thought that Islamabad was justified in feeling betrayed by the US' stance during the 1965 India–Pakistan war. He had himself been particularly sceptical about the loyalty of the Democratic administrations of John F. Kennedy and Lyndon Johnson, which were in office from January 1961 until 1969. At one point, the Shah characterized the Kennedy Administration's human rights agenda as 'more or less an American coup directed against him [the Shah]'.[20] But while the Shah had his deep doubts about the Democratic Party and American liberals, he had been equally disapproving of earlier Republican-controlled White Houses.

The Iranian monarch had been one of the first voices within CENTO to question Washington's commitment to supporting individual members of the alliance. In January 1958, he told US Secretary of State John Foster Dulles, one of America's original 'Cold Warriors', that Tehran would leave CENTO (then still known as the Baghdad Pact) 'unless Washington gave explicit assurances for greater military and economic aid' to Iran.

The Shah, who was also aware and upset that Turkey and Pakistan received more US military aid than did Iran, would tell Dulles that Tehran could 'contemplate declaring a neutralist policy', as had Nehru's India and Nasser's Egypt. In an apologetic note to President Eisenhower, Dulles said that the Shah – who, Dulles claimed, thought of himself as a 'military genius' – was merely bargaining, and would not act on his threats to leave the pact. Dulles urged Eisenhower, the American military hero of World War II, to play to the Shah's vanities on military matters but also asked for Washington to increase aid to Iran, a move that he considered 'reasonable and well within [US] capability'.[21] A US Government assessment from 1961 showed that, of the three CENTO members, Iran was in fact the most 'self-reliant' in terms of meeting its defence-procurement costs as compared with Turkey and Pakistan.[22]

Iran and Pakistan look beyond CENTO

Given their lingering doubts about Washington's readiness to come to their rescue, which predated the 1965 Indo-Pakistani war, Tehran and Islamabad had, from the early 1960s, begun increasingly to look to each other for closer defence collaboration.

There had been much speculation along these lines during the Shah's visit to Pakistan in July 1962. This Iran–Pakistan collaboration, incidentally, occurred at the same time as the Shah was, behind the scenes, urging the Kennedy Administration to cease arms exports to both Pakistan and India – as he held an arms race on the subcontinent to be unsustainable.

Pakistani sources whispered to the media that Tehran and Islamabad were in serious discussions about an alternative to CENTO, a bilateral defence pact that they could each put more faith in to deliver when conditions demanded. The United States observed these tactical manoeuvres, but seemed convinced that Iran and Pakistan would never stray too far from the American orbit. As Dulles had written to President Eisenhower in 1958, Washington continued to see these moves as an ongoing bargaining ploy by seasoned hagglers from the Orient aimed at securing increased US aid and weaponry.

Nonetheless, at the time of Pakistan's 1965 war with India, US diplomats began sending messages back to Washington indicating that the US trust deficit had deepened in Islamabad. One state department briefing paper judged that many Pakistanis believed the then-ongoing Vietnam War had exhausted the US, and that Washington had 'lost its will to support its friends' in west Asia.[23] The Soviet Union, on the other hand, was said to be 'willing to go all the way to back its local allies in Afghanistan, Ethiopia and South Yemen'. Little wonder, then, that in this period both the Iranians and the Pakistanis grew more receptive to Soviet overtures.

The Soviets, for their part, did not hide their intention of ingratiating themselves with Islamabad and Tehran. After Soviet and Chinese communists underwent a decisive split in 1963, Moscow pushed to play a bigger role on the Asian continent, primarily to counter Beijing. As far as Pakistan was concerned, Moscow's major overture came in January 1966 when Soviet premier Alexei Kosygin succeeded in brokering a compromise between Indian Prime Minister Lal Bahadur Shastri and President Ayub Khan of Pakistan, which officially ended the 1965 Indian–Pakistani war.

This was to be known as the Tashkent Declaration, and it was at the accompanying conference that Kosygin first put forward the Soviet proposal for regional economic cooperation and an overland trade route between India, Pakistan, Afghanistan and the Soviet Union. This was Moscow's concept of 'Asian Security'. Moscow was vying for influence in west Asia in ways that it never had before, and it was literally proposing an alternative to CENTO and US-backed regional projects.[24]

Iran feared this Soviet plan and so did the United States and the British, all considering it an attempt by Moscow to encroach on their territory. Ayub Khan was not thrilled with the Soviet initiative either – and not simply because it was a Soviet plan, although that was clearly a major factor. His then foreign minister, Zulfikar Bhutto, had pushed the President towards radically improving relations with Moscow. In an April 1966 letter to Ayub Khan, the ever-populist Bhutto saw such a step as going down well with 'the Pakistani youth and the radical masses'.[25]

Khan was mainly cold towards the idea as he did not believe it to be achievable. Moscow tried some hard selling, knowing that there was plenty of disillusionment about Washington's perceived lack of commitment to Islamabad. The Soviets promised the Pakistanis 'non-interference in [the] domestic affairs of any country that joined its regional economic and military integration efforts'. That meant little to Islamabad, as Soviet interference in domestic Pakistani affairs was a secondary concern. Ayub Khan cut to the chase: 'What help, if any, can the Soviets provide as far as this proposed security plan is concerned if one member state attacked another as in 1965 India-Pakistan war?' The answer the Soviets gave was a fudge. Moscow said its plan would 'put an end to such regional conflicts which the Imperialist countries like [the] USA and expansionist ones like China encourage'.[26]

This sort of Soviet jargon was not much use to the shaken Pakistanis, who were still licking their wounds from the 1965 debacle. However imperfect, they thought it better to stay with CENTO and the United States, and to keep the partnership they had developed with China, than accept the lofty but dubious promises of Moscow. When Moscow in August 1971 signed a friendship treaty with India, it was all too obvious that the Soviets could not deliver what Pakistan wanted. Later, Bhutto was blunt: 'Pakistan has suffered a great deal from pacts. "Asian security" [the name that Moscow gave its plan] against whom?'[27]

While Moscow's greater strategic goal of expanding on the Eurasian landmass failed to gain traction, its role as a useful auxiliary to the United States was recognized by both Iran and Pakistan. One key commodity the Soviets possessed, and were willing to dispense, was arms – which, incidentally, Tehran and Islamabad craved more than anything else. It was in the period starting in 1967 that Islamabad became a recipient of Soviet weaponry.[28]

The same calculations were made in Tehran. When the Shah asked for modern US weaponry and was declined credit by Washington, he turned to Moscow. Tehran's first substantial arms transaction with the Soviets came in 1966, in a $110 million deal.[29] All this was uncomfortably noted by Washington, but no alarm bells were triggered because no one feared that the Shah would jump ship. The Shah, and the Pakistanis, were after all seen to flirt with the Russians with one objective in mind: to make Washington jealous and to persuade the United States to increase its military supplies – or, in the case of Pakistan, to remove the arms embargo imposed after the 1965 Indian–Pakistani conflict. The administration of President Lyndon Johnson, however, did not back down.

On 20-1 April 1967, Secretary of State Rusk went to Ankara to attend the CENTO annual meeting. There, he told the other leaders to 'turn wholeheartedly to economic matters' – in other words, to stop obsessing about US military aid and supplies. London and Washington made it clear that they were not interested in spending large sums of money on joint military ventures. CENTO would have to turn its attention to the development of the food, health and education sectors.[30]

On the one hand, Washington's efforts to promote economic development were laudable. Iran, Turkey and Pakistan had at the time a combined population of some 200 million people. This was a large market by any standards, and all three countries were also at the same time lagging on socio-economic indicators. Yet the level of economic activity between the three partners was dismal.

The by-now open US sneering at the military role of CENTO made Washington's advocacy of economic integration seem both a deliberate distraction and unconvincing. The Shah himself told a French television station that despite years of talk, CENTO still did not have a joint set of military plans and that the term 'defense arrangement could not be applied'. The Iranian leader was, of course, on to something. The CENTO treaty did not itself contain a binding military article. Its Article 1 merely stated that member states 'will cooperate for their security and defense'. If military collaboration was lacking, the economic ideas of the Johnson Administration were simply too far-fetched. As one American official put it, referring to a national US youth organisation, 'CENTO might have turned into some sort of Middle East 4-H club'.

Creating the occasional distance with Western powers had a popular spin-off effect, as so many of the masses in both Pakistan and Iran were at best sceptical toward the West. A CIA special memorandum portrayed the Shah at the time as a 'self-confident potentate, determined to assert his and Iran's prerogatives against all comers'. The memo even admitted that the Shah's 'economic and military deals with the USSR have won him recognition at home as the foremost defender of Iran's national interest'. The Shah's dealings with the Soviets had made it harder for his domestic detractors to label him an American lackey.

Washington concluded that while the Shah 'had often acted against US advice', he was nevertheless a valuable ally and would not abandon his overall attachment to the Western bloc. The British, who unlike the United States were a full member of CENTO, agreed and actually went further in their assessment of the significance of Shah's dealings with the Soviets. A British diplomatic note intended for distribution among American eyes held that, 'It is to Iran's and our advantage that Iran should pursue a cautiously independent policy rather than appear to be a satellite of the West', while also confessing that 'Iran benefits materially from the economic relationship with the Soviet Union'.[31]

Throughout the second half of the 1960s, Washington and London watched as CENTO allies Iran and Pakistan probed various foreign policy options. Islamabad had clearly acted more boldly in establishing a real partnership with Mao's communist China and then weighing Soviet offers. The Shah had been far less experimental in his foreign policy behaviour, but then again he did not have to face down a much larger adversary as Pakistan had to with India.

The challenge for Washington and London was to prevent the Shah from mimicking some of the more audacious steps that the Pakistanis next door had made. On the Shah's rapprochement with Moscow, the British urged that the Anglo–American leadership must constantly be measuring Shah's next steps and be prepared to move in quickly with firm advice if they believed it necessary. The call for this sort for intervention was then justified because, as the British saw it at least, the Shah possessed a darker, irrational side which made him prone to ill-considered actions by the real or imagined neglect of his interests by his allies in London and Washington.

In this contemptuous view of the Iranian leader, the British nevertheless did not want to appear condescending as they merely saw themselves as saving the Shah from himself. In the high-stakes geopolitical manoeuvrings of the late 1960s in south-west Asia, London thought it necessary to guide the Shah lest he 'trip unintentionally over the edge during one of his exercises of brinkmanship'. This sort of patronizing Western stance was equally resented in Islamabad. Ayub Khan's 1967 autobiography was very deliberately titled *Friends Not Masters*.

The Shah's unease about Pakistan's new Arab friends

While they nursed shared grievances against Western allies inside CENTO, Iran and Pakistan clashed as well. Problems began not long after Iran's daring intervention on behalf of Islamabad in the Indo–Pakistani war of 1965. By 1967, there were serious strains in the Shah's relations with Ayub Khan.

The disquiet began as the Shah saw Khan increasingly looking to radical Arab revolutionary regimes such as that in Nasser's pro-Soviet Egypt – an anathema to the Shah – as inspirational movements worthy of Pakistan's admiration and perhaps, even, as collaborators. This diminished Khan's standing in the eyes of many in Tehran – particularly since as far as many Iranians were concerned Khan had never been able to fill the shoes of his predecessor, the jovial Iskander Mirza.

Since the Shah viewed Nasser as a Soviet proxy, Ayub Khan's admiration for the Egyptian president was tantamount to flirting with the enemy. The Shah bitterly complained to US Secretary of State Dean Rusk that when Khan 'wined and dined General Amer [Nasser's vice president, who went to Pakistan for a week in December 1966]' he could not help but be furious.[32] When the Iranians protested against Amer's visit, Islamabad reassured them that the visit was merely part of Pakistani efforts to muster more Arab votes in support of its position on disputed Kashmir at the United Nations, and purely an effort against India.

The Shah, rightly, would point out that there had been 'no public announcements by Amer' suggesting that the Egyptians would side with Pakistan against India.[33] In fact, Nasser had gone on record in the past to defend the Indian claim on Kashmir.[34] But this did not seem to matter. In truth, Nasser and his radical, revolutionary ways had induced a degree of infatuation in both Ayub Khan and, probably, a broad segment of the Pakistani population that the Shah simply could not emulate.

Contemporary accounts given by Iranian officials certainly speak of a deeper emotional disappointment at some of Pakistan's actions at this time than would be suggested by this incident alone. The Iranians chose not take the matter lying down. Assad Homayoun, an Iranian diplomat based in Pakistan in the late 1960s, remembers a telegraph that came from Tehran when he was stationed at the embassy in Islamabad. It instructed the Iranian ambassador, General Hassan Pakravan, to go and see Ayub Khan and ask him 'why is it that Pakistan always turns to Iran when it has material needs but holds instead 100,000-man rallies for Nasser of Egypt?'.[35]

Pakravan, a former head of Iran's intelligence service, the SAVAK, was close to the Shah and had been sent to Pakistan partly because of his prominent stature, which was viewed as reflecting the importance that the Iranian leader attached to Tehran–Islamabad ties. Upon hearing from Pakravan, Khan told him to immediately go to the presidential office where he asked the ambassador to inform the Shah that 'Iran will not come second to any other country for Pakistan'. For the next few weeks, Khan continued to pay lip service to the Shah. In October 1967, when the latter held a pompous coronation for himself, Ayub Khan marked it as a 'fraternal' moment. At the same time, he would let it be known to others that the Shah could not grasp why Pakistan pursued a multifaceted foreign policy to secure its needs.[36]

Soon after Khan had hailed the coronation, the Shah took another jab at the Pakistani leader. On 2 November 1967, *Ettelaat*, Iran's leading newspaper, suddenly stopped publishing translations of Khan's autobiography, *Friends Not Masters*. Instead *Ettelaat*, whose editors got their cue from the royal court, ran an editorial attacking Ayub Khan. It turned out that the Iranians were angry about the praise in his book for Egypt's Nasser. The fact that they stopped publishing excerpts halfway through suggests that no one had bothered to first read the book in its entirety. This Iranian fuss, however, was tied to something much deeper than simply soothing the Shah's bruised ego – although that no doubt formed part of it.

The Shah was worried about how far Khan would take his dalliance with Moscow and courting of pro-Soviet regional leaders such as Nasser. When Khan's quest for a 'multi-faceted foreign policy' led him to ask the Jordanians to mediate between Islamabad and the Baathist leadership in Baghdad, the Shah saw that the Pakistani President was pushing his luck.

At the time, the Shah was already anxious about Pakistan's increasingly close ties with the communist Chinese. In fact, he partly justified Iranian arms supplies to Pakistan as a way of preventing Islamabad becoming entirely dependent on Beijing during the 1965 war. The Pakistanis, though, were now truly striking out on their own path. When Ayub Khan sided with the Arabs in the June 1967 Arab–Israeli War, the Shah called it a 'biased' step, fearing that the degree to which Pakistan was smitten with the radical Arab regimes was becoming hazardous.

The Shah let his reservations be known, and continued to support Israel via the supply of Iranian oil. He even downplayed the impact of the Arab–Israeli conflict. In a meeting at Blair House in Washington, DC, only a few weeks after the June 1967 Arab-Israeli war, the Shah told US Secretary of State Dean Rusk that 'Iran was not being hurt by the closing of the Suez Canal' (by the Egyptians), but that it was a different story with Pakistan.[37] He informed Rusk that it was a difficult balancing act: on the one hand, the Arabs should not feel that they had too much leverage through the control of the canal, but the price to pay was the economic pain that the closing of the waterway imposed on the poorer Pakistan.

Ayub Khan, on the other hand, had virtually become the sponsor of the Arab line within CENTO. At the end of July 1967, when the leaders of Iran, Pakistan and Turkey gathered in Tehran, Khan sought to persuade the other two states to break diplomatic ties with Israel. The Shah and Turkish President Cevdet Sunay, whose country had a similar position to Iran over the Arab–Israeli conflict, listened but Ankara and Tehran did not budge.[38] Iran and Turkey would in effect maintain ties with the Jewish state.

The Arab question continued to generate friction between Islamabad and Tehran. Soon after the 1967 war, the Pakistani media began to refer to the Persian Gulf as the 'Arabian Gulf'. The latter was a phrase coined by Nasser, and part of his revolutionary Arab agenda. The Shah was livid. Iran retaliated, and suddenly Iranian media (largely government-controlled) took a far more sympathetic line towards India, particularly over the Kashmir dispute. Up until then, Pakistan had always been able to count on Tehran's support on the question of Kashmir.[39]

Matters worsened before cooler heads could prevail. The Iranians complained that the Pakistanis had their diplomats under tight surveillance, something they obviously resented.[40] Islamabad, in turn, had its list of grievances. Ayub Khan was particularly averse to the Iranian foreign minister, Ardeshir Zahedi, whose frequent visits to Pakistan were gradually looking to the Pakistanis more like lecture tours. Khan resented Zahedi so much so that he took it on himself to advise the Shah to replace him.[41] Tayyib Hussain, the Pakistani ambassador to Tehran, received Khan's instructions to approach the Shah with this awkward request. This was a highly delicate situation for Hussain: how could he sweet-talk the Shah, the King of Kings, into getting rid of his foreign minister?

The Shah's ties to Zahedi ran deep. Ardeshir's father, General Fazlollah Zahedi, had been instrumental in returning the Shah to the throne in 1953. At one point, Ardeshir had been his son-in-law when he married Princess Shahnaz, the Shah's only child from his first marriage, to Princess Fawzia of Egypt. While the Shah too felt that Ardeshir could at times be indiscreet, he nonetheless viewed him as a loyal confidant. Hussain knew all this very well and shuddered at the thought of broaching the topic. He reached out to the British Ambassador in Tehran in search of advice. The British, themselves often targets of Ardeshir's outspokenness, saw no happy ending in Ayub's request and stayed out of the matter.[42]

Ardeshir Zahedi remained as foreign minister until 1973, and while his frankness had ruffled feathers in Islamabad, Iran–Pakistan problems were broader than the presence of any single individual. The Arab question continued to be the spoiler, but soon Pakistan's overture to an entirely different group of Arabs – the sheikhdoms of the Persian Gulf region – became as worrying for Tehran as Islamabad's earlier overtures to the pro-Soviet Arab revolutionary regimes of Egypt and Iraq.

Rumble in the Persian Gulf

In January 1968, Britain announced that it would pull out its forces from regions east of the Suez Canal. That included a British withdrawal from the Persian Gulf littoral regions where *Pax Britannica* had dominated since London signed its first Arabian treaty with the Sultan of Muscat in 1798.

The decision had taken the Shah somewhat by a surprise. Only three months earlier, London had sent an emissary to Tehran – Baron Goronwy Roberts – to assure him that there was no British plan to leave the Persian Gulf. Shortly afterwards, in July 1969, the newly installed administration of President Nixon proclaimed that the United States 'would no longer maintain its role as the world's policeman'. This declaration would become known as the Nixon Doctrine. As the Shah viewed it, never before had Iran needed to be ready to defend itself without relying on others.[43]

There was, however, an upside to Washington's decision. The Nixon Administration specifically emphasized the role that Tehran could play in safeguarding the security of the Persian Gulf and effectively acting as a US surrogate in the defence of the region. Washington determined that to implement the Nixon Doctrine successfully required Iranian access to the latest American weaponry. Soon, the most sophisticated US military platforms, including Airborne Warning And Control Systems (AWACS), various types of ships and missiles, and the recently launched F-14 fighter aircraft were headed for Iran, a flow that continued until the fall of the Shah's regime in February 1979.[44]

Back in 1969, the Shah was emboldened by the trust that Nixon had placed in him. As he went about sketching Tehran's regional objectives in this new era, the Pakistanis could not help but feel slighted by Washington. In Islamabad, the Nixon Doctrine was considered an inequitable treatment of America's regional allies. Throughout the remainder of the Shah's time on the Persian throne, the Pakistanis enviously watched as he went about fulfilling his new mission.

The Shah's first big geopolitical gamble was his attempt to govern supremely over the Persian Gulf. The British presence and control of the Gulf sheikhdoms had for over a century been an irritant for Tehran as it sought to deal with its smaller Arab neighbours. And there was no doubt that the Shah harboured much mistrust towards the British, particularly as they had forced his father into exile back in 1941 (due to his German sympathies).

Nevertheless, the British had also acted as a protective shield against encroachments by other extra-regional powers. This British function was of paramount importance. The waters and the huge energy fields of the Persian Gulf were critical to the Iranian and the global economies.

Iranian foreign policy historian Rouhollah Ramazani judged that the British decision to withdraw from the Persian Gulf forced three objectives on the Iranian leader: 'To safeguard the Shah's regime against internal subversion; to ensure uninterrupted passage through the Strait of Hormuz; to protect Iranian oil resources and facilities.'[45] To the Shah, these objectives were only attainable if Iran sought and replaced the military role Britain had for so long played in this part of the world. The oil revenue that was now steadily increasing was to be the vehicle that would enable the Shah to reach his ideal destination. On paper, no other littoral state was as well equipped as Iran. The process was set in motion.

A few, somewhat fundamental, obstacles immediately faced Tehran. First, London did not want the Shah's Iran to replace its role in the region. As early as 1965, British Foreign Secretary Michael Stewart advised Prime Minister Harold Wilson to 'disabuse the Shah of the idea that, if and when [Britain] ever leaves the Persian Gulf, Iran can take our place'. As seen by London, the Shah's ambitions in the Persian Gulf posed a threat to a 'post-Britannica' regional balance of power – especially as Tehran continued to press Iranian territorial claims against the British-protected sheikhdoms of Bahrain, Sharjah and Ras Al Khaimah.[46] The more-distant Pakistan was not an immediate participant in the race for influence in the Persian Gulf, but it very early on saw itself as a clear stakeholder in the future of the Gulf states that would emerge once Britain abandoned its colonial possessions. Despite its closeness to Tehran, Islamabad was hardly going to take its cues from the Shah.

Pakistan needed to play a very guarded hand in this transition period in the Persian Gulf. Ayub Khan had already angered the Shah with his flirting with leftist Arab republican regimes, and risked losing his favour over the Gulf Arabs. The fact was that the Shah was convinced that London was conspiring with the Arabs against Iran. Pakistan had to choose whose side it was on. As events unfolded, Islamabad would in fact try to have it both ways: reassuring Iran, but also wooing the sheikhs of the Persian Gulf.

§

The Arab Gulf states that were to emerge once Britain withdrew – Bahrain, Qatar and the United Arab Emirates – were hardly thrilled at the prospect of living under a domineering Iran. There were also territorial disputes in the Gulf that needed to be settled between the Iranian and Arab sides. In the memoirs of Asadollah Alam, the Shah's chief courtier, the British ambassador to Tehran, Denis Wright, was said to have expressed Arab fears about the Shah's plans. 'To hell with it,' Alam retorted, 'What have the Arabs ever done for us? If only they would stop all this nonsense, agree to pay for the defense of the Gulf and let us get to work.' Alam told Wright that Iran was happy to draw up a 50-year defence agreement with the Gulf Arab states, as they had done with the British.[47]

Unbeknownst to the Iranians, the British had, as early as 1967, put together a long-term policy plan in which Iran and Saudi Arabia would share the responsibility for defending the region. This would serve both as a line of defence against the Soviets and to provide an Arab counterweight to Iranian regional supremacy. Before Nixon's arrival in the White House, Washington too felt that Saudi Arabia deserved the same degree of attention as Iran. This was an insult to the Shah. Iran's ambassador to Washington at the time, Houshang Ansary, had a meeting with Secretary of State Dean Rusk on 22 November 1968, in which it was made clear that the Shah was concerned about 'undue support to Saudi Arabia'. Rusk was left with the clear impression that the Shah wanted the United States to 'pick Iran as its chosen instrument in the Middle East'.[48]

What stands out from all the toing and froing between London, Tehran and the Gulf Arabs is the lack of any serious reference to CENTO as a multilateral mechanism that could have filled the void left by the departure of the British. In fact, instead of any collective effort much evidence points to the Iranians and Pakistanis separately racing forward to secure maximum influence among the newly independent Arab Gulf states. In CENTO meetings, Tehran would tout the issue of collective responsibility for the defence of the Gulf but was forceful in maintaining that littoral states had the primary role. This, in effect, only meant one thing: Iranian domination of the Persian Gulf. Within CENTO, Turkey's relative remoteness rendered it an unsuitable candidate for any major role in the Gulf. Nor did Iran consider Pakistan a Persian Gulf state. Meanwhile, the small littoral Arab countries were no match for Tehran.

Tehran tried to coerce the Gulf Arabs into accepting its vision for the region. When that did not work, Iran flexed its muscles. As unfolding events showed, between January 1968 and December 1971 – from London announcing its intentions, until it pulled out from the Persian Gulf – Islamabad and Tehran became the two chief regional players, jockeying for new opportunities in the Gulf's rich waters.

Pakistan and a Trojan Horse

The Pakistani ambassador to Tehran, Tayyib Hussain, soon found himself once again in the middle of the Iran–Pakistan whirlwind. This time, however, his role was public. On 8 January 1968, Hussain caused a fuss when he told Iranian media that Pakistan considered then-British-controlled Bahrain to be 'part of Persia', and that it 'recognizes the Persian Gulf by that name only'. This was not a slip of the tongue. Since December 1967, Islamabad had been trying to calm tensions with Tehran.

On 24 December, the Pakistani newspaper *Observer* even apologized for its use of the term 'Arabian Gulf'. Bahrain's local rulers, anxious about the Shah's claim on the island, were terrified and furious. The Bahrainis asked the British to intervene. London, however, could do no more than ask all parties to stay calm.[49]

The Iranians remained alert to Pakistani conduct, and continued to see some of Islamabad's steps as a threat. It did not help that Ayub Khan sacked Tayyib Hussain, a move that Tehran likened to appeasement of the Arabs.

At times, Tehran would present some of its misgivings wrapped as concerns that Pakistan's actions were making CENTO vulnerable. For example, between 13 and 23 February 1968 Iran and Pakistan held joint naval exercises, nicknamed 'Taj' (Crown). British and American observers were not granted access. The British suspected that this was due to Pakistani insistence, but Tehran had nonetheless gone along with this arrangement.[50] When Iranian officers reported back to Tehran that the Pakistanis had instead let Saudi officers join in during the exercises, eyebrows were raised. The Iranians feared that the Saudis would have noted the 'shortcomings and failures' of their military preparedness, and later discovered that the Pakistanis were also sharing NATO military handbooks – made available to Iran and Pakistan due to their membership of CENTO – with Saudi officers training in Pakistan.

Tehran was alarmed, and raised the question of Pakistan as a 'Trojan Horse'. Washington was sympathetic. Throughout 1968, the US intelligence community assessed that Islamabad was repeatedly in violation of its terms of procurement of American weaponry. One US cable called Pakistani actions 'a partial quid pro quo for Chinese assistance', which meant that Islamabad was giving Beijing access to sensitive US technology.[51]

Attempts were again made to prevent the Iranian and Pakistani fallout from deepening. Between 22 and 26 July 1968, Ayub Khan made another visit to Tehran. He knew exactly the sore point to address, and admitted to his Iranian hosts that Islamabad had been 'over-zealous' in its support for Nasser.[52] The Shah in turn asked Khan not to fall out any further with the Americans. He specifically urged Islamabad to rethink its decision to close down a US surveillance facility in Peshawar, the turbulent Pakistani city on the border with Afghanistan. The Shah called this a 'mistake', but Khan defended the decision by pointing to acute Soviet pressure on the matter given that Moscow saw the presence of the facility on Pakistani soil as 'incompatible with amicable Soviet-Pakistani relations'. Khan went ahead with the move, and by November 1969 the facility closed as its lease had not been renewed. By this action, Pakistan had broken 'a worldwide United States communications chain'.[53] However, Khan did at same time reject Moscow's requests to use Pakistani facilities, despite the flow of Soviet arms and promises of millions of dollars of Soviet aid to Islamabad.[54]

The Shah later informed US officials that he had always told Khan that installations such as the one in Peshawar 'are in reality operations for peace', and that such 'installations are very much in the interest of both

Pakistan and Iran'.[55] Regardless of what the Shah had in fact told Ayub Khan, the version he gave to the Americans was an attempt to inflate his role as the United States' most empathetic ally, looking after Washington's interests.

In truth, he had always shared much of the same reservations about perceived American dithering that had led to the Peshawar closure.[56] In the end, it was not Iran but Afghanistan that helped the United States fill the gap left by the closing of the Peshawar facility. In the spring of 1970, shortly after a visit by US Vice President Spiro Agnew to Afghanistan, a US Air Force C-141 aircraft brought a satellite tracking team to staff a new listening station outside Kabul.[57]

During Ayub Khan's visit to Tehran in the summer of 1968, the other topic under discussion was the pending British withdrawal from the Persian Gulf. The two sides seemingly opted to avoid making this question another area of contention. Khan stressed that regional states would have to deal with the 'legacy of de-colonization', but told the Shah that the problems at hand were not 'insoluble'. The Pakistani President did not, however, make any promises in Tehran. Meanwhile, Khan too had a piece of advice for the Shah, and urged him to 'come to an agreement with the Arabs on the [Persian Gulf] islands disagreement'. Nonetheless, this issue was sensitive enough not to feature in the joint communiqué that followed Khan's visit to Iran.[58]

CHAPTER 5

1969-71: IRAN'S INTERVENTION OVER THE PAKISTANI DEFEAT OF 1971

On 25 March 1969, Ardeshir Zahedi, the Iranian foreign minister who had so greatly offended Ayub Khan, was visiting Hong Kong when he received a sudden telegram from Tehran. He was instructed to telephone the Shah as soon as possible. 'Ayub Khan has been removed', Zahedi was told when he called. A new Pakistani leader was now in charge: General Yahya Khan, the country's army chief from 1967 until his leap into the top post. The Shah asked his foreign minister to hasten to Pakistan for consultations, and to help assess the situation. After all, Zahedi knew the country very well and was the best man for the job, above and beyond his position as the Shah's chief foreign emissary. Zahedi, however, felt that he needed to see the Shah in Tehran before his visit to Pakistan. The matter was serious, and he wanted to ensure that he was 'on the same page' as his king.

As he was preparing for his trip back home to Tehran, Zahedi got another call. This time it was the Indian Ambassador in Japan, who told the Iranian Foreign Minister that India's prime minister, Indira Gandhi, had requested that Zahedi make a stop in India on his way back to Tehran. Zahedi ran this by Tehran, and the Shah himself approved the stopover in India.[1] Zahedi agreed to meet Indian officials, led by Mahommedali Currim Chagla, but only at the airport. Zahedi knew and liked M. C. Chagla: a Shi'a Muslim, he had been one of India's most prominent diplomats, and he and Zahedi had served at the same time as their countries' ambassadors to Washington in the early 1960s. Personal rapport meant that the conversation at the airport could be frank, given that Chagla's mission that day was to assess Tehran's intentions with regard to the power shift in Islamabad.

Zahedi told Chagla that Tehran wanted above all to keep relations between Pakistan and India on an even keel. He then warned the Indian diplomat, 'India knows about [Iran's] affinity for Pakistan and our interests there.' Zahedi added, 'Iran will support Pakistan 100% if India [takes] any military steps against it' in those turbulent times. Chagla, who had himself once been a very close friend of Mohammad Ali Jinnah before the partition of British India, could not have misconstrued the Iranian's message of backing for Islamabad. The Indians took note, and replied that they had no intention of taking advantage of the crisis in Pakistan.

Zahedi then went to see the Shah about Iran's options vis-à-vis events in Islamabad. On the same day, he flew to Pakistan to meet Yahya Khan. On the other side of the world, Zahedi's warning to the Indians against taking advantage of Pakistan's power transition, and the pandemonium that such action could create, was shared by the Nixon Administration in Washington.[2] This was a conformity of perspective that Tehran and Washington would continue to share in the next, eventful, few years.

In Islamabad, Zahedi sought to reassure Yahya Khan, encouraging him to stay on as president. He explicitly told Yahya Khan that Tehran would urge Zulfikar Bhutto to curtail his ambitions in the midst of the political transition in Islamabad: 'I told [Yahya Khan] that Bhutto and I are like brothers. I will ask him not to make any erratic moves.'[3] Bhutto, the flamboyant former foreign minister, was at the time a key rival to Yahya Khan; however, the political contest was devoid of the kind of personal malice that Pakistanis would one day become accustomed to, and the two men were known to privately socialize.

The political situation in Pakistan had, in fact, deteriorated at exactly the time that the Shah had feared. Shortly before the removal of Ayub Khan, the Iranian leader had dispatched another senior Iranian figure on a mission. This time it was Asadollah Alam, his chief courtier, who, in mid-March, went to Kabul with a couple of points to stress. Kabul was urged not to harass Pakistan when it was weak or to raise the issue of Pashtunistan: 'If Pakistan goes red then we [Iran] may be the only guarantee of Afghanistan's survival.'[4]

Based on his recollection in his memoirs, Alam came back empty-handed from that trip. The Iranian Shah, however, would continue to believe that the real danger to Pakistan came from the Soviets, who in turn would prefer to lean on Islamabad through what the Shah called 'proxies' – meaning New Delhi and Kabul. For now, Yahya Khan would be secure in his new role, but his would become one of the shortest and most contentious presidencies in Pakistan's history.

Yahya Khan's reassuring efforts in Tehran

After coming to power in 1969, Yahya Khan, himself a Shi'a and the scion of Persian soldiers from Nader Shah's army that had raided the subcontinent about two centuries earlier, went to Iran for a state visit from 29 October to 4 November.[5] Both countries needed the visit, and the Shah was deeply worried about the situation in Pakistan.[6]

When Yahya Khan arrived in Tehran, the Shah was cheerful. He had, just three days earlier, celebrated his 50th birthday. On a domestic level, he was politically safer than he had been for some time. His ideological soulmate, Richard Nixon, had only months earlier arrived in the White House. With regard to Yahya Khan, it helped the Pakistani cause immensely that both the Shah and President Nixon personally liked the heavy-drinking general. Kissinger once remarked that Nixon 'had a special feeling about President Yahya Khan', noting that: 'One cannot make policy on that basis, but it is a fact of life.'[7] Nixon had, tellingly, included a stopover in Lahore and a meeting with Yahya Khan in his Asian tour of August 1969.

A day after arriving on his six-day visit, Yahya Khan delivered a well-received address to the Iranian Senate.[8] He highlighted key moments when the Shah's interventions had brought great relief to Pakistan. He specially pointed to Tehran's peace mediation between Pakistan and Afghanistan in 1963. But he left his highest praise for Iran's role in the Indian–Pakistani war of 1965. Khan claimed that there was no better case of solidarity and 'intensity of their feelings of togetherness through woe and weal than the spontaneous, timely and most valuable help extended by Iran to Pakistan in its hour of peril in September 1965,' adding: 'Today we march forward hand in hand for the greatest good of our two countries and people.' There was no shortage of pomp.

Yahya Khan sought not only to press the right buttons with Tehran, but also to make the most fitting gestures. Fully aware of the Shah's disapproval of Ayub Khan's admiration for Gamal Nasser and leftist Arab republicanism, Yahya Khan brought along with him Tayyib Hussain, the former Pakistani ambassador to Tehran, who had been sacked by Ayub Khan purportedly for favouring the Iranians over the Arabs in matters involving the Persian Gulf.[9]

Both in terms of symbolism and substance, military matters stayed top of the agenda throughout Yahya's visit – and not just in terms of Pakistan's capabilities or threat perceptions. Tehran had its own challenges to tackle. During his time there, the Iranians treated Yahya Khan to a visit to Vahdati Airbase near the city of Dezful. Here, close to the Iraqi border, the Iranian Air Force was carrying out military drills at a time when Tehran and Baghdad were at loggerheads over a border dispute around the Shatt Al Arab, the river that separates the two countries. Taking Yahya to the Iraqi border was no coincidence. It was a vivid reminder to the new Pakistani leader that Iran had its own version of border disputes and belligerent neighbours to contend with, and that Iranian–Pakistani defence collaboration was a two-way street.

The Iranian hosts also organized a hunting trip for the Pakistani general to the mountains on the Caspian, a few hours' drive north of Tehran. This was not just the region that the Pahlavi family hailed from but also the frontier with the Soviet Union, a 'stone's throw' away across this, the world's largest lake. The original flight had to be cancelled due to torrential rain. It was suggested that they take cars for transportation, but Yahya Khan demurred and said this would be bad for his health. This led to some mocking among the Iranians. 'And he calls himself a Field Marshal!' the Shah's court minister, Alam, wrote in his daily diaries.[10]

Another destination for Yahya Khan was the holy city of Mashhad, home to one of the most revered Shi'a shrines in the world. Mashhad has for centuries welcomed Shi'a pilgrims from all corners of the globe, including legions from the Indian subcontinent coming to worship at the Shrine of Imam Reza. Yahya Khan, a secular Shi'a, might not have known this at the time but the Shah considered himself leader of the global Shi'a community and custodian of the shrine.[11] The fact was, however, that this sectarian kinship, the Shi'a bond, was not at this time a spark that fired Iranian–Pakistani relations.

Yahya Khan would subsequently be remembered more for his soft spot for a stiff drink than religious feeling of any kind. Though the Shah would periodically attempt to brandish his otherwise debatable religious credentials – including beautifying the city of Mashhad during his 37-year reign – his efforts never convinced the Islamist revolutionaries who were later to topple him. Nor did the Shah use his Shi'ism as an instrument to spread his or Iran's appeal among Pakistan's sizeable Shi'a minority. The 'Shi'a card', as an instrument of soft power, would only be wielded by Tehran after the fall of the Shah and with the coming of the Islamist regime in Tehran in 1979.

There is, in fact, no evidence that the Iranian monarch ever resorted to sectarian-based calculations to make inroads among the Pakistani Shi'a, which would otherwise have been a policy option. The founder of Pakistan, Mohammad Ali Jinnah, and three of the first four presidents of that country were Shi'a. Any intentions the Shah had to make an impression on Pakistani soil were limited to the promotion of the treasures of Iranian civilization. He oversaw the launch of a number of *Khane-ye Farhang Iran* (Houses of Iranian Culture) throughout Pakistan, publicizing Iran's rich legacy of art, literature and the Persian language.

As luck would have it, exactly a decade after Yahya Khan's visit to Mashhad, one of the sons of that pious city would take part in the revolution that toppled the Shah. His name was Ali Khamenei, and by 1989 he had become the supreme leader of Iran.

Iran's anxieties about East Pakistan

During this state visit, political exhibitionism aside, the Shah had some concrete advice for Yahya Khan as well. By this point – late 1969 – the winds of separatism were already blowing strongly in the eastern wing of Pakistan, which would soon after break away as a new country called Bangladesh.

The Shah told Yahya Khan that 'it was no use trying to [find] a military solution against the Awami League [the secessionist party in east Pakistan] and its sympathizers' and that Yahya Khan had made a grave mistake in disregarding the wishes of the majority in his nation's eastern wing. It would later emerge that the Shah and the British had, throughout his two years at the helm, advised Yahya Khan in the same vein and urged him to ignore the belligerent advice of radicals such as Bhutto, who argued that force alone could tame the East Pakistanis.[12]

Also during Yahya Khan's 1969 visit, the Shah repeatedly raised the issue of Pakistani policies toward India. Khan, in deference to Tehran's growing economic ties with India, spoke in moderate terms and did not embarrass his hosts in Tehran. The first draft of his speech, circulated before the banquet held in his honour, referred to India as 'the enemy', but this was omitted from the actual speech.

The Shah, however, could not have been pleased when Khan on his way home opted to address the press at the airport. He spoke about Pakistan's willingness to 'cooperate with Iran, Turkey, the Soviet Union and Afghanistan in developing new trade and transit routes as well as other projects for the benefits of the region', but then purposely said that India's participation would be 'unacceptable' to Pakistan.

This sort of stance on India, of course, ran counter to the Shah's ideas about Asian economic integration, something that preoccupied him greatly at the time. How could one keep India out of any effort towards regional integration? But there it was, uttered in so many words by his Pakistani guest and in the full glare of the international press. This insistence by Islamabad that Iran prioritize Pakistan to the total exclusion of India was as impractical for the Shah as it would prove to be for the Islamic republic that came after him.

The dismemberment of Pakistan

Throughout 1960s, the forces of separatism had been gaining ground in East Pakistan, the Muslim-populated regions separated from West Pakistan by some 1,600 km of Indian territory. By March 1971, the Pakistani military engaged in a brutal anti-separatist campaign as part of its Operation Searchlight.

The crackdown was not going well. Yahya Khan quickly found himself short on both diplomatic backing and financial strength. He turned to Zulfikar Bhutto, the former foreign minister who had resigned in 1966 and who now led the Pakistan Peoples Party (PPP), which he had founded in 1967. Bhutto's political fortunes were on the rise, and his party had topped the polls in West Pakistan in the December 1970 elections. Political rivals for the top job, Khan and Bhutto, nonetheless shared a goal in wanting to suppress the East Pakistan separatist movement.

A few months later, in July 1971, Yahya Khan sent Bhutto to Tehran to 'seek more support from the Shah for the anti-insurgency operations in East [Pakistan], which had become more costly and militarily exhausting than any of [Yahya's] generals had anticipated'.[13] Iran had already, in the spring of 1971, lent Pakistan about a dozen helicopters and other military equipment for use in West Pakistan, to replace similar equipment transferred to the east. As war loomed on the horizon, the CIA expected that Iran would again – as it had during the 1965 Indo–Pakistani conflict – act as an armaments broker for Islamabad in the event that Pakistan could not obtain military equipment and parts.[14] The United States had, since the 1965 war, imposed an arms embargo on Pakistan.

A CIA assessment concluded:

> After the 1965 war, Iran acted as an arms purchasing agent for Pakistan, which was having difficulty obtaining military equipment in the West. Iran purchased some 90 F-86 jet fighters, air-to-air missiles, artillery, ammunition and spare parts from a West German arms dealer. The aircraft were delivered to Iran and then flown to Pakistan.[15]

The Pakistanis imagined this Iranian arsenal 'could be tapped without much publicity', particularly as the Shah was sympathetic. Stanley Wolpert, the University of California academic and biographer of Bhutto, ventured to presume that the Shah had a particular soft spot for both Yahya Khan and Bhutto as they were both Shi'a.[16] Iranian officials from the time, however, dismiss this notion about sectarian affinity as a driver in the Shah's calculations vis-à-vis Pakistan.[17]

The Americans did not care much either way about Bhutto's sectarian background. Throughout the 1960s, they judged him on his actions – and there was a deep sense that he was a conniver. Back in December 1965, President Lyndon Johnson could not have been more blunt when he warned Ayub Khan about Bhutto, then his foreign minister. Johnson recounted his advice in a telephone conversation with former US President Dwight Eisenhower:

> I said to him – now Mr. President [Ayub], I know you rely on Bhutto like I rely on Dean Rusk and like Eisenhower relied on

Dulles, but you can't rely on him [Bhutto] that way and I am not entering your internal affairs, but this man is damn dangerous as far as you are concerned and you are my friend and I can give you this warning.[18]

§

The Iranians looked on the developments on the subcontinent with great dismay. The Pakistani military campaign had become a quagmire. India's Indira Gandhi moved closer to the Soviet Union, deepening Iranian trepidation. Moscow and New Delhi signed the 20-year Treaty of Peace, Friendship and Cooperation on 9 August 1971.[19] The Shah's ally, Pakistan, was scrambling to salvage the country from breaking apart when the Soviets arrived on the subcontinent in an unequivocal fashion.

The stakes piled up against the Shah's friend, Yahya Khan. The Iranian leader, like most observers, was convinced that the dismemberment of Pakistan was now just a matter of time. As his last attempt to prevent a disaster for Islamabad, he exerted diplomatic pressure to save Pakistan from collapse. In October 1971, as the Shah wined and dined some 60 kings, queens and other heads of state at the 2,500-year celebrations of the Persian Empire, there were two men he particularly sought to bring together. His mission was to make the Soviets lean on the Indians to cease their support for the East Pakistani separatists.

The Shah wrote in his last memoir before he died:

This is why I wanted to take advantage of the presence in Persepolis of then President of Pakistan, Yahya Khan, on the occasion of the 2,500 anniversary of the Persian Empire. I hoped to arrange a meeting between him and the President of the USSR, [Nikolai] Podgorny, and thus to help avert the impending conflict between India and Pakistan over Bangladesh.[20]

The Shah's efforts were fruitless. But at least he tried, and did so before the conflict in Bangladesh was raging. This was more than the Nixon Administration could claim.

Nixon taps Iran as the go-between over Bangladesh

Throughout the Nixon Administration, from 1969 until 1974, the Vietnam War in South East Asia took precedence over all other foreign policy crises. The December 1971 Indo–Pakistani war was no different. The United States had for most of 1971 ignored alarm bells after the West Pakistan military campaign began in March of that year. By the time Washington began its mediation efforts it was too late, and war could not be averted.[21] On 3 December, the Indian military openly sided with the separatists and East Pakistan was quickly seized. Some 90,000 West Pakistani soldiers were trapped and captured. Indo–Pakistani clashes also erupted in the divided region of Kashmir.

As it had done in the early days of the 1965 Indo–Pakistani war, Islamabad was again quick to look to the United States for help once the conflict was raging. On 4 December, at 10.50 am Washington time, Kissinger told Nixon that Yahya Khan had requested military supplies, asking if 'we can help through Iran'. Khan had been desparate. 'For God's sake, don't hinder or impede the delivery of equipment from friendly third countries', he had implored.[22]

Nixon faced a quandary. Despite the United States' problems elsewhere in Asia, Pakistan was still an ally – and Yahya Khan was owed a particular favour. Only six months earlier, in July 1971, his government had facilitated highly confidential talks between Washington and communist China. The secret flight that took Kissinger to Beijing took off from Rawalpindi, and the Pakistanis had done an excellent job of keeping everything under wraps to the delight of both Nixon and Kissinger. Yahya Khan's mention of Iran as a solution caught Nixon's attention.

Nixon then asked Kissinger, 'Can we help?' Kissinger replied: 'I think if we tell the Iranians we will make it up to them [then] we can do it.' Nixon pondered this: 'If it is leaking we can have it denied.'[23] He wrapped up, 'If the war continues, give aid via Iran', and Kissinger was reassured: 'Good, at least Pakistan will be kept from being paralyzed.'[24] The Shah let it be known that he was happy to oblige, but asked that the United States as soon as possible replenish weaponry that would be transferred to Pakistan. The entire affair would be Nixonite to its core, with secrecy as the glue that held everything together.

Nixon was very anxious that the 'liberals' in the US media would go after him and blame Washington for having given arms to Pakistan in the past. He could do without more bad media publicity. On the other hand, he was very upset about the Indian intervention in East Pakistan and New Delhi's cosy ties to Moscow. 'When the chips are down India has shown that it is a Russian satellite', he said, adding: 'What I am really saying here is and what I am proposing to do – if India pursues this course, then we will reevaluate their program of aid and cut it off. Has anybody told them that?' Nixon feared that the State Department would be in the way: 'I know there are a lot of pro-Indian people in State.' Both he and Kissinger regarded the State Department as being on India's side in the conflict.

The Pakistanis were not blind to Nixon's predicament. As before, Yahya Khan again urged the United States to at least not prevent others from helping. The Pakistanis badly needed air support; they particularly looked to Iran and Jordan. Islamabad let the Americans know that unless they got air supplies they could not intercept Indian air intrusion, 'which would be a prelude to a disaster'. Washington warned King Hussein of Jordan about giving aircraft that he might need himself. According to Kissinger, Jordan nonetheless sent 17 aircraft to Pakistan. Iran was both diplomatically and materially freer and able to assist, and this made a great difference.[25]

Kissinger was also very keen to have the Iranians give him a direct appraisal of the Indo–Pakistan conflict. He asked Iran's ambassador in Washington, Amir Aslan Afshar, to give the 'Iranian assessment of the Pakistan situation', but repeatedly requested that messages not be provided through regular diplomatic channels. Kissinger told Afshar that Nixon was worried, and wanted to hear from the Shah. Afshar was told to bring back the Shah's assessment and give it personally to Kissinger and 'no one else'.[26]

§

Reports appeared in the Arab media that during the opening days of the 1971 conflict, Saudi Arabia, Kuwait and Abu Dhabi together had collected $200 million and sent it to Pakistan for its war effort.[27] In the subcontinental heat of that December month, money was not as nearly valuable as arms and logistics. That made Iran a pivotal player.

Iran was critical as a re-supply route for Pakistan. The eastern city of Zahedan was the nearest place for the safe landing of supplies, as Karachi was under air and seaborne attack from the Indians. The Indian Navy's supremacy over its Pakistani counterpart would prove decisive. 'Neither foreign ships nor Pakistan's own merchant vessels have tried to run the Indian naval blockade of Karachi, and even if they did get into the port, they might have difficulty unloading because of damage to cargo handling facilities', a CIA memo related. A key shortage was in petroleum; Pakistani consumption was 60,000 barrels per day, and it got 50,000 of this from Iran in the shape of crude oil.[28]

Iran seriously considered a request from Pakistan for Iranian-piloted, US-made Phantom F-4 fighter bombers during the 1971 war, but it rejected the idea partly because there were insufficient logistical support facilities in Pakistan.[29] Despite such setbacks, Islamabad differentiated between Iran and the US as far as the likelihood of aid was concerned. 'We expect Iranian aid', a Pakistani spokesman said, distinguishing expectations from those of the United States, 'But we understand Iranian reticence. After all, Iran has something like 10 times the investments in India in oil, that it had in 1965.'[30]

Meanwhile, in Washington the delicate struggle about what to do continued as the war on the subcontinent raged on. Besides a spirited bureaucratic tussle about US policy on the conflict – with the State Department leaning towards the Indians and the White House unquestionably sympathetic towards Pakistan – US legislation enforced its own tricky limitations, as the country had imposed an arms embargo on both India and Pakistan back in 1965.[31]

Kissinger attempted to comfort the Pakistanis. On 8 December, four days into the war and eight days before it ended, Kissinger told Pakistani Ambassador N. A. M. Raza that Islamabad should not despair. 'We will support you', he promised Raza. An altogether dejected Raza was left sceptical; a retired major general himself, he knew that the war was already lost. 'You don't have to say that', Raza shot back, 'Things are getting late.' Kissinger wanted to show ingenuity, but also US loyalty to Pakistan despite its ban on arms to Islamabad: 'I can give you news that we are getting something out of the Shah for ammunition. You can cypher that through me.'[32]

The White House was serious about its support. Kissinger, who had a day before his meeting with Raza, did his utmost during a press conference to hide Washington's tilt towards Pakistan – including the use of numerous dubious assertions of US neutrality – but the White House stood its ground.[33] President Nixon ordered CIA station chiefs in

Iran, Jordan and Saudi Arabia to ignore US ambassadors and go ahead and provide material support to Pakistan despite a ban on US weapons to the country.[34]

The Shah and Nixon held the same opinion as far as India's endgame in the war was concerned. As Kissinger put it: 'India could aim for the kill of Pakistan.' He saw that the Shah viewed the Indian attack on Pakistan as having 'posed a mortal threat to Iran'. Kissinger felt that the 'centrifugal forces in West Pakistan would be liberated, with [Pakistan's] Baluchistan and NWFP [North West Frontier Province] taking off on their own', and likely with Indian–Soviet backing.

The CIA corroborated this assessment. As the agency viewed it, India's Prime Minister Gandhi had a triple objective: 'Liberation of Bangladesh; incorporation into India of the southern Kashmir held by Pakistan; and the destruction of Pakistani armored and air force strength so that Pakistan can never threaten India again.'[35]

From the Shah's perspective, this was tantamount to Iran's entire eastern flank opening up like a gaping hole that would prove irresistible for the Soviet–Indian alliance. The Iranian leader looked to Washington to see what the Americans might come up with as a counter-strategy, but there was little the Nixon Administration could do.

All the Nixon White House could manage was to intimidate the Indians in the hope that they would back off – and this proved futile. Only a month before the outbreak of the war, President Nixon had ordered the mighty USS *Enterprise* – the world's first nuclear-powered aircraft carrier – and its escort warships to move into the Bay of Bengal as a warning to New Delhi. The *Enterprise* would stay in the bay for the duration of the war. The Indians, however, did not back off.

Iran's growing doubts about Pakistan

The two-week military campaign in December 1971 ended in yet another humiliating military defeat for Islamabad. The Indians had deployed the classic concept of *blitzkrieg* – at one point dropping an entire brigade by parachute into East Pakistan – in the face of a defenceless rival.[36]

It was not only a military loss but also a devastating psychological blow to the national psyche of Pakistan. With its eastern wing breaking away, the war raised questions about the viability of the entire idea of a 'Pakistan', a country built around Islam but home to many different ethnic groups including the Punjabi, Sindhi, Baluch and Pashtun.

The further dismemberment of Pakistan was a nightmare vision that the Shah of Iran could not shake off for the rest of his life. He told the British Embassy in Tehran that 'a weak ally often turned out to be a burden', and asked how the British viewed the situation.[37] The British, the CENTO partner of both Iran and Pakistan, were unrepentant, and let it be known that London was still not prepared to side against India in regional conflicts.

The Indians were very well acquainted with the Shah's deep affinity for Pakistan despite Tehran's continuing overtures toward New Delhi. They sought to publicize Iran's role as Pakistan's patron, in what at times looked like a name-and-shame campaign. New Delhi leaked to the Western press that its army had captured many unpacked crates of US-made arms, abandoned by fleeing Pakistani forces. The arms, the Indians claimed, had come from Iran. According to the Indian Army's eastern command headquarters, the captured arms could 'easily equip 60,000 men or 3 divisions'.[38]

Regardless of the authenticity of the leaked report, the aim of the Indians was to paint the Shah's Iran as partisan with regard to the Indo–Pakistani conflict – a de facto participant, whose extravagant assistance was being squandered in the hands of a floundering Pakistani military. From the Pakistani defeat in the war of 1965 onwards, the Shah himself had begun increasingly to doubt the prospect of military parity between Pakistan and India. In the 1971 war, the Pakistanis had not even managed to put any real dents in India's armour. Pakistani failures on the battlefield could not simply be blamed on its foot soldiers alone. The Indian ambassador to Washington, T. N. Kaul, later told Kissinger that Yahya Khan had, in the 1971 war, 'given [India] ten days, notice in a drunken interview with an American correspondent'. As a result, Kaul concluded, the Pakistanis 'never got [their hands on] any of our planes'.[39]

In the face of the humiliating defeat and popular outcry, Yahya Khan resigned on 20 December. The likeable general had been a disaster for Pakistan. Zulfikar Bhutto, whose Pakistan Peoples Party had gained the highest share of the vote in West Pakistan, now became president of the remaining portion of the country.

In the period immediately following the 1971 war, Tehran stuck with Islamabad. Iran's first priority was to keep what was left of Pakistan intact. To do this, two parallel operations were set in motion simultaneously. One related to lobbying for more US arms for Pakistan. The other centred on Tehran's intense diplomatic efforts to disentangle Islamabad as quickly as possible from the entire Bangladesh war fiasco and put a lid on the affair.

First, Tehran wanted to keep Nixon's mind on Pakistan. In Washington, the Iranians remained persistent and kept asking the Americans to provide weaponry to Pakistan. The US reading of the situation was that Iran had a 'desire to aid the Paks as much as possible without becoming directly embroiled in any dispute with India'. The Shah was still firmly of the belief that the total unravelling of West Pakistan could only be avoided if the country's army remained intact as a 'stabilizing force'. The new government in Islamabad kept urging Tehran to act on its behalf.[40] Only three days after Bhutto came to power, Kissinger received a memorandum that assessed 'Iran would undoubtedly like to demonstrate its support for the Bhutto government by responding promptly and tangibly to the Pak request' for Tehran's assistance and mediation. This early US assessment of the situation was spot on.

There was an ironic twist to the Shah's intense efforts in late 1971. Throughout the period from the war in 1965, and in some cases earlier, the Iranian leader had been urging the Pakistanis to restrain themselves. The Shah himself recalled how, as early as 1962, he had sent a letter to President John F. Kennedy urging the US government 'to stop all aid to both Pakistan and India until they buckled down to resolve their differences'.

The Pakistanis were not blind to the heavy costs of the arms race on the subcontinent. Ayub Khan at one point complained to the Shah about the 'wastefulness of large-scale arms expenditures'. Ayub had emphasized that 'through military spending Indians are sapping their country's strength' and Pakistan was also badly hurt, as it had to maintain some attempt at parity. After Pakistan's unqualified defeat in the 1965 conflict, the Shah admitted that his earlier call to Washington to stop the sale of arms to Pakistan, and for Islamabad to 'restrain' itself, was at best 'impractical' in the face of a strengthening India.[41]

Meanwhile, days after the cessation of armed hostilities on the subcontinent, Iran also took it upon itself to see if it could make amends between the two sides. The bulk of its energies were invested at the

United Nations in New York. Fereydoon Hoveyda, Iran's ambassador to the United Nations from 1971 until the fall of the Shah's regime in 1979, needed to put together a compromise deal that would satisfy not only Islamabad and New Delhi but also Bangladesh, the independent country that had formerly been East Pakistan.

It was a tricky undertaking, but Hoveyda, whose brother was the Shah's Prime Minister, had Tehran's backing and he set out to pander to the various UN parties in order to secure an accord. He reached out to Yugoslavia as the most active non-aligned state that enjoyed a fair amount of influence over New Delhi. Hoveyda made the case that any Indian unilateral action at the UN level against Pakistan would fracture the Non-Aligned Movement, as many Arab and Muslim countries were bound to throw their weight behind Islamabad. 'Do you want to split the Non-Aligned Movement', Hoveyda asked the Yugoslav Ambassador at the United Nations. 'No, we don't want to see that', was the reply. An accord was subsequently signed that all parties could find acceptable.

Hoveyda later commented that Tehran's bias was in favour of Pakistan, and the only factor that had allowed it to play the role of mediator was that Iran had by now 'reached a level of status on the world stage and others looked to and listened to [it]'. He continued:

> We [Iran] could see the creation of Bangladesh was a foregone conclusion. But Pakistani pride was at stake and Bhutto had come to the UN [on 15 December] and tore a [ceasefire] resolution up into pieces. [Iran] needed to find an honorable exit for the Pakistanis and that is what we [the Iranian mission at the UN in New York] set out to achieve.[42]

In the end, Tehran let the Pakistanis set the course of Iranian policy toward Bangladesh: Iran withheld recognition of the newly independent state until Islamabad itself recognized it on 22 February 1974.

Pakistan as the junior partner

At the end of the war of 1971, the power balance on the subcontinent had been radically transformed. From 1947 until 1971, Pakistan had been the larger, and often more capable, partner in the Iran–Pakistan relationship. Now, things were different. The dismemberment of

Pakistan and its defeat at the hands of the Indians had coincided with the rise of Iran. The dismembered and weakened Pakistan had become the junior partner, a fact that would be resented deeply by Islamabad throughout the 1970s. In the course of the next six years, Bhutto sought repeatedly to overturn this reality and return to the evenness in relations that had been in place in the 1950s and 1960s.

The Shah, however, no longer regarded Pakistan even as an equal partner. Pakistan's defeats in the 1965 and 1971 wars, combined with the advent of Iran's biggest oil bonanza in the first half of the 1970s, had stripped the Shah of any inclination to pretend that an equilibrium existed or that Pakistan could be entrusted to be Iran's eastern security pillar.

In one of his more eccentric moments, after 1971, the Shah hinted at the possibility of Iran annexing the Pakistani province of Baluchistan if Pakistan was further dismantled due to internal ethnic conflict. In fact, it is from this period onwards that clear signs crop up of the Shah's virtually patronizing attitude towards his Pakistani counterparts. This incensed the Pakistanis, and it is a historical memory that many in Pakistan retain to this day.[43]

CHAPTER 6

1971-77: THE SHAH AND PAKISTAN'S RELUCTANT DEPENDENCE

On 20 December 1971, Zulfikar Bhutto became president of Pakistan after Yahya Khan relinquished power. Bhutto would rule over the country until 5 July 1977, when he was himself topped in a military coup. Some hailed the man as *Quaid-i-Awam*, or Leader of the People. This was to distinguish him from Muhammad Ali Jinnah, the founder of Pakistan, who had been known as the *Quaid-i-Azam* – Great Leader. Others, within and outside Pakistan, thought Bhutto more an opportunist at best and a charlatan at worst. The typical Iranian estimation of him, shared by the Shah, wavered between these two viewpoints.

§

Pakistan's humiliation in the 1971 war – and yet another confirmation that its CENTO membership and Western leanings were of little use in bolstering the country's military capabilities – reinforced Islamabad's turn to the Arab world as a source of diplomatic and, more importantly, financial support.

Suddenly, the Shah found himself in competition with Bhutto for a leadership role in the Muslim world. Right from the outset, Bhutto raised the stakes and ran on a platform that resonated greatly among Arabs and Muslims: the question of Palestine.

On 21 April 1973, Bhutto gave a speech in which he spoke of the 're-awakening' of South Asia's Muslims. He claimed that Muslim empowerment was 'symbolized by the Islamic Republic of Pakistan'. In this blatant dash for the mantle of Islamic leadership, he promptly joined Pakistan's Muslim identity with the fate of the Palestinian people: 'The tragedy of Palestine has agitated Muslim minds for half a century. Israel has gorged and expanded through aggression [...].' He added, 'situations arise in which there is no choice but war against the usurper'.[1] Bhutto would privately strike a much softer tone in his meetings with American diplomats, whom he would inform that Islamabad only wanted to 'facilitate the settlement of these complicated problems',[2] and pledged that Pakistan's membership in CENTO was not at stake because of US support for Israel.[3]

Although this was probably not part of Bhutto's calculations, the fact was the Shah was not willing to play the 'Palestine card'. The Iranian leader recognized that the Palestinian question could be his Achilles heel in any popularity contest in the Islamic World.[4] Yet he still could not stomach the Palestinian Liberation Organization and its inescapable chief, Yasser Arafat, or other Arab leftist-nationalist radicals.

The Shah had rejected Ayub Khan's calls in the late 1960s for CENTO to adopt an anti-Israeli stance. In the interim, nothing had changed his mind on this front and he was not about to be convinced of the merits of such a path by Bhutto either. It probably did not help that in private Bhutto's views on Israel were quite different from his public rancour towards the Jewish state.[5]

Geopolitically, Iran and Pakistan were drifting apart, with Islamabad setting its eyes on Arab plenitude. This fissure opened in those late years of the 1960s, and has yet to heal almost a half century later. Nonetheless, on this path towards separation Iran and Pakistan would still find pivotal moments over the next few years at which common interests prevailed.

A momentous palace coup in Kabul

One such moment came in July 1973, when King Mohammad Zahir Shah of Afghanistan fell victim to a classic palace coup. While the Afghan monarch was away in Europe for medical treatment, his cousin and former prime minister, Mohammad Daoud Khan, struck. A *New York Times* editorial claimed that the overthrow reflected a medieval mentality of palace intrigues and royal loyalties, 'which might be expected in a country about to leap into the sixteen century'.[6]

But this was not just a transfer of power from one loyal family member to another. Daoud abolished the Afghan monarchy and established a republican system with himself as the country's first president. For the Shah, the downfall of yet another regional king was a stark reminder of the anti-monarchy tide in the region. Between 1953 and 1973, royal houses in four states in the region had been toppled: Egypt (1953), Iraq (1958), Yemen (1962) and Libya (1969).

In Tehran and Islamabad, Daoud Khan was considered a dangerous pro-communist sympathizer who would open the door of the region to the Soviets. The Iranians and the Pakistanis equally blamed the Western powers – particularly the Americans – for having ignored the warnings about a coup in Kabul. 'We told you so', was the message from Tehran and Islamabad to Washington.[7]

The Shah had never thought much of Zahir Shah as a potential ally. 'He does not give a damn,' he would say when Zahir Shah was still in power, 'It is as if he were just hanging around waiting for death to take him.' The Afghan king had himself told the Shah that while he was alive 'nothing would change [in Afghanistan]'. The Shah had been aghast: 'It is beyond me how the man can hope to rule a country when he adopts that sort of attitude.'[8]

At the time, in November 1972, there was a famine in the regions around Kabul, threatening the lives of some 200,000 people.[9] Only a few months earlier, Shah had told President Nixon at Theran's Saadabad Palace that he had offered the 'lazy' Afghan king 'everything' in terms of aid and assistance, but that there was an acute absence of foresight in Kabul.[10] Afghan poverty and vulnerability persisted despite significant attention and aid from the big powers. In the two decades prior to the coup in Kabul, Afghanistan had received nearly $500 million in US aid. The Chinese had provided assistance worth $72 million over the same period. Moscow, however, had been the most generous, with aid of some $1.5 billion.[11] Given the existing flow of aid and foreign scramble for influence, Iranian money was not likely to be a game changer in shaping Afghanistan's fortunes, but that did not stop the Shah of Iran hyping his financial punch.

Mohammad Zahir Shah thought the Iranian leader a 'decent fellow', but with an exasperating tendency 'to see the world entirely with Iran as its center'. The Afghan king learned to listen deferentially to, but ignore the Shah's constant lectures about the Soviet threat. He thought the

Iranian monarch was suffering from delusions of military grandeur, and he believed that the Pakistanis 'play[ed] up [the] martial image of Iranian military in order to get access to Iranian armory, if not soldiery, in time of conflict'.[12]

Zahir Shah let it be known that he for one was not impressed about all the latest military build-up in Iran. 'Iranians are not much as fighters,' he remarked at Kabul airport as he was leaving for his ill-fated trip to Europe, 'If [I] was to bring down, say 3,000 [Afghan] Pashtun fighters against [the] Iranian army, [the] world would be treated to [an] impressive view of Iranian retreat.'[13] He did not get his chance, as shortly afterwards he learned of his ousting while taking a mud bath on the Italian island of Ischia and he was never to be reinstated as King of Afghanistan.

Iranian intelligence had repeatedly warned Zahir Shah about the dangers of a *coup d'état*, and even a communist takeover.[14] Nonetheless, once the Afghan king was in exile, the Shah ordered that he receive from Tehran a monthly allowance of some $11,000 to cover the expenses of his children's school fees, and additional monies were to be allocated to 'buy him a house in Rome'.[15] Mohammad Zahir Shah may have been ousted, but Tehran would keep him in reserve to be resurrected if the opportunity ever arose. It never did.

Tehran in the Kabul–Islamabad firing line

Mohammad Daoud Khan was a very different man from his cousin. As prime minister between 1953 until his forced resignation in 1963, Daoud had pursued progressive and often controversial domestic policies in the highly traditionalist society of Afghanistan. The trademark issue of his foreign policy was his raft of anti-Pakistani programmes, which nearly brought the two nations to full-scale war. The fact that post-Partition disputes with Pakistan had cost Afghanistan dearly in economic terms was to a large extent the catalyst for his eventual removal, on 10 March 1963.

Daoud, who had been promoted to major general at the tender age of 23, had had a meteoric political rise. Nonetheless, he had been waiting on the sidelines for a decade thanks to the 1964 Afghan constitution, which barred royals from participating in government. He had grand ideas, and longed to make an impression now that he was in command.

At an official level, Daoud proclaimed that he would pursue a 'non-alignment policy' – or neutrality – in the context of the Cold War. He denied that the Soviets had helped bring him to power: 'Anyone who says this *coup d'état* was helped by a foreign country – I will deny that emphatically and it is a great mistake.' Tehran and Islamabad rejected this vigorous denial as a red herring.[16]

They pointed out that nearly the entire officer corps, which had participated in the coup, was Soviet-trained. The Shah and the Pakistanis, therefore, both saw Moscow as kingmaker in Daoud's coming to power – although this assumption would, in time, prove to be wrong. At the time, however, Tehran and Islamabad detected an elaborate Russian conspiracy playing itself out in Afghanistan, and feared that its tentacles might soon spread across the regional map.[17] At first, such anxieties would appear justified.

Within weeks of coming to power, Daoud once again resuscitated the issue of Pashtunistan with Pakistan, and masqueraded as an ethnic Pashtun concerned about the plight of his brethren on the other side of the Durrand Line. In fact, Pakistan was the only country singled out by Daoud in his first statement after the coup. He promised friendship with all, but pointed out the issue of Pashtunistan as an unsettled dispute.[18]

Western intelligence services by and large did not detect Soviet sponsorship of Daoud's crusade for Pashtunistan. In fact, some saw him as personally deeply committed to this case. His great-great-grandfather, Sultan Muhammad Khan, had been the last Afghan governor of Peshawar until he was ousted in 1823. Peshawar was now the capital of North Western Frontier Province in Pakistan. Sir Olaf Caroe, the last British governor of that province, once testified that for the Afghan descendants of the sultan, 'the lure of Peshawar is a passion, deep in their heart'.[19] This was a passion that could only create fear in Islamabad.

A couple of months later, Daoud went further and suggested that the ethnic Baluch in Pakistan were also looking to Kabul for rescue from neglect and poor living conditions. The Afghan Government resorted to the Iranian Embassy in Kabul as a conduit to let Islamabad know that: 'Afghanistan can no longer turn a blind eye to the sufferings of Baluchis living [on the] Pakistan side of the border.'

The question of the Baluch peoples was suddenly catapulted to new heights. Historian Selig S. Harrison put it this way:

A glance at a map of southwest Asia quickly explains why strategically located Baluchistan and the five million Baluch tribesmen who live there could all too easily become a focal point of superpower conflict. Stretching across a vast desert expanse of western Pakistan and eastern Iran bigger than France, the Baluch homeland commands more than 900 miles of the Arabian Sea coastline, including the northern shores of the Strait of Hormuz. Soviet control of the Baluch coast would not only give Moscow a powerful new springboard for spreading its political influence throughout the Middle East and south west Asia but would also radically alter the military balance in the region.[20]

Daoud's aggressiveness was unsettling not just the Pakistanis; Tehran, too, was greatly alarmed. Any inciting of minority groups in Pakistan had the potential for further dismemberment of the country, a prospect that was both frighteningly believable – the loss of Bangladesh in 1971 was still very fresh in everyone's mind – and consequential, as an independent Baluchistan carved out of Pakistan could easily set a precedence for Iran's separatist Baluch.

Iran's ethnic Baluch had genuine grievances with Tehran. As long as anyone could remember, Iranian Baluchistan had been the poorest region of the country. The Baluch themselves say that:

[A]lmighty [Allah], when making the world, used all the water, and grass, and flowers, and trees to make other beautiful countries, and when He had used all these, and had nothing left but [a] heap of rubbish, He threw that down and made Baluchistan.[21]

On both sides of the border, the Baluch saw Pakistani and Iranian neglect. Between 1967 and 1972, a five-year drought had killed off 80 per cent of shepherds' flocks in Iranian Baluchistan. Things were so bad that some 200,000 Iranian Baluch were estimated to have moved to Karachi or to the Arab countries of the Persian Gulf in search of a livelihood.[22] Many of these migrants and their descendants are today found across the Arab states of the Gulf, in places such as Dubai, Abu Dhabi, Oman and Bahrain.

Such abject poverty, at a time when Iran's oil revenue was on the rise, made the Baluch people an ideal target for communist and other anti-Shah propaganda. The Shah had sought to jolt the economy of the province into life, but was unable to make significant strides. Meanwhile, he saw the fortunes of Iranian Baluchistan intimately tied to Pakistani Baluchistan. Unsurprisingly, he would from the early 1970s increase the aid to Islamabad that was specifically linked to launching new economic enterprises.[23]

The Shah envisaged the Soviets pushing ahead, via Kabul, with an agenda that was ultimately aimed at the creation of Greater Baluchistan and the inevitable dismemberment of both Iran and Pakistan. The fear was that Daoud's Soviet-friendly policies were designed to push over the whole box of south-west Asian dominoes.

Shah's chief courtier, Asadollah Alam, wrote that the 'position of Afghanistan [had become] even more ridiculous', adding:

> On top of their long-stated ambitions in Pashtunistan, they've now laid claim to Pakistani Baluchistan. It is India and the Soviet Union that have egged them on. The idiots [Afghans] can't appreciate that even if they manage to snatch Baluchistan and so get access to the sea, the Soviets would march straight in and claim the spoils.[24]

From Tehran's perspective, however, Daoud was only one component of a much larger Soviet scheme to clip the Shah's wings. Another key player in this plot was Iraq and the pro-Soviet Baathist party led by Saddam Hussein, which had controlled Iraq since 1968. The Iraqi Baathists and the Shah were arch-rivals, engaged in a competition that spanned the Middle East from the Kurdish mountains of northern Iraq to the barren Baluch soil of eastern Iran. In Iranian Baluchistan, the Iraqis had launched destabilization efforts against the Shah before Daoud had come to power in July 1973.

Iraqi anti-Iran plots and Bhutto's campaign in Baluchistan

It was Saturday morning on 10 February 1973, and George G. B. Griffin, a political officer at the US Embassy in Islamabad, had stepped out for a stroll with his daughter. He lived a block away from the Iraqi Embassy, and suddenly all hell broke loose. The area around the Iraqi Embassy was swamped with police and security troops, while helicopters roared overheard. The Iraqi Ambassador, helpless and bewildered, had been unable to prevent raiders from barging inside.[25] This, however, was anything but a routine raid.

A few days earlier, the Iranian intelligence service had passed information to Pakistani officials about the arrival of an illegal shipment of weapons from Iraq to Pakistan.[26] It was intended for Baluch separatists in Iran. Iraq was clearly extending its reach.It had previously launched an office for the separatist Baluch Liberation Front (BLF) and begun radio broadcasts in the Baluch language from Baghdad.

Less than an hour after the raid at the Iraqi Embassy, Griffin saw large crates being brought out. 'I'm talking about truckloads of such stuff', he recalled years later. Bhutto had made sure to invite the media before the seizure of the weapons by Pakistani Special Forces. The incident made international headlines. The Pakistanis would claim that the Soviets had also been involved, hand-in-glove with the Iraqis.[27] Three hundred sub-machine guns and crates containing 40,000 rounds of ammunition were captured. Tehran said it would 'not allow a third country [to] become a channel for the smuggling of arms into [its own] territory'. The Iraqi Embassy in Islamabad was closed and the Ambassador expelled.

This delighted the Shah, but the embassy raid soon had a twist to it, which, to some observers, was of a nefarious nature. Bhutto was handed an opportunity to lash out against nationalist parties that controlled the provincial assembly in Baluchistan, and who opposed Bhutto's policies at a federal level in Islamabad. He linked these moderate Baluch politicians to the Iraqi arms seizure.

On 14 February, Bhutto dissolved the elected provincial government in Baluchistan, which had been led by the National Awami Party, a leftist group that promoted ethnic-based autonomous regions within Pakistan. Soon, NAP leaders found themselves in prison and the party's foot soldiers retreated to the mountains, waging an insurgency that would not come to an end until 1977 after Bhutto himself had been removed from power.[28]

On 29 April 1973, Bhutto mobilized the Pakistani Army and pro-government Baluch tribesmen to pursue the insurgents across Baluchistan's rugged terrain.[29] Some 20,000 insurgents roamed an area of up to 260,000 square kilometres, and weekly clashes with government forces became the norm.[30]

Four divisions, about 80,000 Pakistani soldiers, were stationed in the province, and Iran's Shah provided critical financial and military air support to Bhutto's military campaign.[31] The Pakistani Army's access to air assets, such the US-made Cobra gunships provided by Iran, was instrumental in its tactical military gains. These air assets delivered a notable advantage in terrain that the Baluch insurgents knew far better than the national force, which needed all the help it could get. The Pakistani Army was, after all, structured for a conventional military conflict with India, not to engage in anti-insurgency operations inside Pakistan itself.[32]

Besides loaning helicopters – some reportedly manned by Iranian pilots – to Pakistan, Iran also transferred four US-made C-130 transport planes, a step approved in advance by Washington although Tehran would later seek to haggle over the cost of the replacement aircraft.[33] In any event, modern American weaponry was suddenly in action in one of the most desolate corners of the world. In 1962, visiting Pakistan on a trouble-shooting mission for President Kennedy, Henry Kissinger had famously declared: 'I would not recognize the Baluchistan problem if it hit me in the face.'[34] A decade later, Kissinger would no longer have any excuses on that score.

In Islamabad, Iran was gladly regarded as a likely conduit for such advanced platforms as it was due to receive more such aircraft from the United States.[35] In all of this, the Shah played a very hands-on coordinating role. He was, after all, Iran's real – rather than merely symbolic – commander in chief.

During the four-year duration of the insurgency, Iran would remain a partner of Islamabad despite the increasingly rocky personal relationship between the Shah and Bhutto. NAP supporters claimed at the time that Bhutto's heavy-handed tactics against the Baluch were meant as an unmistakable gesture of faith towards the Shah, who was fearful of the conflict in the Pakistani Baluch regions spilling over into Iran.

There is no question that the Shah initially pressed Bhutto to flex his muscles against the Baluch. He wanted the whole affair taken care of promptly – and certainly not for the eastern border to become a distraction for the Iranian military. At the time, some 80 per cent of Iran's armed forces were deployed in the west on the border with Iraq, and the Shah intended to keep them there to track a rapidly rising Iraqi military.[36]

More radical elements among Baluch nationalists were demanding the unity of all Baluch in Iran, Pakistan and Afghanistan in a Greater Baluchistan. They were a minority faction, but that was not much solace to the Shah. The Afghans, both when Mohammad Zahir Shah was still in charge and under Daoud, told the Americans that Bhutto would not have acted with such zeal in Baluchistan had he not been encouraged by the Shah of Iran.[37] However, the Shah was not in the business of hiding his actions in Pakistan. When anti-Iranian protests broke out in front of Iran's consulate in Quetta, the provincial capital of Baluchistan, the Shah sent his sister, Princess Ashraf, to arrange for counter-demonstrations. At the rally, she was to be accompanied by Bhutto and members of his cabinet.[38]

However, Bhutto's strong-arm tactics and temperament were becoming an issue. The Prime Minister, who himself controlled a large paramilitary organization – the Federal Security Force (FSF), which he created in 1972 – was roundly accused of fascist tendencies.[39] If their tactics were fascistic, the Shah did not mind. He simply wanted the insurgency in Pakistani Baluchistan to come to an end, and Bhutto was keen to ease the Shah's fear about the Baluch problem spilling over into Iran.[40]

Bhutto had waged an all-out and divisive war on the Baluch opposition, but the Shah was at this stage preoccupied with only one objective: keeping what was left of Pakistan intact so as to keep the Soviets out. Fear that the violence from Pakistani Baluchistan could spread to other areas of the country, particularly to North Western Frontier Province – the heartland of the Pashtun people – mounted when Daoud came to power in July 1973 and committed himself to another round of battle with Pakistan over the issue of Pashtunistan.

The Shah told the British ambassador that Iran: 'has nothing to hide. Our intervention is at the request of Pakistan and aimed solely at defending her integrity.'[41] When the British Broadcasting Corporation (BBC) subsequently ran a story about the heavy-handed crackdown in Baluchistan and the centrality of the Shah's money and arms to the Pakistani counter-insurgency, the Shah viewed it as a personal slight. Were London and Moscow in cahoots to undermine him in Baluchistan?[42] He was later persuaded that a joint British–Soviet plot in Baluchistan was bizarre beyond belief. Nonetheless, here was the Shah – in a formal alliance with London via CENTO – seriously entertaining such thoughts about the deviousness of the British. Throughout his life, the Shah would never trust the British.

During the Baluch conflict, both Pakistan and Iran wanted obsolete US-made Iranian military to go to Pakistan. The Iranian military was modernizing, and its older military hardware was ready to be decommissioned. Between 1966 and 1972, Iran's defence budget increased fourfold, and $700-million-worth of US arms were exported to the country in the period 1967-71. As the Pakistanis saw it, Iran was awash with American arms, some of which it was happy to offer to the Pakistanis.

The United States again dragged its feet. 'Since most of this is U.S.-supplied, such transfers require USG approval', the US State Department insisted. Still, there were no discernible American objections to what the Shah was doing in Pakistani Baluchistan. In fact, as one diplomatic cable read: 'Iranian action in supporting the government of Pakistan could not in any way be said to contribute to tensions in the area.' It continued: 'Quite the contrary, moderate, timely and limited aid to Pakistan could head off possible troubles in the in future.'[43]

Zulfikar Bhutto kept looking for more Iranian arms and financial support. He went to Tehran on a five-day trip in May 1973. The *New York Times* said of the visit, 'Seated in a horse-drawn coach, Pakistan's president Zulfikar Bhutto rode through the streets of Tehran' in a 'remarkable display of old-fashioned panoply – usually reserved for visiting royalty'.[44]

This display of warmth extended to the state banquet, where the Shah said, 'it is obvious to all that our relationship is one of the best of its kind in the world'. Bhutto praised his hosts, saying that 'relations have stood the test of times' and that those 'who desired to create some schism between the two countries could never succeed'.[45]

US officials in Tehran were 'struck with the unusually warm reception' that the Shah gave Bhutto, while his esteem for the Pakistani leader was seen to 'border on the line of being patronizing'. This reading of a 'patronizing' Shah could have been simply a mistaken interpretation by American observers of the kind of adoration so common among peoples living in that part of the world. While the Shah might have made a 'very special effort' to enchant Bhutto, there was no sign at that time that he was on some kind of Machiavellian venture to lure the Pakistani leader into anything he did not otherwise want to do.

By all accounts, what *Keyhan* – Iran's principal newspaper – stated at the time held true: that 'a strong and prosperous Pakistan shelters Iran from a turbulent Asia'.[46] The Shah's commitment to Bhutto appeared unconditional. A joint communiqué claimed that his discussions with Bhutto 'were marked by complete identity of views' about regional affairs.[47] This would soon prove to be a colossal US misjudgement, and within months this façade of unity would be all but shattered. For the Americans had not taken into account Bhutto's personal ambitions and the concealed envy he had for the Shah, which would shortly rise to the surface.

In Tehran, meanwhile, Bhutto asked the Shah to urge Washington to be more understanding of Islamabad's predicaments. Following the visit, Iran and Pakistan again agreed to strengthen defence cooperation.[48] As the CIA assessed at the time, despite official denials speculation continued that a formal 'mutual defense pact was in the works'.[49] The intrigue heightened when shortly after Bhutto's visit the Pakistani Army's chief of staff, General Tikka Khan, paid a low-profile visit to Tehran. The unusual, inconspicuous nature of Tikka Khan's visit alarmed the Western embassies in Tehran. What were the Shah and Bhutto up to? Were they planning to cut themselves loose from CENTO? The US Embassy concluded, 'there may be more to the Tikka visit than now appears likely'.[50]

There was no doubt that Iran and Pakistan were militarily now the closest they had ever been, and they certainly stood out compared with the rest of CENTO. On the Shah's request, Bhutto even agreed for his country to take part in CENTO's air and naval exercises, something that Islamabad had refused to do after the 1965 Indian–Pakistani war and its disappointment at not receiving much support from its CENTO allies.[51]

Bhutto's decision to retain Pakistan's membership of CENTO reversed his 1970 election campaign pledge to withdraw from the treaty. The Shah's persuasive attempts probably had an impact as well, but the signing of the 1971 India–USSR Friendship Treaty no doubt also inclined Bhutto to keep his country in CENTO as a minimum insurance policy, although he would regularly threaten over the coming years to withdraw from the body.[52]

When Bhutto went to Washington, DC in July 1973, he took a leaf out of the Shah's book and told the US President that: 'Iraq, Afghanistan and USSR {were} after {Pakistan} because of her allegiance to Washington.'[53]

This fell on deaf ears in Washington. As with the Lyndon Johnson's presidency before it, President Nixon's administration still saw Bhutto's actual target as India. Bhutto was merely raising the coup in Kabul and the insurgency in Baluchistan as pretexts to beef himself up militarily against his perennial rival on the subcontinent.

Bhutto was enraged, particularly since the brush-off had come at the same time as Nixon told him in Washington that: 'Pakistan is the corner stone of American foreign policy in South Asia.'[54] Bhutto would quip, 'solemn commitments are becoming a piece of paper in the hands of the superpowers', another sign of his despair at what he thought to be fumbling in Washington.

The American reading of Pakistan's motives might have been accurate. Bhutto had cried wolf many times before. Still, by the end of 1973 the Pakistani leader was genuinely convinced that Daoud had an active role in sustaining the insurgency in Baluchistan. He declared the NAP 'not a national opposition party' but 'anti-national' and guilty of treason for aligning itself with the regime in Kabul. Western sympathy for Bhutto, however, was again in short supply.

The Pakistani President was seen to have overreacted with his military campaign in Baluchistan, and was now falsely casting himself as a democrat and the Baluch insurgents as Soviet-controlled anti-democratic extremists. As one Western diplomat in Islamabad commented at the time, 'Democracy is a fig leaf here. Bhutto likes to have just a hint of it around to hide his true instincts of a one-man rule.'[55] Bhutto himself provided the ammunition for this view. He once said that the: 'Pakistani temperament [is] such that people either wanted too much or too little government. No happy medium [has] yet been evolved.'[56]

This was an instinct that Bhutto shared with the ruler in Tehran. The Shah espoused the view that the struggle against global communism should be the principal unifying factor for anti-communist states such as Iran and Pakistan. Democracy was dismissed as a dangerous distraction. He said about his own people, 'when the Iranians learn to behave like Swedes, I will behave like the King of Sweden'.[57]

Both men saw their respective peoples as needing a steady but firm hand to guide them forward. It is still not clear which first inspired the other. Did the Shah's authoritarian streak influence Bhutto, as the Pakistani opposition claimed? They taunted him as the 'want-to-be the Shah of Pakistan'.[58]

Bhutto in turn scolded the opposition for its 'deliberate efforts to harm relations with friendly countries' such as Iran and the United States. At one point, he likened the Pakistani opposition to the 'Zionist Lobby' in the United States in attempting to undermine US–Pakistan relations. Bhutto explicitly named the National Awami Party leader, Wali Khan, as someone hell-bent on sabotaging Islamabad's relations with Iran and Turkey.[59]

One thing was for sure: the Shah initially welcomed Bhutto's crackdown on the leftist opposition and media, including the eventual closure of 15 independent newspapers in the year 1974-5. In turn, when in 1975 the Shah returned from a trip to Pakistan and promptly banned all political parties in Iran, creating the one-party system (*Rastakhiz*), Bhutto and the Pakistani state-run media hailed the decision.[60]

To Iran's dismay, the Afghans raise the stakes

In Kabul, after coming to power in July 1973, Daoud kept telling foreign visitors that Islamabad was plotting against him. There had been three coup attempts: in September and December 1973, and June 1974.

Things became so tense that American analysts predicted outright war between Afghanistan and Pakistan.[61] As the Shah saw it, Daoud was asking for trouble. He declared that any Pakistani interference in Kabul – including suggestions of it having planned a counter-coup against Daoud – was entirely justifiable: 'When the Afghans are making public statements to the effect that Baluchi dissidence in Pakistan is nothing but an extension of the Pashtunistan problem', then 'the Afghans are meddling in Pakistani affairs and therefore should not complain when the same is done to them'.[62]

For the Shah, the Afghanistan–Iran–Pakistan security triangle was inseparable. If the Afghan–Pakistani spat were left to degenerate, the two countries would become more dependent on their respective communist friends – the Soviet Union in the case of Afghanistan, and China in the case of Pakistan. The Shah told US Ambassador in Tehran Richard Helms that whether 'Afghanistan disintegrate[s] into a country of tribal factions or become[s] a genuine police state under communist control', he saw nothing but trouble for Iran.[63]

On 19 August 1973, the Shah told Alam, his close advisor, that several Iraqi-trained guerrilla units had infiltrated Iranian Baluchistan from Pakistan, and: 'I want these men caught, tried and executed.'[64] Any hint of Iraqi involvement was almost certain to terrify the Shah. He had foreseen the arrival of the Iraqis in Baluchistan; exactly a year earlier, the Shah had raised his concerns with the US Embassy.

A cable sent to Washington from Tehran read, 'The Shah is concerned about literature and maps appearing out of Baghdad calling for independent Baluchistan' in Iran.[65] Iran's secret service, the SAVAK, had infiltrated Baluch nationalists based in Baghdad and determined that Moscow was involved in the scheme. The Iraqis, backed by the Soviets, were edging closer to him from the east, and the Shah knew that he could not afford to blink.[66]

The Shah arranged for loyal Iranian Baluch tribal leaders to hunt down the anti-Shah Baluch insurgents. The irony of resorting to the help of tribal leaders was that it came at a time when the Shah and Bhutto had committed themselves to the eradication of feudalism among the Baluch peoples on both sides of the border.

'Confronting them [the Baluch insurgents] along a single front will get us nowhere', Alam told the Shah.[67] His advice came at a time of soul-searching by the Shah. He was not happy with Western assessments of the situation in Afghanistan before and after the July 1973 coup. Western assertions that 'Afghans were hard to get to know' because, among other things, they 'do little official entertaining for the foreign diplomatic corps in Kabul' were roundly dismissed by the Shah as designed to intentionally mislead.[68]

The Shah had until then received bi-monthly reports from the CIA and British Intelligence on regional and international security developments. In September 1973, he began to refuse to read them unless they could give him real intelligence: 'They expect me to accept as intelligence reports what are no more than transcripts of broadcast news items.'[69]

Alam, a confidant of the Shah from the days of their childhood, opined that attack is the best form of defence. His advice on cowing Daoud was simple: 'Why doesn't your majesty allow me to raise [the issue of] western Afghanistan against the regime in Kabul? It could be done quite easily.' The Shah agreed, and requested that a plan of action be prepared.[70] Western regions of Afghanistan bordering Iran, including the historic city of Herat, had been Persian territory until the mid-nineteenth century, when they were lost to the British.[71]

Alam suggested that Iran instigate an uprising in Afghanistan and return Zahir Shah to power in Kabul: the [Afghan] city of 'Herat can always reunify with Iran'. The Shah was nervous about the Soviet reaction to such an act but Alam dismissed his fears, claiming that the Soviets could not send troops anyway and the exiled Zahir Shah could be manipulated even if he was spineless.[72]

§

Bhutto, meanwhile was in principle willing to talk to Daoud, but Kabul's insistence on 'negotiations' over Pashtunistan was 'anathema to him'. From a US perspective, it was clear that neither side wanted war, and that 'better communications between the two governments might help moderates on both sides'. The Iranians were among the very few parties possessing the influence to press both the Afghans and the Pakistanis, but the Shah, too, had a stake in the matter. Washington still urged the Iranian leader to reprise the role of mediator that he had successfully played in the early 1960s.

What had, however, grown in the interim decade since Iran's successful mediation of 1963 was a noticeable Afghan unease about Iran's rise and the Shah's zeal for regional hegemony. Many Afghans believed that the Shah's dream was to revive the Persian Empire.[73] They thought that Afghanistan was no more than a minor obstacle in the Shah's path.

Daoud was particularly concerned about the Iranian military build-up and the free hand that Nixon had granted the Shah to achieve his regional ambitions. Daoud's brother, Naim, told Western envoys that Kabul 'deplored the Iranian military build-up except when it was related to the defense of the Persian Gulf and oil outlets'. Meanwhile, officials in Kabul had for years, even during the reign of Zahir Shah, been very anxious about Iran–Pakistan military ties.[74]

As the Afghans saw it, the Shah's professed intentions to give military help to Pakistan if asked to do so was creating strain in Afghan–Iranian relations, since its only effect was to 'make Bhutto more intransigent about the Pashtunistan problem'. Naim was said to have urged the 'Shah to take a more realistic attitude toward Pashtunistan', and stop backing Bhutto so unreservedly on the matter.[75]

Kabul, however, could also not resist provoking the Shah. Shortly after coming to power, the Daoud Government revived an old water dispute about the Helmand River. Tehran believed that this had been settled only a few months earlier, in March of 1973 when Iranian Prime Minister Amir-Abbas Hoveyda had succeeded in securing a deal after intense negotiations.[76]

Kabul's revival of the Iran–Afghanistan water dispute had, at the time, lessened Daoud's standing in Tehran even further. Alam, who soon afterwards travelled to Kabul to press the Afghans, told the Shah that:

> [...] many factors incline them towards closer relations with Iran but they are greedy and will only supply us with more water on a commercial basis. They want credit facilities, [a] development program down stream along the Helmand River, and [demand that we] grant them access to our ports.[77]

The Shah agreed; he often complained to American visitors that 'Afghans are perfectly willing to take but are rarely in a frame of mind to give'.[78]

Soon afterwards, Daoud appointed his son-in-law, Mohammad Ghazi, ambassador to Tehran to make the point that Kabul was committed to Iran and that there was no danger of a Soviet overrun of Afghanistan. Such efforts proved to be worthwhile, and arguably helped change the trajectory of relations between the two nations.

The United States anxiously watches Daoud

The view in Washington too was that Daoud had been 'testy' towards the Shah. A US diplomatic cable concluded that the latter's attempts to mediate between Afghanistan and Pakistan 'during the previous 15-16 years' had been viewed by Daoud as 'unsuccessful', but that his efforts had in 1963 led to Daoud's ouster as prime minister, a fact that the now President of Afghanistan still held against the Iranian monarch.[79]

Kabul was hardly in a position to be too provocative towards its far more powerful Iranian neighbour, and the first six months of the Daoud Government became a balancing act to keep Tehran–Kabul relations in a 'reasonable shape', as Naim – Daoud's influential brother and de facto foreign minister – put it.[80] The US State Department concluded that during his October 1973 trip to Moscow, Naim had 'obtained political encouragement tempered by cautionary strictures about danger of getting in too deeply' against the Pakistanis and the Shah.[81]

An American summary of the situation from October 1973 read: 'Obvious signs of close Iranian-Pak coordination on a tough Pakistani diplomatic line, plus at least some concrete Iranian military help in Baluchistan, has probably convinced [the] Afghan[s] that they are treading on very dangerous ground at moment.' It continued: 'it [Kabul] desperately hopes [to] avoid simultaneous confrontations with both Iran and Pakistan and has no fundamental dispute with Iran in any event.'[82]

While the Americans assessed Daoud to be besieged and too frightened to make any rash moves against Tehran, they assumed that the 'Shah would be highly unlikely to take any advice from [the United States] very seriously on this particular issue'.[83] American diplomats in the region knew that the Shah was still fuming over what he perceived to be Washington's inaction over the July coup in Kabul. Washington was urged to maintain high-level contact with Tehran about Afghanistan, and that US policy 'dispel some exaggerated perceptions which seem to be endemic in Tehran' about America's endgame. The same US diplomats had some hard truths for the Shah ears:

> Basic fact still remains that Iran's best hope for avoiding the great increase in Soviet influence here which it legitimately fears lies more in holding out carrots to Afghanistan than in helping Bhutto to wield the stick against his xenophobic, emotional, cantankerous and extraordinarily proud neighbors.[84]

In the end, the Shah did just that. He would, over the course of Daoud's tenure in Kabul, seek to placate him rather than topple him at any cost. Alam's proposal to make territorial claims on western regions of Afghanistan came to naught. The Shah even believed that luring Daoud away from the Soviets was within his grasp. Iran–Afghanistan relations improved throughout 1974–5.

The Afghans were suddenly open to discussing a new treaty on the Helmand River water distribution, and hoped that Iran would help them economically while opening itself up as a transit route.[85] Iran, on the other hand, began an extensive cultural and educational soft-power campaign aimed at the Afghan people, mainly through the distribution of Persian-language books, newspapers and other popular-culture exports such as Iranian films. Iran also, as early as 1975, began to offer Afghan students scholarships at its universities.[86]

The Shah's mediation efforts between Afghanistan and Pakistan included pressing Bhutto to apologize for Pakistani helicopters entering Afghan airspace. The burden on the Shah was less than initially met the eye. Despite the public acrimony, the Afghans still preferred to have Bhutto in charge in Islamabad and believed relations would be much worse if the Pakistani military took over reins of power. As one senior Afghan official put it: 'we hope [Bhutto] will stay in the saddle. The alternative to Bhutto would be so unpleasant that they make him look preferable'.[87]

The Shah invited the Afghan president to Tehran for a four-day state visit in late April 1975, and gave him a splendid ceremonial welcome at Niyavaran Palace. Iranian newspapers took their cue from the Shah's office and praised Daoud as a 'strong man and a modernizer', but carefully omitted any mention of him having overthrown a crowned head to become president of a country that he then promptly turned into a republic.[88]

Daoud meanwhile sought to hit the right notes for the Shah's ears. In a blatant appeal to the Iranian leader's ego, Daoud insisted that the 'security of the Persian Gulf should be maintained with the cooperation of the littoral states free from foreign interference'. Tehran considered this kind of gesture from the Afghan leader a snub to the Soviets and Moscow's then-increasing naval presence in waters south of Iran.

The Shah's patience with Daoud prevailed, despite his many misgivings about the Afghan leader. Bhutto, however, took the warming in Tehran—Kabul ties as a rebuff to him and to Pakistan's diminishing strategic importance in south-west Asia.

Meanwhile, the Iranians would claim – as they had done back in 1973, in foretelling the coup that brought Daoud to power – that more coups should be expected in Kabul. How secure was Daoud's grip on his own military, given that the top echelons of the officer corps were mostly Soviet-trained? A coup by communist officers did finally remove Daoud in April 1978.

While Daoud held power, however, Tehran always kept the door open to him as there was no Afghan alternative – at least not from Iran's vantage point. Although the Shah was not able to repeat the peace deal that he mustered back in 1963, he was nonetheless able to ease the mounting tensions between Afghanistan and Pakistan during the Daoud Government's tenure.[89]

The Shah–Bhutto falling out

Throughout the difficult years when the insurgency in Pakistan's Baluchistan raged on, the Shah stood by Bhutto. This was of no small significance to the Pakistani President, who would, over the course of the conflict, find his domestic political support base increasingly eroded.

Nonetheless, the support that the Shah could provide did not match the quality and quantity of what Washington had the power to put at Bhutto's disposal. So instead of asking the Shah to do his bidding for him in Washington, Bhutto set out to make the case for why he, and not the Iranian leader, ought to be America's principal 'regent' in south-west Asia. Two primary realities pushed Bhutto towards the United States at this time, despite the fact that as foreign minister in the 1960s he had been avidly critical of Washington.

First, Bhutto deeply appreciated the Nixon Administration's support for Pakistan in the 1971 war, when most of the world sided with India and Bangladesh. Meanwhile, from the conflict in December 1971 until April 1973, Nixon provided Islamabad with a total of $306 million in aid, a generous amount by the standards of the day.[90] Second, Washington was at this moment in time involved in a process of detente with China, Islamabad's key ally against India. Thus, the way was paved for closer relations with Washington.

Nixon himself helped to give the impression that Bhutto's fortunes were in the upswing. As a CIA staff memo stated, 'few foreign leaders [had] at the time been invited twice to the White House in less than 18 months'. The Americans completely understood why Bhutto wanted to get closer. 'Even if China, Iran and all the Arab States come to her aid, it would not be a substitute for US backing', the memo read.[91] That 'US backing' meant, in effect, a US agreement to supply Islamabad with arms and make Pakistan her regional military anchor. The trouble was that that role had already been promised by Nixon to the Shah of Iran.

The fact that Bhutto went as far as promising to let the United States establish air and naval bases in Pakistan's Baluchistan did not change that equation. Bhutto had genuinely believed he had been on a winner with the port offer, and was 'so engrossed in talking to Nixon that he forgot and left his papers on this subject in the White House'.[92]

Bhutto made this particular offer when the Shah had already announced an $8 billion plan to create a 'blue-water' port in Chabahar, on Iran's southern shore facing the Arabian Sea.[93] Elsewhere, Tehran planned to upgrade its port facilities at Bandar Abbas. With such steps, the Shah no doubt had the accommodation of large US Navy ships in mind. Bhutto was now on the Shah's tail.

When Kissinger asked the Pakistani President about his 'real motive', he replied that such a large port would 'bring development to a badly underdeveloped area'. Kissinger did not challenge this assertion, although he might have known that Bhutto had, back in 1972, offered the development of the same port facility to the Soviets.[94] The US, however, did not have the money needed for such an ambitious project. The port, located in Gwadar, would eventually be built, but not for another 30 years and then with Chinese funding and technical assistance.

Bhutto's profound longing to catapult Pakistan to new geopolitical heights became known to Tehran thanks to his tendency to speak his mind. This soon got him into trouble with the Shah on a personal level, a situation that was never to be corrected.

In September 1973, with the insurgency in Baluchistan mounting, Bhutto visited Nixon. Bhutto himself recounted in his diary how he had managed to antagonize the Iranian king:

> In good faith I hinted to [Nixon] that the Shah was not all that stable as they [the Americans] thought and that they should look beyond Iran and lift the arms embargo on Pakistan. It was one of the arguments I used to get the ten years arms embargo lifted but it was my honest view as well. Kissinger was present in the meeting. Either Kissinger or Nixon or both passed on my views on the Shah. The Shah was mad as hell with me. He was infuriated. He sulked and spoke against me.[95]

Bhutto was right: the Shah never forgave him for this transgression. The personal bond between the two men was ruined for good despite Bhutto's repeated pleas for the Shah's forgiveness. From then onwards, dispassionate reasoning would steer the Shah's policies toward Pakistan even though the two men would still see plenty of each other in the years to come. Bhutto's indiscretions, however, would not stop.

Bhutto's big push for Arab support

In early October 1973, Egypt and Syria, backed by other countries from the Arab world, launched an attack on Israel. By the end of the month, the war ended with an Israeli victory. The Arabs were demoralized. The timing of the war, however, was opportune for Pakistan, and provided Bhutto with an excellent opening to gain the Arabs' favour in order to support his country's economy with surplus oil money. To do this, the Pakistani leader had to bolster his Islamic credentials. Islamabad's close ties to Iran would swiftly come under the spotlight. In light of Pakistan's membership in CENTO and close association with Iran, Arab leaders would ask, 'is it possible for any [country] to believe that an Islamic State as that of Pakistan should accede to those who have joined hands with Zionist Jews?'[96]

Bhutto set out to pacify Arab concerns, and provided material support to the Arabs in their war against Israel. Squadrons of Pakistani-piloted aircraft were stationed in Syria. They saw combat in 1973, and were reportedly responsible for destroying a few Israeli aircraft in Syrian skies.[97]

Thus the Shah faced yet another dilemma involving the Arabs. There was little doubt that his instinct was to sit on the fence during the 1973 Arab–Israeli war. The Shah's bottom line on the issue was clear: as he put it, Israel 'exists' and the Arabs should learn to live with it. In his mind he was convinced that the Arabs were 'after' Iran as much as they were after Israel. It was only a matter of time before the Arab countries would turn their collective wrath towards their Persian neighbour. This was a trend that Egypt's Nasser had most recently set in motion, from the 1960s, and now the oil-rich Arab Persian Gulf countries had taken the anti-Iran lead thanks to the territorial dispute in the Persian Gulf.

Yet the Shah was not oblivious to the Arab majority in the Middle East, and he played to Arab sensitivities during the 1973 war. He replied positively to a sudden Iraqi request for 'friendship', which meant that three Iraqi battalions could be moved from the Iran–Iraq border to the front against Israel.[98] These, however, were tactical measures, dictated by the circumstances at the time. For the Arabs, the Shah was never a convincing ally, and he had simply too much Persian baggage. Bhutto on the other hand, and his toddler nation of Pakistan, were not saddled by such Arab scepticism and the Pakistani leader sought to tap into that reality.

Between 22 and 24 February 1974, four months after the Arab–Israeli war of October 1973, Bhutto gathered dozens of Muslim leaders in Lahore for a pan-Islamic conference. Bhutto's speeches at the summit were peppered with Islamist and pro-Arab slogans: 'Islam is our religion', 'At no cost shall we compromise against it' and 'Pakistan is uncompromisingly committed to the Arab cause.'[99] He unashamedly targeted Muslim passions: 'Except for an interval during the Crusade [sic], Jerusalem has been a Muslim city – I repeat, a Muslim city.'[100]

Such anti-Israeli theatrics earned Bhutto kudos from even the most radical corners of the Arab world. Afterwards, the Libyan leader, Muammar Qaddafi, hailed Bhutto as his 'older brother', dubbed Pakistan the 'citadel of Islam in Asia' and declared that Libya was ready to sacrifice its blood for Pakistan.[101]

The conference was in effect one big sales pitch to the Arabs – and it worked. The Pakistani media rejoiced, glorifying all things Arab. Suddenly the secular, socialist-leaning, alcohol-consuming and womanizing Bhutto presented himself as a Muslim leader and spoke about the necessity of jihad. Some in Tehran had seen this coming. Asadollah Alam wrote, as early as March 1969, that Bhutto was a 'bon-vivant, a heavy drinker and above all an extraordinary ambitious demagogue. Despite being one of the richest men in Pakistan he's as thick as thieves with communist China.'[102] Alam was not the only one in Tehran who harboured doubts about Bhutto.

Bhutto's sudden transformation, and the political contradictions that came with it, at times seemed comical. When he received King Faisal of Saudi Arabia, someone he lionized to a great extent and who had co-sponsored the Islamic conference in Lahore, Bhutto showed up at the airport wearing a Mao hat given to him by the communist Chinese leader himself. The symbolic contrast was both blatant and baffling.

There stood Bhutto, essentially a secular Shi'a, on the tarmac next to Faisal – the titular custodian of Islam's two holy mosques in Mecca and Medina, an unyielding anti-communist from a country where Shi'as are often considered heretics. Yet both men basked in the fantasy of a pan-Islamist front. The Shah, for one, was far from convinced about this show of brotherhood in Lahore.

The Shah had earlier decided not to attend the conference, despite Bhutto's multiple attempts over months to persuade him.[103] The Arabs were again at the heart of the disruption. 'Why the hell should I let [King] Faisal dictate the [conference] date?' fumed the Shah, deliberately ignoring the advice of his own court minister, the same Alam who had no high regard for Bhutto but who nonetheless believed that the Shah not going to Lahore would be slap in the face for the Pakistani leader. 'Send our prime minister and tell the Pakistani ambassador that I consider the conference to be a waste of time. Let's see what they make of that,' the Shah ordered.[104]

The Iranian prime minister, Amir-Abbas Hoveyda, was even more sceptical. 'What common interest can Islamic countries from the Pacific to the Atlantic find to talk about?,' he asked, fearing that some 'counterproductive resolution might get adopted' at such a forum. The Iranians strongly suspected that such a detrimental resolution would have invariably targeted the Israelis, to whom they were relatively close.[105] When Islamabad then asked the Shah to push the Israelis to deliver anti-tank guns that Pakistan had purchased after Iranian brokering, Shah claimed the delay was predictable given the way Bhutto was 'openly provoking the Israelis'.[106]

Still, Bhutto desperately wanted the Shah to attend. He invited Princess Ashraf, the Shah's sister, to Pakistan. Besides trying to convince the Iranian leader to go to Lahore, Bhutto wanted to explore the possibility of 'cut-price Iranian oil'. Ashraf asked if this was something that Tehran could do. 'Never!' replied the Shah, adding, 'Mr. Bhutto is so anxious to please the Arabs that he's even started talking about the "Gulf" without a hint of the all-important adjective "Persian". If he wants cheap oil, then he [should] damn well sort something out with his Arab friends.'[107]

On that particular occasion, in late December 1973, Shah had Ashraf cancel her planned trip to Pakistan. He himself toyed with the idea of going to Lahore after Bhutto agreed to postpone the conference, and then the Shah wavered for a while. Bhutto sent two of his cabinet ministers to secure the Shah's consent, but again to no avail. Washington and London were now seriously concerned that the dispute over the Lahore conference was weakening the Iran–Pakistan link, and that this was sure to harm CENTO.[108]

In the end, the Shah dispatched his foreign minister to Lahore. The Shah's absence was made further conspicuous by the presence of the personalities who did opt to attend. Besides King Faisal from Saudi Arabia and Libya's Qaddafi, those in attendance included Idi Amin, the maverick leader of Uganda, Yasser Arafat of the Palestinian Liberation Organization (PLO) and Hafez Al Assad, the Baathist strongman of Syria. This was hardly a gathering of anti-communist figures, but Bhutto was oblivious to any bruised feelings in Tehran, London or Washington.

The Shah's objections aside, the Lahore conference paid handsome dividends for Islamabad. In all, 38 states – represented by prime ministers, presidents, monarchs and sheikhs – came to Lahore to hear Bhutto's call for Islamic solidarity.[109] Shortly afterwards, Libya became the first Arab oil producer to ship its oil to Pakistan at the cost of production. Following the conference, five Arab countries plus Iran together gave Pakistan some $993 million in financial aid.[110] The timing was opportune, as the impact of devastating floods and the global oil crisis were badly hurting the Pakistanis. Before 1974, Islamabad had not received direct financial aid from any Arab country, and with a single stroke Bhutto had changed that and Arab oil money started flowing.

The Shah, particularly, ridiculed Bhutto for his closeness to Qaddafi and for eyeing Libya's oil wealth. In an interview with the *Washington Post* on 3 February 1974, after Qaddafi called for 'revolution against the crime of peace with Israel' – a blatant jab at the Shah – the Iranian monarch said that one 'should not take seriously everything Mr. Qaddafi says' and called the Libyan leader a 'crazy fellow'.[111] After Bhutto signed military and economic pacts with Libya, the Shah would not even receive the Pakistani leader and, for a good while, continued to ignore him.[112]

In adopting such a sneering stance, the Shah constantly underestimated the tangible aspects of Islamabad's new rapport with so many countries in the Arab world. It would become a functional, if not a transactional, relationship that is in place to this day.

The Kish Summit, and salvaging relations

The Shah was clearly displeased with Bhutto. The latter knew full well, however, that the Shah's absence in Lahore was about more than just his inability to control the list of conference attendees. Bhutto was only too

aware of this because he had himself, by his own account, set the stage
for the rivalry and was an enthusiastic participant in this duel.

The Shah was displeased, not so much because of Bhutto's newfound
pro-Arabism and Islamism – which the Shah did not take at all
seriously – but for his unrelenting dash to monopolize relations with the
smaller Arab states of the Persian Gulf. This the Shah considered a very
unfriendly act of poaching in Iran's backyard.[113]

Bhutto, however, was undeterred, and Pakistan moved full force
ahead in consolidation ties with the Arab countries. Islamabad did not
discriminate against likely Arab donors as such. By August 1974, it
would even sign off on a $10 million loan for 'economic development'
from tiny Qatar, which, with a population of some 50,000 in those days,
was the smallest country in the Middle East.[114] The support that
Islamabad would secure from the larger Arab states – notably Saudi
Arabia and Libya – ran into the hundreds of millions of dollars.

Gulf leaders, including Sheikh Zayed of the United Arab Emirates,
would become regular visitors to Pakistan, where they were often treated
to all sorts of extravaganza including rare-bird hunting excursions, much
beloved of Arab sheikhs. The personal ties that were cultivated were
accompanied by generous Arab financial support.

§

Conversely, by the early 1970s civilian technicians and military
personnel from Pakistan were to be found throughout the Arab
world. Libyan air operations were assisted by a large number of
Pakistanis. Training missions went to Egypt and Saudi Arabia.[115]
When the Egyptians opted to pull out their military forces from Libya,
Pakistan filled the gap.[116] In Jordan, one of those deployed Pakistani
officers was a man by the name of Zia ul-Haq. Within a few years,
he would carry out what was to be yet another military *coup d'état*
in Islamabad.

Kuwait and other Persian Gulf sheikhdoms also received Pakistani
manpower. In 1974, 3,600 of the 11,500 military forces in Oman were
Baluchis from Pakistan. In the emirate of Abu Dhabi, 115 officers and
1,800 servicemen out of a 13,000-strong force were Pakistanis.
Meanwhile, hundreds of thousands of Pakistanis found employment in
the fast-growing, oil-rich countries that had acute labor force deficits.
The billions of dollars in remittances that these Pakistani expatriates

would send home each year has since become a vital of economic source for Pakistan.

In early 1970s in the newly independent Arab countries of the Gulf, Pakistan had found a cash cow and it was not going to let the Iranians or anyone else stand in the way. For Tehran, Pakistan's dependability was on trial. At the same time as the Shah was embroiled in a territorial dispute with the United Arab Emirates over three islands in the Persian Gulf, Pakistani military officers were on the ground in Abu Dhabi training the Emirati armed forces.[117]

§

The Pakistanis even competed with their former colonial masters. London watched anxiously as the Pakistanis convinced Sheikh Zayed of the United Arab Emirates to replace British military personnel in that country with recruits from Pakistan. The British saw Zayed as so fond of the Pakistanis that he had taken it on himself to try to persuade the Sultan of Oman to do the same, and replace the remaining British officers in his armed forces with Pakistanis. As one British diplomat put it: 'Pakistani denigration of British motives and performance has gone beyond the norms of customary commercial and political competition.'

Meanwhile, the US ambassador to Islamabad, General Henry Byroade, warned Bhutto about his regional manoeuvring. 'Don't move away from your old friendships with Iran and Turkey,' Byroade advised, 'Don't substitute Southern friends for older Northern friends.' Bhutto sought to reassure the US Ambassador. He said there had been some 'difficulties in semantics, but all was solid as far as real substance' with Iran was concerned.[118] That was, of course, at best a half-truth.

§

Following the Shah's refusal to go to Lahore, Bhutto asked and the Shah again declined to visit Pakistan.[119] Bhutto could tell that the Shah's fury was not fleeting, and that Tehran was now unquestionably ignoring him. After Bhutto's September 1973 visit to Washington, the flow of Iranian dignitaries to Pakistan had come to a halt. Something was amiss, and Bhutto desperately wanted to find out the reason. At this point, he did not yet know that his badmouthing of the Shah at the White House had reached Iranian ears.

Bhutto turned for help to a friend, Mohammad Aslam Khan Khattak – a former ambassador to Iraq and Afghanistan, and a political player in his own right. Khattak writes in his memoirs that he was vehemently against rejoining Pakistan's foreign service, but Bhutto persisted. The Pakistani President asked him to go to Iran as his ambassador: 'Go for only six months if you want and come back every week.'[120]

Bhutto told Khattak: 'I have a problem. The Shah is cold-shouldering us, and I need to know why he is annoyed with us. On the matter of placating the Shah, you would deal with me alone.' Khattak guessed that Bhutto was not particularly bothered about having fallen out of the Shah's good graces, but the fact was that Iran still provided the 'lion's share of help [Pakistan] received from the Muslim world'.

Khattak acquiesced, and went to Tehran. He could not fail to notice that the Shah was single-handedly the force behind shaping Iran's posture toward Pakistan. In Khattak's estimation, most of the Iranian intelligentsia, and even the inner circle around the Shah himself, were of a pro-Indian disposition.

Khattak observed that Iranian Prime Minister Amir-Abbas Hoveyda, Finance Minister Houshang Ansari and Foreign Minister Amir-Abbas Khalatbari were being 'meticulously cultivated by the Indians'.[121] India did not need not throw a wide net to capture the Shah's inner circle at the court, which at the time was estimated by some to be made up of only ten individuals.[122] When the Iranian Foreign Minister turned down two visiting senior Pakistani financial representatives who had come to Tehran to secure a low-interest loan, Khattak overturned the decision by appealing directly to the Shah himself.[123]

In other words, the usually friendly ties between Iran and Pakistan had been due to the favoritism of the Iranian king. Bhutto had made a potentially ruinous mistake for his country by taking cheap shots at the Shah in Washington and courting the Arabs at Tehran's expense.

When presenting his credentials to the Shah, Khattak used the opportunity to make an impression. He told the Shah that: 'Iran, Afghanistan and Pakistan are linked by unbreakable ties. Some great man would one day arise and weld them together.' The Shah listened and expressed satisfaction, undoubtedly charmed by the flattery bestowed on him by this senior Pakistani diplomat.[124]

The Shah's smile put all his men in the room at ease. Khattak saw himself as having passed the test, and recalled the warmth. The Iranians were clearly also keen to put the bad blood behind them. Khattak, an ethnic Pashtun, was approached by Assadollah Alam, the Shah's court minister and an ethnic Baluch, who roared, 'Pashtun and Baluch are one, as you and I are one.'[125]

Soon after arriving in Tehran, Khattak discovered that the unflattering remarks made by Bhutto in Washington had reached the ears of the Shah. The new ambassador set out to undo the damage. At first, and on Khattak's urging, the Shah's politically active twin sister, Princess Ashraf, paid a visit to Pakistan, something that had earlier been postponed at the Shah's insistence.

After some further prodding, the Shah finally agreed to see Bhutto. The visit took place between 28 and 31 March 1974. The location was the Persian Gulf island of Kish, the Shah's deluxe playground – with its large casino, nightclubs and even an airport custom-made to handle supersonic Concorde aircraft from Europe – which only the Shah's inner circle were allowed to visit.

The meeting was designed to clear the air.[126] The Shah agreed to further oil supplies and financial loans. By 17 May, Bhutto was back in Tehran with his defence and foreign ministers. The Pakistanis insisted that in Kish they had been promised $1.2 billion over three years, but now the Shah agreed to $450 million. Bhutto had to plea with the Shah: 'I may have accepted a military agreement with Libya but I did so only because the military told me that we need to procure arms from whoever will supply them, the devil himself if needs be.'[127] By end of June that year, Iran agreed to lend Pakistan $580 million.

Khattak judged that he had achieved the core objective of his mission to Tehran.[128] The Shah could be charmed on a personal level but his fundamental readings of the geopolitical situation were at this time still unchanged. He was very frank, and pleaded with the Pakistanis to reconsider their policies against India.

'Is it possible for Pakistan to fight India and win?' he asked Khattak. Taking a shot at Bhutto's latest experiments with the Arabs, the Shah nonetheless posed a very poignant question. He asked: 'Do you have reliable friends and allies who will come to your assistance? Iran's entire defense capability is not enough to deter or defeat an Indian attack on Pakistan. India is the great power of the region and we all have to accept that.' The Shah's efforts to mediate between Pakistan and India intensified from as early as 1972.[129]

The Shah was busy working toward assuaging New Delhi himself. In late 1974, Tehran gave India a loan of $1 billion on easy terms for the purchase of Iranian oil imports. One British newspaper speculated, 'in befriending India, the Shah hopes to render it less hostile to Pakistan'.[130] The terms that the Indians received for the loan were in fact very similar to those that the Pakistanis had been asked to agree only a few months earlier for their $580 million loan package.[131] Between 1974 and 1976, Iran would provide Islamabad with $800 million in credits and loans.

Incidentally, at the same time as he was dishing out loans to the Pakistanis and Indians, the Shah's efforts within OPEC (the Organization of the Petroleum Exporting Countries) to ramp up oil prices was having a devastating impact on oil importers, including Pakistan and India. Bhutto complained to US officials that Pakistan's 'balance of payment is terrible and we need fertilizer which has become extremely expensive. The increased oil prices are having a disastrous effect.'[132] The oil-price hike, however, was a colossal windfall for Iran. Its oil export income went from $4.9 billion in 1973 to $25 billion in 1975.[133] Iranian–Pakistani trade at the time was dominated by oil, other trade standing at a meagre $10 million per year in 1973.

The Shah was telling the Pakistanis to learn to live with their military defeat in 1971, and that Islamabad had to accept India as the regional power. His message for the Western powers was different, and here he continued to champion Pakistan's case. He repeated many times the same message: that Iran would 'protect Pakistan against Indian aggression'.[134] When the Indian foreign minister, Swaran Singh, went to Tehran in late 1973 and suggested a 'non-aggression' treaty, the Shah replied he was 'prepared to enter such a pact provided that Pakistan was included in it'.[135]

The Shah's posture was part of what the CIA concluded was an increasingly 'paternalistic' attitude towards Pakistan. The CIA was not alone in detecting this 'paternalism'. Despite his eagerness to find his way back to the Shah, an irritated Bhutto would let it be known that it seemed the 'Shah seems himself as the protector of Pakistan'. In response to the Shah's frequent references of the dangers of the dismantling of Pakistan, Bhutto would say, 'the fears of unmanageable problems after the separation of East Pakistan {Bangladesh} are behind us'.[136]

The Iranians' reservations did not end with concerns about Islamabad's unwinnable competition with India. The conclusion of the Iranian intelligence service, the SAVAK, was that Bhutto's political grip in Pakistan was itself tenuous.

On one occasion at a social gathering in Tehran, a senior Iranian general asked Khattak about 'when the Pakistani generals would once again come to power?'. Khattak laughed it off at first, but was alarmed by the remark and took it on himself to raise the 'joke' with the head of SAVAK, General Nematollah Nasiri. Nasiri downplayed it, and explained that SAVAK was closely monitoring developments in all of Iran's immediate neighbours. He told Khattak that anyone 'who travelled in Pakistan or followed the news could see there were signs of a military intervention'.[137] It would later be revealed that the Shah had feared a military coup against Bhutto from as early as 1973.[138] Bhutto later complained that the Shah had had prior knowledge about the coup that finally toppled him in July of 1977.

By his own account, Khattak had managed to improve relations between Tehran and Islamabad but Bhutto was soon resentful of the close ties that his ambassador had built with the Shah. He was perhaps even fearful of what the friendship could lead to, and raised questions about the advice the Shah was receiving on Pakistan. He told Khattak that the 'Shah used to tell us to crush and hang people who worked against [us]. Now he is telling me to make peace with opponents, compromise with them and bring them into government.'[139]

On a visit back to Pakistan, Bhutto's wife – Nusrat Bhutto, Pakistan's Iranian First Lady – told Khattak that he had been 'bad at public relations'.[140] The writing was on the wall. Bhutto shortly afterwards asked Khattak to run as a candidate in elections for the national assembly. When the latter pointed out that he could not do this while he was ambassador to Iran, the foreign ministry in Islamabad went ahead and issued Khattak's backdated resignation on his behalf.

Despite his efforts, Khattak had not broken the confidence deficit in Islamabad–Tehran ties. Besides the increasingly patent geopolitical rivalry, their squabbling at times looked juvenile. In one highly symbolic instance in September 1974, the Shah chose not to stop in Pakistan en route home from a trip to India, despite pleas by Islamabad. On that occasion, the Shah had been annoyed that the Pakistanis had decided to join Arab countries and the Chinese in boycotting matches with Israel during the Asia Games held in Tehran.[141] Bhutto would write about the Shah that there was 'an uncomfortable perversity about him', and that the Iranian leader could be 'jealous and mean in small things'.[142]

India's view on the Shah and Pakistan

The fluctuations in Iranian–Pakistani relations were keenly watched by the Indians. Since Iran's open support for Pakistan in the 1971 war, New Delhi had redoubled its efforts in lobbying the United States to act on Iranian support for Islamabad.

In August 1973, just a couple of weeks before Bhutto's trip to the White House, the Indian ambassador to the United States, T. N. Kaul, had a meeting with Henry Kissinger, President Nixon's national security advisor. Kissinger would within a few weeks become the secretary of state. At first, Kissinger brushed off the US support for Islamabad in the 1971 war as history. He assured the Ambassador that Washington had now no 'great arms programs for Pakistan'. 'Bhutto,' Kissinger said, 'will not come here with any great illusions.' He sought to close that chapter, and proclaimed that Washington was 'not going to do stupid things as long as we are on [the] course of improving relations with [India]'.

What of Iran's role? Was the United States thinking of more 'subcontracting' to Tehran? Kaul got straight to the point, and asked Kissinger if the Shah was willing to 'restrain arms shipments' to Pakistan. According to Kissinger, this was something that the Shah had been willing to do but only if India limited its Soviet arms imports. Kissinger informed Kaul that his impression was that the Shah would give arms to Pakistan if there was another Indian–Pakistani conflict.

Knowingly ignoring what Iran was doing in Pakistani Baluchistan, Kissinger said that the Shah would rather have the arms 'kept in reserve in Iran'. Nor, he said, should New Delhi worry about advanced US armaments sold to Iran ending up in Pakistan. In response to a specific question, Kissinger said that Tehran would not send any recently purchased F-4 fighter aircraft to Pakistan, adding: 'They are highly technical equipment and need trained pilots.'[143]

Kissinger assured Kaul that the Shah was not out to antagonize the Indians, but that 'he genuinely feared an Indian attack. He is worried about Baluchistan,' adding, 'He is not consciously anti-India. He is sincerely worried about a weakened Pakistan.' Only two weeks earlier, the Shah had told Kissinger that he would 'consult the Indians before Iran made any irrevocable decisions in regard to its stance in the Indian-Pakistan dispute', but he clearly did not think his actions in Baluchistan constituted an 'irrevocable decision'.[144]

The Indians were far from convinced. When New Delhi kept the heat on the United States over its suspicion that Iran was providing arms to Pakistan (this time, 70 M-47 tanks), Kissinger was infuriated. 'It is a bit insulting that the Indians should ask us about an action allegedly taken by the Iranians. The Peacock Throne is still in Tehran,' he bemoaned, adding, 'I conclude they don't have the balls to face up to the Persians on these things, and consider it routine to present us with accusations.'[145]

The American Embassy in Islamabad determined that the United States 'would have known if anything like this number [of tanks] had been transferred between Iran and Pakistan'.[146] The embassy thanked US Ambassador to New Delhi, Patrick Moynihan, for his 'spunkiness' in rejecting the 'groundless' Indian charge, but Moynihan – later to become one of America's most prominent senators – had in fact done this before the embassy staff in Pakistan, by their own admission, had done any 'digging around' to establish the facts.[147]

In another cable two days later, this time from the US Embassy in Tehran, Ambassador Richard Helms – himself America's top intelligence official as CIA head from 1966 to February 1973 – declared, 'it is exactly this kind of Indian rumor mongering that filters back to Tehran and fosters new suspicions'.[148] Helms said that US military advisors on the ground in Iran were 'virtually certain that the report is false', and that it was 'almost impossible for 70 of some 400 M-47 tanks to have disappeared' from the Iranian military's inventory without US knowledge.[149]

American analysts were simply baffled by Indian concerns about a rising Iran. One cable read:

[...] with only a twentieth of India's population and a lower average level of skills, it is difficult to understand how Iran's military build-up causes anxiety in New Delhi. Furthermore, Iran has to worry about the ambitions of a latently hostile Soviet Union whose power it can never match and in the aftermath of the latest

[1973] Middle Eastern war, Iranian concern over Arab potentials will be greater.

The US verdict, though, was somewhat curious, as it deemed 'psychological factors to be at the root of the rivalry'. It concluded, 'Iranian pride is matched by Indian self-righteousness.'[150]

This may have been true, but the fact was that the Indians could not ignore Tehran continuing to play a two-pronged game vis-à-vis Pakistan: despite the unfolding Bhutto–Shah fallout, the Iranians would remain Islamabad's principal strategic ally for some time to come; the only other country that could claim such a position was China.

Nonetheless, the Indians had been on to something. First, the United States partially lifted its arms embargo against Pakistan and India. A full lifting of the embargo was in the works, a development that was to be expedited by an epic Indian accomplishment.

When Indian Prime Minister Indira Gandhi made a historic four-day trip to Tehran in May 1974, the Indians were reportedly amply reassured. One US diplomatic note judged that: 'India now is more relaxed about what Iran might do in event of another India-Pakistan confrontation, no longer fearing Iran would come to PAK assistance under any circumstances.'[151] The Shah returned Mrs Gandhi's visit in October 1974. Trade deals and other agreements were signed, initiating a flow of Indian technicians, doctors and engineers to Iran.[152] The Iran–India relationship had hit a new high.

The Shah still felt that Pakistan's security was tightly connected to Iran's, but few believed he would actually commit Iranian troops.[153] This was not a question of political will or military capacity. Many in Pakistan viewed the Iranians as 'soft' people, lacking the martial spirit of Pakistanis. They deemed it ironic that vast oil reserves should be located next door in Iran, which had enabled Tehran to buy huge amounts of US arms. This sort of Pakistani put-down was unfair. When Iran's security interests were threatened, the Shah was immediately willing to wade into the fray.

Most notably, he deployed two Iranian battalions in Oman in 1973-6 to combat a communist revolt. Victory for the Omani rebels would have meant communist control of the southern shore of the Strait of Hormuz – the strategic choke point of global oil flow from the Persian Gulf, and Iran's economic lifeline. However, besides necessity, Iran's intervention with two battalions – or about 4,000 men – in Oman was very different from giving the Pakistanis a blank cheque in terms of military support against India. For the Shah, a military entanglement against India was an entirely different matter.

Generally, the Shah's focus would, throughout the remainder of his reign, be on Iran's southern and eastern flanks. He stayed out of broader regional disputes such as the Turkish–Greek or Arab–Israeli conflicts, or the Lebanese civil war. At this stage, the Iranian king was at the height of his regional power, but he was by no means the senseless daredevil that some painted him.

Nukes and the race to become 'gendarme' of the Persian Gulf

When India detonated its first nuclear weapon at 8.05 am on 18 May 1974, the Islamic world was largely quiet. Pakistan was, of course, an exception; Islamabad had some catching up to do. Bhutto began a coordinated campaign, culminating in a speech in December 1974 in which he said that, failing a resumption of US arms aid, 'we will take the big jump forward and concentrate all our energies on nuclear capability'. The warning about a 'big jump' was linked to the fact that a year earlier, in 1973, Bhutto had already reviewed and evaluated atomic bomb designs.[154]

Iran's reaction to the Indian test was entirely different. State-owned newspapers were overwhelmingly ambivalent. The most critical commentaries fell short of condemning it, and suggested that India joining the nuclear club necessitated that Tehran re-evaluate its 'defense needs and [. . .] at least increase its scientific preparedness'.[155] They were calling for Iran to do something that many knew the Shah had already started.

Iran's nuclear programme had commenced in 1956, after the United States agreed to provide Tehran with nuclear know-how as part of the 'Atoms for Peace' initiative.[156] Over the next 24 years, Tehran's multi-billion dollar nuclear interests and collaborative efforts with countries such as the United States, the United Kingdom, Canada, France, Germany and South Africa mushroomed under the auspices of the Shah.

In the same year as Pakistan's (1973), the Shah launched Iran's nuclear programme. His chief nuclear scientist, Akbar Ettemad, recalls that the

'Shah did not at first say he wanted a nuclear weapon, but he clearly wanted to have the option'.

Ettemad remembers a meeting in the Shah's office prior to the Indian test. The king pointed out that if the situation changed and one of Iran's immediate neighbours should go nuclear, then Iran would have to reassess its nuclear policy. 'I pushed the Shah to see what he really meant,' Ettemad says, 'What options do you want to be available to Iran in 10 years time in the event one of our neighbors becomes nuclear? Do you want the nuclear weapon option: "Yes," the Shah said, "why not?"'

That night, as Ettemad left the Shah he thought about what the king had said. It was very clear that he wanted both civilian and military nuclear options to be available: 'If the situation changed, I could not simply tell the Shah to wait for another 10 years before we can pursue the bomb. We had to be ready for that call.' Accordingly, Ettemad told research directors at Iran's atomic agency that Iran should be 'open to any kind of nuclear research'. He recalls, 'We had a lot of scientists at the time returning from abroad. We would tell them they could conduct research into anything as long as the overall nuclear capacity of Iran increased.'

In Ettemad's estimation, Iran's nuclear programme had to have a weaponization path if regional circumstances shifted and Iran's security requirements suddenly changed.[157] The Shah told him that, for the time being at least, 'Iran's conventional armed capacity is enough' and there was no immediate need for a nuclear weapon.

The Shah would not even mention the 1974 Indian test in its immediate aftermath. Was his silence an indication of his prior knowledge about the impending test? Ettemad dismisses any such suggestion.[158] Sixteen days before the nuclear test, however, the Indian prime minister, Indira Gandhi, had visited Tehran. Here, discussions were held about 'nuclear cooperation' between the two countries.

Iran viewed India through a different, nuclear prism. It was scientifically ahead of Iran, and could be a source of knowledge for the country in the nuclear and other fields. As a result, Ettemad would travel to India many times. Iran sent trainees there to learn the craft of nuclear science. In the realm of such technology, India was of course both an alternative to unwilling Western states and also shared a very similar outlook about the future of nuclear technology.

Thus, Iran and India would paradoxically often find themselves collaborating in the 1970s as the defenders of the smaller regional powers on nuclear-related matters in international forums such as the International Atomic Energy Authority (IAEA). Ettemad recollects that in his meetings with Mrs Gandhi, Tehran and New Delhi in effect agreed to have a common front against the West.

According to Ettemad, the Shah did not like the idea of either India or Pakistan going nuclear, but did not panic after the Indian test of 1974. For him, there was an element of inevitability to India becoming a nuclear power. It was the country's destiny, and a deserved one given India's size and regional status. By most accounts, he did not believe in the same inevitability for the Pakistani quest for the bomb.

What is known is that by late June 1974, the Shah was in France and it was thought that he discussed nuclear technology procurement. When asked by a French newspaper if Iran, too, would go nuclear, he replied, 'certainly, and sooner than is believed but contrary to India we have first thought of our people and then of technology'. He later denied having made this comment. The US Ambassador to Tehran, Richard Helms, dismissed 'the off the cuff' comment as insignificant, and reported to Washington that the Shah was not – for now – looking for a nuclear bomb.[159]

There had also been some passing discussion at this time between Tehran and Islamabad on ways of obtaining nuclear technology. What is clear is that the Iranians were reluctant to consider Pakistani requests for nuclear cooperation seriously. Ettemad recollects the frequent visits of Munir Ahmad Khan, the chief of Pakistan's nuclear programme, to Tehran, where he requested Tehran's financial support and collaboration in the nuclear field.

Khan would tell the Iranians about the 'need to go around Western powers'. According to Ettemad, the Iranians never directly said 'No' to the Pakistanis but simply kept them waiting. In Ettemad's view, Pakistan wanted Iran for dual purposes: 'both as a financial source but also to share the blame if the two states were discovered to conduct nuclear work behind closed doors'. Iran was, in other words, to be both a cash cow and a cover:

We listened to Pakistani overtures but never took them seriously. [The] Shah made sure there was a lot of ceremony in place in relations with Pakistan but it was never really that deep in substance. How could we enter into any serious cooperation with them given the state of that country? [...] The problem was always about the high degree of decentralized power in Pakistan. Who was really running the show? Our assessment at the time was that Pakistan was politically too volatile and unpredictable for Iran to agree to close partnership in the sensitive field of nuclear technology. In general, we did not trust the Pakistanis and nor did we want to be caught up in the US–Pakistani dispute about what Islamabad was up to with its nuclear ambitions.[160]

Following the Indian test, both Tehran and Islamabad turned to the United Nations to push for ways to combat nuclear proliferation, but their emphasis varied. While Iran sought a 'Middle East Nuclear Free Zone', Pakistan unveiled plans for a 'South Asia Nuclear Free Zone' – although on the latter, the Indians were predictably dismissive.[161] Iran and Pakistan thus went their separate ways with different priorities when pushing for anti-proliferation measures – in much the same way that they had separately raced toward nuclear capability in the first place. That estrangement was also evident in other areas as the nuclear era arrived in south-west Asia.

America between Iran and Pakistan

The Pakistanis were, of course, angered by what they saw as US double standards on the question of access to nuclear technology. This time, the Shah was not entirely unsympathetic. He remarked that both Pakistan and Iran were 'prisoners of U.S. goodwill', adding: 'If we cannot get sufficient supplies of enriched uranium, this entire [nuclear] investment goes up in the air.' He told the Americans, 'Suppose I do put pressure on Bhutto. What will he say? It seems clear he is determined to obtain [nuclear] reprocessing plant [...] Do they really care if your [US] Congress gets mad at them?'[162]

The Iranians and the Pakistanis were in agreement that the United States applied different rules to different countries on the question of nuclear proliferation. Washington had continued to supply nuclear fuel to India despite its May 1974 nuclear explosion. Nor did Washington at the time see fit to do anything about Israel's and South Africa's well-known nuclear activities.[163]

Nonetheless, the Shah saw Pakistan's economic case for a full nuclear fuel cycle on its soil as weak.[164] As a way out, the United States suggested a regional, multinational facility that could do this job. When American officials told the Pakistani nuclear chief Munir Ahmad Khan that 'Iranian-Pakistani co-operation in this regard would make a lot of sense', Khan was lukewarm toward the idea.[165]

Khan had, in fact, approached the Iranians earlier on this issue, but he still believed the idea of a multinational plant to be 'unrealistic' and insisted that 'control of [the] fuel cycle' within Pakistan was paramount. Tehran, too, took this position, and wanted the fuel cycle to be on its soil.[166] This US-initiated idea was thus a back-up option for both Tehran and Islamabad, but each envisaged themselves hosting it. When Bhutto at one point suggested that the Shah had agreed to such a facility on Pakistani territory, the Shah pointed out to US Ambassador Helms in Tehran that Bhutto 'must have misunderstood' him.

The Americans seemed to prefer Iran as a site for such a facility. A cable from the US Embassy in Tehran stated:

> The successful outcome of the current negotiations between US [government] and government of Iran on arrangements to build American nuclear power plants in Iran would seem to be a sine qua non if we expect any useful assistance from the Shah in dissuading Pakistan from its drive to obtain reprocessing facilities.[167]

Unbeknownst to the Pakistanis, the Shah had as early as August 1971 accepted a proposal by Kissinger to establish 'regional' centres for reprocessing spent nuclear fuel. However, at the time, no particular site had been discussed. Back in 1971, Iran's agreement had been needed before a deal could be signed for the United States to supply Tehran with eight nuclear reactors.[168] Kissinger had let the Iranians know that acquiescence to US demands – and effectively a US veto – on its nuclear projects would open the door to American high-tech conventional weaponry. It was a grand bargain of sorts, but one that Washington at that time would only offer Iran and not Pakistan.[169]

Aside from assenting to a de facto American veto in regards to its nuclear activities, it also helped that Iran had, upon its launch in 1968, signed the nuclear Non-Proliferation Treaty (NPT), which Pakistan – along with India – had refused to do. As they doggedly battled to catch up with the Indians, the Pakistanis could not afford the adjustments the Shah was willing to make to accommodate Washington's concerns. For Bhutto, the Shah had thus become 'a stooge for Western interests'.

America's preferential treatment of Iran over Pakistan extended to the fact that Washington would even run with one of the Shah's ideas about convincing Bhutto to forego his nuclear ambitions. The Shah had specifically told the Americans that 'Pakistan has no air force' to speak of, and that this should be a focus for the United States as far as providing incentives in Washington's evolving 'carrots-and-sticks' policy.

In August 1976, Kissinger went to Lahore and offered Bhutto 100 A-7 attack aircraft in exchange for 'his willingness to drop the idea of acquiring a [nuclear] reprocessing plant', which was due to come from France and be financed by Libya. Earlier in 1976, the US intelligence services had discovered Islamabad's 'crash program' for a nuclear bomb using fuel from this plant.[170] Given that the 'aircrafts-for-nukes' package had been the Shah's idea, he thought that Bhutto 'would be wise to accept it'.[171] The Pakistani President did not, and pushed ahead with his nuclear aspirations. In retaliation, the United States suspended all economic and military assistance to Islamabad.

In its preferential treatment of the Shah, the United States continued to put Bhutto's nose out of joint. In the same month, August 1976, Washington signed a $10 billion arms deal with Tehran. In late October 1976, Kissinger again visited Bhutto in Pakistan. This was a highly anticipated summit. Both men were anxious and wanted to do well. Bhutto threw a banquet for Kissinger. By one account, Kissinger wanted to deliver 'an extraordinary speech because he knew that Bhutto was a superb after-dinner speaker and of course Kissinger did not want to be outshone'. Kissinger did deliver a brilliant address, but then Bhutto spoke and upstaged him. The Americans had worked on their speech for three weeks, but it turned out the Pakistanis had spent three months preparing Bhutto for his homily.[172]

In his toast to the US Secretary of State, a visibly indignant Bhutto told Kissinger: 'If there is to be a big bang, we cannot conceive of Iran's security separate from Pakistan's.' 'What is sauce for the goose is sauce for the gander,' he griped, 'If the United States considers that Iran's security is so important to the vital interests of the world, it must come to the conclusion that the same applies to Pakistan.'[173] Thomas

Lippman, the *Washington Post* reporter travelling with the US Secretary of State thought that the Kissinger–Bhutto toasts that night in Islamabad gave a new meaning to 'two scorpions in a glass'.[174] An 'apoplectic' Kissinger gave his staff hell for not having produced a better text, but agreed that Bhutto had been the cleverer orator that night.

§

Brent Scowcroft, the air force general who became President Ford's national security advisor, later remarked that the Ford Administration had hoped the Shah would commit himself to a 'major act of nuclear statesmanship: namely to set a world example by foregoing national [nuclear] processing'.[175] It was not to be.

In December 1976, in the dying days of the Ford Administration, the Shah informed Bhutto after 'extensive discussions' that Iran had given up on the idea of a nuclear reprocessing plant altogether, and that Islamabad should do the same. The Shah believed he had convinced Bhutto, but acknowledged that he had made it very difficult for himself to climb down from his nuclear stance after his populist stance on the matter.

The Shah urged Washington to reassure Bhutto about the prospect of conventional arms, and hoped that American 'military transfers and economic assistance to Pakistan [would] not be forgotten with the advent of the new [Jimmy Carter] administration' in 1977.[176]

The Carter Administration would, in the end, prove highly sceptical about military and nuclear cooperation with Third World countries. On that list, Pakistan stood out prominently. President Carter swiftly killed off the idea of selling A-7 attack aircraft to Pakistan.[177] Bhutto maintained that he was shocked, but it probably hurt more that the same Carter Administration within months sold the Shah five sophisticated aircraft with a $1.1 billion price tag.[178]

Cyrus Vance, Carter's secretary of state, had quickly been dispatched to Tehran. He told the Shah that Carter would honour 'prior sales commitments to Iran'. Pakistan was again left standing on the sidelines, bitter both at Iran and the United States.

§

The Iranians did not want to let the 1974 nuclear test stop them from improving relations with New Delhi. With the British withdrawal from the Persian Gulf, Iran and Pakistan – and also India – all looked to increase their interests there. The Iranians were suspicious of India's monopolizing intentions. Farther afield, they were particularly sensitive to India's extensive ties with Iraq.

New Delhi was uncomfortable about the Shah eyeing an important role for his country in the Indian Ocean region. The Shah's ambitions were grand, and made worse due to the ambiguities around his intentions. For example, Tehran agreed to provide an undisclosed amount of aid to the island nation of Mauritius in return for port facilities being made available to the Iranian Navy and the same facilities being denied to the Soviet Navy.[179] Indian anxieties were reinforced by the Shah's twin 'sins': his support for Pakistan and the role he played as America's key regional proxy.

Still, as the Shah himself would put it, no regional effort in this part of Asia could happen without India's participation. When he floated the idea of an 'Indian Ocean Economic Community', he sensed a Pakistani indifference to the project, which he resented. From 1974 onwards, Iran's economic ties with India expanded considerably, and soon dwarfed Tehran's with Islamabad although Iranian–Indian trade had always been considerably greater than its Iranian–Pakistan equivalent.

It quickly became clear that Pakistan had to work hard if it wanted to counter the improvement in Iran–India relations. Bhutto told Kissinger that the Shah's advances towards the Indians would ultimately fail, but that he did not 'intend to lecture the Shah on this'.[180] The Pakistanis were now less bitter and more apprehensive.

They sought to bring the Shah back on board. Bhutto aimed to do this through a rebirth of the RCD. On the eve of the April 1976 RCD summit in Izmir, Turkey, Bhutto wrote: 'Iran, Pakistan, and Turkey constitute a single civilization [. . .] permeated by a common faith. Our three countries have a complementarity in resources and skills and a common held Weltanschauung which would be the envy of many another region.' He urged collective action and warned that 'turmoil and tension seethed beneath a thin layer of tranquility'. Despite this passionate plea, Bhutto's problem was that neither the Shah nor the Turks trusted him or his intentions.[181]

Bhutto, the Afghans and the Indian nuclear bomb

For Bhutto, the Indian nuclear test was akin in significance to the July 1973 coup in Kabul. He set out to link the nuclearization of India to the ongoing tensions with Afghanistan. In an intentional step in 1974, he chose to give an important speech in the Pashtun-populated North Western Frontier Province on the border with Afghanistan in which he lambasted both Kabul and New Delhi. He had strong domestic political priorities in such foreign policy announcements.

Facing a tribal audience largely oblivious to Cold War politics, Bhutto spoke in black-and-white terms. He linked the godless Soviets with the recent Indian nuclear test, and connected Afghanistan's close ties to New Delhi to a spate of bombings that had recently shaken the tribal Pakistani province, and which Islamabad blamed on Indian–Afghan sabotage.[182] It might have sounded like another conspiracy to some, but this was Bhutto's call for unity against outsiders. In May and June of that year, the Pakistani public was even treated to a short-lived scare when the Bhutto Government claimed to have detected coordinated and threatening military manoeuvres along both the Afghan and Indian borders.[183]

It was about this time that Islamabad began to cultivate Afghan Islamists in order to rattle Mohammad Daoud Khan. Many of Daoud's foes, the future Afghan Mujahedeen commanders, had found sanctuary and support in Bhutto's Pakistan. It was in 1973 that Peshawar first became the main hub for Afghan opposition and militant forces.

In June 1974, Kabul aborted a coup attempt by the Afghan branch of the Muslim Brotherhood.[184] The secular Bhutto saw Afghan Islamists as a convenient instrument against Kabul, a strategy that eventually came to be known as 'forward policy'. Afghan Islamists who began to receive support from Pakistan included Gulbuddin Hekmatyar, an engineering student at Kabul University who would over the next few decades rise to become one of Afghanistan's key warlords.[185] Another was Ahmad Shah Massoud, another Kabul University engineering student, who became a hero against the Soviets and later led the fight against the Afghan Taliban in the 1990s.

Bhutto reached out to Iran and Turkey as well. He called for a new 'organic association' to better defend their collective security needs.[186] While that initiative failed, attempts were also made to reinvigorate CENTO. The largest-ever CENTO naval exercises in November 1974, combined with a CENTO meeting attended by the US Chairman of the Joint Chiefs of Staff, unnerved the Indians. Still, it did not change the trajectory of Tehran's foreign policy.[187]

With Islamabad wanting to consolidate ties, and with India in its sights, the Shah was now arguing for India's inclusion in regional efforts. For example, he argued that both India and Afghanistan should be part of the RCD as it made economic sense. This was anathema to Islamabad.[188] However, a cash-strapped Pakistan needed the Shah, and could not explicitly reject his regional ideas. Islamabad stood in the path of Indian membership of the RCD, but would reluctantly agree to its road and rail network being used by Iran in its trade with India.

§

Between the Indian nuclear test of May 1974 and the lifting of the US arms embargo, Bhutto assiduously cultivated the Americans. In early 1975, he travelled again to Washington. This time, however, unlike in 1973, he would steer clear of smearing the Shah in the process of coaxing President Gerald Ford. It almost seems as if Bhutto wanted the Americans to convey to the Shah his loyalty to Tehran. The Americans, on the other hand, were unsure about the state of affairs between the Shah and Bhutto. The Pakistani President's one-day stay in Tehran on 26 October 1974 had been a mystery to the US Embassy in Tehran. They did not know what to make of it, and had been unable to 'develop any inside information' on that occasion.[189]

When Bhutto arrived in Washington in early 1975, Kissinger set out to gauge his mood in a roundabout way. He asked Bhutto about the increasing Iranian–Saudi rivalry in the region, particularly over divisions in OPEC. Bhutto replied, 'Iran is our neighbor. Saudi Arabia is far away.'

Sensing an atypical circumspection in Bhutto, Kissinger egged him on. He raised the question of the Shah's oil money, and said, 'You are a martial people, but there is no evidence of the Persians fighting anyone for the past 1,000 years!' Bhutto did not bite. He knew better, and must have sneered at either Kissinger's lack of familiarity with Persian conquests on the subcontinent or his attempt to trick him into a new cascade of badmouthing of the Shah.[190] The latter situation was probably far more likely, given Kissinger's known proclivity for mind games with foreign leaders.

Bhutto's trip was the pinnacle of what the *Sunday Observer* at the time called a 'two-year campaign to get the American arms embargo lifted'.

His message to Washington was simple: give us arms and we will stop the approaching nuclear race with India. He put it this way:

> [Pakistan] is not racing for the bomb. If we get even a modest contribution we shall not find it necessary to proceed. We don't want to do what India does and destroy half the economy. India is becoming a giant with clay feet. Spiritually and morally it will fall apart, in spite of its glorious victories.[191]

Bhutto's bid for more conventional arms worked. Only a few weeks later, on 24 February 1975, the United States finally lifted its ten-year arms embargo.[192] The Shah, too, was pleased with this move. A few weeks after the lifting, he told President Ford and Kissinger that Washington had done the right thing vis-à-vis Pakistan: 'They can't go in for an aggressive war because India is too big. But we should give them the ability to defend themselves.' Kissinger responded that the Pakistanis had not bought anything yet. The Shah replied, 'They have no money. They asked me for a $1 billion. I don't have it. The Saudis do but they don't have the close relations we do.'[193]

The Shah could claim to have heard the latest news straight from the horse's mouth as he had, just prior to his arrival in Washington, spent three days with Bhutto in Pakistan. The two leaders would publicly claim that the question of military supplies was not part of that discussion – a highly implausible claim, as everyone knew that Islamabad was preparing a long shopping list for US military equipment now that the embargo had been lifted.

Bhutto told the Americans that he would rather have money to purchase weapons than third-party arms transfers from Iran that still faced American restrictions, particularly from the US Congress.[194] However, his best bet was still the Shah, for a number of important reasons. Key among them was the fact that by now the Shah had moved from acting as the unqualified guardian of Pakistan to a moderating hand, if not mediator, in the Indo–Pakistani conflict. This gave the Shah sway both with the Americans – as the intended, but anxious, weapons suppliers to Pakistan – and also the Indians, the focus of any Pakistani military modernization. This was, under the circumstances, the best that Islamabad could hope for.

In October 1975, Bhutto paid one of his regular visits to Tehran. He told the Shah that he 'found it embarrassing to ask for assistance' with financing of military purchases, but he had no alternative. 'I have decided to help you', the Shah replied.[195] The previous year, Iran had supplied some $700 million in aid to Islamabad.

Iran had overtaken the United States as the largest aid provider to Pakistan. Despite Tehran's generosity, Bhutto could not help but find the Shah increasingly overbearing. His 'dependence on the Shah and the Shah's aloof acceptance of the cordial and gracious Bhutto hospitality left unpleasant memories of "Pahlavi" in [Bhutto's] mind'.[196]

The Shah insisted that Pakistan set its eyes only on defensive military equipment.[197] He thought that offensive equipment was too expensive for the Pakistanis and would also aggravate the Indians. This was the Shah at his best as a broker. Kissinger remarked, 'Shah's policy has thus in fact contributed to promotion of stability and moderation among countries of South Asia – objectives which completely accord with our own.'[198] Another way of looking at the matter was that by now neither Iran nor India wanted Pakistan to become too strong. Both countries were content to have Pakistan as a buffer state.

Bhutto's fall

Over his six years in power, Zulfikar Bhutto had managed to generate a sizeable opposition to his rule. He was ultimately overthrown in a military coup led by General Zia ul-Haq in July 1977, and would spend the rest of his life in a prison cell. Bhutto had himself hand-picked ul-Haq as chief of the army in March 1976, in the belief that the religious-minded general had no political ambitions.

Only a couple of weeks before he was toppled, Bhutto told the Shah that the Americans were after him. The administration of President Jimmy Carter had been in office for only a few months when Bhutto went public with his worries about US plans for Pakistan. Bhutto's people claimed to have intercepted a phone conversation coming out of the American Embassy, which they said showed Washington was keen to see the Pakistani President go.

In May 1977, Bhutto decided not to send his foreign minister to Tehran for the annual CENTO meeting. This was in protest against Washington, as Bhutto charged that US money was behind the increasingly vocal domestic opposition in Pakistan.[199] Going public was bold and controversial, but this pugnacity was short-lived. Behind the scenes, Bhutto was looking for a way out.

On 21 June 1977, on his way home from Kuwait, he stopped in Tehran and told the Shah that the US Embassy in Islamabad was in contact with various members of the Pakistani opposition. Bhutto did not stop there. He told the Shah that he 'regretted his tirade against Washington and that he was anxious to make it up to the USA by whatever means possible'.[200] Asadollah Alam wrote in his memoirs at the time that the 'Shah agreed Bhutto's days were numbered'.

Bhutto would have sensed this inevitability in the Shah's stance, and he clearly resented it. Later on, from his prison cell, he claimed that the 'Shah definitely knew that a *coup d'état* was about to take place in Pakistan within days and with his approval'.[201] He wrote at the time that the Iranian leader 'had a complex' towards him. 'He respected and feared my capabilities', Bhutto said about the Shah. Nonetheless, the Shah's campaigning on behalf of Bhutto would have a final chapter.

CHAPTER 7

1977-1988: ZIA, THE SHAH AND THE COMING OF THE AYATOLLAH

Within a few months of coming to power, Zia ul-Haq urgently needed to shore up his standing at home. When he unseated Bhutto, Zia had promised his people that free elections would be held within 90 days. He chose not to deliver on that promise. Instead, he looked to the outside world for political support and as a financial stopgap to staunch the economic haemorrhage at home. After his foreign emissaries repeatedly returned empty-handed, Zia sensed the need to push his agenda abroad with a greater force.

In October 1977, he embarked on a tour to shore up support. It included Iran, Saudi Arabia, the United Arab Emirates and Afghanistan. Iran was key, as it had for decades been Pakistan's regional linchpin. The Gulf Arab countries had by this stage become critical sources of money for Islamabad – both in direct aid and through the roughly $2 billion that Pakistani migrant workers sent home each year from the Arab Gulf states. Afghanistan was, historically, the stormy neighbour, which could create more distress at any moment and needed to be mollified as Zia could do without any external distractions. Zia chose later on to add Kuwait, Turkey, Libya and Jordan to his itinerary.[1] This was intended to be his big tour of deliverance. He had a lot of bruised egos – particularly, old friends of Bhutto – to calm down and keep in with Pakistan.

Once he arrived in Tehran, Zia tried hard to endear himself to the Shah. Over the next 18 months, he would push for meetings with the

Iranian ruler even when he had nothing urgent to discuss, a pattern that proved annoying for the Iranians. Since a US Senate resolution in 1976 – the Symington Amendment – to ban economic and military aid to countries that engaged in illegal nuclear activities, Islamabad's need for money had intensified.

This pushed Pakistan further into the arms of the Saudis. The Shah did not look too kindly on it at that. As with Bhutto before him, Zia wrapped himself in the flag of Islam – although he would end up going much further in his attempt to cultivate the Saudis. 'If Saudi Arabia is attacked, I will personally lead its defense', he once declared. On another occasion, he simply said that an 'attack on Saudi Arabia is an attack on Pakistan'.[2]

There was little sign of the Shah attempting to pull Zia away from the Saudis. In fact, the former's munificence would now increasingly come with strings attached. When Zia asked him for more financial aid, he was condescendingly informed that Pakistan needed to improve its economic performance and launch reform.[3] If the Saudis were the source of hard cash, the Shah was still the one with the longest reach into the White House.[4] That reality provided the Shah with leverage over Zia. He pushed for the release of Bhutto, but this call was gently ignored.

A frustrated Shah would soon publicly threaten that the execution of Bhutto would lead to total severance in relations between Tehran and Islamabad. Nonetheless, Bhutto remained behind bars.[5] Were the Shah's efforts to save him genuine? It would later emerge that the imprisoned Bhutto, by most accounts, did not think so. After all, if he had been approached, how could Zia have refused the *Shahanshah*, the King of Kings! There can be no doubt that the Shah in those volatile days would have still perceived Bhutto as a known entity irrespective of his irritating traits and personal rivalry with him. Bhutto had delivered when called on during the 1973–7 Baluch insurgency that the Shah so deeply feared would spill over into Iran. He had stayed in CENTO as the Shah had asked him to do. However, on balance the Shah regarded Zia as a naive successor with an unknown political agenda, at the time mostly famous for his endless media gaffes. At worst, Zia was a huge liability for the anti-communist cause in the region. This was, of course, a misguided appraisal of him, but it was nonetheless the Shah's view at the time.

Bhutto remained in custody. While no one on the international scene at the time believed that his execution would bring an end to the multiple distresses of Pakistan, the former leader had cut so many corners and created so many enemies at home and abroad in his six years in office that calls for his freedom were never overwhelming.

§

On 5 February 1978, the Shah of Iran concluded a four-day state visit to India. The Iranian monarch, accompanied by Queen Farah, had come to New Delhi to push for closer ties between the two nations.[6] The Shah's stay in India, which had included the promotion of his precious grand ideas of regional, political and economic integration by the littoral states of the Indian Ocean, went smoothly. By the end, he was suffering from exhaustion aggravated by ongoing medical troubles (linked to his then-secret cancer treatment) and wanted to fly home.

The Pakistanis pleaded with him to stop in Islamabad on his way back to Tehran. The Shah chose not to offend the ul-Haq Government, and at the last minute arranged for a stopover in Islamabad. However, his heart was not in it: India had received four days, and now ul-Haq was given only four hours.[7]

The eager Pakistanis wanted to hear from the Shah himself what Tehran was discussing with the Indians with regard to economic aid to New Delhi. They were particularly worried about Iran's decision to agree to fund an irrigation canal in India's Rajasthan state, which borders Pakistan. Islamabad would claim that it was concerned about the environmental impact of the canal, and whether this could affect water availability for Pakistan further downstream. In reality, it feared the military implications of this project that a hitherto ally had agreed to sponsor for India.

The Indian military had failed in the 1965 and 1971 wars to make quick breakthroughs into Pakistan's hilly Punjab and Kashmir regions. Indian military planners were now looking further south, to the desert terrain of Rajasthan, as territory better suited to a quick Indian military offensive in the event of another land war. The Pakistanis guessed, correctly, that there was at least some military purpose to the canal.[8]

Pakistani fears were about far more than a single Indian canal. By this time, the ul-Haq military regime feared that in the near future Iran and India would have tangible overlapping interests – such as the idea of the Indian Ocean Economic Community – to the detriment of Pakistan. This appraisal was shared by the US Ambassador to Islamabad, Arthur

Hummel. Five days after the Shah's brief visit to Islamabad, Hummel sent a telegram to Washington raising questions about the future of Iran–Pakistan ties.[9] The Shah's Iran and ul-Haq's Pakistan were perceptibly drifting apart. CENTO, the only significant institutional linkage that might have acted as a 'glue', was by now an open farce.

In the April 1978 annual CENTO meeting, held in London, the British foreign secretary, David Owen, once again made it abundantly obvious that CENTO was not to be turned into another NATO. Stop dreaming, was Owen's message to the Iranians, the Pakistanis and the Turks. As he put it, the politico-military structure and activity of the alliance was 'about the right amalgam', adding, 'if you tried to fit it into too tight framework [it] would be trying to make it more than it can be'.[10] London and Washington were still in agreement that CENTO should focus on its economic development mission and not become a NATO-style military alliance. At that 1978 summit, there were no actual references to the Soviet threat. Its final communiqué simply stated: 'We [the CENTO ministers] see no significant recent development in Soviet policy towards CENTO.'

The communiqué did say that 'the Soviet Union will continue to look for opportunities to extend her influence in the region'.[11] This was, however, a mere rhetorical warning, rather than any pre-emptive measure to deter Moscow. This sort of indecision on the part of CENTO was least surprising to Tehran and Islamabad.[12]

One topic that was not on the agenda at the CENTO summit was Afghanistan. This impoverished neighbour had been a security ordeal for both Iran and Pakistan for decades, and its omission from the agenda turned out to be an omen.

1978: Another coup in Kabul

As fate would have it, it would once again be political events in their common neighbour – Afghanistan – that created a common cause for the Shah and the Pakistani regime.

On 27 April 1978, only a few days after the conclusion of the CENTO ministerial meeting in London, communist military officers overthrew and killed President Mohammad Daoud Khan in Kabul. The coup was backed by Moscow, precisely the sort of move that the CENTO communiqué had predicted only days earlier.

Reactions in Tehran and Islamabad to events in Kabul were matched. Fears expressed about some master plan concocted by Moscow were identical to reactions the last time a coup had taken place in Kabul, back in 1973. After the 1978 coup, ul-Haq said that Afghanistan was no longer a buffer – that it was now a full-fledged Soviet satellite, and that 'Pakistan now shared a common border with Soviet Union'. Iran was flanked by the Soviet Union to its north, and now to the east as well. Again, there was plenty of anger at the West for its perceived negligence in letting Afghanistan slip uncer communist control.

The Iranian intelligence service, SAVAK, would claim to have seen the redrawn borders as envisaged by Moscow on an intercepted map showing a Greater Baluchistan arising from Iranian and Pakistani Baluch territories.[13] The British Embassy in Kabul estimated that the number of Soviet advisors in Afghanistan had doubled in a few short months after the coup to some 4,000. By December 1978, Moscow and Kabul had signed a new friendship treaty, which the communists in Kabul looked on as a security bond.[14] For the Iranians and the Pakistanis, the Soviet plot was thickening.

Islamabad repeatedly made the point that the coup in Kabul was a disaster for its security, and that unless CENTO came to its 'aid and comfort' Pakistan would 'have to reassess her position as a member of CENTO'. The British were undeterred. 'There are good grounds for believing that these arguments are at least in part tactic to loosen the purse strings of those who might assist Pakistan', the British in Islamabad concluded in reference to London and Washington. The Pakistanis were seen as wanting to use Afghan crisis as 'a means of applying pressure on the US to relax [its] attitude to the French [nuclear] reprocessing plant' that Islamabad had relentlessly pursued.[15] The same cables, however, did also raise some concern that Pakistan's 'threat of leaving CENTO cannot safely be dismissed as merely tactical'.[16]

While the Iranian and Pakistani penchant for seeing Soviet plots around every corner was often excessive, they could not be blamed if they sensed a high degree of Western apathy in the face of monumental events in Kabul. Tehran said it was preparing to intervene militarily, to shore up the stability of its neighbours if they faced pro-communist subversion.

The Shah's global anti-communist crusade was still alive, despite mounting troubles at home. A few weeks before the communist coup in

Kabul, he had warned the socialist regime of Ethiopia that if they crossed into Somalia, then Tehran would intervene. Now the communists were at his eastern doorstep. The Soviets were going to create a Pashtunistan and a Baluchistan – and then dominate the region through these vassal states.

The Iranian leader was unwavering: 'In certain geographic areas of the world, there is no alternative but chauvinism. Iran is [located] in one of these regions. Otherwise, we will disappear and our name will no longer be Iran, but Iranistan.'[17] The Shah was in panic mode, and Moscow did not help one bit. In early July, the Soviets shot down two Iranian Army helicopters that they claimed had entered Soviet airspace in fog. Eight Iranian soldiers were killed. The Shah again pressed the Americans for the most sophisticated US-made anti-aircraft systems, to deter the Soviets as they regularly encroached into Iranian airspace. Ultimately, the coup of 1978 in Kabul became the first step in a chain of events that led to the Soviet invasion of Afghanistan the following year.

Paradoxically, there had been heightened speculation in the West that the Shah had caused Daoud's fall by seducing him too far and too quickly away from Moscow. From the moment he took office in 1973, Daoud's declared 'neutrality' had seemed gradually less convincing in Moscow's eyes. Daoud had been expected to take Kabul closer to Moscow, but had done the reverse. Kabul under Daoud had instead set out to diversify Afghan foreign policy. Besides Iran, he had looked to Saudi Arabia, India, Egypt and even increasingly Pakistan for cooperation.

That became a factor in Daoud's undoing, and he misjudged where the internal threat would emerge. As a strongman-modernizer who centralized power in Kabul, he had anticipated a backlash from the fundamentalist right among the ranks of Afghanistan's roughly 300,000 unhappy mullahs. The country's diehard communists had not been deemed politically mature or numerous enough to pose a challenge.[18] That turned out to be Daoud's fatal misreading. With communist rule in Kabul now a matter of fact, on 6 May 1978 Iran and Pakistan reluctantly granted diplomatic recognition to the Democratic Republic of Afghanistan. After decades of anticipation, the angst had become a reality and Iran and Pakistan now had a bona fide communist government in charge of a neighbouring country.

What to do with communists in Kabul?

As had happened when Daoud came to power in 1973, the new communist Afghan regime, under President Nur Mohammad Taraki, chose to raise the issue of Pashtunistan as soon as it was in power. This upset ul-Haq no end.

Taraki was himself from ethnic Pashtun peasant stock. He had been the only son from his family to be chosen for an education – a pursuit that took him to India at one point, where he learnt English and was introduced to the ideals of national liberation and Marxism. In 1965, he co-founded the Soviet-leaning People's Democratic Party of Afghanistan.[19] His deputy, the fiery and merciless Hafizullah Amin, was also an ethnic Pashtun, but far more enthusiastic about the use of the 'Pashtunistan card' in Kabul's dealings with Pakistan.

Two weeks after seizing power, Taraki and Amin invited Khan Abdul Ghaffar Khan, the leader of the Pashtunistan secessionists in Pakistan's North West Frontier Province, together with his son Wali Khan, to Kabul. The visit caused huge alarm in Islamabad. This was only to be exacerbated in the weeks that followed. In June of that same year, Amin travelled to New York to attend a UN event on global disarmament. If he had set out to pester the Pakistanis, his speech here made sure he did just that.

Amin spoke about Kabul's desire for the 'expansion of friendly relations with our great northern neighbor the Soviet Union' and with India. He then turned and gave Islamabad what sounded like an ultimatum. Relations could only be normalized, he warned, if a 'solution of the national issue of the Pashtun and Baluch people [those living in Pakistan] on the basis of their own will and historical background' could be found.[20]

As Daoud before him, Amin was raising the prospect of Afghan incitement of Pakistan's ethnic Pashtun and Baluch. As Bhutto before him, ul-Haq saw this as a direct threat to his country's territorial integrity. He was indignant, and ruled out political dialogue with Kabul. The only difference between the Afghan coups of 1973 and 1978 was that Daoud had come to power only as sympathetic toward Moscow but ended up genuinely enacting a non-aligned foreign policy. The group that had come to power in Kabul in April 1978 was in the pockets of the Soviets, as the passing of only a few months would vividly show.

The communist coup in Kabul quickly led to a massive influx of Afghan refugees into Pakistan. The majority of these were God-fearing ethnic Pashtuns, and hardly amenable to the atheist dogma of the communists. Among the refugees were some of Afghanistan's leading religious families, including the Gailani and Mojaddedi. The size of these extended families ran into thousands of individuals. These very same fleeing crowds were to become Pakistan's abettors. As a way of countering the communist regime in Kabul and making it rethink its crusade for 'Pashtunistan' and 'Baluchistan', Islamabad opted to provide financial and military assistance to the refugees who were mobilizing for an armed insurrection against the Afghan communists and Moscow. The anti-communist insurgency was in motion over a year before the Soviet military invaded Afghanistan.

In this Pakistani game plan, the Iranians were by this stage largely missing.[21] The Shah was facing his own revolution, as a broad-based opposition to his dynasty – ranging from local communists to Islamists – combined to try to bring him down. 'The [domestic] troubles in Iran have increased the feeling of isolation that has grown in Pakistan since last April [1978]', a US intelligence summary concluded.[22] However, the Shah's predicaments at home did not stop Afghan rebels from soliciting help from him.

Haji Mangal Hussain, a prominent Afghan Pashtun warrior who would later became a minister in the government of Hamed Karzai, was one of these rebels. He and a few members of his group travelled from their base in Peshawar to call on the Iranian Embassy in Islamabad in order to explore possible assistance. He remembers the Iranians being open to the idea, and initial steps were taken in the autumn of 1978 for the flow of aid to begin. As winter set in, and the political situation in Iran deteriorated, the Afghan rebels could only watch as the Shah's regime crumbled.[23]

In Kabul, British and American diplomats observed the developments between Afghanistan and Pakistan with a keen eye, but were undaunted. There was certainly no sense of alarm. After one of the regular meetings with their American counterparts in Kabul, a British cable said the two sides had 'briefly touched on border problems with Pakistan' but that the 'Americans seem to share the [British] view that the Afghan leaders have so much on their plate at present that they would not wish to meddle in Pakistan'.

The same British diplomats who wrote that note in August 1978 knew that their judgement about Afghan intentions would not persuade the sceptical Pakistanis: '[Britain's] major concern at the moment is to limit the damage from the Afghan coup which in practice means trying to keep Pakistan from swerving too far towards non-alignment and instead staying within the CENTO framework.' Iran, the same cable astonishingly noted, 'is much steadier'.[24]

As the Taraki Government persisted in pushing the Pashtunistan question, the views of the Western diplomatic and intelligence services hardened. US and British diplomats began expressing fears about the coup's broader implications: 'Uppermost in the minds of KGB planners may have been the need to have a regime in Kabul that would give full support to Soviet-backed subversion in Iran and Pakistan.'

As the weeks passed, Western intelligence services became convinced that the growing domestic political instability in Iran had made provocation among Baluch peoples more attractive for Moscow. The opinion was, and it turned to be true, that the communist Afghans would lump the cases of Baluchistan and Pashtunistan into one sedition campaign to aggravate their larger neighbours, Iran and Pakistan. As early as 14 February 1979, a meeting of representatives from NATO countries in Brussels determined that 'Baluchistan is [a] more likely source of future trouble than the Pashtunistan issue'. The British, the old hardened European hand in the region, were specific in their warning at that NATO meeting:

> It is questionable whether the Afghans will be able to exploit the
> Pashtunistan issue against Pakistan, whatever they say about it in
> public, but the possibilities for creating trouble in Baluchistan,
> where new, radically inclined leaders have been reported to be
> replacing the traditional tribal leadership, are probably greater.
> Unrest in Baluchistan could have incalculable consequences for the
> cohesion of Pakistan itself.[25]

Within months, this diagnosis had more or less become reality. If the conclusions of the Western intelligence services were far-reaching, the action plan that they put forward was at first feeble. As they had argued in 1973, any Afghan administration − be it that of Daoud or Taraki − would be busy with internal problems and threats, and have little capacity to provoke Tehran and Islamabad. But Taraki's government turned out to be far more zealous than that.

This forced a reassessment on the part of Western intelligence services. 'There are clear indications that the Russians are developing Afghanistan as a base for their efforts to destabilize the pro-Western governments of Iran and Pakistan', the British warned.[26] Still, the Western powers – the Americans and the British in particular – sat tight. A British diplomatic note at the time read: 'There has been some talk recently of the Moscow-Kabul-Delhi axis. This usually comes from the Pakistanis [...] the Iranians have also spoken on similar lines in discussions in CENTO.' The 'idea is non-sense [sic]', the memo suggested dismissively, doubting whether even those who propounded it really believed it.[27]

India argued that confronting the communists in Kabul would only intensify Soviet efforts to create havoc in Afghanistan and beyond. The Indians took this message directly to the Shah. One British diplomatic report from Tehran said that the 'Indians have advised the Iranians to not act in a way of isolating Afghanistan to the extent of pushing the Afghans further into the arms of Russia. It would be a "self-fulfilling prophecy".'[28]

Whereas the Shah had been at the top of his game when Daoud had come to power in 1973, things were very different for him in 1978, his *annus horribilis*. The oil bonanza of the first half of the 1970s was over, restraining his financial capacity to induce those he needed to cajole. The Shah's hands were tied and his mind was on events at home, as the winds of revolution inside Iran steadily gathered force.

This, however, was only part of the picture. While the Shah and ul-Haq reacted with identical horror to the communist power grab in Afghanistan in April 1978, there was no common understanding about joint efforts as had been the case when the 1973 coup had happened. A month after communists had taken hold in Kabul, the Shah was sitting in Tehran threatening to sever ties with Islamabad if ul-Haq executed Bhutto.

Personal memoirs and declassified material have since made it clear that by this stage – the spring of 1978 – the Shah's relations with Bhutto had, during the previous five years, experienced what can be mildly described as creeping deterioration. This was no longer a life-and-death friendship – if, indeed, it ever had been. The notion that the

Shah, the self-declared grand strategist would prioritize Bhutto's life over joining with the ul-Haq Government to contain the Afghan communist coup is far-fetched to say the least.

It is more likely that the Shah's keenness to save Bhutto was driven by his fears about his own fate. Over the course of his reign, the Iranian ruler had seen many of the region's leaders toppled or unceremoniously killed at the hands of coup makers and revolutionaries. He had most recently watched Daoud – along with his family members – gunned down by communist mutineers in Kabul. Perhaps seeking to preserve Bhutto's life was about preventing more precedents being set that might rouse the anti-Shah hordes back home in Iran.

In any event, there is no evidence of a coordinated Iranian–Pakistani strategy to go after the Afghan communist regime of Taraki. A few months before he was toppled, the Shah chose to send General Nematollah Nasiri to Islamabad as his ambassador. Nasiri had been the boss of the SAVAK, Iran's intelligence service, from 1965 to 1978. The Shah, in his attempt to appease his domestic critics, removed Nasiri and gave him the ambassadorship. This move, however, was seen in Pakistan as puzzling. Even though it was a political act to remove him from SAVAK and send him away, ul-Haq said Nasiri's 'appointment had started rumors' in Islamabad. The Pakistanis were offended by the appointment, but the preceding months had already signalled that Iranian–Pakistani relations were about to take a turn for the worse.[29]

§

A few months earlier, in February 1978, as the Shah took his seat in the royal aircraft that would take him to Tehran from Islamabad en route from New Delhi, a senior aide approached him with an envelope. Amir Aslan Afshar, chief of protocol at the imperial court, had quietly been handed it during the official luncheon that the Shah had just finished with General ul-Haq. The anonymous person who had delivered the envelope claimed to be a friend of Zulfikar Bhutto.

The Shah asked Afshar to read the letter out loud. The handwritten two-page note turned out to be an impassioned plea by Bhutto to the Shah, in effect asking the Iranian monarch to save him from his jailor. In the letter, Bhutto dismissed the array of charges laid against him by the ul-Haq regime as baseless, but then swiftly moved on to the crux of the matter in asking the Shah for a substantial favour. Over the years,

Bhutto had often asked the Shah for support, be it financial assistance or military supplies to bolster Pakistan's armed forces. But this one was different, and of a personal nature. Bhutto wrote: 'I am willing to prove my intentions [to ul-Haq] by leaving Pakistan and come and live [sic] in Iran. I consider Iran my second home. My wife is Iranian. And I have always considered you [the Shah] my friend.'[30] It was the ultimate plea from a broken man.

When Afshar stopped reading, he noticed that an aura of profound sadness had filled the Shah. The latter's efforts to seek Bhutto's freedom, as with the attempts of many other world leaders, had fallen on deaf ears. Given the close ties up until then between Iran and Pakistan, ul-Haq's refusal to release Bhutto was by all accounts not made lightly, but it was one that he would stick to despite the intense pressure that subsequently fell on him, and the unmistakable chill in Tehran–Islamabad ties.

The turnaround in relations that began with the coming to power of ul-Haq stood in sharp contrast to the period when Tehran acted as one of Islamabad's main supporters when Pakistan faced catastrophic defeats at the hands of India in the 1965 and 1971 conflicts.

The Shah might have looked to hit back at ul-Haq's intrasigence, but his opportunity never came. In the midst of his many overtures toward the Pakistani general, the Shah himself was overthrown in the Iranian Revolution in the winter of 1978-9. On 4 April 1979, less than three months after the Iranian monarch had been forced into exile, Bhutto was unceremoniously hanged at the central jail in Rawalpindi, the city housing headquarters of the Pakistani Army.

Ul-Haq, the evasive Islamist

The Shah never took a liking to the drab ul-Haq – a striving Islamist who stood in sharp contrast to the flamboyant Bhutto, but whose secular lifestyle nonetheless matched that of the Shah. Bhutto had also been considered by many around him to be a formidable intellect, if not ruthlessly ambitious. But the Iranian monarch was certainly not motivated merely out of his personal loyalty toward Bhutto.[31]

The Shah had expected ul-Haq to be more accommodating about the fate of Bhutto. He felt that whoever ruled in Islamabad owed Tehran as much due to decades of Iranian–Pakistani cooperation in many areas and millions of US dollars in aid. But the Shah's greater concerns were also tied to ul-Haq's then still ambiguous Islamist agenda, and Pakistan's future regional trajectory.

Fereidoon Zand-Fard, the Shah's penultimate ambassador to Islamabad writes in his memoirs that in his final letter to ul-Haq, the Iranian monarch had two requests. First, he sought the release of Bhutto. Second – and far more consequentially for future global security, as time would show – the Shah urged the Pakistani leader to abandon the quest for a nuclear weapon. In no uncertain terms, the Iranian leader warned ul-Haq that Washington was deadly serious about opposing Pakistan's nuclear ambitions at the time. He offered his services as a go-between with the Americans.[32]

For the Shah, the occupier of the Peacock Throne, Pakistan's nuclear ambitions posed a major challenge to his regional ambitions. Throughout the 1970s, he had eagerly cultivated an image of a man with great ambitions for the country he had ruled since he came to the throne as a 21-year-old in 1941. Some saw him as the reckless, tyrannical ruler of a Third World nation, with outlandish ideas that he nonetheless could entertain thanks to the oil bonanza that Iran enjoyed in the 1960s and 1970s. A CIA psychological profile of the Shah from the mid-1970s painted him as a 'brilliant but dangerous megalomaniac who [was] likely to pursue his own aims in disregard of US interests'.[33] Those who stood to defend him saw in the Shah a strategist who rightfully envisaged Iran as a natural leader in the Middle East and beyond in greater Asia.[34] And in the Shah's world view, Pakistan could absolutely not become unfriendly territory.

On 21 July 1977, Zand-Fard had met with ul-Haq in Islamabad. The Pakistani general had come to power only days before, on 4 July.[35] Iran's foreign minister, Abbas Ali Khalatbari, had asked his ambassador to travel to Pakistan as quickly as possible, but had also given him meticulous instructions. Zand-Fard had been told to treat ul-Haq very sensitively, but to nonetheless urge him to seriously reconsider Pakistan's quest for a nuclear weapon. Otherwise the United States would be forced to abandon close military ties with Pakistan, the Shah's emissary was tasked with explaining to his Pakistani hosts. During the meeting, Zand-Fard stressed that neither Iran nor Pakistan could afford that prospect, given the larger Soviet threat on the horizon. Iran and Pakistan needed each other, and their joint fortunes were tied to the United States. And the United States had made it abundantly clear where it stood on the matter.

The Pakistanis, of course, knew only too well about America's opposition to Islamabad's rush for the first 'Islamic bomb'. Benazir Bhutto, Zulfikar's daughter and a future Pakistani leader, later said that her father's quest for nuclear arms was a pivotal reason for Washington's withdrawal of support for him. She even hinted that it was a central factor that led to her father's downfall.

She wrote about the visit of US Secretary of State Henry Kissinger to Pakistan in 1976, in which he told Zulfikar Bhutto that Islamabad's agreement with France for a nuclear reprocessing plant 'had the potential to result in a nuclear device'. In her words, Kissinger had told her father that Washington was against an 'Islamic Bomb' and that Zulfikar Bhutto had to 'reconsider the agreement with France or risk being made into a horrible example'.[36]

But Bhutto had by then already invested heavily, both politically and materially, in the nuclear programme, and to walk away from it all was said not to be an option. As early as 1965, when he was still only a foreign minister, Bhutto had vowed: 'If India builds the bomb, we will eat grass or leaves, even go hungry, but we will get one of our own. We have no other choice.' Bhutto looked to the Islamic world for support and asked Muslim leaders that if 'the United States, England, France, China, Russia and Israel were entitled to the bomb, why shouldn't a Muslim nation have one?'.[37]

In the 1970s, this brand of nationalist rhetoric by Bhutto was not that dissimilar to the language of the Shah of Iran, who also blasted the notion of nuclear 'haves' and 'have-nots'. The oratory of Bhutto and the Shah on nuclear technology and weapons was certainly similar as long as it was cast in response to Western criticism and anxieties about nuclear proliferation. But as Zand-Fard's mission to Islamabad clearly demonstrated, Tehran and Islamabad each considered the nuclear question differently and with their own distinct interests at play.

On the nuclear issue, two key factors separated Bhutto from the Shah. For Pakistan, a nuclear weapon was seen as an essential military capability just to put Pakistan at military parity with already nuclear-armed India, which had joined the exclusive club in 1974.[38] While the Shah entertained great ambitions for his country, and considered joining the nuclear club as an important step in the direction of fulfilling his goals, Iran unlike Pakistan did not at that time face any mortal threats at the hands of adversaries that were nuclear armed. If the Pakistani quest for nuclear weapons was seen as a necessity, the Shah of Iran was not as hard pressed.

Another factor that separated Pakistan from Iran on the nuclear question was the matter of money. Iran could self-finance its nuclear ambitions thanks to its plentiful oil revenues. Pakistan was not in the same enviable position. Later in 1978, when Iran faced a major economic contraction thanks to a fall in the price of oil, the Shah voluntarily put his nuclear ambitions on hold. Bhutto's motto of 'we will eat grass but have a bomb' would not have worked for the Shah given the economic malaise that Iran was facing at the time and the popular mobilization that was building up around socio-economic grievances.

The need for financing led to Bhutto astutely touting the idea of an 'Islamic Bomb' in the hope that oil-rich Arab and Muslim states would help bankroll Islamabad's nuclear goals. Bhutto's plan worked. After his much-anticipated February 1974 Islamic conference in Lahore, largely engineered by Bhutto for the purpose of building Muslim momentum against India, aid from Arab oil states to Pakistan indeed began to flow on an unprecedented scale.[39]

In Lahore, a host of Arab dignitaries, including the conference co-sponsor King Faisal of Saudi Arabia, pledged financial support. The young dapper Colonel Qaddafi of Libya turned to Bhutto and famously told him 'Our [Libya's] resources are your resources'; soon afterwards, Libya began sending its oil to Pakistan at the cost of production.[40] Later, the Pakistanis would name one of the country's largest stadiums after the Libyan leader. The Lahore conference, however, was a turning point in more ways than one.

The Shah recognized Pakistan's financial predicaments but he did not at all appreciate Bhutto turning for support to the Arab sheikhdoms of the Persian Gulf or to Colonel Qaddafi, a man the Shah deeply detested. Many Iranian and Pakistani accounts point to Qaddafi as the reason the Shah shunned the Lahore conference. But still, according to Ardeshir Zahedi, the Shah's son-in-law and then Iranian ambassador to Washington, the Shah was a 'bigger man than [to] simply let his personal dislike of Qaddafi keep him from the conference'.[41] The truth was that by then, the early 1970s, previously innocent Iranian–Pakistani relations had begun to show signs of growing conflicts of interest and divergent paths ahead.

Zand-Fard writes that despite the Shah's misgivings, Bhutto's and now ul-Haq's nuclear ambitions were of much more concern to the

Americans than even to the Iranians, their next-door neighbours. Washington wanted Iran's subtle but direct involvement in mediation on this sensitive issue, in the hope that Tehran could sway Pakistan to change course.[42] What the Iranians did not know at this stage was whether ul-Haq would pursue the nuclear bomb as vigorously as Bhutto, the father of the programme, who had begun the project in January 1972.

Zand-Fard writes:

> I expressed the Shah's message in the context of the friendly ties between the two countries. I said [to Zia ul-aq] that [the] Shah, as a true friend of Pakistan, would like to raise the possibility of Pakistan ceasing her nuclear activities [...] and explained about American opposition to spreading of nuclear weapons and that by insisting Pakistan could lose the economic-military support of America and create conditions for further instability in the region.[43]

On hearing the Iranian views, ul-Haq remained unbending. He told Zand-Fard, 'as with the Shah, we [Pakistan] only seek to strengthen our armed forces and modernize our country'. Zia ul-Haq then lectured about Indian hostility toward Pakistan and the fact that New Delhi was already armed with nuclear weapons.

The self-ordained military leader stood his ground while Zand-Fard's instructions, which he suspected had been minutely put together by the Shah himself, advised him not to persist in making the point. If the Pakistanis would not abandon their nuclear aims, the Shah urged them to at least go about their nuclear project without creating much international attention. In retrospect, this piece of advice was prescient, yet it was scorned by the Pakistanis. In time, Pakistan would become an unrivalled global nuclear proliferator, with the world's eyes fixed on its atomic arsenal.

In Zand-Fard's estimation, Iran's mediation efforts in the nuclear realm had an adverse impact on the otherwise close relations between the two countries. Ul-Haq, and probably many more in the ranks of the Pakistani state, looked at such Iranian efforts as blatant interference in their affairs. And they made sure their misgivings were clear and noted at the highest levels in Tehran.

At Zand-Fard's farewell dinner, arranged by the host country, the Pakistani foreign minister, Agha Shahi, was noticeably absent. The deputy foreign minister, Shahnawaz Khan, attended instead, and he did not mince his words on the occasion. Khan flabbergasted Zand-Fard by suggesting in his after-dinner remarks, in front of top Pakistani figures and other foreign ambassadors, that 'Iran should act in a way to dispel any hint of interfering in Pakistan's affairs'.[44]

Zand-Fard left Islamabad for Tehran empty-handed, convinced that Iran's push for Islamabad to scale back its nuclear programme represented the first ever serious rupture in their bilateral relations. The fate of the imprisoned Zulfikar Bhutto simply lingered as a constant irritant in relations from the day General ul-Haq came to power until the downfall of the Shah.

Ul-Haq's advice to the Shah

In all, the Shah and ul-Haq met three times in Tehran. On the latter's third visit, it was the Shah's turn to make a point. He opted not to receive the Pakistani general at the airport as per protocol. If the Shah's gesture was designed to frighten ul-Haq into rethinking his policies, it failed. Instead of letting it be known that he was offended, ul-Haq sought to give the impression that he was deeply concerned about Shah's grip on power.

At the official reception at Mehr Abad Airport, he told Afshar, the chief of protocol at the imperial court, that the 'Shah had to act boldly in the face of the political upheaval' that Iran was undergoing at the time. As if to put a vision in the mind of the Shah, ul-Haq advised Afshar that he himself practised what he preached, and that he had had '200 of his own private guards arrested' and 'even killed some of them to gain control' when the general's own rule in Pakistan had been challenged.

Regardless of the worthiness of ul-Haq's advice in hindsight, the trouble was that he had by this time built up a serious trust deficit with the Iranians. His continual promises to the Iranian Embassy in Islamabad that the 'Shah's friend [Bhutto] will be treated in a friendly manner' turned out to be lies. Even the Shah's twin sister became embroiled in the Bhutto affair.

Ashraf Pahlavi, a close personal friend of Bhutto's, desperately wanted to contact him in prison. Given that he was Pakistan's No. 1 political prisoner, passing correspondence to him broke diplomatic protocol. Instead, Ashraf asked Iran's ambassador to Islamabad, Zand-Fard, to quietly improvise and find a way to deliver the letter to Bhutto, a request that Zand-Fard reluctantly accepted but, by his own account, never fulfilled.

Ul-Haq would surely have been aware of, and resented, such Iranian efforts on the behalf of his political arch-foe. Until the Shah was toppled, he continued to pay lip service to Iranian requests. He needed the Iranian leader for his larger, strategic objective. As the Americans remained cool towards him, the general wanted the Shah, with his close ties to Washington, to act as a bridge for Pakistan. That was why, in Zand-Fard's words, ul-Haq looked for 'every possible opportunity to meet with the Shah' but without ever intending to give in to the latter's key demands.

The Shah's fall

On 16 January 1979, after months of violent protests against his rule, the Shah left Iran. Over the next year and a half, he would criss-cross the world in a pitiful search for permanent exile. The King of Kings, the holder of the Peacock Throne who had ruled Iran for 37 years, was now politically so toxic that his former allies universally deserted him. Only two countries – Egypt and Paraguay – offered him asylum. The cancer-stricken Shah ended up in Egypt in March 1980, and he died there on 27 July in that same year.

§

As had long been quietly known on both sides of the Iran–Pakistan border, and as was later confirmed by Bhutto's memoirs, the Pakistani president had for a long time held considerable disdain for the Shah. Some time between January and April 1979, between the overthrow of the Shah and Bhutto's own hanging, the imprisoned former Pakistani leader mused over the character of the man who went by the title 'King of Kings'.

From his prison cell, Bhutto wrote about the Shah's downfall: 'If only he had been a bit more human, he might have survived [...] as an enlightened Oriental Monarch of a great Nation. If only he had not been such an obnoxious tool of Western interests.' He wrote that the Shah had been a superstitious man, who was both easy and difficult to please. 'He possessed a certain modesty in his vanity,' Bhutto added, 'He spoke disparagingly about almost all his neighboring countries and their leaders. There was an uncomfortable perversity about him.'

At the same time as he disparaged the Shah, Bhutto insisted that he had been a loyal friend to the King of Kings:

> I knew his doom was at hand. I had a stubborn premonition that he was about to depart. I tried to warn him of it [. . .] when he and Queen Farah came to Larkana in 1976. He [the Shah] must have said to himself 'Look who's talking. The man is about to fall himself in the near future!' I say this because when I went to Tehran in the end of June 1977, the Shah definitely knew that a *coup d'état* was about to take place in Pakistan within days and with his approval.[45]

Bhutto's account sums up so much about a relationship that, to this day, is often depicted as a close friendship. History shows that there was much more to it than that. In Bhutto's mind, the Shah had always been 'intensely envious', of him because, as Bhutto saw himself, he was an original. The Shah was not. Instead, oil money had led the Shah astray, pursuing his 'grandiose designs and fanciful ambitions', which in the end 'contributed in no small measure to his ruin'.[46]

In reality, the Shah was never much of a popular figure in Pakistan despite his oft-touted devotion to that country's defence. The likes of Qaddafi and Gamal Nasser of Egypt were preferred by the Pakistani masses. This applied to the country's elite as well. The 'disparity between Iran and Pakistan in almost every sphere has sparked evident resentment', as US diplomats reported from Islamabad in the summer of 1976, 'Resentment of Iranian good fortune is not diminished by Iranian arrogance, ultimately personified in the Shah himself.'[47]

Ul-Haq and the Ayatollah

Pakistani reaction to the fall of the Shah was both swift and, at first, enthusiastic. Ayatollah Khomeini's regime was immediately recognized by Islamabad, and two congratulatory messages sent to Tehran. Ul-Haq himself quickly sent a personal message to Prime Minister Mehdi

Bazargan, who headed the provisional government from 4 February to 6 November 1979. On 10 March, Pakistan's foreign minister, Agha Shahi, paid a visit to his counterpart, Karim Sanjabi. Many regarded this explicit enthusiasm as driven by necessity rather than genuine deference toward Iran's new rulers. As the CIA put it, 'the Shah, while occasionally irritatingly paternalistic to his poorer ally, was a known factor in regional relations; Khomeini is not.' This left the Pakistanis uncertain, but they had been careful to hedge their bets.

As Iran's revolution-in-waiting progressed in the winter of 1978, Islamabad had established contact with the Khomeini camp through the Pakistani Embassy in Paris. Khomeini, who from October 1978 lived in Neauphle-le-Chateau on the outskirts of the French capital, had by then emerged as the Shah's principal foe, and ul-Haq's government began in earnest to approach the revolutionaries. That move turned out to be cynical but smart. One of ul-Haq's cabinet ministers, Khurshid Ahmed, had openly supported the anti-Shah movement in Iran. Ahmed went to see Khomeini in early January 1979, days before the Shah's final departure from Tehran. The message from his government to Khomeini was simple: Pakistan wants friendship with the emerging Islamic government that was to come in Iran.[48]

On 1 February 1979, Khomeini returned to Tehran after 15 years of exile in Turkey, Iraq and France. Within days, Iran's 2,500-year-old monarchy would be abolished. In its place came a Shi'a Islamist regime with Ayatollah Khomeini as Iran's supreme leader. The Pakistani press was largely favourable towards the new government. Pakistan's Islamist parties were much more enthusiastic.

Ul-Haq, in his message to the new regime emphasized the 'simultaneous triumph of Islamic ideology in both our countries'. 'Khomeini is a symbol of Islamic insurgence', he said. Ul-Haq had himself experimented with political Islam from the outset of his rule. 'Pakistan, which was created in the name of Islam, will continue to survive only if it sticks to Islam. That is why I consider the introduction of [an] Islamic system as an essential prerequisite for the country,' he said.[49]

Up until his rise to power, ul-Haq's fame, or notoriety, had lain elsewhere. Nicknamed the 'Butcher of Palestinians', he had been based in Jordan as a brigadier general from 1967 to 1970. There, he had been involved in the training of Jordanian military forces. He was commander of the 2nd Division and instrumental in helping King Hussain crack down on Yasser Arafat's PLO in 1970, in what became known as Black September. Several thousand Palestinians were killed in this mini-civil war, when Palestinians living in the country rose up against the king. Ul-Haq was later awarded Jordan's highest honour for his services. Moshe Dayan, the Israeli defence minister, once commented that: 'King Hussain, with the help of Zia ul-Haq, killed more Palestinians in 11 days than Israel could kill in 20 years.'[50]

Islam became ul-Haq's primary political vehicle and claim to legitimacy. His plea to Khomeini for Islamic solidarity was aimed at increasing Iranian aid to Pakistan where the Shah had been lagging. Ul-Haq, however, was in reality open to any non-communist government in Tehran.

While Khomeini was a dogmatic puritan, ul-Haq was malleable. His official biography said he was 'fortified by deep religious conviction', but that he was also 'an enlightened and progressive soldier-statesman'. At state visits, ul-Haq would pour wine for his guest but never touch a drop himself. Like Khomeini, he chose to live a simple life. He set up Islamic courts and introduced public flogging. As with the Khomeini regime, ul-Haq pushed for more conservative dress codes for men and women. At the same time as Khomeini banned the tie as a symbolizing subservience to Western culture, civil servants in Islamabad were pressed to give up wearing suits and ties. Foreign films were banned, banks were not allowed to pay interest and mullahs were asked to see to it that people prayed five times a day.

Ul-Haq 'so skillfully exploited the [Islamic] fundamentalist terminology in [his] country that he threw the fundamentalists off balance. He blunted their revolutionary edge.'[51] At times even ul-Haq himself openly stressed the practical usefulness of tapping into Islam for political ends. After four years in power, he told a British magazine in 1981 that 'Pakistan is like Israel, an ideological state. Take out Judaism from Israel and it will fall like a house of cards. Take Islam out of Pakistan and make it a secular state; it would collapse.'[52]

Khomeini, although from the start deeply suspicious of ul-Haq, played along in the public show of solidarity with Islam as the cement that would keep Tehran and Islamabad together. Ul-Haq waxed lyrical:

> It is my heartfelt desire that the two brotherly peoples of Pakistan and Iran, who have always been friends and brothers, would

henceforth get closer under the banner of Islam, strengthen their unity and help and support each other like two brothers.[53]

In reality, the Khomeini camp from the very beginning did not consider ul-Haq an Islamist of any sort but an American pawn. Abol-Hassan Bani Sadr, one of Khomeini's chief lieutenants and Iran's first president after the Shah's fall, put it this way:

> Just because someone was Muslim did not make them an Islamist. That was true for Pakistan as it was for the House of Saud [in Saudi Arabia]. And we saw Islam as only one of three pillars that we [Iranian revolutionaries] advocated. The other two were independence and freedom. We did not consider Zia's regime to be independent [from the United States] and definitely did not think the Pakistani military junta was about people's freedom.[54]

Asad Durrani, a top general and the future head of the Pakistani intelligence service, the ISI, recollected years later that Khomeini hardly hid his disdain when he met visiting Pakistani officials in Tehran. The elderly Iranian religious leader would urge the Pakistanis to 'get rid of Zia', and mocked ul-Haq, calling him 'Zia ul-Batel'. *Haq* means 'truth', whereas *batel* means the exact opposite: 'false' or a bogus pretender.[55]

Iran abandons the West

With Khomeini's coming to power, Iran's military ties to Washington came to a halt. Iran unilaterally cancelled the Iranian–American Defense Agreement of 1959. Some $12 billion in US arms orders were halted by Tehran. American listening posts on Iran's northern borders with the Soviet Union were dismantled. In March 1979, Iran withdrew from CENTO.

Within 24 hours of Iran leaving CENTO, Pakistan had followed its lead. Both countries had abandoned the Western camp and were now officially part of the Non-Aligned Movement. In April of that year, Prime Minister Bazargan stated, 'Iran will not play the role of gendarme in the Persian Gulf and the Indian Ocean.'[56]

Pakistan, once it left CENTO, had its own basic 'bottom lines' for Washington. It wanted bilateral agreements with the United States such as its 1959 defence treaty, but with clarifications or it would not join any multilateral US-inspired security mechanism similar to the now-defunct CENTO.

Islamabad saw such a move as making Pakistan seem like a US stooge without giving it what it wanted: US guarantees against India. So it opted for maximum US concession but minimum visible coordination with Washington. A good example of this was its position on the Persian Gulf. As with the new Iranian Islamist regime in Tehran, Islamabad made it clear it had no desire to contemplate any military relationship with the United States for Persian Gulf security when the issue was raised.[57]

Soon after leaving CENTO, Islamabad looked for an alternative mechanism to serve its defence needs. The US Embassy in Pakistan cautioned that the Pakistanis were not sure where to go – after quitting CENTO – but Islamabad in March 1979 still insisted on a new defence mechanism to include Iran and Saudi Arabia, and exclude India.[58] This was part of ul-Haq's ongoing efforts to extend Bhutto's policy of shifting Pakistan's foreign policy away from the subcontinent and putting more focus on relations with the Middle Eastern countries. This approach at first included Khomeini's Iran, although Pakistan would with time become Arab-centric in its regional advances.[59]

§

By this stage, early 1979, relations between Western states and the new regime in Tehran were still more or less intact. There were even cases of security cooperation. When, in March 1979, fighting broke out in the Afghan city of Herat between communist government forces and anti-communist rebels, the British in Kabul quickly turned to the revolutionaries in Tehran for information and support about the well-being of stranded British citizens. The Iranian Consulate in Herat was the only source available. The Iranians were more than just gatekeepers, however; Kabul radio blamed the fighting on infiltrators from Iran.[60]

The riots in Herat became the first catalyst for the CIA to initiate its anti-communist crusade in Afghanistan. Washington's attention had locked on Afghanistan, as a couple of weeks earlier – on 14 February 1979 – US Ambassador Adolph Dubs had been assassinated in Kabul. On 30 March, at a secret session of the Special Coordination Committee, a representative of the State Department announced that the Carter White House firmly intended to stop Soviet expansionism in that region. There was no clear strategy at the time, but Carter's national security advisor, Zbigniew Brzezinski, admitted that on 3 July 1979 President Carter signed the first directive for secret aid to the Afghan anti-communist rebels. Brzezinski claims that on the very same day he wrote a note to the President in which he explained to him that 'this aid was going to induce a Soviet military intervention'.[61]

Iran was at this point not part of Washington's planning, but the Americans were happy that the ayatollahs in Tehran shared their anti-communist stance. When Khomeini received the Soviet Ambassador to Tehran in June 1979, he told the Russian in 'undiplomatic language' about Moscow's interference in Iranian and Afghan affairs. A week later, things worsened when Iran cancelled two basic treaties between Iran and the USSR. This was no small matter. It was important because the 1921 treaty gave Moscow 'the right of inspection', amounting to granting it a say in Iran's foreign dealings and for the Soviets to send troops to Iran if a third party used the country as a base against the USSR. This treaty was the basis for the November 1978 warning by Soviet leader Leonid Brezhnev to Washington that it should not intervene in favour of the Shah, which in Moscow 'would be viewed as an attack on its security'.

Moscow had been one of the first capitals to recognize Khomeini's regime and offer assistance. The Soviets were ecstatic that Khomeini eliminated the US presence in Iran, closed US electronic monitoring stations, withdrew from CENTO, cancelled multi-billion-dollar defence contracts with American firms, severed ties with Israel and broke with Western oil consortiums.[62]

Khomeini, however, did not feel that he owed the Soviets anything. His regime treated them as it did the United States. The Russians were lampooned as expansionary imperialists, just of a different orientation to the Americans.

§

By the middle of the spring of 1979, the Pakistanis were quietly letting Western embassies in Islamabad know that they regretted the Shah's departure. Perhaps they could feel the standoffishness of Khomeini and his cohorts. Ul-Haq's government made it known that at least the Shah had given Pakistan material support in combatting Afghan-incited Baluch and Pashtun separatism in Pakistan. By this stage, Afghanistan had been under communist control for over a year and Zia was worried that the Khomeini Government was distracted and that Iran was no longer a partner on the question of Afghanistan.

Despite such reservations, ul-Haq was not yet ready to give up on Iran. He had been one of the first foreign leaders to visit the Ayatollah. His foreign minister, Agha Shahi, soon became his interlocutor with the Iranians. Shahi was a lifelong bachelor, whose prominent Shi'a family hailed originally from southern India. Khomeini, too, had some ties to India, as his clerical ancestors had at one point settled there in the mid-nineteenth century.

Whether ul-Haq, a strict Sunni, thought that Shahi's Shi'ism would carry any favors with Khomeini is unclear but highly doubtful. Still, sectarianism inside Pakistan − the divide between Sunni and Shi'a Muslims − was already fermenting, and would one day soon contaminate Khomeini's relations with ul-Haq's Pakistan.

§

Shahi's reports back to the Americans about matters in Tehran were not heartening. In his trips to Tehran, he had quickly tired of the new elite. Shahi told the British that Iran was now 'run by ignorant mullahs with no idea of international affairs and with sinister left-wing elements behind them'. He was disillusioned, and judged that Khomeini's regime was 'incapable of formulating any coherent policy'.[63]

In October 1979, three weeks before hard-line students seized the US Embassy in Tehran, the foreign minister told officials in Washington that Khomeini was 'against anything US-inspired'. Shahi was frank, and let it be known that Islamabad was struggling to keep Iran from abandoning the Regional Cooperation for Development (RCD), the only significant remnant of Iranian−Pakistani institutional linkage, which had been fostered with US encouragement over the previous decade.

Shahi urged the United States to establish a direct line of contact with Khomeini, to put a stop to Iran's disintegrating ties with former allies.[64] This advice was soon overtaken by events. Suddenly Pakistan was forced to play the role of mediator between Tehran and Washington, a mission that it peddled a little too enthusiastically.

US embassies under attack in Tehran and Islamabad

On 4 November 1979, radical Iranian students and followers of Ayatollah Khomeini attacked the US Embassy in Tehran and took 52 Americans hostage. Early on in the crisis that followed, the United States made it clear that it expected Pakistan to help in making the Iranians understand the gravity of what they had done. Islamabad was squeezed and at US request ul-Haq sent a private appeal to Khomeini asking for the release of the hostages, but he took no further action. Shortly afterwards, Islamabad in fact became disapproving of Washington's handling of the hostage crisis in Tehran.

§

The saga of this American–Iranian–Pakistani triangle soon had another twist to it. It all began with the siege of the Grand Mosque in Mecca, Saudi Arabia. On 20 November 1979, an armed group of extremist Sunnis opposed to the House of Saud stormed the mosque, Islam's holiest site. They barricaded themselves inside, said they were preparing the ground for the Mahdi's [Messiah's] coming, and a two-week-long stand-off followed.[65] Back in Tehran, Khomeini quickly blamed the United States and Israel. His indictment was false, and purely part of his own war of words with Washington about the fate of the hostages in Tehran. His words, however, mattered.

Khomeini's charge spread like wildfire. On 21 November 1979, Pakistani cities – as elsewhere in South Asia – witnessed anti-American demonstrations. Iranian state media aired Khomeini's baseless charges about a US role in the attack on the Grand Mosque, showing the degree of anti-Americanism that Iran's new regime was willing and able to tap into. This presented ul-Haq with a golden opportunity to play the role of unwavering ally of the United States in the face of an Iran that was seemingly forsaking Washington for good.

Shortly after lunch on 22 November, an angry Pakistani mob ransacked and burned down the US Embassy in Islamabad. Before overrunning the embassy compound, protesters had stood outside and shouted, 'Kill the American dogs'. Some 90 staff and visitors hid in the embassy's six- by nine-metre vault for seven hours to escape the rage of the protestors.[66] During the attack, a 20-year-old US marine was killed by gunfire. Another American was killed by a building fire after being trapped in his room.[67] Two Pakistani embassy-staff members were also killed. Other US and Western facilities across Pakistan were also attacked that day.[68]

The United States at time suspected that the initial plan to attack the facility 'may have been planned and initiated by Iranian and Palestinian students': adding, 'The evidence that Iran was behind was at best sketchy. The mob had in fact been recruited in the streets of Islamabad and Rawalpindi.' A perception among the Americans that the Pakistani police and army had been slow to disperse the protestors generated its own theories. Everyone knew that the ul-Haq Government had for months been upset with the Carter Administration for its decision to cancel aid and for its reprimanding of Islamabad for its nuclear activities. As one US diplomatic cable put it: 'The Pakistanis are mad at us for reasons of their own.'

Ul-Haq went on radio and television to say that there had been no American or Israeli involvement in the Mecca incident. The Pakistanis then downplayed the attack on the US Embassy, declaring that there had been 'a little lapse here and there' in the army's response. The Pakistani President promised US Ambassador Hummel that Pakistan would cover the $21 million cost of the embassy's rebuilding.[69] Ul-Haq's first year and half in his post had not boded well for US–Pakistani relations. However, events in Iran and Afghanistan would quickly lift Pakistan's strategic value in Washington, and ul-Haq set out to capitalize on this.

§

The United States concluded that Khomeini's influence in Pakistan was at this point considerable, and that: 'Zia, not in a strong position, would be most reluctant to cross him.'[70] In the weeks and months after the start of the Tehran hostage crisis, it increasingly became evident to the United States that the Pakistanis were playing to both sides. Islamabad was claiming to work towards the release of the hostages in Tehran. However, Cyrus Vance, the US secretary of state, wrote to President Carter that Islamabad 'placed a higher priority on cultivating Pakistan's image as a supporter of the Iranian revolution.'[71]

That conclusion, accurate as it was, did not mean that Washington was totally unsympathetic to Islamabad's predicament. One US assessment stated that the continuing US-Iran crisis:

has acutely strained Pakistan's sense of where its interests lie. Pakistan's security policy had always been based on a strong relationship with both the US and Iran. As the crisis has dragged on, Pakistan's public posture has been inexorably drawn closer to the Iranian side, and its private actions with respect to the crisis [have] wavered.[72]

As President Carter contemplated a military operation to bring the American hostages out of Iran, the US Embassy in Islamabad transmitted back the likely Pakistani reaction to such a US military operation. The assumption was that US action against Iran would make it nearly impossible for Pakistan to preserve close ties with Washington. When Carter did commission a military rescue mission to free the hostages – the unsuccessful Operation Eagle Claw in April 1980 – the Pakistani Government reacted with 'shock and dismay', and called it an 'adventurous' and 'flagrant violation of international norms and law'.[73]

The Pakistanis praised the Khomeini Government's 'moderation', and let it be known that 'Pakistan would stand by Iran in its struggle to defend its sovereignty and national honor'. Such language was, of course, used in public not because of any real sympathy for what Khomeini and his people were doing in Tehran. It was because a still-fragile ul-Haq Government could not ignore the lurking anti-Americanism inside Pakistan itself, or the popularity of the Iranian Revolution among ordinary Pakistanis. The United States, however, took the wrong lessons from it.

In the belief that ul-Haq had some genuine leverage in Tehran, a desperate Carter Administration relentlessly asked Islamabad to put its supposed influence to use. US officials told Foreign Minister Shahi that 'the crisis over the American hostages in Iran has unified and galvanized American public opinion as no other issue since World War II'. Washington kept urging Pakistan to continue its mediation on the matter. Shahi, who had just been to Iran, was complimented as a representative from 'one of the few countries with real influence in Iran'.

Shahi would later remark that the Pakistanis were captured by the hostage situation too. He was told when he visited Washington: 'You can play a key role in encouraging a prompt release of the hostages so that this confrontation no longer encumbers regional resistance to the USSR.' Well aware that Pakistan had a problem in being seen to be too close to the United States, Washington made it clear that it was happy for all initiatives to be seen as if made in Islamabad.

In the end, the Pakistani role in the Iranian hostage crisis was negligible. Bani Sadr, a top advisor to Khomeini at the time, did not recall the Pakistanis having ever pushed the case of the American hostages with the Iranians:

The Pakistanis were motivated to appear in front of the Americans as players and with weight in Khomeini's early days in power. That was not the case. What they told the Americans at the time was probably intended at exaggerating Islamabad's sway so [as] to curry favors with the Americans.[74]

How much of all this was recognized at the time in Washington is difficult to gauge. The Americans were, however, not ignorant of some of the most pertinent facts. 'Khomeini's view of Pakistan apparently continues to be colored by his recollection of Pakistan's close relations to the Shah', one of the US diplomatic cables from Islamabad read.

Disquiet moves to Iran's Baluchistan

As the Iranians and the Pakistanis had feared, the communist regime that emerged in Kabul in April 1978 persisted in inciting the Baluch in Iran and the Baluch and Pashtun in Pakistan. This time around, with a new Islamist regime in Tehran evidently eager to export its revolution, Iran's Baluch minority suddenly became a focal point for Kabul. It was soon obvious that Kabul's support for the region's ethnic Baluch and Pashtun was as much about deterring Tehran and Islamabad as anything else. This was the quintessential 'forward defence' strategy, as the British had termed it. The Afghan message to Khomeini was simple: If you incite against us, we will agitate against you.

It had been quite different at first after the Shah's fall. The state-run communist Afghan media had welcomed the end of the 'despotic and terrorist regime of the Shah', and announced, 'the revolution of the toiling Iranian brothers [has] succeeded'.[75] Privately, however, the same Afghan communist leaders were far less sure about what the post-Shah era would mean for Afghanistan. The earliest consequences of the Shah's downfall had not been heartening. There was a loss of Iranian oil supplies, which the Shah's government had delivered at a heavy discount. The return of Afghan immigrants from Iran meant a loss of remittances. Such setbacks were minor compared with the ideological threat that Khomeini posed once the communists in Kabul realized what the Islamic republic would come to represent. Within a few weeks of the Shah's departure, the communists in Kabul made a dramatic U-turn on Khomeini.[76]

On 1 April 1979, the *Kabul Times* declared that Afghanistan 'condemn[s] the ominous encroachment of narrow minded religious leaders of Iran and reactionary circles of Pakistan.'[77] Communist chief Taraki, by now given the title of Great Leader in a typically whimsical piece of North-Korean-style cultism, quickly launched a counter-attack when Iranian and Pakistani leaders and religious groups labelled his government an 'infidel' entity. In highly traditional Afghanistan, that verdict was tantamount to a death sentence.[78] Taraki responded:

> The fanatics of Iran who interfered in our domestic affairs were given such a bloody nose [in Herat] that I don't think they will have the courage to repeat their encroachment. The reactionary circles of Pakistan have some imperialistic forces and international reaction that want to use Pakistan as the springboard for their activities.[79]

Taraki's mention of giving Iran a 'bloody nose' referred to the earlier uprising in Heart, a major city close to the Iranian border. On 15 March 1979, a group of farmers from Herat's surrounding areas had come to town where they – by the Afghan Government's account – were promptly encouraged by local mullahs to attack the communist government's headquarters.

Soon other government buildings had been seized. As the rebellion grew a number of local soldiers joined the anti-communist revolt. A frantic Taraki asked for Moscow to intervene but the Soviets hesitated at first. This was despite the fact that during the week-long revolt some Soviet advisors had been killed in the fighting, which all-told took the lives of hundreds of people. Once the dust had settled, Taraki accused Iran, but also Pakistan, of being behind the entire episode.

The *Kabul Times*, the communist mouthpiece, claimed that those who had rebelled were in fact '4,000 Iranian agents'. A month earlier, some 7,000 Afghans had returned home from Iran. Kabul was now claiming that the 4,000 agents had been part of this larger group of returnees, and that these Iranian agents had disguised themselves as Afghans. While the fighting was going on, the Soviets claimed that '3,000 Afghan rebels' had also been dispatched from Pakistan. 'Most of them are religious fanatics', concluded the chairman of the KGB, Yuri Andropov, as the members of the Soviet Politburo were contemplating what to do to help Taraki against the insurgents.[80]

The transcripts from the politburo meetings in Moscow show that the Soviets were highly apprehensive about losing Afghanistan to a rapidly expanding insurgency. Alexei Kosygin told the other Politburo members, 'We can expect that Iran, China, Pakistan and certainly [US President Jimmy] Carter will position themselves against Afghanistan and do everything in their power to interfere with its lawful government.'

Both Iran and Pakistan had been identified by Moscow as the key instigators. 'New masses of rebels, trained in Pakistan and Iran' were ready to join the fighting, Soviet leaders were warned. There was, however, an important caveat: in Soviet transcripts, there is no sign that Moscow actually spotted any Iranian–Pakistani collaboration of any kind in the Herat insurgency. The Afghan Government's focus solely on Iran appeared to be more credible.

Kabul's claim that Tehran had organized the rebellion was self-serving. Taraki magnified Iran's role with the single aim of discrediting the rebels as foreign proxies.[81] This was readily recognized by the Soviets, who at the time pressed the Afghan communists to stop their campaign of massacring internal opponents, and staging an economic agenda that had single-handedly turned the entire 'Muslim people of Afghanistan' against Marxism.[82]

Nonetheless, the fact that most of the rebels had been Shi'a Afghans – no doubt emboldened by the revolution next door in Iran only a few months earlier – made Taraki's accusations against Tehran stick. Even if his charges against Tehran and about what had occurred in Herat in March 1979 were opportunistic and exaggerated, there was no denying the fact that the Khomeini Government subscribed to a Shi'a-centric Islamist dogma. His regime was dedicated to spreading Iran's Islamist revolution, and the global Shi'a were deemed the most receptive to its ideas. In the years that followed, the Iranians would fine-tune the application of sectarian calculations when crafting policies towards Afghanistan and Pakistan.

§

The battle lines were drawn, and over the remainder of 1979 Kabul increased its support for ethnic Baluch nationalists across the border in Iran in retaliation for Iranian interference.[83] In the summer of 1979, tensions reached unprecedented levels. Kabul accused the Iranian military of a build-up on the border. The cycle of quid pro quo continued. While Kabul was undeniably in the business of agitating disillusioned Baluch in Iran, Khomeini's own discriminatory policies at home were no doubt the far bigger culprit.

In early December 1979, only days before the Soviets invaded Afghanistan, Iranian troops had moved into the city of Zahedan, the capital of Iran's Baluchistan Province. Unrest had shaken the region for days, leaving dozens dead. Traditional ethnic rivalry between the province's Shi'a Sistani and Sunni Baluch was exacerbated when, in that month, the Khomeini Government in Tehran made Shi'a Islam the official religion of Iran.

The province's Sunni majority was resentful. The Baluchis had arguably been the most successful of Iran's minorities in resisting the 'Persianization' that the Shah's late father, Reza Shah Pahlavi, had instigated back in the 1930s. 'What we want is for the outside officials to be gone and for them to have some respect for our religious customs', said Mowlavi Abdolaziz, the Baluch religious leader. There was much anger that a Shi'a outsider had been appointed provincial governor by the Khomeini-led government.[84]

The situation was not helped by the deployment of young, rash members of the Islamic Revolution Guards Corps (IRGC) from outside the province. In the final weeks of 1979, some 100 IRGC were killed in clashes with Baluch militants – often in urban firefights – and martial law was imposed on the province.

The Iranians claimed that leftist groups from outside the province were behind the violence as part of a nefarious attempt to topple the Khomeini regime. The communists in Kabul were among those incriminated. Ebrahim Yazdi, the US-trained Islamist who had been foreign minister until 12 November, went to Zahedan as Khomeini's troubleshooter. He told reporters that 'foreign elements' were behind the ethnic tumult. After the Shah's overthrow, a number of ethnic disturbances had rocked periphery provinces in Iran: Kurdistan on the border with Iraq; Azarbaijan on the border with the Soviet Union; and the pivotal oil-rich Khuzestan province in the south-west, on the shores of the Persian Gulf. Now it was the turn of Baluchistan. Were they all the work of the CIA as Khomeini's men kept telling the world?[85]

What the Islamists in Tehran did not know was that the CIA was preoccupied with exactly the opposite challenge: keeping Iran intact.

A CIA research paper from March 1980 outlined the problem that the United States faced. Fragmentation in Iran only heightened the likelihood of Soviet encroachment into the country as most of the separatist movements there, including those in Baluchistan, were inherently leftist and considered susceptible to Moscow's advances.

The fear in Washington at the time was that the Soviets might want to link their rail line from the Soviet south in Central Asia through now Soviet-occupied Afghanistan and then, via Iran's eastern regions, to the Iranian port of Chabahar. 'This would require Soviet annexation of much of eastern Iran, a far more ominous development than a takeover of Baluchistan alone', a CIA reported warned. It continued: 'While they do not yet pose a serious threat to government control of the province, provision of arms, equipment and training either from fellow Baluchis in Pakistan or from Soviet surrogate[s] in Afghanistan could make the Baluchis [in Iran] a much more serious disruptive force.'[86]

Khomeini's people were not totally ignorant of these realities. In Tehran, the verdict was that Moscow would possibly resort to the 25,000 ethnic Baluch who lived in Afghanistan at the time to foment and support the establishment of an autonomous Baluch state in Iran. In exchange, the Soviets would get access to Chabahar. The Shah's plans to build a $1 billion military facility around the port had been cancelled by the Khomeini regime, which found the project to be too expensive. The venture had been abandoned, with cranes left hanging. The Soviets could have easily revived those dormant cranes if they made it that far south to the warm waters of the Arabian Sea.

From Tehran's perspective, the Iranian Baluch minority had always been hard to crack. In 1972, the Shah developed a long-range strategy for the economic development of the province. The main reason behind such efforts were to act pre-emptively and to avoid the situation that was plaguing Baluch regions across the border in Pakistan, where political unrest and militancy had become a perilous fact of life. These efforts abruptly ended with the 1979 revolution, and the Shah's accomplishments were quickly rolled back.

The Soviet invasion of Afghanistan

Factional infighting had plagued the communist government in Kabul since it came to power after the coup of April 1978. By September 1979, the feud reached its zenith. The communist leader, Nur Mohammad Taraki, was murdered in a palace coup. Taraki's killer was his own deputy and protégé, Hafizullah Amin. Amin was a ruthless autocrat whom Moscow had never really liked or trusted. His very short tenure as leader would last from 14 September until 27 December in that year.

On 25 December, Soviet troops invaded Afghanistan, and Amin was shortly afterwards targeted and killed when Soviet special forces raided his compound. The Soviet Politburo's justification for the invasion was that the Afghan communist government was in dire need, and that Kabul's enemies – the United States, Iran, Pakistan and Saudi Arabia – were plotting to impose a 'reactionary' non-communist government in Afghanistan. Moscow installed Babrak Karmal, until recently an exiled rival of the Taraki Government, as the new head of the communist regime in Kabul.

President Jimmy Carter reacted with strong denunciations. He called on world leaders, including ul-Haq in Islamabad, to coordinate a collective response. There was no one in Tehran to talk to now that the Shah was gone. The Russians had moved into Afghanistan just as the United States was busy with the hostage crisis in Iran.

If CENTO was ever created to act as an anti-Soviet bulwark, this would have been its moment – however, it had been disbanded only nine months earlier. Whether the continuing existence of CENTO would have made much difference to Soviet actions is debatable. The Soviet military's invasion of Afghanistan occurred at the exact same time as the United States had its largest military presence in the Persian Gulf – including two aircraft carriers, some 150 fighter-bomber aircraft, hundreds of helicopters and some 40,000 American combat troops.[87]

The Russians had never in history been so close to the Indian Ocean; they sat in barracks less than 500 km away in Afghanistan. Pakistan, now with Soviet troops on its border, felt totally vulnerable.[88] The fear that Moscow would intensify its efforts to incite Baluchi, Pashtun and Sindhi separatists inside Pakistan made officials in Islamabad cringe. As with the Shah and Bhutto, Khomeini and ul-Haq felt that Moscow, operating through a compliant government in Kabul, intended to eventually secure access to the Indian Ocean, reshaping the national boundaries of the region through the creation of puppet states. The US intelligence community detected the twin threats to Pakistan.

In a memo to William J. Casey, the head of the CIA, Robert Gates – then deputy director of intelligence – put it bluntly: 'Separatism and sectarianism are the most serious long term threats to Pakistan.' Moscow attempted to ease Islamabad's fears. They offered economic and even military aid, and 'hints that Kabul would recognize the Durand Line as Afghanistan's border with Pakistan'. The CIA estimated that Islamabad's hints that it might some day seek an accommodation with Moscow and Kabul represented not only genuine considerations of policy alternatives but also subtle efforts to elicit more Western support.

The Soviet threat to Pakistan from Afghanistan provided strong impetus to the resurrection of US–Pakistani security ties. Had the Shah still been in power, this doubling of American attention and support would surely have also been extended to Tehran, but Washington kept the offer on the table even for the Khomeini Government. Tehran's falling-out with Washington, however, stifled the possibility that Iran could be relied on as a promoter of US polices in Afghanistan, even though they shared the same goal in wanting an end to communism in that country.

This reality by and of itself made Pakistan the sole de facto US channel into Afghanistan. It was without doubt true that geography in this case helped make Pakistan the kingmaker. Afghanistan was bordered by the Soviet Union to its north, by Iran to its west and by China to its east. Pakistan was the only feasible conduit for America to reach the anti-communist Afghan Mujahedeen.

Pakistan had two options. It could seek assurances from its allies or attempt to reach an accommodation with Moscow. The Carter Administration provided strong statements of support, but Islamabad was wary. The United States had walked away before or acted hesitantly – as in the Indo–Pakistani wars of 1965 and 1971 – and many in Islamabad felt that combining forces with the United States was a risky business. This was not least because the Soviets were now massed on Pakistan's borders.

Before the Soviet invasion, the United States had indicated an inability to express its 'support in practical terms', which, it said, 'would remain constrained as long as differences [with Pakistan] over the nuclear issue were unresolved.' Once the Soviets were physically on Afghan soil, even the nuclear issue would remain an obstacle to US aid for Pakistan.

General Zia ul-Haq jumped at the opportunity. On 4 January 1980, he spoke to President Carter on the phone. On 5 January, US

Ambassador Hummel was called in for a meeting at ul-Haq's residence. Waiting with him were Foreign Minister Agha Shahi and other key foreign policy personalities, including Foreign Secretary Sardar Shah Nawaz. Afghanistan was the only topic on the agenda, and ul-Haq's pitch was dramatic. He told Hummel that: 'Pakistan faces [a] decision on which direction to take. Pakistan has two options. It can toe the Soviet line or it can again line up with the free world. If the latter, the question is who will support Pakistan and in what magnitude?'

Ul-Haq said that he 'appreciate[d] President Carter's assessment that a qualitative change had taken place in the region with the Soviet invasion of Afghanistan'. 'If they can enter Afghanistan, they can enter Pakistan too', he pointed out to Hummel. Then came ul-Haq's reassurance: 'We will confront them, no doubt, but we must know where we stand.' He moved on to say that he had told Carter over the phone that he would be discussing with Hummel himself 'how to approach Pakistani requirements and how best to proceed from here in light of events in Afghanistan'.

The Pakistani leader saw no need to shun the nitty-gritty. He made the point that President Carter's statement of 4 January 'gives the impression that nuclear issues need not be an obstacle' for a revival of US–Pakistani collaboration. Zia ul-Haq had some things to say about the Iranians as well. As they had done with the fate of the American hostages in Tehran, the Pakistanis again offered to act as a bridge for the United States to Tehran.

Ul-Haq said that he was willing to 'aid in easing [the] Iran-US dispute'. Hummel thought that this was clearly as important as anything else he was offering. He stressed to him that from Washington's perspective, 'Khomeini's policies were providing [an] opportunity for Soviets to meddle' across the region. Shahi interjected that he had made this very point to Sadeq Ghotbzadeh, the Iranian foreign minister at the time, and other members of the revolutionary council when he had last been to Tehran.

The meeting with ul-Haq and his advisors must have made a strong impression on Hummel. He wrote back to Washington: 'Now it is the time to reorder our priorities, and to decide which of our objectives is most important. In my strong view our longer-range non-proliferation actions should be temporarily subordinated to the more immediate necessity of making an effective response to Soviet aggression.'[89]

Not everyone viewed it the same way, and some feared that the Carter Administration was about to give ul-Haq a blank cheque. At a congressional hearing in Washington, DC, a few weeks after ul-Haq's conversation with Hummel, a congressman asked witnesses from the State Department: 'Are we asking President Zia to be our stand-in, in that part of the world, such as the Shah of Iran?' 'Are we propping up a government that at best might last less than a year? Is there any kind of talk like that in the State Department?'[90]

There probably was, but the hawks in the White House had convinced the dovish Carter that the restoration of a defence barrier against the Soviets in south-west Asia was urgently needed, and that Pakistan was a pivotal – if not the only – component of this strategy.

Pakistan's coordination with Washington continued. At the end of January 1980, Pakistan hosted an extraordinary session of foreign ministers from the countries of the Islamic Conference, a 57-state bloc. The 40 states that sent representatives to Islamabad took strong objection to the Soviet invasion. This was seen as a threat to the survival of Islam in Afghanistan.

In his 29 January speech at the Islamic Conference gathering, the Iranian delegate said that 'had the US not created the US-Iranian crisis [by admitting the fleeing Shah to the US], the Soviet Union would not have been able to make use of this opportunity to implement' its intervention in Afghanistan. Iran and Pakistan jointly drafted the resolution adopted, condemning Moscow.

After the Islamic Conference event, Washington again asked ul-Haq whether he saw a 'useful role for the Islamic governments, singly or as a group, in resolving the Iranian [hostage crisis] so that energies can be directed towards resolving the region's strategic problems.'[91] The United States wanted the Iranians on board, but to no avail. Instead, the Pakistanis were soon knee-deep in Washington's Afghan policy.

§

When Zbigniew Brzezinski, Carter's hawkish national security advisor, visited a training camp for Afghan anti-communist insurgents on the Afghanistan–Pakistan border, he told ethnic Pashtun and Baluch fighters there: 'The American people admire your fight and we are sure you will succeed.' Kabul was fuming. A *Kabul Times* editorial warned Brzezinski that this was 'close to an undeclared war against sovereign Afghanistan'. The US Embassy in Kabul wondered if this was 'the opening propaganda offensive to justify a possible offensive Soviet military action against Pakistan as some point'.[92]

Ul-Haq's demands on the United States soon became crystal clear. He wanted significant American military assistance without strings attached on such issues as the Pakistan nuclear programme. Islamabad's big gamble that Washington would stay on side worked. In April 1979, the Carter Administration had acted on evidence that Pakistan had covertly acquired uranium enrichment technology; US aid was suspended. This cut-off had brought US–Pakistan relations to a new low. Thanks to the Soviet invasion of Afghanistan, in February 1980 Carter offered ul-Haq $400 million – half in military aid, half in economic aid – in security and economic assistance, and a promise to ask Congress to waive or suspend the Symington Amendment, which barred the United States from providing aid unless the US president could certify to Congress that the receiving country was not pursuing nuclear weapons. Ul-Haq called Carter's package 'peanuts', and rejected it. Carter's offer nonetheless represented a new chapter in US–Pakistan relations.

Brzezinski and Deputy Secretary of State Warren Christopher visited Saudi elders in Riyadh on 30 January 1980 to ask for money for Pakistan. This kind of shuttle diplomacy continued until US persistence paid off and the Saudis eventually became the top financial donor to Pakistan. Carter's successor, Ronald Reagan, soon after coming to the White House accelerated aid to Pakistan. In September 1981, Washington provided a six-year $3.2 billion aid package to Islamabad. By now, the early 1980s, ul-Haq's lucky star was on the rise. Since his coup of 1977, he had been handsomely served by four successive years of good weather, landing bumper crops for his people. The United States was now providing top-quality arms – such as a batch of 40 F-16 fighter aircraft – in unprecedented quantities.[93]

The United States sought to shield ul-Haq from being seen to associate too blatantly with American policies. Washington told the Pakistanis that it could 'strengthen Pakistan's hand, though we must recognize that Pakistan must play its own cards its own way.'[94]

Iran and Pakistan in the early days of Afghan jihad

By the end of 1979, south-west Asia was in chaos. A revolution in Iran had replaced a secular pro-United States monarchy with a radical

Islamist regime. Next door, the USSR had invaded Afghanistan. And Pakistan would soon be deeply involved in the Afghan jihad against the Soviets.

Immediately after the Soviet invasion, Zia ul-Haq regretted that 'Iran can no longer be counted on for support'. The country was in a 'state of total xenophobia', he said, and its leadership 'believes the whole world is against them'.[95]

From a US perspective, the Soviets were in a better position to exploit changes in the Iranian regime. A top-secret White House memorandum, 'U.S. Policy toward Iran', made it clear that 'preventing the disintegration of Iran and preserving it as an independent strategic buffer' separating the Soviet Union from the Persian Gulf was Washington's top priority.[96] The memo exposed the fact that the US–Soviet rivalry was the overriding factor even when dealing with Iran, the country that by then had held the 52 US diplomats hostage for 98 days.

Carter, widely blamed for having let the Shah fall, was upfront about its intentions. 'White House and other senior officials [. . .] say that if the Soviet Union carries its expansionism into Iran or Pakistan, the United States will have little choice but to oppose it militarily', newspapers told a US readership that must have been confused by Carter's commitment to Iran given the anti-Iran mood in the United States at the time.[97] The country had been lost to an anti-American clique in Tehran, but Carter refused to believe that Iran had abandoned the US orbit for good.

§

By July 1980, there were some 80,000 Soviet troops in Afghanistan, together with 30,000 to 40,000 Afghan Government forces. They faced some 50,000 to 100,000 rebels, the Mujahedeen.[98] The Soviets, even when combined with the Afghan National Army, did not have the numbers to seal the border with Iran and Pakistan. Foreign supplies kept flowing into Afghanistan. Pakistan's support for the Afghan Mujahedeen had started in earnest in 1978 after the communist coup in Kabul. Iran now jumped on the bandwagon in supporting the Afghan jihad. The Iran–Afghanistan border rapidly developed into an important passage for weapons and fighters into Afghanistan and refugees fleeing the country.

At first, the communist government in Kabul sought to lessen tensions with Iran and Pakistan. The Afghan communist leader, Babrak Karmal, called for regional talks 'on lowering the level of military spending, reduction of arms and armed forces with appropriate guarantees of security'.[99] This was Kabul's bid for admission among Islamic states after they had denounced its communist government as an 'un-Islamic invention' at the January summit of Muslim states in Islamabad. Iran and Pakistan, unlike with the first communist government of April 1978, refused even to recognize the Soviet-installed Karmal Government.[100] As Iran and Pakistan kept up efforts to foster and sustain Afghan rebels, a frustrated Soviet occupation power in Kabul weighed its options.

A few weeks after the Soviet invasion, Iranian Foreign Minister Sadeq Ghotbzadeh held a press conference in Tehran. All the Western journalists were fixated with the fate of the US hostages held by the radical Iranian regime. As if to give a signal to Washington, Ghotbzadeh said: 'We are the most concerned nation about the situation in Afghanistan. We cannot tolerate this Soviet invasion.'

When Ghotbzadeh claimed in June 1980 that Iran, Pakistan and the Afghan Mujahedeen had formed a 'three-man commission' to aid the 'freedom fighters if the Soviet do not vacate their aggression', Islamabad denied it strongly. The hot-headed Iranian revolutionaries were getting ahead of themselves. Agha Shahi was forced to denounce the idea, and said that Iran and Pakistan had only agreed at the Islamic Conference gathering to have a body to 'coordinate humanitarian assistance'.[101]

Khomeini's foolhardy followers had already brought Iran to the brink of war with the United States by snatching its diplomats as hostages. Now they were out to rile the Soviets. While Iran was carrying out its slogan of 'No to the West and No to the East', Islamabad was not yet ready to dive in against the Soviet Union.

There were very good reasons for that caution. Shortly after the Soviet arrival in Afghanistan, Moscow went public with its warnings. Soviet Foreign Minister Andrei Gromyko threatened as early as February 1980 that 'Pakistan risked its independence by aiding the insurgents'. The Pakistani Ambassador to Moscow was repeatedly warned that Islamabad's support for the Mujahedeen 'would eventually lead to war with Afghanistan in which Moscow would support Kabul'.[102] Nonetheless, the frenzied Iranians were soon stopped in their tracks.

§

On 22 September 1980, Iraq invaded Iran. Tehran's focus and resources would, for the next eight years, be allocated towards its war effort against

Saddam Hussein. It was Pakistan that eventually metamorphosed into the backbone of the anti-Soviet struggle in Afghanistan.

Pakistan's Inter-Services Intelligence Agency (ISI) started to channel aid to the Mujahedeen groups based in Pakistan. The various factions soon consolidated into seven major groupings, each with a particular regional grip inside Afghanistan. Three of the groups were moderate Islamists; four were hard-core fundamentalists. Pakistan required that the Mujahedeen groups join one of the factions in order to receive aid. Islamabad – influenced by Saudi financial weight – preferred the most fundamentalist Sunni Islamist groups. Four further factions were headquartered in Iran. The Shi'a factions were smaller and less well supplied, but they too had regional strongholds inside Afghanistan.

Islamabad saw Iraq's invasion as part of the same Soviet expansion across the region. After all, Baghdad and Moscow were allies, having signed a friendship treaty in 1973. Six days after the outbreak of the Iran–Iraq war, ul-Haq together with seven other Muslim leaders went to Tehran to urge an end to the conflict. Khomeini received the delegation and heard them out.[103] Islamabad was particularly keen to find a quick solution to the conflict. Pakistan held the chairmanship of the Islamic Conference, a group of 57 Muslim states. It wanted to exercise this chairmanship to the fullest extent against the Soviets, and the Iran–Iraq war was a major distraction.

The pan-Islamic attempt at conciliation failed. Tehran insisted that Iraq pull out of Iranian territory first. An anxious ul-Haq tried to convince the Iranians that Saddam was hanging on to captured land only as 'bargaining chip'.[104] The Muslim delegation left Tehran empty-handed.

Tehran's focus on its western border and Iraq suddenly left its eastern flank and Iranian Baluchistan vulnerable. Iranian Baluch dissidents now set up lines of communication both with Moscow and, increasingly, the Iraqis as well as Pakistani Baluch militants. Everyone was looking to gain leverage against Khomeini.

Even Iranian monarchists, those still loyal to the dead Shah and dedicated to the restoration of the Peacock Throne, linked up with anti-Khomeini Iranian Baluch forces. Bizarre alliances were forged. Iranian monarchists were suddenly in cahoots with leftist Baluch groups, unthinkable only a few years earlier when the Shah had implemented an eradication policy against these same Baluch militants. Declassified

British documents show that some Iranian Baluch leaders travelled to various European capitals to explore options against Khomeini.

In Paris, the Baluch dissidents met with the Shah's last prime minister, Shapour Bakhtiar, and General Gholam Ali Oveisi, a former top general who had managed to flee Tehran and was looking for ways to stage a counter-revolution in Iran. These British documents suggest that the Shah's widow, Queen Farah, who was living in Cairo at the time, also invited the Baluch leaders to visit her there to see what could be done.[105] The movement's aim was to give ethnic groups autonomy within Iran, but they had to overthrow Khomeini first. This in itself makes the Pakistani complicity in such manoeuvrings puzzling.

Some of the Iranian Baluch who were criss-crossing Europe were travelling on Pakistani passports. The British believed that 'it was clear that the Pakistanis were assisting' them. 'They [the Baluch militants] were getting rifles and ammunition from Dubai and Peshawar', one official report said. The British claimed that while the British Embassy had nothing to do with the Baluch, the United States 'had active contact with them' although the Iranian Baluch thought that the Americans 'were playing politics with them'.[106] Those Baluch were on to something. There is no evidence that the United States seriously aided any separatist Iranian ethnic movement, at least not in the early 1980s.

Pakistan was not without a say in all this. The Shah and Bhutto had made a secret pact pledging that Iran and Pakistan would aid each other in case of any security emergencies. This was probably meant for Iran to help the Pakistanis, but the tables had since turned. The United States knew about this secret deal. A CIA report read: 'A 1975 Pakistan-Iran military agreement suggest[s] some of the specific actions the Zia regime might take to advance its own interests rather than to preserve the Iranian government as envisaged in the agreement.' The agreement called for Pakistani support for any remnant of the central government in south-eastern Iran, including provision of weapons, supplies and staff to aid military units, and sanctuary for Iranian leaders in Pakistan. There was little chance of a Soviet invasion of Iran, but the Iranian Baluch could have seceded and this would have forced the Pakistanis to react.[107]

CHAPTER 8

THE ARRIVAL OF THE SHI'A–SUNNI SCHISM IN RELATIONS

At no point since Pakistan's independence in 1947 had sectarian factors adversely influenced governmental relations between Shi'a-majority Iran and Sunni-majority Pakistan. In fact, most of Pakistan's earliest leaders had been Shi'a in faith, with a close affinity to Iran.

The Shah of Iran never advocated himself as a leader figure for the Pakistani Shi'a. If he ever had a pan-regional fixation, it was to promote the notion of a 'Greater Iran' – which was not a territorially expansionist or sectarian concept, but a call to promote the Persian language and culture. He launched Iranian cultural centres (*Khan-e Farhang*) across Pakistan, and pushed the idea of *Iran Zamin* (the Land of Iran) in regions outside the boundaries of the modern nation but where Persian cultural influence from ancient times was still apparent. There is no evidence of the Shah funnelling cash to Pakistani Shi'a organizations.

With the arrivals of Sunni-centric ul-Haq and Shi'a-centric Khomeini, this calm sectarian balance was soon transformed. When Khomeini first came to power, pan-Islamism was very much alive and attracted many of those who came to the cause both from Shi'a and Sunni backgrounds. The amicable tone was set at the very top, among the ideologues of the day.

In Pakistan, Abu Ala Maududi was the 'superstar' of Sunni Islamists. He had in 1941 created his Islamist party, the Jamaat-e-Islami (Islamic Assembly), Pakistan's foremost revivalist faction. As with Khomeini, Maududi was highly critical of the Western world. He shunned mainstream party politics, and from the sidelines cursed Islamabad's close ties to Washington. Maududi was thus a soulmate of the Iranian ayatollah, who had met him during a pilgrimage to Mecca in 1963 and subsequently translated Maududi's books into Persian. In Qom, his teaching base, Khomeini's pupils learned from Maududi's works that all of Pakistan's troubles were due to its politicians abandoning Islamic principles and adopting depraved, secular ways of life.

Maududi went out of his way to curb sectarian customs. He would admit to disparities between the various Islamic schools of thought, but looked for common ground. He attacked anti-Shi'a Sunni voices in Pakistan, declaring, 'every Muslim has the right to follow the Sharia [Islamic religious law] according to his understanding'. Most notably, Maududi did not regard Iran's 1979 uprising as a revolution by Shi'as for Shi'as – as so many Arab Islamists had done – but as an Islamic revolution. He hoped that the blaze that had started in Iran would spread. Maududi, who was said to be anxious about the durability of Khomeini's revolution, did not live long enough to see the evolution of Islamist rule in Iran. He died in September 1979. Maududi's vision of unity between Shi'a and Sunni Islamists never really transpired. Pakistan's Sunni Islamists quickly turned on Khomeini and his 'Shi'a' revolution.

§

Within a year of Iran's revolution, ul-Haq's government was deeply angered by Tehran's new crop of diplomats, whom they regarded as inciting the Pakistani Shi'as. There were even open calls in the Iranian media for the overthrow of the ul-Haq regime. Pakistan was merely another victim of Khomeini's push to export Iran's revolution, but the attraction for the Shi'a of Pakistan was glaring. In absolute numbers (20 per cent of the population, or about 16 million in 1980) they comprised the second-largest Shi'a population in the world after Iran.

In September 1980, only two weeks before ul-Haq travelled to Tehran, Pakistan for the first time publicly criticized Iran for these media attacks. The government-owned press denounced Tehran for its 'tirade', inciting the people of Pakistan to revolt against ul-Haq's government.[1] Agha Shahi, Pakistan's foreign minister, sought at first to brush it off. He privately told the Americans that the Soviets were using leftists in Tehran to create a wedge between Iran and Pakistan by playing the sectarian card and by depicting ul-Haq as America's minion.

All kinds of spurious stories were floating around. At one point, there were claims that relations between Tehran and Islamabad had become so hostile that the Iranians had secretly allowed the Soviets to 'set up an electronic listening post to spy on Pakistan'.[2] The tale was nonsense, but it was a reflection of troubles in Iranian–Pakistani relations. As the following years would show, the situation was much more intricate than that. Nonetheless, both governments – in Iran and Pakistan – were guilty of whipping up sectarian emotions.

Ul-Haq's 'Shi'a card'

It has become commonplace to regard Pakistan's Islamization as a project begun by Zia ul-Haq when he came to power in 1977. It was not him, however, but that Shi'a 'drunkard' and 'socialist' Zulfikar Bhutto who first initiated this process immediately after the Pakistani defeat against India in the war of 1971. Following that humiliating rout and the loss of Bangladesh, Pakistan experienced an identity crisis of sorts and the nation entered a period of soul-searching.

Bhutto at the time opted to further enhance the role of Islam as the common bond between Pakistan's distinct 'nationalities'. The additional logic behind this rotation toward Islam was twofold. The first was rooted in domestic politics: Bhutto needed to appease Islamic traditionalists at home. In September 1974, he had caved in to pressure from Islamic radicals and agreed to a constitutional amendment that rendered the Ahmadis, a minority Islamic community with tens of thousands of adherents, 'non-Muslims'. This was Bhutto's big moment of truth with the Islamists, and he passed it.

Second, Bhutto had international goals. The oil crisis of 1973 had badly hurt energy-importing Pakistan whilst landing billions of dollars in windfall revenue in the treasuries of the oil-exporting Arab states of the Persian Gulf region. For Bhutto, to turn to the likes of Saudi Arabia and the United Arab Emirates made sound financial sense. If this transactional relationship could be greased through lip service to Islamic causes, then Bhutto was game.

Ul-Haq simply took over where Bhutto had left off. He, too, sought to Islamicize for chiefly practical reasons. There was one major difference, however. Many of Pakistan's Shi'a political elite viewed ul-Haq's agenda as a sectarian one, and tantamount to the 'Sunnification' of Pakistan at the expense of all religious minorities, including the Shi'a.

In February 1979, ul-Haq decided to impose a 2.5 per cent *zakat*, an Islamic tax, on personal income. The government at first ruled that the tax would be automatically collected from people's bank accounts. There was, unsurprisingly, a backlash. The Shi'as, however, were upset not because of the new tax but because Shi'a and Sunni Muslim traditions on *zakat* are different. Ul-Haq wanted to go with Sunni Islamic laws and many of the Shi'a were not willing to put up with this.[3] They wanted the Shi'a community to regulate its religious life through its own doctrine and organizations.

Suddenly the Pakistani Shi'as were politically mobilized in ways never seen before. In April 1979, rural-based Shi'a organizations threatened ul-Haq with mass mobilization unless he changed his mind on pursuing the implementation of the new legal code based on Sunni Islamic dogma. They demanded that ul-Haq invite Ayatollah Khomeini to make an official visit to Pakistan.[4] Ul-Haq held a tough line when in Sunni company, but privately told foreign visitors that if the Shi'a insisted then he would eventually give in to their demands for a separate Shi'a-based *zakat*. He promised, however, that he would make sure that Pakistani Shi'as 'can't get the money out to Iran'. The foreign visitors could not tell if ul-Haq was genuinely irritated or merely play-acting.[5] He finally conceded on the religious tax. The joke in Pakistan was that ul-Haq had done more than anyone to create new Shi'as, as many Sunnis declared themselves Shi'a to escape the tax.

Khomeini himself never visited Pakistan, but his influence would gradually become apparent to anyone who cared to look. Sectarian killings were becoming a part of everyday life, and there were fears that ul-Haq might be open to calls among some of the radical Sunnis for the Shi'a to be declared non-Muslims, as the Ahmadi community had been in 1974.

For most of his tenure, the Sunni clergy in Pakistan remained largely supportive of ul-Haq. At its core, his political grip was based on the loyalty of the Pakistani Army, a well-trained and -led military, supplemented by the state bureaucracy. But the backing of conservative Sunni religious groups gave ul-Haq's military dictatorship an air of legitimacy. This was important for him as the clerics were a major influence on the urban middle classes, who were the likely feeder for any political mass opposition to ul-Haq.

Much of the Sunni Islamist support ul-Haq received was tactical, if not downright unenthusiastic, but it was available to the teetotal general because the Sunni Islamists feared that a leftist Pakistan Peoples Party Government led by Bhutto's widow – the Iranian Nusrat – would be even worse. A PPP Government would also disturb the standing line against Moscow. Within weeks of the Soviet invasion of Afghanistan, Nusrat Bhutto had expressed a willingness to engage in dialogue with the Soviet-backed communist regime of Karmal in Kabul. She declared that she would send Afghan refugees home as a goodwill gesture to the Soviets. This was the PPP's line for the first half of the 1980s. A CIA assessment said, 'US-Pakistani relations would be impaired if a leftist-dominated mass movement seized power'.[6]

Meanwhile, some radical Sunni Islamists thought that ul-Haq was proceeding too slowly along the path of Islamization. Some of them, like the activists who attacked the US Embassy in November 1979, were willing to go to the streets to pressure ul-Haq. US intelligence services predicted that the 'emergence of Muslim radical groups, answerable only to themselves and bent on destroying the Army is a real possibility'.

This prediction quickly came true, but with a twist. The fury of some Sunni radical groups was aimed not at the State but at the country's Shi'a community, which rapidly became Enemy No. 1 – a process that was both ideologically and financially sustained and supported by Saudi Arabia, the world epicentre of anti-Shi'aism. A vicious retaliatory cycle, pitting extremist Sunni and Shi'a groups against each other, had been born and began to ravage Pakistani society.

A common perception among the Pakistani Shi'as was that the United States was encouraging ul-Haq to attack them out of fear that they might become a conduit for an Iranian-style revolution.[7] The Pakistani Inter-Services Intelligence Agency (ISI) was, on the other hand, regarded as the instigator and patron of the Sunni mobs that went after Shi'as. There is still debate about the role of the ISI in forming anti-Shi'a groups in Pakistan, but many of the country's Shi'as believed that elements of the State were colluding with Sunni extremists.

Some Pakistani Shi'as look to Iran

Among the radical Pakistani Shi'a, eyes were directed at Tehran for guidance and guardianship. They had historically turned to Shi'a clergy outside Pakistan's borders – especially to Iran and Iraq, where the major Shi'a scholars are based. With the coming of Khomeini, however, it was no longer just theological interpretations and textbooks that arrived from Iran but a new kind of revolutionary dogma and a call for Shi'a resurgence.

Inside Pakistan by the early 1980s, Shi'a–Sunni violence had become commonplace. In spring 1983, rounds of clashes between Sunnis and Shi'as rocked Karachi, Pakistan's commercial capital. The popular perception was that Iran was fanning the flames of Shi'a unrest in Pakistan.[8] Not everyone was convinced, however, that the blame could be attributed solely to Tehran. As one Pakistani Islamic scholar put it at the time: 'Zia is learning that once he gets beyond superficialities, Islamization is more divisive than unifying.' Ul-Haq had misjudged. 'The desire for Islam is strong in Pakistan but it is an emotional thing. It is not loaded with dogma', the same scholar said. Meanwhile, the sectarian violence spread. It soon moved north towards regions that bordered Afghanistan.

The town of Parachinar, located in a far-flung corner of western Pakistan, is bounded on three sides by Afghanistan, is fondly called 'Little Iran' by some Iranian religious Shi'ites. The majority of the town's residents are ethnic Pashtuns, who – unlike the vast majority of Pashtun people – belong to the Shi'a sect. It is also the capital of Kurram Agency, one of the seven tribal districts that make up Pakistan's volatile Federally Administered Tribal Areas. The Shi'as of this region are vastly outnumbered.

Sectarianism has been a frequent plague here, going back to the mid-1980s, but the latest round that began in 2007 was particularly vicious. A wave of violence killed hundreds of Shi'as in Parachinar, making a potent symbol of Shi'a suffering in Pakistan. The plight of its Shi'a residents became a rallying cry for elements of the Iranian regime.

Parachinar happened to also be the home town one of Ayatollah Khomeini's chief representatives in Pakistan. His name was Syed Arif Hussain Hussaini. He had been born in 1946 in the village of Pewar just outside Parachinar. Hussaini had the appearance and mannerism of a typical mullah, with full jet-black beard and black turban, signifying that he was a *syed*, a descendent of the Prophet Mohammad. He shared this heritage with Khomeini, who was also a *syed*. Nonetheless, Hussaini was anything but a typical mullah.

Hussaini had first met Khomeini when in exile in the Iraqi city of Najaf in the 1970s, and later followed him to Iran where he continued his religious studies in Qom.[9] Hussaini represented a new breed of Pakistani Shi'a political activist, who had abandoned the traditionalist practices of the Shi'a community and adopted the revolutionary rhetoric of Khomeini. His circle of activists grew in numbers, and Hussaini was soon the 'Pakistani Khomeini'.[10]

Following his old mentor, Hussaini taunted Zia ul-Haq for his relationship with the United States. As Khomeini had called the Shah 'a dog of the Americans', so Hussaini delighted his followers by adopting a fiercely nationalist and anti-American line. He blasted 'American Islam' – a formulation denouncing Muslim rulers, such as ul-Haq, who cooperated with Washington – with a revolutionary zeal as fierce as anything from Tehran.

Iran was never too far away in Hussaini's mind. He often warned that if the United States took any action against Tehran the Pakistani people 'will not sit idle'. There were grounds to take such warnings seriously. If Hussaini and his pro-Tehran ilk could manage to send Pakistani volunteers to fight on the side of Iran against Iraq – as they had managed to do – then organizing anti-American action at home was well within their reach.[11]

Nonetheless, the Pakistani Shi'as did not all share one single view of Khomeini. Even among those pious Shi'a who followed a particular religious voice, Khomeini was often not the first choice. It was, rather, Iran's Ayatollah Mohammad Shariatmadari, a progressive figure, who commanded the largest Pakistani Shi'a following. Shariatmadari, a critic of Khomeini's draconian Islamization policies inside Iran, was, soon after the Iranian Revolution, hounded by Khomeini's henchmen and put under house arrest, dying in 1986.[12]

Rivalry and conflicting visions within Iran's Shi'a religious establishment invariably reached Pakistan. At a convention of Shi'a activists belonging to Tehrik-i-Nifaz-Fiqah-i-Jafria (TNFJ) in February 1984, Hussaini was elected the leader of this pan-Shi'a group. His pro-Khomeini orientation was a key reason why a split subsequently occurred in the TNFJ, and traditionalists broke away from the organization.[13] In 1985, Hussaini became Khomeini's official emissary in Pakistan.

Hussaini became more cautious in choosing his words, but his anxieties about Sunni supremacy in Pakistan were crystal clear. As he said, 'Let the Sunnis as well as the Shiites live in Pakistan', but he then quickly grumbled about the broken promises of the ul-Haq Government, which Hussaini accused of political opportunism and stirring religious discrimination in the country at the time.[14]

Prior to his assassination by Sunni militants in 1988, Hussaini openly spoke of the theocratic political system put in place in Iran by Khomeini serving as a 'working model' for his Shi'a organization.[15] Iran's influence on parts of the Pakistani Shi'a community was unwelcome, but the astute ul-Haq kept a lid on his anxieties about Iran.

§

In January 1986, Iran's then-president, Ali Khamenei (a future supreme leader), made a very rare foreign visit, and chose Islamabad as his destination. Khamenei received a 21-gun salute at the airport, and the four-day visit was enough of a success that he returned a month later. As ul-Haq stood next to Khamenei in the motorcade that took them from the airport to the presidential palace, he must have scanned the cheerful crowds and been troubled by some of the passions on display from the pro-Iran Shi'a Pakistani activists who came to greet Khamenei.

Placards that read 'United States is Islam's enemy' and 'Death to American Imperialism', by association, made ul-Haq a target too, as he was one of Washington's closest allies at the time.[16] Incensed by Shi'a activists who made 'obscene gestures' at him in front of Khamenei, ul-Haq ordered the security forces to 'check closely into the operations – and funding – of the radical [Pakistani] Shias'. Pro-Iranian Pakistani newspapers taunted him and called his decision to invite Khamenei a mistake. 'Stolen clothes never fit', one report read, wondering why ul-Haq, a pro-American military general, ever thought he could outmanoeuvre revolutionary Islamists such as Khamenei.[17]

US officials in Islamabad assessed that Iranian funding had played a role in the pro-Khamenei rallies, but concluded that Tehran was not the architect of the spectacle. It was the radical Shi'a activists themselves who had gone over the top with the anti-American and anti-Zia display.[18] This was part of a domestic Pakistani power struggle. Khamenei and the Iranians would probably not have ventured out so recklessly at a time when they were putting feelers out to the ul-Haq military regime. At no point since the Islamist takeover in Tehran in 1979 had radical Pakistani Shi'a organizations been able to turn Iran into a sanctuary of the kind that Iraqi, Lebanese, Bahraini, Afghan or Saudi Shi'a radicals did throughout the 1980s.[19]

The militancy that Hussaini embraced, and which resonated so well with some Shi'a activists in Pakistan, occurred at a time of great sectarian tensions in the country. Iran and Khomeini did not create these conditions – that was done by ul-Haq's Sunni-centric policies. The regime change in Tehran in 1979 had merely come at an opportune moment, when a Sunni resurgence in Pakistan compelled some Shi'a activists to look for external patrons.

Ul-Haq, Arabs and the Iran–Iraq war

Even while such tensions were rife in relations, Pakistan could not afford to make Khomeini's Iran into a public enemy. Larger geopolitical factors were in the way. The Soviet invasion of Afghanistan and the fall of the Shah in Iran had completely altered Pakistan's strategic situation. Perhaps revealingly, India had not condemned Moscow's Afghan invasion.

Someone had to fill Shah's rather large shoes as Pakistan's benefactor. The United States put the Arabs on the case immediately after the Shah's fall. When Agha Shahi went to Washington on 20 April 1981, the State Department made it clear that it looked very favourably on closer Pakistani–Saudi ties. Shahi was told:

> We are gratified by the progress already made in establishing closer ties with Saudi Arabia. The Saudis recognize the magnitude of your military modernization needs. The Saudis are prepared immediately to make substantial funds available so that you can begin to [fulfill] your most urgent military needs.[20]

Within two years, Pakistan had some 18,000 troops in the Middle East and North Africa. By the end of the decade, there were some 40,000 Pakistani troops in Saudi Arabia alone. These deployed Pakistani military forces became an important source of income.

Arab money continued to roll in as Pakistan's status as a security custodian built up. By the close of the 1980s, as it had done exactly a decade earlier, Riyadh re-committed itself to funding Pakistan's arms purchases in return for Pakistani troop assistance in Saudi Arabia's defence.[21] The small Arab states of the Persian Gulf region were worried about the impact of the Iran–Iraq conflict, the civil war in Lebanon and Iranian agitation of the Shi'a in the Middle East generally.

Washington was, by and large, happy for Pakistan to play this role. As US intelligence assessments concluded:

> The United States generally benefits from PAKs military assistance programs. It helps PAK financially and minimizes US visibility in this sensitive region. Only in the training of Libyan pilots and small number of Palestinian guerrillas do Pakistan's military ties run counter to US interests.[22]

At times, Pakistan was walking a tightrope. In August 1987, when Iranian pilgrims and Saudi security forces clashed in Mecca, leaving some 400 people dead, the Pakistanis were highly uneasy about the role they found themselves playing. They were in the midst of a sectarian conflict. Their Saudi Sunni paymasters financed them and yet many of the Pakistani troops deployed there were Shi'a. Some sources claim that at this juncture Khomeini issued a fatwa, a religious decree, and banned any cooperation between Iran's military and that of Pakistan due to the latter's close collaboration with the House of Saud.[23] The contrary partnerships that ul-Haq had put together proved cumbersome to synchronize. Most notably, ul-Haq refused the Arab call to back Iraq in its war against Iran.

§

A number of reasons lay behind this stance. The most obvious one was that ul-Haq did not want to open up a new, hostile front on Pakistan's western flank. He was already preoccupied with India to its east and Afghanistan to its north. Additionally, siding with Saddam in the war would have real potential to exacerbate sectarian tensions inside Pakistan. When the Saudis asked him to withdraw Shi'a Pakistani soldiers, ul-Haq did not flinch: the Saudis could not pick and choose, he said, and Pakistani soldiers would not be dispatched based on sectarian background. Ul-Haq was also not blind to the fact that, for a number of reasons, public opinion in Pakistan was overwhelmingly on the Iranian side in the Iran–Iraq war.

Instead of becoming entangled in the minutiae of that conflict, ul-Haq looked for ways to profit from it both diplomatically and materially.

It was an internationally isolated Iran that offered the best opportunities. Ul-Haq's support for Tehran during the Iran–Iraq war had several elements. First, and probably most important, Pakistan became a conduit and trading partner for Iran as never before.

Iran, whose main shipping outlets in the Persian Gulf were increasingly threatened by the Iraqi Air Force, began quietly making use of the port of Karachi as a back door for imports. Goods would then travel by train or be trucked via the Iran–Pakistan land border. After the fall of the Shah, imports from Pakistan increased fivefold. Iran became Pakistan's second-largest foreign trading partner.

A desperate, war-scarred Iran needed cheap imports, and Pakistan was on hand with wheat, sugar, oil, textiles and other commodities. Iran sold Pakistan oil at a $5–6 discount per barrel. Their mutual trade went from $47 million in 1978 to $250 million in 1983. A 1983 agreement provided for the export of 120,000 tonnes of Pakistani wheat and 100,000 tonnes of sugar, rice and fertilizer to Iran. Iranian imports from Karachi were less well documented, but in one year alone – between 1982 and 1983 – Iran brought 109 times more fertilizer through the port than hitherto.[24]

Pakistan was also a conduit for East Asian military hardware destined for the Iranian war effort. It is impossible to calculate the volume of such arms channelled through Pakistan during the 1980–8 Iran–Iraq war, but the sum was in the billions of dollars. According to CIA estimates, China and North Korea, both with excellent ties to Pakistan, were by the mid-1980s the two largest suppliers of arms to Iran. The Chinese alone provided about $500 million in arms to Iran per year at the time.[25] From small arms to the large Silkworm anti-ship missiles, the Chinese and the North Koreans relied heavily on Pakistan as a pipeline for arms to Iran.

American arms were also a big part of Pakistani offers to Tehran. After the US Embassy hostage crisis in Tehran, the United States blocked arms sales to Iran. From 1983, the United States launched and led Operation Staunch, a global drive to stop the flow of third-country arms into Iran. This was cataclysmic for the Iranian armed forces, which over the previous half-century had been equipped with American weaponry but no longer had access to parts from US manufacturers. Critical US military parts found in Pakistan therefore attracted a premium Iranian price.

Nonetheless, American arms would arrive in Iranian hands in all sorts of ways. US-made weapons, such as the shoulder-fired Stinger missiles, were supplied by the CIA to the Afghan Mujahedeen through Pakistan, and some of them ended up in Iranian possession. On one occasion alone, 30 Stingers were lost to the Iranians.

Some American officials were later forced to scratch their heads when a US Navy ship patrolling in the Persian Gulf stopped an Iranian military vessel and found Stinger parts on board. The Pakistanis were among those suspected of having transferred them to Iran in return for payment.[26] It cannot be established with any certainty the profits that ul-Haq and his government reaped at the time from such transactions, but a number of subsequent investigations point to sizeable sums.[27]

Reviving ideas from the days of the Shah

By the mid-1980s, the fanaticism of Khomeini's revolution had begun to show signs of waning. The Iranians were feeling particularly isolated, and sought ways of breaking their ostracism. One of the first steps was to revive the old RCD, the same American-motivated mechanism for regional integration that Khomeini had so thoughtlessly abandoned in the immediate aftermath of the 1979 revolution. By March 1985, the RCD was revived, albeit under a new name: the Economic Cooperation Organization (ECO). As with the RCD, Iran, Turkey and Pakistan were the only members, but were later joined by Afghanistan and former Soviet republics that became independent in 1991. Tehran was chosen as the ECO headquarters.

According to Shamshad Ahmad, former Pakistani ambassador to Tehran: 'The Iranians revived the ECO in 1985 because they were by then – six years after the revolution – tasting the costs of regional and international isolation.'[28] Such Iranian efforts were not only about Pakistan, but Islamabad saw no need to turn Khomeini down. As the Pakistanis saw it, at a very minimum paying lip service to such regional attempts by Iran would not cost Islamabad anything, and there was always a slight chance that benefits might come from it. Moreover, Tehran's change of heart did not end there.

§

In September 1985, a delegation from the Pakistani Foreign Ministry held talks with Iranian representatives about the sale of nuclear technology and transfer of expertise. In 1983, Tehran asked the International Atomic

Energy Organization (IAEA) for assistance in restarting its Bushehr nuclear power plant – another Shah-era project that Khomeini at first deemed 'satanic' and anti-Islamic, and had shut down. In the middle of the war with Iraq, Tehran was now re-evaluating the value of a nuclear programme.

Tehran knew that Saddam Hussein still harboured ambitions for a nuclear weapon. Eight days after he had invaded Iran, the Iranian Air Force had bombed Iraq's Osirak nuclear facility, albeit only a partial hit. The Israelis attacked Osirak the following year, and destroyed the facility. Saddam continued his nuclear ambitions. The Iran–Iraq war and anxieties about Baghdad's nuclear designs were the reasons behind Tehran's rethinking of its own nuclear options. When it approached the IAEA, however, Iran was cold-shouldered. No doubt the IAEA was under US pressure to ignore the Iranians. In such circumstances, Pakistan suddenly appeared in Iran's nuclear plans. Islamabad was open to Tehran's overtures. General Khalid Mahmud Arif, a top advisor to ul-Haq, declared, 'Having seen the US so flexible in the past, everyone doubted that [Washington would] sanction [. . .] us at all' for giving Tehran assistance in the nuclear field.[29]

In February 1986, Iran's president, Ali Khamenei, returned to Pakistan. During this visit nuclear talks were expanded, and by 1987 nuclear officials from Tehran and Islamabad entered into a formal agreement.[30] The Pakistani media later reported that ul-Haq had approved a long-standing request from Tehran for peaceful nuclear cooperation. However, he did not intend to help Iran acquire a nuclear bomb. A senior Pakistani official claimed that when he had told ul-Haq about the Iranians probing into non-peaceful nuclear matters, he was instructed to 'play around [with them] but not to yield anything substantial at any cost'.[31] Ul-Haq's trepidation was completely justified. He had spent most of the 1980s denying that Pakistan itself was after the bomb, and did not want to irk the Americans.

By summer 1987, ul-Haq was under scrutiny in Washington, and a sceptical Reagan Administration and US Congress needed to be reassured that Islamabad had nothing to do with attempts by Pakistani citizens to purchase illicit nuclear material, which US intelligence services had picked up. A new $4 billion American aid package was in serious jeopardy. Ul-Haq needed to be careful, including over his ties to

Tehran, as America mattered.[32] In the 1980s, Pakistan had become one of the top five recipients of US aid.

It was at this point that the Western press began to pay attention to the Iran–Pakistan nuclear issue – and in a fairly sensationalist way. An article in the British newspaper, the *Observer*, claimed on 12 June 1988 that the two nations had signed a deal for the training of Iranian nuclear scientists. The paper spoke of a 'secret pact', which had been signed in 1987 between Dr Reza Amrollahi, head of the Atomic Energy Organization of Iran, and Dr Munir Ahmad Khan, chairman of the Atomic Energy Commission in Pakistan.

The latter was the same Mr Khan that the Shah of Iran and his nuclear chief Akbar Ettemad had turned down back in the 1970s, when Islamabad first raised the issue of nuclear cooperation. This latest cooperative effort, however, was being pursued through ECO, the British newspaper claimed.[33] Attention focused on Kahuta, a uranium-enrichment facility some 40 km from Islamabad where Pakistan's efforts to produce weapons-grade nuclear material were said to take place.[34] Pakistan denied that there were any bomb-making plans involved, although nuclear cooperation was not denied per se. In any event, the US State Department monitored these events at the time, and did not see fit to object.[35]

The journalist who wrote the piece for the *Observer* – Farzad Bazoft, an Iranian-born British citizen – was later executed in 1990 in Iraq by Saddam Hussein on charges of spying for Israel. As was subsequently revealed, Pakistan's infamous A. Q. Khan trading network began from 1987 providing Tehran with nuclear assistance.[36]

On the one hand, ul-Haq did not want to turn down the Iranians outright. He had himself set the tone for nuclear cooperation with foreign countries back in 1981, when he said that Islamabad would make every effort to acquire nuclear technologies and expertise and share them with the Islamic world. Agreements were signed with Malaysia and Indonesia, with Pakistan agreeing to establish an atomic research centre in Malaysia. There was also a tripartite agreement with Iran and Turkey, which included provisions for the exchange of scientists and assistance in developing Iran's nuclear power.[37] Additionally, ECO's scientific directorate was based in Pakistan.

However, Pakistan could do without US and other international scrutiny at a time when it was itself engaged in building a nuclear weapon. This explained the limited nature of the cooperation, and ul-Haq's order to his scientists to 'play around' with the Iranians on sensitive nuclear requests.

The race to aid the Afghan Mujahedeen

Throughout the 1980s, multi-track Iran−Pakistan relations continued. In Afghanistan, Pakistan continued its support for the jihad despite concerted Soviet pressure that included numerous violations by Soviet/Afghan aircraft and shelling of Pakistani territory. In the first half of the 1980s, UN-sponsored talks for a negotiated settlement went nowhere. The Afghan communists did not want to include discussion of the withdrawal of Soviet forces, which was a precondition for both Iran and Pakistan.

By 1983−4, the Afghan conflict suddenly did not seem as menacing. Five years after the Soviet invasion, the Pakistanis still had not moved any major military units from the Indian border to the border with Afghanistan.[38] While the Soviet military presence was still a threat to both Iran and Pakistan, the United States no longer believed that a domino effect was imminent. In Washington, there were even calls not to overestimate the utility of Soviet bases in Afghanistan to 'project air power deep into the Middle East (except eastern Iran)'.[39] Outside powers continued to supply the Afghan Mujahedeen, and the Soviets were bleeding on Afghan soil. That was good enough reason for Islamabad, Tehran and Washington to stay in the war.

§

Even if they were in the same boat on Afghanistan, Iran and Pakistan coordinated policies to a diminishing degree. By 1983, Afghan resistance groups based in the Pakistani city of Peshawar recognized the dominant Iranian influence over Afghan Shi'as, particularly the Hazara community in central Afghanistan. Sectarian divisions were becoming marked. No doubt, sectarian tensions and killings in Pakistan itself were having an impact on the dynamics between the various Afghan forces. The impact of Saudi and other Arab money and anti-Shi'a dogma was also by now undeniable.

Tehran's ties to Peshawar-based Sunni Mujahedeen groups were minimal. All Sunni groups were based in Pakistan; all Shi'a Afghan groups were based in Iran. Tehran did not feel comfortable with the Pakistan-based groups due to the heavy reliance they had on supplies of money and arms from the United States and Gulf Arabs. The level of Iranian aid to Afghan insurgents had increased in 1981 when the Khomeini regime began to consolidate its control at home, and this continued throughout 1982–3, but a cash-strapped Tehran had no prospect of matching what the United States and the Arabs were bringing to the table.

Throughout 1980–2, Iran had also flirted with aiding Sunni-led Islamists based in Pakistan. The United States estimated that unspecified numbers of rifles (M-1s and G-3s), landmines, shoulder-fired anti-tank rockets, heavy machinery, uniforms and boots were supplied to, at least, the Hezb-e Islami of Gulbuddin Hekmatyar for operations in southern and eastern Afghanistan, away from Iran's buffer zone in western Afghanistan. Hekmatyar was one of the key Sunni fundamentalist Mujahedeen leaders. Tehran liked his anti-US rhetoric, even if he was in fact a recipient of American aid.

Hekmatyar had openly said that the only reason the United States supported the jihad was because it wanted influence, so that it could stop Afghanistan from becoming another Islamic republic like Iran. The United States could not afford for this line of thinking to gain ground, however, and opted to lower its public anti-Soviet role in supporting the Mujahedeen. Among the Afghan Mujahedeen leaders, only the moderates – such as Ahmad Gailani and Sibghatullah Mojaddedi – were open to a stronger political role for the United States. Hard-line Islamists such as Hekmatyar, Burhanuddin Rabbani and Abdul Rasul Sayyaf desired an Islamic republic in Afghanistan, and were suspicious of US intentions. They also happened to be the most capable fighting forces. Some of the Afghan commanders, such as Sayyaf, were anti-Shi'a and suspicious of Iran, and instead became conduits for radical Saudi Sunni doctrine and Arab volunteers who came to Afghanistan to wage jihad.

'Pressure from Pakistan is acceptable [to the Afghan] insurgents generally, and many US objectives probably can be best effected through Pakistan,' the CIA assessed. Its recommendation went even further: 'Because anti-US rhetoric from resistance leaders like Gulbuddin provides the alliance with an aura of independence, it might be wise for the US to promote such criticism [of Washington] occasionally and quietly.'[40] This was exactly the suspicion that the Iranians had: that the

United States was the hidden puppetmaster behind Pakistan-based Afghan groups, and that Washington had ulterior motives.

There was another angle to the Iran–Pakistan differences over the war in Afghanistan. Iran had, from the outset, refused to take part in peace talks that included Moscow and its puppet Afghan communist government. As a compromise, when the 'tripartite proximity talks' were held – between the Soviets and the Afghan communist government, Iran and Pakistan – Tehran agreed to the so-called empty-chair formula whereby it would not attend the talks on the understanding that the Pakistanis would keep it informed.

This made Iran–Pakistan relations on the issue appear far more cordial than was the case. Iran was now playing second fiddle to Pakistan. 'In fact, what we are witnessing behind the smokescreen of the tripartite talks is really a bilateral Pakistan-Soviet Union dialogue', said a well-placed Western diplomat at the time. Ul-Haq was talking peace with the Soviets despite Washington's objections. The Reagan White House and the ayatollahs in Tehran both refused to negotiate with the Soviets. This might have been a major common platform, but by now the Pakistanis had moulded themselves into an essential component of America's Afghan strategy and cutting them loose was not an option for Washington.[41] Furthermore, the cries of 'Death to America' after Friday prayers in Tehran hardly helped Iran's allure in the eyes of US strategists.

Pakistan-based Mujahedeen groups were also anxious. While the Pakistanis made headway in talks with the Soviets during the 'Geneva II' round of discussions in April and June 1983, nervous Mujahedeen leaders Hekmatyar and Rabbani travelled from their camps in Peshawar to Tehran to see whether they could find a base in Iran in case they needed to leave Pakistan.[42] They needed a country with land borders with Afghanistan, in order to sustain the flow of men and arms. If Pakistan was out, only Iran could fulfil that function. It was that simple.

In the context of the UN-sponsored Geneva negotiations, which lasted from June 1982 to April 1988, Iran never stopped suspecting hidden Pakistani motives and Islamabad's close ties to Washington. Publicly, the Iranians proclaimed that they would not block a settlement to which Pakistan could agree. This would signal considerable trust, and perhaps indicate a new chapter in Iran–Pakistan relations given the tensions in the first half of the 1980s. In fact, the Iranians had no such trust. Behind closed doors they kept insisting that the Pakistanis were playing a game, selling out the Afghan Mujahedeen to the Soviets. Even when the final Geneva Accords on a peace settlement were signed in April 1988, Iran still remained suspicious of Pakistan's intentions in Afghanistan.[43]

It was not just the Iranians. Islamabad also tried to control Saudi influence over the Afghan rebels. Ul-Haq simply did not want the Afghan Mujahedeen to become too independent or to find alternative patrons to Pakistan. This was, at least, the US assessment, and they were in a very good position to know. As the CIA calculated: 'Relocation [of Mujahedeen political offices] to Saudi Arabia or Western Europe would virtually eliminate their [Pakistan's] role in supplying insurgent bands and severely reduce the influence of the exiles on the insurgents.' Islamabad did not want to lose its cash cow, and Iran never really competed on this front. Thus, Pakistan remained the crucial conduit of aid from most third parties.[44] Whereas Pakistan cashed in billions of dollars in US and Arab financial compensation, Iran was in the anti-Soviet fight for practically zero financial reward.

America, and Iran's anti-Soviet agenda

Meanwhile, Iran's war with Iraq was a huge drain, and it limited Iran's ability to provide aid to the Afghans. What aid Iran could provide, it did so in a very targeted way. A growing number of Iranian military advisors from its Revolutionary Guards were suddenly on the ground training Afghan Hazara militiamen. Such hands-on commitment provided political openings for Tehran. 'We judge that the degree of discipline and responsiveness to the Iranian-led Khomeini regime has also increased with the presence of these guards', a US intelligence study found.

Moscow kept warning Tehran about its activities in Afghanistan. After 1982, when the Soviets concluded that Khomeini's regime would not reply positively to Moscow's advances, they tilted openly towards Iraq.[45] Moscow vowed that relations would continue to suffer unless Tehran halted its activities in Afghanistan.

Some of the largest Soviet military operations of the war were already taking place in western Afghanistan, aimed at preventing the Mujahedeen from taking Herat, the city on the border with Iran. Western Afghanistan had always been an Iranian zone of interest, and Tehran was heavily invested here. The city's key rebel leader – Ismail

Khan, from the Jamaat-e-Islami party – closely coordinated his operations with officials in Tehran. Khan's hit-and-run operations put the Soviets on his tail, and Iran would complain about Soviet incursion into Iran. A good part of Herat's population had already fled to Iran. By the mid-1980s, there were some 1.8 million Afghan refugees in Iran – half of them located in Iran's Khorasan and Baluchistan provinces.[46] Another 3 million Afghans had fled to Pakistan. Both Tehran and Islamabad reacted to Soviet cross-border raids with a harder line against Moscow.

From Tehran's perspective, by the mid-1980s the Soviets were not engaged enough in Iranian Baluchistan to incite ethnic rebellion against Tehran. Still, Iran, despite its ongoing war with Iraq, stayed in the anti-Soviet coalition. This was music to American ears. A top-secret national security decision directive called 'Policy Toward Iran' made no bones about where Washington stood. The decision said that the most immediate US interest included 'preventing the disintegration of Iran and preserving it as an independent strategic buffer which separates the Soviet Union from [the] Persian Gulf'.[47] Iran, the study continued, has to come back as a 'moderate and constructive member of the non-communist political community'. Khomeini's Iran had to be encouraged to further resist 'the expansion of Soviet power in general'.

The US verdict at the time was that 'Tehran's support for the Afghan resistance has been continuous but selective'. Tehran provided military aid and guerilla training to pro-Iranian Shi'a groups in western and central Afghanistan. Unlike Pakistan, however, Iran refused to participate officially in the UN-sponsored indirect talks on Afghanistan until Soviet troops first withdrew. Iran's aid to the Mujahedeen, its refusal to have anything to do with the communist Kabul regime and its insistence that Mujahedeen leaders be included in any political talks helped frustrate Soviet efforts to consolidate control of Afghanistan. The United States hoped for more Iranian involvement: 'The spirit of religious crusade now driving [Iran's] war against Baghdad could be turned on Kabul', agency analysts told their bosses in Washington.[48]

This American fixation with Tehran's Afghan policies was natural, as Iran was the only alternative to Pakistan given Afghanistan's geography. While the general American perception was that Pakistan was in the fight in Afghanistan for the long haul, substitute strategies nonetheless needed to be prepared.

Even if the Iranians might have seemed to operate more from principle – unlike Pakistan, which enjoyed billions of US dollars in aid – from Washington's perspective, Iran's support was not nearly as crucial to the resistance as Pakistan's.[49] By 1985, the tilt by Afghan Mujahedeen groups towards Pakistan was highly pronounced. Meanwhile, infighting amongst the Afghan Shi'a weakened Tehran's hand. In June 1985, Iran brought all the Afghan Shi'a groups to Qom, where Ayatollah Hossein-Ali Montazeri, Khomeini's deputy at the time, asked them to stop fighting each other and 'concentrate on the invaders'. This sort of Iranian arbitration was helpful to the cause of the highly fragmented Afghan anti-Soviet opposition.

On 24 October 1985, an Afghan Mujahedeen delegation went to the United Nations in New York. This Ittihad Islami – or Islamic Unity – umbrella gathering was a major achievement. Created to focus international attention on the Soviet occupation, it was the first time since November 1980 that such a cross-section of factions (from supporters of former King Zahir Shah to Islamist leaders) had come to the United Nations together. Pakistan did not like the initiative, as it feared that this sort of highly visible Afghan campaign would anger Moscow, which might retaliate against Pakistan. Open squabbling about the distribution of aid, the role of the United States, positions on Saudis and Iranians and other issues always lay under the surface. Washington could see that the Pakistanis wanted full control over the Mujahedeen, and to prevent US officials from gaining influence over the insurgents.[50]

Some in Tehran look to Afghanistan for US arms

As the Iran–Iraq war dragged on, some regime figures in Tehran looked for ways of breaking Iran's international isolation. They believed that rethinking relations with the United States must be at the heart of any foreign-policy rebirth. The anti-Soviet struggle in Afghanistan was viewed as the perfect shared cause.

Iranian supporters of reaching out to the United States had a case. As various declassified US intelligence and diplomatic papers illustrate, during the first half the 1980s much of the American posture towards Tehran was often driven by the American–Soviet battle in Afghanistan. Yet the Reagan White House repeatedly failed to establish a formula to reconcile conflicting US policy goals concerning Iran. Reagan's policy towards Iran ranged from indifference at first to moments of cooperation and then outright confrontation.[51] The Reagan Administration wanted Tehran's help in Afghanistan, and yet worried non-stop about the spread of Iranian power in the region. The Iranians were familiar with this American dichotomy – after all, the United States from 1983 onwards had tilted on the side of Iraq in its war with Iran. Somehow, however, enough people in Tehran felt that a finite but advantageous deal could still be struck with the Americans.

On 26 May 1986, a team of US officials arrived in Tehran on a secret mission. The team included Lieutenant Colonel Oliver North; Howard Teicher from the National Security Council; and George Cave, a subject expert from the CIA. By that time, American weapons had for nine months secretly been shipped to Iran via intermediaries. This would later be known as the 'arms-for-hostages' deal, whereby US weaponry was provided in return for Tehran's help in freeing American hostages held by pro-Iran militants in Lebanon. During these tough talks in May 1986, the Iranians wanted to expand cooperation.

Two issues kept coming up: that the Soviet Union was a mutual threat, and that Iran and the United States could collaborate in Afghanistan. Teicher told the Iranians that 26 Soviet divisions were surrounding Iran. 'The Soviets are increasing the frequency of their cross-border strikes into Pakistan and occasionally Iran,' he told his already convinced Iranian hosts.

The over-eager Iranians quickly acknowledged the Soviet threat. 'There are training camps for [Afghan] Mujahedeen in Iran. Weapons and logistics support are provided. We are ready to send troops into Afghanistan,' one of the hosts told the Americans. The Iranians forged ahead along this track, arguing that Iran was the epicentre of anti-communism in the region, claiming: 'The Russians already complain about Iranian bullets killing Russians;' 'If there is only one other country in the world against the Soviets [besides the United States], it is Iran;' and 'You see the [Russian] threat [in Afghanistan] with high technology [from a distance]. We feel it, touch it, see it. It is not easy to sleep next to an elephant that you have wounded.' The man who spoke those words was a 37-year-old senior foreign affairs advisor in the Iranian Government. His name, it was revealed later, was Hassan Rouhani, the man who nearly three decades later was elected president of the Islamic Republic.[52]

In 1986, these pragmatic Iranians were offering the United States not only a helping hand to crush the Soviets in Afghanistan, but to facilitate bringing an end to the Soviet empire. 'Millions of Soviet Muslims listen to our influence. Many believe that [Khomeini] is their leader, not [Mikhail] Gorbachev,' one of them told the Americans. At this secret meeting, both sides agreed on the need for dialogue on the Soviet Union.[53]

Washington most likely would have looked at this Iranian offer very differently had it been put on the table five or six years earlier. By now, a new Soviet leader – Mikhail Gorbachev – had arrived in the Kremlin. The Soviets were clearly looking for an exit strategy from Afghanistan, and Iran's offer to help in Afghanistan just did not grab much American attention. For the United States, Afghanistan was no longer the mother of all battles against the Soviets. Pakistan, too, soon felt the impact of Washington re-weighing its priorities in south-west Asia.

Ul-Haq rediscovers Iran

During Iran's eight-year war with Iraq, Zia ul-Haq did his best to portray his country as neutral. As US–Pakistani relations soured in the last few years of his rule – principally due to the resurfacing of Pakistan's nuclear activities – the Pakistani military leader made some overt, but clearly calculated, pro-Iran noises. By now, in the period 1987–8, the regime in Tehran was deemed the principal threat to US regional interests. Washington was doing its utmost to prevent Tehran's victory in the Iran–Iraq war – including providing satellite imagery to Baghdad of Iranian military formations. Then, the US military, on 18 April 1988, directly engaged the Iranian Navy, sinking a frigate and a few smaller gunboats. This was in retaliation for the Iranians mining the Persian Gulf.

In the midst of this volatile regional situation, Pakistan's army chief of staff, General Mirza Aslam Beg, openly advocated an axis with Iran (as well as Turkey and Afghanistan).[54] Why was ul-Haq's deputy speaking in such terms? Was ul-Haq suddenly playing the 'Iran card' to keep Washington on its toes?

US officials were angered by Pakistan's criticism of the US military build-up in the Persian Gulf without condemnation of Iranian attacks on shipping traffic.[55] Pakistan had started to openly tilt towards Iran. This upset Washington and Pakistan's Arab friends. Ul-Haq said that the

Pakistani and US views about what should happen in the Persian Gulf were not similar. Islamabad raised the stakes and suspended port calls at Karachi by US Navy ships, ostensibly after anti-US riots there in July and August 1987. This displeasure, however, went beyond a few zealots in the streets of Karachi. Some influential circles in Islamabad argued that the United States was increasingly unreliable, and advocated continued non-alignment, dependence on moderate Arab countries, friendship with Iran and a degree of accommodation with the USSR.[56]

The Pakistanis would also hit back at American criticism. An unnamed official said, 'People must understand our position on Iran has a domestic aspect to it. A large section of Pakistani population genuinely believes in promoting Iran's interests.' There was – as always – a leverage issue tied to the shift in Pakistani policies on Iran. In September 1987, Pakistan was no longer exempt from a law barring US assistance to countries that imported material to develop nuclear weapons. A waiver had been in place in the previous six years as part of Washington's gratitude for Islamabad's help in Afghanistan.[57]

And yet, that unnamed Pakistani official was not lying when he told the *New York Times* that Iran was a factor in Pakistani domestic politics. A crowd estimated at 100,000 had gathered in Lahore in early July 1987 to launch a new Shi'ite party – Movement for Implementation of Shi'ite Jurisprudence – which openly advocated closer relations with Khomeini's Iran. The party's spokesperson said that no opposition to Khomeini by Pakistan would be tolerated. Within 48 hours of the Lahore rally, 13 houses occupied by anti-Khomeini Iranian refugees in Quetta and Karachi were attacked with sub-machine guns, grenades and bazooka-type weapons. A handful of members of the Mujahdeeen Khalq (MEK) – the leading armed Iranian anti-Khomeini organization – were killed. Iran was clearly a factor in Pakistani political life in more ways than one.

The Pakistani police made arrests, and about a dozen suspects were identified as belonging to Iran's Revolutionary Guards. Still Islamabad made no public protests, and instead began to round up anti-Khomeini Iranian refugees. A high-ranking Pakistani official asked, 'Tell me, we are fighting with India, with Afghanistan, with the Soviets; how can we open another front with Iran?' Ul-Haq, never too sure about his domestic political grip, was constantly reminded that local Shi'a radicals would not hesitate to wound him. Arif Husseini, Khomeini's top

Pakistani pupil and envoy made it crystal clear: 'Shiites [in Pakistan] will topple the [Zia] government in Islamabad if it helps the US to launch any anti-Iran operations from Pakistan.'[58]

§

On 17 August 1988, General Zia ul-Haq was killed in a mysterious air crash. On board the C-130 aircraft were a number of other top figures, including US Ambassador Arnold Raphel and Pakistani Chief of Staff Rahman Akhtar. Akhtar had been the architect of Pakistan's support for the Afghan Mujahedeen. They were returning to Islamabad after viewing a demonstration involving US M-1 tanks, which Pakistan was considering buying. The crash happened halfway through the Soviet withdrawal from Afghanistan.[59] To this day, there is no certainty about the culprits.

In less than three months, Zulfikar Bhutto's eldest child, Benazir Bhutto, would become Pakistan's civilian-government prime minister after 11 years of military rule. This daughter of an Iranian woman became Pakistan's, and the world's, first female Muslim head of state. Her first foreign-policy test was Afghanistan, with the Soviets only a few months away from a full and humiliating withdrawal.

CHAPTER 9

1988-2001: GEOPOLITICAL FOES, SOMETIME PARTNERS

On 25 August 1988, the Pakistani Army chief Mirza Aslam Beg gave a lecture to a group of army commanders at a Rawalpindi garrison. Ul-Haq had died just a week earlier, in that mysterious aircraft crash. The Soviet military was in full swing withdrawing from Afghanistan after an eight-year occupation. No one in the audience would have been surprised when Beg told them that they were 'witnessing the dawn of a new era'; it was self-evident. What came next, however, was anything but. Beg told the commanders that:

> These [are] historic moments and a turning point for the Afghanistan-Pakistan-Iran struggle against global hegemony. It bonds the three nations together for a common cause ultimately forming into a union. It is the realization of my dream of 'strategic depth'.

Beg was not just talking about the liberated post-Soviet Afghanistan as the new arena for 'strategic depth' for Pakistan. He had Iran in mind as well. Tehran had, only five days earlier, agreed to a ceasefire that brought to an end the bloody eight-year war with Iraq. Beg faced his commanders:

> Iran has emerged stronger after eight years of brutal war with Iraq and the Islamic Revolution has consolidated. Pakistan has opted for democracy after 11 years of military rule. This is the moment

of triumph of freedom for all the three countries. Freedom beckons us to unite and gain strategic depth to safeguard our national security interests.[1]

Beg was flogging a dead horse, but he was not looking back but ahead. Over the course of the turbulent 1980s, dozens of bilateral agreements had been signed between Iran and Pakistan – from commerce and transportation to defence accords. Earlier in 1988, after an eight-year halt, even direct flights between Iran and Pakistan resumed.

Nonetheless, Beg's mention of Iran as part of Pakistan's 'strategic depth' represented a tectonic shift in ambition. Some attributed the so-called pro-Iran orientation to his Shi'a background. This point, though, is altogether unsubstantiated and generally only a bone of contention among those with a sectarian agenda or sectarian-centric prism.

Beg had spoken of a new 'strategic depth' a year earlier in 1987 when he was ul-Haq's deputy as vice chief of the army. He talked about a 'putative axis between Iran, Pakistan, Turkey and Afghanistan'.[2] Beg had presumably trumpeted such a sensitive topic only with his boss's prior blessing, and no one could have accused ul-Haq of pro-Shi'a or pro-Iran inclinations. This would suggest that Beg's Shi'a background had nothing to do with this latest pitch from Islamabad. It was a geopolitical manoeuvere, pure and simple, and free of any sectarian motivation.

This idea of unity was, of course, a throwback to the 1950s and 1960s. In those days, the question of a 'confederation' would emerge each time Iran and Pakistan felt vulnerable to external threats or faced geopolitical trials. This time was no different. As the United States began to roll back its intervention in Afghanistan, its need for Pakistan plummeted. Instead, Washington started to again press Islamabad over its nuclear activities. In 1990, US Ambassador Robert Oakley told the Pakistanis to halt their nuclear programme or the United States would drop all aid. That year alone, US aid stood at $560 million.[3] Beg's anti-Americanism was growing, which is how Iran suddenly re-entered the equation.

General Beg's Iran plan

The authorities in Washington did not like Beg's turn towards Tehran. After ul-Haq's death, Beg was told that Washington would not look kindly on any collaboration with Iran. The United States feared that the new Pakistani military boss had bid for unfettered collaboration with the Iranians. The concern was that the Pakistanis wanted oil in return for passing on nuclear bomb-making expertise to Iran. Once he was pressed, Beg ultimately agreed to abandon the idea of Iranian talks.[4]

Beg defended his views on Iran, but qualified them as well. He denied that he had sanctioned the transfer of nuclear parts to Iran, despite many rumours. As army chief, many suspected that Beg must have known that the A. Q. Khan network was shipping such parts to Iran on Pakistani military aircraft. Beg claimed that A. Q. Khan was not 'answerable' to him but to the president and the prime minister.

Robert Oakley, the US ambassador, claimed that as late as March 1991 Beg had personally told him about his seriousness in pushing ahead with a 'strategic alliance' with Iran. According to Oakley, the general had said that he wanted conventional military capability from Iran in return for nuclear technology. Beg emphatically denied ever having said such a thing. He told an American news organization, 'Of all the people, I would not go to Robert Oakley because, I didn't talk to him because I did not like his face, to be very honest.'[5]

Beg later claimed that he had never 'thought of sharing nuclear technology with Iran':

As a member of the nuclear command authority as early as 1989, [when] Benazir Bhutto was prime minister, we took a very strong policy decision – a policy of nuclear restraint, and we said there would be no transfer of technology to anybody, and we have shown not only responsibility, we have stood by what decisions were taken.[6]

Beg's insistence, however, flies in the face of the facts. Only a few years earlier, Pakistan and Iran had publicly announced a deal to pursue nuclear collaboration, albeit only in the civil field. Beg himself never made that distinction between civil- and military-related nuclear collaboration. As it turned out, the devil was in the detail, and much depended on the two countries' implicit understanding with regard to nuclear cooperation. However, this lay undetected until the A. Q. Khan network was publicly revealed in early 2004.

When Beg visited Iran in February 1990, he told Iranian President Ali Akbar Hashemi Rafsanjani that he was ready to assist Tehran with nuclear technology.[7] In return, he wanted direct military support for Pakistan in the event of another war with India. Beg, on his return from his 1990 trip to Tehran, is reported to have said, 'with the support Iran promised me, we will win in case of war over Kashmir'.[8]

In fact, when Beg's successor, General Asif Nawaz, went to Tehran in October 1991, Iran's President Rafsanjani took him to one side and asked, 'when can [Iran] expect the technology your predecessor promised us?'. Once back in Islamabad, Nawaz claimed to have asked whether the President and the Prime Minister knew anything about this nuclear deal with Iran. This was purportedly denied.[9] Regardless of the truth, in subsequent years it has become expedient to put the blame for nuclear deals with Iran at the door of General Beg.

The finger is often pointed at his Shi'a background as the motivator. While Beg's Shi'a heritage might, in the context of Iran–Pakistan relations, be an attention-grabber, the genesis of this nuclear partnership went back to a decision that Zia ul-Haq had made a few years earlier. Beg merely continued a policy that ul-Haq, that fervent Sunni, had set in motion. After he retired, Beg ignored entirely the question of Iran in the two autobiographies that he published.[10]

Nonetheless, there can be no doubt that as Pakistan's military boss from August 1988 to his retirement in August 1991, Beg sought to revive the spirit of the old CENTO despite its shortcomings. In July 1989, Iran and Pakistan signed a new defence agreement, including exploration of the joint production of military tanks.[11] By 1993, Pakistan and Turkey had signed a new military-to-military cooperation agreement and a year later Iran and Pakistan held a joint naval exercise, the first in two decades. In the end, however, as had been the constant fear during CENTO's 24-year existence, the common interests of Iran and Pakistan were simply not enough to keep them hand-in-hand. In fact, a storm was already in the making – and the biggest rift in Iran–Pakistan relations was just around the corner.

The race for Kabul

On 15 February 1989, the last Soviet troops left Afghanistan. With that Soviet withdrawal, Iranian–Pakistani rivalry over influence in Afghanistan entered a new, and soon deadly, phase.

Afghanistan had lost over 1.3 million people to the war, the bulk of them civilians. The Mujahedeen had not defeated a superpower but they fought it to a standstill, and then stayed in the fight until the Soviets tired and went home. The Afghan national economy was smashed, the population was scattered in neighbouring refugee camps and across the globe. Some 6 million Afghan refugees were in Iran and Pakistan alone.

Afghan society had been shattered. It was no longer a traditionalist Islamic country under secular rule. Tribal law and customs no longer controlled the swelling ranks of rural youth. Anarchic conditions prevailed and a state of free-for-all was in existence. Afghanistan was fertile ground for ethnic and sectarian conflict. In this cocktail of misery, Iran and Pakistan were not spectators but guilty of exacerbating existing rifts among the Afghans.

§

Within weeks of ul-Haq's death, the Pakistani military under the leadership of General Beg decided on an end to military rule. Elections were held in November 1988, and the PPP won the vote. Zulfikar Bhutto's daughter, Benazir, was elected prime minister in December 1988. When the Soviets had arrived in Afghanistan in December 1979, she and her PPP party had been critical of ul-Haq's policy of confronting the Soviets. Benazir's Iranian mother – Nusrat Bhutto, then the chairwoman of the PPP – had even 'pleased Moscow by saying she would recognize the Kabul [communist] government, stop [Afghan] insurgent infiltration from Pakistan, and send the Afghan refugees home if she [Nusrat] gained power'.[12]

In her 1989 autobiography, Benazir defended this stance by her family and party. She was bitter about 'America's lack of commitment to Pakistan'. In the 1971 war against India, 'military help from America never arrived', she complained. US–Pakistani security agreements, she said, 'suffered from mistaken identity', adding, 'Americans were prepared to defend us from their enemy, the Soviet Union. But Pakistan's real threat has always been India.' In other words, Islamabad did not feel that it owed the United States anything.

Once in power, however, her position on the question of Afghanistan was considerably hardened. There was no more talk of compromising with the Afghan communists, as the PPP had reasoned in the early 1980s. Bhutto insisted that the Afghan communist government of

President Mohammad Najibullah – who had emerged as leader in 1987 – had to go before Islamabad could partake in negotiations about Afghanistan's future.

Najibullah asked the United States to ignore Benazir Bhutto's call for his government's removal before a process of political dialogue for post-Soviet Afghanistan could commence. He warned about the 'Lebanonization' of Afghanistan, and promised non-alignment as his foreign policy if he was able to stay in power. He warned about Islamic fundamentalists taking over, and pointed to Iran as a lesson: 'For the United States, which is more appropriate: a non-aligned Afghanistan – free, independent, demilitarized, and professing democracy – or a fanatic, extremist and fundamentalist regime? Hasn't the United States already tasted the bitterness of fundamentalism [in Iran]?'[13]

Najibullah sought to woo the doubters and tilt the balance in his favour. He dropped Marxism, renamed the Communist Party the Homeland Party and at the same time embraced Islam. His was authentic Afghan Islam, he said, as he warned about the dangers of Arab Sunni extremists aligned with some of the Afghan Mujahedeen, a fear shared by the Shi'a Iranians.

Alas, such warnings were left unheeded. In the first six months of 1989, despite the cooling ties, the Bhutto Government and the United States were in agreement that Najibullah had to go. Despite his visceral aversion to the clerical regime in Tehran – where he had, only a few years earlier, been the Afghan ambassador – Najibullah was forced to make overtures towards Tehran. He knew full well that whatever the United States was for, Iran would be against and vice versa. Najibullah's ongoing transformation now included overt attempts to endear himself to the clerics in Tehran.

Najibullah between Islamabad and Tehran

On 3 June 1989, Iran's supreme leader, Ayatollah Khomeini, died. Najibullah quickly ordered three days of national mourning and large, elegant memorials were held. He personally went to the Iranian Embassy to sign the book of condolences, and the Afghan national flag flew at half mast. The lavish symbolism aside, Najibullah guessed that he and Tehran really shared only one fundamental common interest – and that was a deep sense of antipathy towards most of the radical Sunni Afghan groups that were waiting in Peshawar for the right moment to seize Kabul.

Iran was no small player in the Afghan saga. By early 1989, seven of the Afghan resistance groups were based in Pakistan, but nine such groups had picked Iran as their base. The Iranians thus exerted considerable influence over at least part of the Afghan Mujahedeen.

Tehran weighed its Afghan options as it considered Najibullah's overtures. At one point, the Afghan President even seemed open to the idea of self-determination for the ethnic Hazara, the Shi'a community in central Afghanistan, which Iran so heavily backed during the Soviet occupation.[14] It all seemed as if Iran was preparing to learn to live with a communist government in Kabul.

When Rafsanjani, then Iran's powerful speaker of the parliament, visited Moscow in June 1989 – the first visit by an Iranian official since the 1979 revolution – he told Mikhail Gorbachev, '[now that Soviets] have resolved to pull out of Afghanistan we are prepared to assist you, so that after your departure there will be no American domination in Afghanistan'.[15]

Six weeks after his trip to Moscow, Rafsanjani became president of Iran and suggested that pro-Iran Afghan groups should reach an agreement with the government of Najibullah. To press this point, a meeting was held in Tehran to which Afghan commanders based in Peshawar were also invited. Four of the seven Afghan commanders in Peshawar, including Gulbuddin Hekmatyar and Abdul Rasul Sayyaf, refused to go to Tehran.[16] The latter two commanders were the main Sunni and ethnic Pashtun Afghan warlords, whose alliance at the time was with Pakistan, the Saudis and the United States. Those Afghans who went to Tehran heard from the Iranians about the importance of holding talks with the Soviets on the future of Afghanistan. One of those Iranians giving such advice was a man with long, greying beard. He was none other than Ayatollah Ali Khamenei, Iran's new supreme leader who had succeeded Ayatollah Khomeini.[17]

The Pakistanis, too, began to show some openness to a political deal with Najibullah. This policy turnaround was partly due to the various Mujahedeen factions starting to fight amongst themselves, meaning that the fall of the Najibullah Government no longer seemed imminent. This was a break with US policy – which insisted on the removal of Najibullah – but Islamabad could not afford to let Najibullah's manoeuvrings outdo its own bid for supremacy in Afghanistan.

It certainly did not help that Tehran was jockeying for maximum influence, and leaving the door open to a possible compromise with

Najibullah. General Beg might have introduced the idea of 'strategic depth' to the Pakistani lexicon and advocated the virtues of partnership with Iran, but in practice Islamabad and Tehran engaged in a zero-sum game as far as Afghanistan was concerned. It only escalated with time.

In this race for Kabul, Tehran competed against not just Pakistan, but Saudi Arabia too. Tehran was horrified about the prospect of a Saudi-beholden regime in charge in Kabul. At the same time, the Iranians recognized that they could not bring about a Shi'a or non-Pashtun government after Najibullah. The demographics – with the Pashtun as the largest community in Afghanistan – were simply stacked against such an outcome.

The best the Iranians could hope for was a moderate Sunni Pashtun Islamic government that would not be beholden to Saudi Arabia or Pakistan. Iran's options were limited, and this explained its receptiveness to Najibullah's advances.

In late 1988 and early 1989, as the Soviet withdrawal from Afghanistan was nearing completion, Tehran accelerated its efforts to consolidate the Afghan Shi'a and non-Pashtun factions that were close to Iran. This was a response to developments in Peshawar. In 1988, as soon as Moscow announced its intention to withdraw, Afghan Mujahedeen groups in Pakistan created an interim government in exile. Afghan Shi'a groups were excluded from this process. In early 1989, as formation of a second post-Soviet interim government was under way, Tehran again pushed for the Shi'a parties to be involved – but it was yet another disappointment. The Pakistan-based groups in effect excluded the Shi'a parties and formed a government in exile. This interim administration was recognized only by Saudi Arabia, Sudan, Bahrain and Malaysia.[18]

After the Afghan Shi'as were excluded from the interim government, and on Tehran's insistence, the main Afghan Shi'a parties based in Iran formed a coalition called Hezb-e Wahdat (the Islamic Unity Party of Afghanistan). The Iranian objective was to bolster the Afghan front to compete with Pakistani- and Saudi-backed Pashtun factions such as warlord Abdul Rasul Sayyaf's vehemently anti-Shi'a outfit.

With the creation of Hezb-e Wahdat, Iran's consolidation efforts had paid off – but this had not been without hurdles, nor was it an unconditional win for Tehran. Throughout the 1980s, Afghan Shi'a groups that did not subscribe to the Iranian Islamist model – the concept of *velayat-e faqih* (rule of the Supreme Jurisprudent) – had been forced out of Iran.[19] By 1989, Tehran no longer had the same appeal to the Afghan Shiʻa as it had a decade earlier. This was true even among those who had chosen to stay in Iran. Accordingly, Hezb-e Wahdat definitely had more Afghan 'colour', and the detachment from Iran was perhaps greater than ever before. While Iran was not able to completely control Hezb-e Wahdat, it was comforted by the fact that no country could back the Shiʻa Afghans like Iran could, and that kept Tehran in the Afghan 'play'.

Iran did not limit itself to the Afghan Shiʻa. In 1991, Tehran brokered a cultural agreement between the Tajik-dominated Jamaat-e-Islami party and the Hazara-dominated Hezb-e Wahdat. While the Afghan Tajik are predominately Sunni, they are Persian-speakers. Iran, therefore, focused on the common ground, the Persian language, and not the sectarian split. The Iranians would only play the Shiʻa card if it sustained or complemented an otherwise broader geopolitical objective. Tehran's aim was to unify as much as possible the non-Pashtun Afghans, Shiʻa or otherwise, since Pakistan already had a near-monopoly over Afghan Pashtun-dominated Mujahedeen groups.

From an Iranian perspective, the principal dividing issue revolved around Pakistan's continued preference for hard-line Islamist Pashtuns. This Pakistani partiality hardened with time. A watershed moment came in March 1990, when the Pakistanis concocted a coup attempt in Kabul. Najibullah's defence minister, Shahnawaz Tanai, switched sides and joined forces with the Pakistan-backed Gulbuddin Hekmatyar in the battle for Kabul.

The coup attempt took Tehran completely by surprise, and was the gravest reminder to date that Islamabad had in reality no intention to include Iran in shaping the future of Afghanistan. After all, a month before the coup attempt General Beg himself had visited Tehran and told the Iranians that Pakistan would not take any steps in Afghanistan before consulting Tehran first. That was proven flatly false.[20]

On 6 August 1990, General Beg removed Prime Minister Benazir Bhutto from office. She was accused of corruption and abuse of political power. Her departure meant fewer hurdles for the Pakistani military and intelligence services, and their ambition to install a pro-Pakistan Pashtun Islamist government in power in Kabul. Before her removal, Prime Minister Bhutto had advocated for pro-Iran groups to be accommodated, and generally adopted a more moderate line on

Afghanistan. She would later claim that she wanted a political solution to the Afghan civil war. The Pakistani military–intelligence complex did not agree on the need to find a political compromise, and forged ahead with military plans for Pakistan-backed Afghans to capture Kabul.

Iran was forced to intensify its Afghan efforts. It was to be a multipronged game plan. Tehran never abandoned the seven Afghan groups in Peshawar, but focused on the moderates among them – namely, Sibghatullah Mojaddedi and Ahmad Gailani. On the other hand, secret talks with Najibullah's regime continued.

Shortly after the March 1990 coup, Iran's former Ambassador to Pakistan secretly visited Najibullah in Kabul to assess common interests. This high-level personal channel between Kabul and Tehran would remain active for the rest of Najibullah's time in power. That Iranian ambassador was Mir Mahmoud Mousavi, a handsome man with a gentle demeanour whose family background had deep ties to the Islamist regime in Tehran. His brother, Mir Hossein Mousavi, had been Iran's prime minister for most of the 1980s, and would, two decades later, emerge as the key leader in Iran's Green opposition movement. Mir Mahmoud never reached such political heights, and devoted himself to a diplomatic career with a focus on south-west Asia.

Pakistani officials in Islamabad still remember Mir Mahmoud as a 'difficult' ambassador with little sympathy for Pakistan.[21] He was for most of the 1990s Iran's top emissary on Afghanistan, with an eagerness to give the Pakistanis a good run for their money in the race for influence in the country.

Mir Mahmoud's consultations with Kabul were a glimmer of hope for the beleaguered Afghan President. In November 1990, Najibullah paid a low-profile but important visit to Iran. On his way back from Geneva, where he had held an unprecedented reconciliation meeting with Pakistan-based Afghan Mujahedeen leaders, he arrived in Mashhad, Iran's main eastern city on the border with Afghanistan. No top figure came to see Najibullah. Those who did apologized profusely and explained that senior officials in Tehran, such as President Rafsanjani and Supreme Leader Ayatollah Ali Khamenei, hoped that the Afghan leader would understand the need for prudence and secrecy. The Islamic Republic of Iran, the self-declared Islamist revolutionary regime, was after all secretly dealing with a communist – albeit one who claimed to have been rehabilitated. Iran had no option but to be cautious.

Najibullah, a Pashtun with a hulking physical presence, said that no apologies were needed. He focused on topics of mutual interest. He was very keen on Iranian oil now that Soviet supplies were slowly vanishing. He also highlighted the shared animus toward the Americans – who, at the time, had deployed half a million troops in the Middle East to throw out the Iraqis from Kuwait – and the Saudi version of Islam: Wahhabism. 'We Afghans have been Muslims for 1,300 years but we cannot accept Wahhabism', he once told Mir Mahmoud Mousavi.

Najibullah had nothing good to say about the Pakistanis either. Instead, he urged his Iranian hosts to start working on ways of mediating between all Afghan factions – a pointed dig at the Pakistanis, with whom Najibullah had reluctantly just signed an agreement in Geneva.[22] Despite his pledge about secrecy when talking to officials in Mashhad, once in Kabul Najubullah held a press conference and spoke of Iranian 'warmth' towards him. The Iranians quickly downplayed Najibullah's comments. Nonetheless, the hard truth was that the regime of the ayatollahs in Tehran was by now the old Afghan communist's only real hope for political survival in Kabul.

§

Despite rising tensions over Afghanistan, at no point did Iran and Pakistan stop communicating. Attempts were even made to see if a mutually agreed understanding could be attained. General Asad Durrani, who was the head of the Pakistani intelligence service, the ISI, travelled to Tehran in September 1991. Talks about Afghanistan had been ongoing for months. 'The Iranians', he said, had played an 'excellent game in Afghanistan during the 1980s, and now they wanted a big role for the Iran-based groups in the government that would come after Najibullah's inevitable fall'.[23]

Durrani and the Pakistanis felt that Tehran was asking for a lot more than it deserved, based on its contribution during the anti-Soviet jihad. Nonetheless, talks continued. Their joint efforts irked many of the Afghans, who felt left out of discussions about the future of their own country. When Tehran and Islamabad set up a tripartite forum – known as the Consultative Committee – on the future of Afghanistan, most of the Afghan Mujahedeen commanders boycotted the process. They were angry that the Iranians and the Pakistanis assumed the prerogative of choosing the Afghans that could join the committee. The 'tripartite' Consultative Committee was seen as unrepresentative.

What tilted the balance in favour of Pakistan-based groups in this race for Kabul was US opposition to anything associated with Iran. Anti-Iranian sentiment among the Americans and the Saudis was so innate that opportunities – when the ethnic–sectarian tangle could have been undone – were ignored. In one case, some Shi'a Hazara petitioned the US special envoy to Afghanistan, Peter Tomsen, for American help to bring them into the interim Afghan Government that they had been excluded from. The Shi'a Hazara made it abundantly clear that they were not acting on the behest of Iran, but in spite of it. Tomsen, who held his unenviable role from 1989 until 1992, gave the written petition to Prince Turki bin Faisal, the Saudi intelligence chief and a key player in the Afghan game. Prince Turki heard Tomsen out, but nothing came out of the matter. The Saudi intelligence boss made it clear that neither Iran nor the Afghan Shi'a could play a role in Kabul once Najibullah was gone. Tomsen assumed that Prince Turki feared that the Iranians would seek to take over the Afghan Mujahedeen movement.[24] Meanwhile, the Saudis kept up pressure on the Pakistanis to continue favouring Afghan Sunni hardliners over all other factions. Tomsen knew that the same allergic reaction to Iran and the Shi'a existed within parts of the US Government.

The State Department wanted a broad diplomatic solution to include the Soviets and the Iranians. The CIA pushed for a decisive military victory for the Mujahedeen, and wanted to keep the Pakistanis and the Saudis in the forefront. President George H. Bush's team in the White House were somewhere in between. This American policy dispute was only exacerbated by the fact that the Iraqi invasion of Kuwait in August 1990 and the crumbling of the Soviet Union in 1991 preoccupied the George H. Bush White House to such a degree that all matters relating to Afghanistan were consigned to the back-burner.

The 1990 Iraqi invasion of Kuwait proved to be a watershed in another crucial way. After feeding from the hand of the United States for over a decade, two key Pashtun Afghan commanders – Gulbuddin Hekmatyar and Abdul Rasul Sayyaf – decided to back Saddam Hussein in his invasion of Kuwait and threats against Saudi Arabia. The horrified Americans and Saudis cut off aid to both Hekmatyar and Sayyaf. Pakistan stayed with the two renegades, and kept supporting them.

Pakistan itself came out publicly against the US plan to expel Saddam Hussein from Kuwait. Tension in US–Pakistan ties led to the

October 1991 decision by US President George H. Bush to invoke the Pressler Amendment, as he now suddenly refused to certify that Pakistan did not have a military nuclear programme. US sanctions were then imposed on Islamabad, in accordance with the amendment. This American–Pakistani falling out was, on paper, welcome news from Iran's perspective, but in fact it did nothing to bring Tehran and Islamabad any closer.

Pakistan's commitment to radical Sunni Afghan groups was exacerbating its rivalry with Shi'a Iran.[25] Nonetheless, these self-inflicted wounds meant that the most likely anti-Shi'a contenders for power in Kabul – Hekmatyar and Sayyaf – were significantly weakened.

§

The collapse of the Soviet Union in December 1991 ended Soviet support for Najibullah. In March 1992, the UN brokered a deal and the Afghan interim government in Peshawar took charge.

The fall of the Najibullah regime in April 1992 was, however, not to be the end of the Afghan civil war. Within days, armed clashes began between key Mujahedeen groups. Iran's Revolutionary Guards, under diplomatic cover, coordinated and distributed weapons to the Afghan Shi'a in Kabul and elsewhere in the country. On 7 June 1992, fighters from the Iran-backed Hezb-e Wahdat clashed in Kabul with supporters of Ittehad-e-Islami, a coalition supported by Saudi Arabia. By now, Riyadh was again back in the game of propping up hard-line Sunnis such as Ittehad-e-Islami, which was led by the anti-Shi'a Sayyaf. Sayyaf's fighters targeted ethnic Hazaras in systematic sectarian killings, while Hezb-e Wahdat retaliated by killing Pashtuns. This was an Iranian versus Pakistani–Saudi proxy war, leaving hundreds dead in that summer of 1992.[26]

Fighting between Afghan factions continued, but it did not always follow a sectarian or ethnic-based script. Nor were Afghan loyalties to either Iran or Pakistan rock-solid. When, in January 1993, the president of the interim Afghan government, Burhanuddin Rabbani, a Persian-speaking ethnic Tajik from the Jamaat-e-Islami, was controversially re-elected for a second term, the provisional government he led in Kabul collapsed. Rabbani was the commander with most support among Afghan Mujahedeen leaders. Among his lieutenants were Ahmad Shah Massoud and Ismail Khan, two of the most prominent non-Pashtun

Afghan warlords. They belonged to the Persian-speaking and ethnic-Tajik-dominated Jamaat-e-Islami party.[27]

At the time, however, in order to face down Rabbani's bid for a second term, the Iran-backed Shi'a Hezb-e Wahdat forged an alliance with the Sunni Hekmatyar and fought Rabbani's government troops.[28] This kind of no-nonsense jockeying for power and shifting alliances among the Afghan factions became commonplace. There was, however, one certainty – and that was that Iran and Pakistan would back different horses in competition for power as Afghanistan plunged into a deep civil war.

The collapse of the Soviet Union

The collapse of the Soviet Union in 1991 had immense geopolitical implications for Iran and Pakistan. For nearly half a century, the two countries had been the pillars of the anti-communist front in south-west Asia. With the end of the Soviet system, their principal common interest was gone. The ongoing Iranian–Pakistani zero-sum race for influence in Afghanistan had the potential to be broadened to the new independent states that emerged from the former Soviet south. The five 'Stans' – Kazakhstan, Kyrgyzstan, Tajikistan, Turkmenistan and Uzbekistan – became the new nearby neighbours of Iran and Pakistan.

Some have called it a repeat of the 'Great Game' of the nineteenth century, with rival states racing for the natural riches in Central Asia. In the meantime, the raging Afghan civil war to the south was seen by all of Afghanistan's neighbours as a threat to their national security. In some cases, this was more than a mere perception. Shortly after gaining independence, Tajikistan became embroiled in a civil war that lasted from 1992 to 1996. Among the warring factions in Tajikistan were Islamists who had working ties with Afghan Mujahedeen groups. Afghanistan was morphing into the regional command post for militant Islamists. Iran was suddenly no longer alone in fearing the consolidation of Sunni fundamentalist control of Afghanistan. Russia, the Central Asian states, China and even India all shared this fear. Pakistan stood out as a benefactor of Sunni radicalism, a tendency that rapidly consolidated when Islamabad banked on a new emerging Sunni Islamist movement in Afghanistan.

The Taliban and the Pakistani bomb

By 1994, the former Soviets had been out of Afghanistan for five years. Yet there was no end in sight for the Afghan civil war. By this time, a new movement, the Taliban, emerged from the Pashtun regions of southern Afghanistan. The fighters of this new movement were Sunni and ethnic Pashtun. Most of its early combatants had been born, or spent many years, in refugee camps in Pakistan. Pakistani indoctrination and tutelage of the Taliban were unmistakable. Islamabad opted to facilitate the rise of the Taliban as its former favourites – commanders Hekmatyar and Sayyaf – had failed to bring about total military victory in Afghanistan.

A pivotal moment in the rise of the movement came in October 1994, when the Pakistanis helped some 200 Taliban to rout Hekmatyar's fighters in the strategic border town of Spin Baldak. Then, in one of the Taliban's earliest political decisions, Afghan roads were opened up to Pakistani vehicles. By December of that year, 50 Pakistani trucks brought cotton south from Turkmenistan via Afghanistan to the Pakistani city of Quetta. As it turned out, the Taliban's rise had coincided with a new regional trade initiative launched by Islamabad. Tehran was again taken by surprise.

Within the next few months, the Taliban effected speedy capture of dozens of Afghanistan's 31 provinces, greatly helped by Pakistani assistance. By February 1995, Taliban fighters were on the outskirts of the capital, Kabul.[29] By September of that year, the western-province city of Herat fell – and, suddenly, Iran and the Taliban shared a border. Meanwhile, the Saudis, under the supervision of intelligence chief Prince Turki, agreed to financially support the Taliban. Relations between Tehran and Islamabad were now totally dominated by Afghanistan.

§

In November 1995, Prime Minister Benazir Bhutto paid an official visit to Tehran. The pomp and ceremony of the days of the Shah were long gone, but President Ali Akbar Hashemi Rafsanjani was at hand on the tarmac at Mehr Abad Airport to welcome the Pakistani leader. As she was disembarking to set foot on the land of her maternal ancestors, she was seen quickly to put on a traditional Iranian cloak and a tight and intensely white headscarf. The elder Rafsanjani could not help himself and blurted out, 'Dear, why have you covered yourself so much?'[30]

Rafsanjani's blundering comment might have duped poor Benazir. She was a woman who had spent years studying on liberal campuses at Harvard and Oxford universities, but was evidently not equipped to disarm emphatic Shi'a clergymen. Later, at the residence of Supreme Leader Ayatollah Khamenei, she was in fact asked to cover up some more. Khamenei gave Bhutto such a lengthy monologue about Islamic chastity that she was left nearly in tears. 'My daughter,' Khamenei is said to have remarked, 'You are a child of Islam, a Muslim and a Shi'a.' All she could reply was, 'pray for me that I am forgiven on [the] Day of Judgment'.[31]

A scolding for immodest dress code was, of course, not all that Bhutto received while in Tehran. She also got an earful from Rafsanjani and Khamenei on her country's support for the Taliban. She could not charm herself out of this one. The government of Benazir, this daughter of a Shi'a father and an Iranian mother, had been instrumental in giving life to the Taliban, the most anti-Shi'a and anti-Iran movement that the region had seen in centuries.[32]

On being re-elected in October 1993, she appointed as minister of the interior Major General Naseerullah Babar. Babar had been her father's advisor on Afghanistan in the 1970s, at a time when Islamabad first began fostering ties with Afghan Islamists who had fled to Pakistan after the 1973 coup in Kabul by the leftist Daoud Khan. Some 20 years later, as interior minister for Zulfikar Bhutto's daughter, Babar still saw value in Afghan Islamists. He set out to help the Taliban, and with Benazir's blessing.[33] Babar pushed the line that a protracted civil war in Afghanistan would split Afghans along ethnic lines – a prospect that Islamabad could ill afford, as the dormant question of Greater Pashtunistan could once again emerge and threaten the territorial integrity of Pakistan.

The Iranians had every reason to be anxious about Pakistan's actions. While many worldwide at first reckoned Taliban leader Mullah Omar to merely represent popular anger at the brutality of the Mujahedeen commanders during the Afghan civil war, onlookers in Tehran were busy calculating the ramifications of Afghanistan in the hands of this rising band of Sunni puritans.

Not only was Pakistan behind this new movement, but its leader, Mullah Omar, appeared as particularly bad news from Tehran's vantage point. Omar, the 'one-eyed mullah', as the world would subsequently know him, had been a member of Hezb-e Eslami-Khalis, one of the seven Peshawar-based anti-Soviet Mujahedeen groups led by Younis Khalis, a commander who was known as being profoundly anti-Shi'a and anti-Iran.[34] The dangers of sectarianism loomed increasingly larger in Iranian minds.

Only a few months earlier, on 20 June 1994, a massive bomb had shattered the holy Shi'a shrine of Imam Reza in the city of Mashhad, killing 27 worshippers. Tehran publicly blamed it on an Iranian dissident group,[35] but Pakistani sources linked the bombing to Ramsi Yousef, a Kuwaiti–Pakistani later convicted of the 1993 bombing of the World Trade Center's twin towers in New York. Yousef's uncle, Khalid Sheikh Mohammad, later became infamous as one of the principal architects of the 11 September 2001 attacks in the United States.[36]

Tehran opted not to blame extremist Sunnis for the June 1994 bombing in Mashhad, in order to prevent a sectarian backlash inside Iran. Nonetheless, developments in Afghanistan were not encouraging. The anti-Shi'a Taliban was shortly afterwards considered by Tehran a principal national security threat to Iran. The fact that a Shi'a Pakistani leader – Benazir Bhutto – had been instrumental in the movement's rise only served to irritate the Iranians further.

The Pakistani ambassador to Tehran, Khalid Mahmood, remembers meeting President Rafsanjani. 'What are we competing for in Afghanistan?' the former had asked, 'There is nothing there to fight for?' This odd statement, of course, fell on deaf ears in Tehran. Mahmood had not been lucky with the timing of his ambassadorship. In the Pakistani diplomatic service, an ambassadorship in Tehran is a prestigious posting, but Mahmood had arrived at an all-time low in relations. A few months later, he had the unenviable task of having to go to the airport in Tehran to be part of a ceremony to receive the bodies of five Iranian Air Force cadets killed in a targeted terrorist attack in Rawalpindi. In the 1990s, dozens of Iranians were killed in armed attacks in Pakistan – including diplomats, teachers and engineers.[37] Anti-Shi'a and anti-Iran militant groups were invariably blamed, but in Tehran's eyes the Pakistani state was somehow complicit.

Iran, and Pakistani nuclear offers

There remained, however, some areas of cooperation – a testimony to the intricacies of Iranian–Pakistani relations over the decades. Nothing stands out more than the ongoing nuclear collaboration that began under ul-Haq in the mid-1980s and continued in the 1990s despite the intensifying rivalry in Afghanistan.

An International Atomic Energy Agency report from 2004 – a decade after Benazir Bhutto's trip to Tehran – concluded that it was about that time (the year 1995) that 'Pakistan was providing Tehran with the designs for sophisticated centrifuges capable of making bomb-grade nuclear fuel'. US officials claimed that they had no evidence throughout the 1990s that Iran was receiving nuclear assistance from Pakistan. One senior US intelligence official called this 'a fairly major failure despite the fact that we were watching Iran and Pakistan quite closely' in the 1990s.[38] Other players have since given a different interpretation of the American attitude at the time.

Hossein Mousavian, who later became Iran's chief nuclear negotiator and was subsequently hounded out of the country by a rival political faction, claims that the history of Iranian–Pakistani nuclear dealings has been altered retrospectively to better fit an official US narrative: 'The Americans forced the Pakistani authorities to publicly pretend that they had not known that A. Q. Khan [network] was giving Iran nuclear material. We [in Tehran] were able to live with this and chose not to make a big deal out of it.'[39] In other words, the US policy-making community did not want to have to punish Islamabad for its nuclear proliferation activities, and offered the Pakistanis an exit option from the mess they had created for themselves.

Meanwhile, despite the clash over Pakistan's support for the Taliban, Rafsanjani looked for ways to engage Benazir Bhutto. By now, Iran's Islamic revolutionary zeal had subsided and Tehran began a policy of detente towards its neighbours. At first, this policy was extended to Pakistan, although it was not to last long.

The Rafsanjani Administration – in office from 1989 until 1997 – stressed the economic rehabilitation of Iran after the devastating eight-year war with Iraq. In what became known as the 'Reconstruction Era', President Rafsanjani first pushed for closer economic integration with Pakistan and other neighbours in the context of the Economic Cooperation Organization. ECO, revived in 1985, was the successor to the American-backed RCD, which the Shah and Ayub Khan had pioneered back in 1964 but which had been dissolved in 1979 following the Iranian Revolution.

This new attempt to foster regional trade and integration was expanded to encompass a total of ten countries, including Afghanistan and six former Soviet republics. At the headquarters of ECO in Tehran, the zeal to advance the organization's goals was at first great, but too many snags on its path quickly turned ECO's agenda into a pipedream. Member states were mostly distracted by other foreign-policy priorities, or simply did not see ECO as a viable instrument.

§

At one point, progress made on a bilateral level appeared far more promising. In 1994, Iran and Pakistan signed their first Memorandum of Understanding, to build a 2,700 km multi-billion-dollar pipeline to ship Iranian natural gas from a field in the Persian Gulf to energy-starved Pakistan. This gigantic project was at first regional in its scope. It was designed to continue southwards and also deliver Iranian natural gas to the huge Indian market. Pakistan was, in turn, due to collect pipeline transit fees for the gas destined for India. It was dubbed the Peace Pipeline. After years of negotiation, India withdrew from the project citing pricing disputes for the gas and concerns about being beholden to Pakistan for its reliable delivery. The United States, however, also pressed New Delhi to abandon the deal as part of Washington's broader efforts to isolate Tehran.

Islamabad remained committed, and let the Iranians know that American pressure would not stop the project. Still, the Pakistanis were by no means putting all their hopes in Iran to satisfy their acute energy needs. While in talks with the Iranians, Pakistan was also in discussion with tiny but gas-rich Qatar – although finding means of transporting the gas eventually proved too arduous. The other option for Pakistan was to haul natural gas from Turkmenistan, the Central Asian state located north of Afghanistan. The Turkmen gas on offer was cheaper than Iran's, but there was a major drawback. A pipeline from Turkmenistan south to Pakistan needed to traverse Afghanistan, a country that was still engulfed in a civil war. That reality made the project at first unfeasible, but a major turnaround in the Afghan civil war suddenly gave new momentum to Islamabad's regional plans and the Turkmenistan pipeline project stayed on the Pakistani drawing board.

On 27 September 1996, the Taliban took Kabul. The post-Soviet Rabbani Government had to retreat northwards and westwards, and most anti-Taliban non-Pashtun commanders joined forces in a new coalition. This alliance was named the United Islamic Front for the Salvation of Afghanistan, better known as the Northern Alliance. Tehran refused to recognize the new regime, a policy that it stuck to throughout Taliban rule, and Iran became one of the principal backers of the Northern Alliance. Battle lines in Afghanistan had not been this pronounced in years, with the Iran-backed Northern Alliance pitted against the Pakistan-backed Taliban.

Only three countries recognized the new 'Islamic Emirate of Afghanistan': Pakistan, Saudi Arabia and the United Arab Emirates. Thousands of radical Sunni Islamists – Saudis, Yemenis, Iraqis, Tunisians, Libyans, Algerians, Chechens and Uzbeks – all found a safe haven there.[40] At its peak, some 12,000 foreign Islamist combatants were in Afghanistan fighting alongside the Taliban against its enemies.

The Pakistanis and the Saudis tapped into their extensive networks in Washington and painted the Taliban as a popular grass-roots movement that could, on the one hand, be a bulwark against the anti-American Iranian model whilst, on the other, becoming a geographical conduit to the economic riches of the newly independent states of Central Asia. Pakistan was a critical component of this channel from Central Asia to world markets. For a while, the United States pondered relations with the Taliban. Assistant Secretary of State for South Asian Affairs, Robin L. Raphel, visited Afghanistan and pointed out that the Taliban had to be 'acknowledged' as an 'indigenous movement' with 'staying power'.[41]

Iran was seemingly isolated. Instead, Tehran called the Taliban the 'ones who made ugly [...] this beautiful religion', renouncing what it called Taliban's alien Islam. The Russians, the Indians and the Central Asian States all banded together in opposing the Taliban; Tehran led the pack.

Iranian state radio – broadcasting into Afghanistan in Dari, Pashtun and other Afghan languages – waged a massive propaganda campaign against the Taliban. The movement was endlessly denounced as barbaric and un-Islamic. Worst still, the fighters of Mullah Omar were portrayed as planted by Washington to implant 'American Islam' in Afghanistan. This was not just a swipe at the Taliban and the United States but also at the Pakistanis, the Saudis and the ultra-conservative Sunni creed that they now spread by backing the Taliban.

As before, Islamabad publicly downplayed any differences with Iran over Afghanistan. In June 1997, Prime Minster Nawaz Sharif, who had taken over the reigns from Benazir Bhutto a few months earlier, told the Iranians in Tehran point-blank that all factions in Afghanistan 'should sit behind a negotiating table and try to resolve their differences in a peaceful manner'.[42] No one in Tehran believed Nawaz's words. Pakistan was seen to be entirely dedicated to the Taliban.

Despite urging the Afghans to rise up and overthrow the Taliban, Tehran did also at times sound out the potential for some kind of understanding with the new rulers in Kabul. One of the most notable instances was in late 1997. Iran was due to host the 56-nation Organization of the Islamic Conference. President Mohammad Khatami, who a few months earlier had been elected on a platform of moderation at home and abroad, could not ignore the situation next door. A few weeks before the summit, the Iranians invited the Taliban to take part in a reconciliation seminar in the historic Iranian city of Esfahan. The Taliban leadership refused to attend.

At the summit in Tehran, President Khatami spoke to the Islamic dignitaries from the podium and said:

> What is happening in the dear land of Afghanistan is indeed a massive human tragedy as well as a fertile ground for foreign intervention and disruption of security and stability in the whole region. Muslim countries, and for that matter, the Organization of the Islamic Conference, should insist that there is no military solution to the Afghan problem.[43]

There can be little doubt that the Pakistanis were at the heart of the 'foreign intervention' that Khatami spoke of at that conference. However, whether Khatami knew it or not, the fact was that at the same time that the Iranian president discounted a military solution in Afghanistan, Iran's elite Revolutionary Guards were working around the clock to train and arm anti-Taliban fighters.

§

On 11–13 May 1998, for the first time since its initial test back in 1974, India detonated nuclear weapons in a series of underground tests only 150 km from the border with Pakistan. Iran's President Khatami told Prime Minister Nawaz Sharif that 'the security of Pakistan, as a brother, friendly and neighboring state is crucial to us'. It sounded just the kind of promise that the Shah of Iran had repeatedly made to hearten the Pakistanis whenever they came off worse in a conflict with India. This time, however, Islamabad proved ready and equipped to respond to India.

On 28–29 May 1998, Islamabad detonated six nuclear weapons at a mountain test site not far from the Iranian border. By doing so, Pakistan had become the seventh declared nuclear-armed state in the world. Iran's foreign minister, Kamal Kharazi, was the first foreign dignitary to visit Islamabad after the tests, and he declared that: 'Now they [Muslims] feel confident because a fellow Islamic nation possesses the know-how to build nuclear weapons.'[44] Kharazi defended Islamabad's tests and blamed India for forcing Pakistan to react, making Iran one of the very few countries not to fault Islamabad for its action.

There was an element of diplomatic hyperbole to Iran's public stance on Pakistan becoming a nuclear-armed state. Khalid Mahmood witnessed this first-hand as the Pakistani ambassador to Iran. He recalled that officials in Tehran had, a year earlier, anticipated that Pakistan was soon to become a nuclear state. They told Mahmood, 'We know what you are doing on the nuclear project, and we don't like it. But we understand.'[45] In his subsequent assignment, Mahmood was sent as ambassador to Saudi Arabia. He was there in May 1998, when Pakistan became a nuclear power. He remembered being called in by the Saudi King Fahd. He was driven to a royal palace outside Jeddah, where the Saudis expressed the same sentiment as the Iranians had done a year earlier: 'We don't like what you did but we understand.'[46] Nonetheless, the Saudis, unlike the Iranians, continued to look upon Islamabad as a strategic ally. Riyadh ratcheted up its financial aid to Pakistan as international sanctions were imposed as a penalty for going nuclear. Pakistan becoming a nuclear-armed state, however, did not alter the fundamentals in Tehran–Islamabad relations. The key issue that still mattered in bilateral ties was Afghanistan, and there was no sign of the rivalry subsiding.

A massacre in Mazar-e Sharif

That same summer, on 8 August 1998, Taliban forces overran the northern Afghan city of Mazar-e Sharif, until then a stronghold of the Northern Alliance. They went on a 'killing frenzy', and targeted Shi'a Hazara. According to Human Rights Watch, some 2,000 people were systematically killed in the attack on the northern city.[47] Once in Mazar-e Sharif, the Taliban fighters quickly arrived at the Iranian Consulate.

Eight Iranian diplomats and one journalist from Iran's IRNA news agency were rounded up and summarily executed. This would become a turning point. Only one among the Iranians present survived. That sole individual, Allahmadad Shahsoon, managed to escape, and after 19 days of walking made it back to Iran. He spoke about how the city had been taken by the Taliban and that the foreign ministry in Tehran had insisted that they stay put at the consulate. The Taliban had spared Iranian diplomats in the past − when they took Herat and Kabul, for example. The Iranians at the consulate had offered the intruding Taliban fruit, and one who spoke Pashtun tried talking to them. But they soon realized that the Taliban had come on a specific mission.

According to Shahsoon, the Taliban asked whether the phone in the consulate could make calls to Pakistan. They then made a call. Afterwards, the Iranians were taken to the basement. Shahsoon recalled the chilling moment when they realized that they were about to be murdered. They were machine-gunned, and Shahsoon claimed that he only survived by playing dead.

The Iranian authorities blamed Pakistan. Iran reduced its diplomatic staff in Islamabad, and an anti-Pakistan media campaign was launched by Tehran that further undermined relations. Some accounts suggest that the Taliban group had included members from the militant Pakistan-based anti-Shi'a group, the Sipah-e Sahaba.[48] Tehran was so rattled by the incident that everyone became suspect. They never believed Shahsoon's escape story, and that lone Iranian survivor has ever since been an outcast.[49]

In response, the Iranians put their military on alert and some 70,000 troops and military equipment were amassed on the border.[50] The Taliban did not bring any reinforcements to the western border region, but those already stationed there were told to confront the Iranians if they crossed the border. The Iranians never did. After a few days of deliberations, the consensus in Iran's Supreme National Security Council (SNSC) in Tehran was that an invasion of Afghanistan would be militarily relatively easy, but becoming bogged down in this historical graveyard of invaders was a real possibility. In such a scenario, Iran would in effect be fighting Pakistan, whose many military advisors had become an intrinsic part of the Taliban. No one in Tehran could ignore the fact that Pakistan had, just weeks earlier, become a nuclear-armed state.

Many in Tehran detected a Pakistani conspiracy to drive Iran and the United States into an open conflict over Afghanistan. In other words, the Pakistanis sought to have rival Iran removed from the Afghan scene by bringing the Americans into the equation. As Abbas Maleki, a deputy foreign minister in Tehran at the time, saw it: 'The ISI [Pakistani intelligence service] had urged the Taliban to attack Mazar-e Sharif and the [Iranian] consulate to compel Iran to retaliate against the Taliban. This way the ISI wanted to force Washington to embrace the Taliban.'[51]

Iran's supreme leader, Ayatollah Khamenei, sensitive to popular outrage at home about the Taliban's misdeeds, sought to spin Tehran's paralysis. He argued that the Taliban had not legally violated Iran's soil. Instead, Iranian troops were asked to slap down the Taliban. Within 48 hours, Iranian troops destroyed a number of Taliban stations on the border.

Other key Taliban targets were bombarded shortly afterwards. However, this was not at the hands of Iran but its arch-foe, the United States. On 7 August, a day before the Iranian Consulate was ransacked in Mazar-e Sharif, al-Qaeda operatives carried out bombings at US embassies in Nairobi and Dar es Salaam in east Africa. President Bill Clinton vowed that the attacks, which had been operationally planned by the al-Qaeda organization based in Afghanistan, would not be left unanswered.

In retaliation, on 20 August, some 70 American cruise missiles rained down on al-Qaeda and Taliban targets in Afghanistan, in Operation Infinite Reach. The Iranians, usually swift to denounce US unilateral military action, were conspicuously silent. The Pakistanis, by contrast, condemned the strikes – their anger exacerbated by the fact that many of the missiles had passed over Pakistani airspace from US Navy ships in the Arabian Sea, whilst no one in Washington had bothered to notify nuclear-armed Pakistan first.[52]

The Taliban and the energy riches of Central Asia

In September 1998, Iran's President Khatami travelled to New York to attend the UN General Assembly. Here, in a hard-hitting speech against the Taliban, he urged an international coalition to come together to resist the Afghan regime. However, as some 20 years earlier when the Soviets had invaded Afghanistan, suspicion and bad blood prevented tangible Iranian–American cooperation against the Taliban. The Iranians were guilty of holding back when the United States this time extended a hand. After much agonizing, the two sides agreed to meet on the sidelines of the UN assembly to discuss mutual interests. When US Secretary of State Madeleine Albright showed up for the meeting, her Iranian counterpart, Kamal Kharazi, was nowhere to be seen.

§

Tehran still blamed Pakistan for the killing of its diplomats in Mazar-e Sharif. Its minimum demand was an apology, which the Taliban leadership refused to grant. They insisted that the Iranians killed in the northern city had not been diplomats but military instructors aiding the Northern Alliance. Recriminations continued. When Tehran closed the border with Afghanistan, the Taliban stopped water flowing from the Helmand River to south-eastern Iran, forcing Iran to take the issue before the United Nations.

As the Taliban's grip on power increasingly looked permanent, Tehran slowly began to rethink its stance. What followed was a pure geopolitical gambit on the part of the Iranians: Tehran reopened the border in November 1999. This was highly unpopular in Iran, but a clever step nonetheless. The reopening of the border and resumption of trade meant that Pakistan no longer had a monopoly over the flow of goods in and out of Afghanistan. Iranian imports now challenged Pakistani goods, while at the same time Iran became an alternative transit option for the Afghans. This, of course, left the Pakistanis less than pleased.

Tehran had decided that it was not about to let Pakistan be the de facto master in Kabul. The Iranians launched periodic talks, and envoys visited Kabul. This sentiment was, to a degree, reciprocated. In 2000, Mullah Omar appointed Wakil Ahmad Mutawakel as foreign minister, and he wanted to reach out to Iran. Mutawakel was part of the so-called anti-Pakistan faction within the Taliban. Nonetheless, the killing of the diplomats was never settled. Mutawakel wrote a letter to Kamal Kharazi, the soft-spoken Iranian foreign minister, and blamed the killings on 'elements' that did not want Taliban–Iran relations to improve. He meant, of course, the Pakistanis. Even so, the Iranians never believed that there was an anti-Pakistan faction in Taliban, and Kharazi never replied to Mutawakel's letter.[53]

§

The fate of Iran–Taliban relations could perhaps have been very different had there been more receptive ears in Tehran. Unfortunately, there never were – and Iranian suspicions even crippled international efforts to solve the ongoing Afghan civil war. The Taliban might have captured Kabul in 1996 but it never actually controlled all of Afghanistan, as remnants of the Northern Alliance went on fighting.

One of the principal multilateral forums was the Group of '6 + 2', an initiative run under the auspices of the United Nations from 1999 until the Taliban's fall in 2001. It involved all six of Afghanistan's neighbours: China, Iran, Pakistan, Tajikistan, Turkmenistan and Uzbekistan. Two extra-regional powers, Russia and the United States, were also participants. In this forum, as Islamabad argued the Taliban's case Iran kept stressing the illegitimacy of Taliban rule and that regional security was at risk.[54] Little wonder, then, that the initiative never yielded any results. Lakhdar Brahimi, the UN's special envoy for Afghanistan from 1997 to 1999, later concluded that the Iranians were convinced from the outset that Pakistan, Saudi Arabia and the United States were behind the Taliban in order to undercut Iran's influence in the region.

One issue that probably fed such Iranian angst was the proposal to build a natural-gas pipeline from Turkmenistan in Central Asia, through Afghanistan, to Pakistan. For Tehran, a Pakistani–Saudi–American plot was all too visible. The consortium behind the project – CentGas – was led by the US energy firm UnoCal. Other main finances for the project came from Saudi Arabia and Pakistan. The realization of the multi-billion dollar, roughly 1,500 km pipeline through Afghanistan to Pakistan amounted to a major strategic setback for Tehran. Iran badly wanted to become an energy conduit to world markets for the states that emerged from the former Soviet south.

Other events fuelled Iranian anxieties. Not only had the United States welcomed a Taliban delegation to Washington to discuss the pipeline in February 1997, but the same delegation had, en route back to Kabul, stopped off in Jeddah to discuss the project with Saudi spymaster, Prince Turki. In the end, however, the Taliban's ties to al-Qaeda wrecked any chance of Western firms working in Afghanistan. On 21 August 1998 – a day after the US missile strikes on Afghanistan, and in punishment for hosting al-Qaeda – UnoCal suspended, and later ended, its commercial activities in Afghanistan.[55]

§

A new military coup in Pakistan, in October 1999, brought General Pervez Musharraf to power. As his first foreign visit, he chose to go to Tehran in December of that year. The choice was puzzling, but the intention behind it was clear: as Pakistani military coup makers before him had, he wanted to strengthen the legitimacy of his rule. However, during his nine years in power, Musharraf never became close to the Iranians.

Things started badly. Bitter Iranian–Pakistani rivalry in Afghanistan was continuing. Musharraf – who agreed for the deposed prime minister, Nawaz Sharif, to be sent into exile in Saudi Arabia – had no quarrel with Benazir Bhutto's and Sharif's previous support for the Taliban. In fact, he argued that such support went beyond domestic Pakistani politics and served the country's strategic interests. In his 2006 memoir, while still in power, he wrote:

> We [Pakistan] have strong ethnic and family linkages with the Taliban. The opponents of the Taliban [were] the Northern Alliance, composed of Tajiks, Uzbeks, and Hazaras. How could any Pakistani government be favorably inclined toward the Northern Alliance? Any such inclination would have caused serious strife and internal security problems for Pakistan.[56]

Musharraf set out to convince a very sceptical world community about the benefits of diplomatically recognizing the Taliban. As he put it, this would have enabled 'collective pressure' on the group for it to change its ways. If Tehran was going to deal with the Taliban, it definitely did not seem prepared to take its cue from Islamabad. Musharraf's problems with the Iranians did not stop there. Mohammad

Khatami, Iran's president – an aspiring democrat of sorts – had misgivings about associating with the military dictator.[57] It would be three years before Khatami accepted Musharraf's invitation to visit Pakistan – and then only after the fall of the Taliban in Afghanistan.

The fall of the Taliban

The al-Qaeda attacks on the United States on 11 September 2001 instantaneously altered the trajectory of the ongoing Afghan civil war. The fortunes of both Iran and Pakistan, the hitherto twin key foreign players in the Afghan conflict, were to experience something of a rollercoaster ride. At first, Tehran was the primary beneficiary of the US actions but it was by no means an idle bystander in what was about to unfold.

As President George W. Bush vowed to annihilate the Taliban for providing sanctuary to the 9/11 al-Qaeda plotters, officials in Tehran sat back and sighed with relief. The imminent US invasion was hugely welcomed across the political spectrum in Iran. It was considered a golden opportunity for Iran to regain what had been lost to the Taliban and its Pakistani–Saudi backers in the 1990s. Only a tiny minority of voices in Tehran bothered to raise the question of a lasting US military presence in Afghanistan, although this issue subsequently became a key concern for Iran.

Mullah Omar dispatched a delegation to gauge Iran's stance. A group of Taliban officials met with their Iranian counterparts on the border, and asked them about Tehran's position should the United States attack Afghanistan. If the Taliban envoys anticipated any sympathy, they were disappointed. The one piece of advice from the Iranians was that the Taliban should abandon the battlefield and 'retreat south'. This left them distraught, as it obviously meant that Iran wanted the Taliban to lose in the clash against the invading Americans.[58] As it turned out, the day after this very meeting the Afghan city of Herat fell to coalition forces in an operation in which the United States and the Iranians closely collaborated.

Unbeknownst to the Taliban delegation, Tehran had by then already agreed to help the US military campaign. It had assented to close its border with Afghanistan, return any US troops forced to land in Iranian territory during the invasion of Afghanistan and proactively ask the Northern Alliance to facilitate the US war against Taliban. Meanwhile,

Iran also pledged to the US to actively work with Pakistan to form a new post-Taliban government in Kabul.[59] In the end, this last point became the only unfulfilled promise that Tehran made to Washington in the staging of Operation Enduring Freedom.

The role of Pakistan was far less clear-cut. Immediately before the US military began its Afghan campaign, the George W. Bush Administration had given Islamabad an ultimatum. Faced with the wrath of the United States, President Musharraf promptly backed Washington – but Pakistan still needed to deal with the legacy of its seven years of support for the Taliban. By some accounts, what followed was an expedient arrangement. In one instance, Pakistani intelligence agents stranded with Taliban fighters in Afghanistan were quietly permitted by the US military to return home. The Pentagon denied that it had cut a deal with Islamabad, but the fact was that Washington desperately wanted Pakistan on its side and was not about to hold Islamabad's prior backing of the Taliban against it.[60]

§

Once the Taliban was militarily routed, the United States again engaged the Iranians. While this temporary collaboration proved tactical in nature, it was definitely worthwhile while it lasted. At the Bonn Conference in December 2001, a gathering to establish the post-Taliban political order for Afghanistan, it was Iran that took the lead in many ways. Pakistan, on the other hand, was largely sidelined. Jim Dobbins, the US special envoy at the conference, found himself working closely with the Iranians. In his assessment, he found them to be by and large helpful to the US agenda.

According to Dobbins the Iranian negotiators were the trailblazers at that conference. They insisted, for example, that the final document to emerge from the conference 'commit the Afghans both to democracy and to cooperation with the international community and the war on terror'. 'No one else had thought of [that],' Dobbins remarked. As far as he could tell, the Iranians had one serious reservation – and that was any mention of the return of King Mohammad Zahir Shah to power in Kabul. The Islamist rulers in Tehran were still hypersensitive to any precedent of toppled monarchs returning to power, given that Iran's own monarchists still harboured similar ambitions.[61]

The situation with the Pakistanis was very different. Members of the Northern Alliance were naturally very suspicious of the Pakistani representative, who very quickly became a lonely figure during the conference. Islamabad had also ill-advisedly sent to the gathering their last ambassador to the Taliban regime, which understandably raised eyebrows among the other emissaries. At the conference, the discord between the Pakistani and Iranian sides was all too evident, but was not allowed to turn into a spoiler.[62]

Unlike the Iranians, who were brought on board to actually help shape a political solution, the Pakistanis were mainly a token presence at the conference. 'They weren't likely to be helpful. We just didn't want them to be unhelpful,' Dobbins later recalled. Still, the 9/11 attacks had fundamentally changed the equation and Washington's resolve, and Pakistan could not stop the outcome of the conference.

In the end, the consensus candidate who emerged at Bonn as Afghanistan's next leader was Hamed Karzai, a 44-year-old congenial Sunni and ethnic Pashtun former anti-Soviet operative. Both the Iranians and the Pakistanis made it clear that Karzai was an acceptable candidate. Later on, the cheerful Iranians dispatched their foreign minister to a still highly volatile Kabul to attend the 22 December 2001 swearing-in ceremony for Karzai. The Iranian Kamal Kharazi became one of only three foreign ministers to attend the festivities. The other two were from Pakistan and India.[63] When Ismail Khan, Tehran's key rebel Afghan ally at the time, dithered on whether to attend Karzai's inauguration in Kabul, Kharazi's aircraft made sure to stop off in Herat on its way from Tehran to Kabul and pick him up. There was to be no doubt about Iran's full support for Karzai.

Tehran had hoped collaboration with the United States in removing the Taliban might continue and even expand into other areas. Dobbins heard first-hand from the Iranians that they were willing to work under US command in order to establish a post-Taliban Afghan national army. From Pakistan's vantage point, such an Iranian–American compromise was tantamount to defeat of its decade-long Afghan strategy aimed at making Islamabad the principal foreign power broker in Kabul.

The Pakistanis, however, need not have worried for long. Within few short weeks of the Taliban's fall, President Bush had rejected all Iranian overtures and, in his January 2002 State of the Union speech, branded Iran as part of an 'Axis of Evil'. Washington instead looked to Pakistan as a partner in Afghanistan. This was akin to the subcontracting of the Afghan policy that Washington had pursued in the 1980s in order to confront the Soviets. By 2004, the George W. Bush Administration made Pakistan into a 'Non-NATO Major Ally', while Tehran remained part of the Axis of Evil.

Pakistan was suddenly at the forefront of the US global campaign against terrorism. This did not make sense in Tehran. The Iranians had abetted the United States in removing a Pakistan-created movement that had hosted al-Qaeda, but now Washington was rewarding Islamabad. To the Iranians, including its then reformist president, the policies of the Bush Administration could only be explained as knee-jerk, anti-Iran reaction.

As Mohammad Khatami later put it, Iran–US relations were now lower than they had been in 1979 when the Shah had been toppled. Iran's collaboration with the United States in Afghanistan was to be short-lived, but Tehran still had no intention of letting Washington make Pakistan the commanding influence in Kabul. The Iranian–Pakistani rivalry in Afghanistan was destined to go on.

CHAPTER 10

2001-PRESENT: AFGHANISTAN, THE ARAB CHALLENGE AND IRAN'S SOFT POWER IN PAKISTAN

On 10 December 2001, Iran's, foreign minister, Kamal Kharazi, arrived with an 18-person, high-level delegation on a three-day visit to Islamabad. The aim was to restore normality in relations and put the last six years of Taliban rule in Afghanistan behind them. The Taliban was now gone, and both sides claimed that nothing stood in the way of improving relations.

Kharazi's counterpart, Foreign Minister Abdul Sattar, was visibly excited. '[The] Taliban are [a] matter of past and shadows that marred our relations do not exist any more. [The] Sun is shining and we should take full advantage of it,' he told Kharazi. Numerous joint ventures, including the multi-billion-dollar Iran–Pakistan gas pipeline that had been left frozen, could now be revived. Kharazi, too, was joyful: 'Relations between Pakistan and Iran are back to normal and the two sides now share absolute unanimity on all issues including Afghanistan.'

It was here during this summit that the two sides again paid lip service to a common understanding about Afghanistan. A decision was made to establish a joint Iranian–Pakistani committee for the reconstruction of Afghanistan under the UN Development Program (UNDP) and other international aid agencies. This public posture casually omitted to mention that whereas Iran had wheeled and dealed with the Americans, the Pakistani delegate in Bonn had in effect been shunned. In Islamabad, Sattar put on a smile and – for now – let bygones be bygones.

An early post-Taliban duel

As Kamal Kharazi was in Islamabad, his nephew was a few hundred kilometres east in Kabul. Sadeq Kharazi was the deputy foreign minster at this time. A graduate from New York University, he had been Iran's Ambassador to the United Nations from 1989 until 1995. His appointment to the United Nations at the tender age of 26 had much to do with his family background. Not only was his father a prominent ayatollah, but Sadeq's sister had married into the household (*bayt*) of Iran's supreme leader, Ayatollah Khamenei. His bedrock was solid, but his politics were not always to the liking of traditionalists in Tehran.

At the fall of the Taliban, Sadeq Kharazi was dispatched to Afghanistan to see the situation first-hand. Kharazi's team arrived in an aircraft belonging to Iran's Revolutionary Guards, as there were no commercial airline connections. They arrived at Bagram Airbase, north of Kabul, and from there boarded a Russian-made helicopter which took them to the Afghan capital. Sadeq Kharazi recalled paying visits to Afghan ministries in offices often with no windows, electricity or furniture.[1]

Nearly a quarter of a century of war had pulverized Afghanistan. The awestruck Iranian delegation included representatives from various governmental ministries and members of the Iranian Parliament. Meetings were held with all the top Afghan officials who were in town. While these Iranian representatives were in Kabul scouting, there were those back in Tehran who remained sceptical. Iran's leading hard-line newspaper, *Kayhan*, went public and asked why Kharazi was in Afghanistan on a haphazard mission that looked likely to only expedite US interests in Afghanistan. This kind of indictment of Kharazi, and the reformist government that he belonged to, was by now a routine affair in Tehran in the midst of the political struggle between hard-line and reformist factions. In fact, Kharazi's mission was anything but haphazard.

Back in 1989, when the Soviets left Afghanistan, Tehran had taken its eye off the ball. The Pakistanis and their Saudi backers had then swiftly filled the vacuum, a move which culminated in the rise of the Taliban. Sadeq Kharazi's hasty stopover in Kabul in that lonely winter of 2001 was designed to capitalize on the years of sponsorship that Tehran had provided to the Northern Alliance, which was now destined to dominate the post-Taliban era in Kabul. And Iran's key rival in Afghanistan was still Pakistan.

§

On his December 1999 visit to Tehran, President Musharraf had formally invited President Khatami to Islamabad. During the tête-à-tête in Sadabad Palace, Khatami graciously accepted the invitation. It would take him exactly three years to make good on his promise. When he arrived, it had been seven years since an Iranian head of state – President Rafsanjani – had visited Pakistan. Unsurprisingly, this hiatus had coincided with their decade of intense rivalry in Afghanistan.

During Khatami's December 2002 visit, the leaders focused on economics and trade. The question of Afghanistan was still impassable anyhow, even though the two sides would not admit this publicly. Economic cooperation made sense: south-west Asia remains one of the least economically integrated regions of the world. Trade volumes between Iran and Pakistan have long been dismal – standing at around $200 million in total for the year 2002, and massively in Tehran's favour thanks to oil exports. In comparison, total Iranian exports worldwide for that year stood at $110 billion.[2]

Pakistani Foreign Minister Khurshid Kasuri, only a handful of weeks into the job, set the tone when he said, 'we have spent 50 years on photo opportunit[ies] and we should take concrete steps to promote economic ties'. As one Iranian official later remarked, the 'absence of political warmth stood in the way'. Somehow, the Iranian official said, 'We cannot work together, even though the potential for trade is very high.'[3]

The 'elephant in the room', Afghanistan, continued to hamper closer relations. Attempts to find tangible common ground were going nowhere. A year before President Khatami's fruitless trip, another top Iranian delegation had also unsuccessfully sought to mend ties. That time, in April 2001, it had been Hassan Rouhani – the future Iranian president, but then the secretary of Iran's Supreme National Security Council (SNSC) – who travelled to Islamabad for talks. He was there specifically to discuss two topics: Afghanistan and trans-border security threats. Javid Husain, the Pakistani ambassador to Tehran who had arranged for Rouhani's trip, was very upbeat.

Husain found Rouhani and his colleagues at the SNSC 'extremely well-informed with deep insight into the strategic issues of the day'. Husain felt that the Iranians now – in the spring of 2001 – 'fully realized the gravity of the situation in Afghanistan and the need for improvement of Pakistan-Iran relations in the best interest of the two countries'. In April of that year, a road map for 'undoing the damage of the past years' was signed. That, however, was not the end of it. As Husain put it, 'the Iranian offer to reach an agreement with Pakistan on the coordination of the Afghanistan policies of the two countries was summarily rejected by Islamabad'.

As so many times before, Pakistan's diplomatic and military–intelligence communities were following different agendas.[4] The Iranian–Pakistani zero-sum race for Afghanistan, which had started in 1989 following the departure of the Soviets, was proving impossible to abandon. Within five months of Rouhani's trip to Islamabad, the 9/11 attacks had occurred, and the Afghan question was hugely transformed. With the Taliban gone, Iran was no longer in need of a political accommodation with Pakistan. Instead of closer cooperation, another point of contention soon emerged. Iran's Baluchistan Province quickly plunged into unprecedented violence. As time went on, Tehran would claim to detect a hidden Pakistani hand behind its Baluch troubles.

Iran's Baluchistan: a tinderbox

By early 2003, a new militant Sunni Baluch group had arrived on the scene in Iran's province of Baluchistan. The group called itself Jundollah (Soldiers of Allah). It claimed that it was fighting for the rights of Iran's ethnic Baluch and minority Sunni population. The Baluch make up roughly 2 million of Iran's 77 million population. They are also part of the country's Sunni minority, at about 10 per cent of the population – although most Iranian Sunnis are found on the opposite side of the country, among ethnic Kurds on the border with Iraq.

Jundollah's uncommonly violent operations and hit-and-run tactics not only brought havoc to the province, but soon loomed as an embarrassing threat that Iran's otherwise gung-ho Revolutionary Guards could not counter. The Revolutionary Guards, constitutionally mandated to protect Iran's frontiers, were put on the defensive like at no other time since the end of the Iran–Iraq war in 1988.

Jundollah's 23-year-old leader, Abdol Malek Rigi, was a daredevil unlike anything the Iranian security forces had encountered in many decades. He taunted the Iranians by posting regular video announcements on the internet, which at times included gruesome treatment of its prisoners – usually made up of young Iranian regular-army conscripts. In June 2005, Jundollah carried out a jihadist-style beheading of a captured Iranian officer.[5] This was a first for Iran, and anxious officials in Tehran began to fear Jundollah as Iran's weak link whose actions could open a Pandora's box, given the country's ethnic and religious diversity. By now, ethnic and sectarian conflict had become commonplace in the region in places like post-Saddam Iraq, and Tehran feared a spillover of this regional radical Sunni resurgence.

Rigi was a member of the Rigi tribe, one of the largest Baluch tribes in Iran and historically one of the most progressive. In 1970, the Rigi tribe had claimed the honour of having Iranian Baluchistan's only Baluch university graduate. Still, many of the country's ethnic Baluch had never felt totally at ease in the Persian-dominated Iran. In the 1960s and 1970s, they had mainly rallied around a leftist, Soviet-leaning and Moscow-backed Baluch separatist agenda. That campaign had necessitated a joint response by Tehran and Islamabad. Zulfikar Bhutto and the Shah of Iran had risen to the task, and much of their common efforts against the Baluch at the time succeeded. Among the Pakistani Baluch, leftist habits had stayed strong; however, different political realities impacting Iran's Baluch since the 1979 revolution had profoundly altered the trajectory of Iranian Baluch ethnic nationalism and political aspirations.[6]

In the 2000s, many Baluch in Iran sought to cling to religion and their Sunni faith as a way of resisting the Shi'a-centric Islamist elite in Tehran. At first, Rigi's foot soldiers adopted Sunni jihadist rallying cries over long-established Baluch nationalist slogans, and often clung on to al-Qaeda-type black flags over the leftist insignia of yesteryear. Jundollah's adoption of radical Sunni Islamism, inherently anti-Shi'a, did not emerge out of the blue. In fact, the group's birth and outlook was largely shaped by events and like-minded organizations across the border. The young Abdol Malek Rigi had himself first studied in a madrassa in the small Pakistani town of Mashkel. From Mashkel, Rigi had entered the Binori Town seminary in Karachi, which happened to have also been the starting point for many future Afghan Taliban officials.[7] Here, he was indoctrinated in puritan Sunni ideas and, by some accounts, first joined Lashkar-e Jhangvi, one of Pakistan's premier anti-Shi'a terrorist groups.[8]

Despite the jihadist cloak, on home turf Jundollah claimed merely to fight for socio-economic justice and equal treatment of Sunni Muslims. It avoided any overt association with extremist jihadists in Pakistan or the Taliban in Afghanistan. The group even denied that it had any secessionist aspirations. This was a wise step. Thanks to widespread poverty and general alienation, the Jundollah 'brand' for a while took off among Iranian Baluch. The province was already massively plagued by common banditry associated with the drug trade and other smuggling. It was in this explosive context that Jundollah was born.

As Rigi and his unknown number of militiamen – probably numbering in the few hundreds at most – continued to stage a string of high-profile assassinations and kidnappings of Iranian military personnel and officials in the Iran–Pakistan border regions, Tehran transferred authority in the province to the Revolutionary Guards. As in 1979 – the last time that the Guards had been given the task of neutralizing anti-government elements in this far-flung province – they adopted a militaristic approach. The strategy failed, and tanks and other heavy armour quickly proved inappropriate for the task of combatting Jundollah's violent campaign.

The Revolutionary Guards then re-evaluated, and focused on two points. First, pursuing cooperation with local Baluch elders and pushing for socio-economic regeneration; second, doing a much better job of monitoring the border with Pakistan given that after nearly all hit-and-run attacks Jundollah's fighters had slipped over the border and disappeared in Pakistani Baluchistan. The first priority turned out to be the easier of the two tasks.

The Revolutionary Guards' soft-power application was remarkably close to earlier experiments. As under the Shah in the 1970s, the emphasis was on economic cooperation with Islamabad to turn this volatile border region around. A whole host of economic projects were floated, including an Iranian promise to build a $4 billion refinery in Pakistani Baluchistan, something that Shah had promised nearly 30 years earlier.

In November 2004, the governor of Iran's Baluchistan – Hussein Amini – signed an agreement in Quetta with Owis Ghani, his counterpart as governor of Pakistani Baluchistan. They declared their regions 'Twin Provinces'.[9] Some of their promises never left the drawing board, while others materialized. The supply of Iranian electricity to Pakistani border regions still means that they are some of the very few inhabitants of Pakistan who do not experience the acute power shortages common in the rest of the country.

The second task, to better monitor the border jointly with the Pakistanis, has proven much harder. As administrators had before them, the Guards discovered that the Baluch peoples living on both sides of the Iranian–Pakistani border do not recognize international boundaries. Baluch from both sides frequently cross the border for various purposes: to see relatives, celebrate marriages and seek employment among other things.

There was another twist to this matter, and that was the overlap that existed between Jundollah and traditional criminal syndicates that have for long operated with near impunity in this vast and barren region. The improved border control that Tehran sought, in effect threatened cross-border smuggling. The smuggling operations here are immense, lucrative and an important source of income for many of the inhabitants. For example, cheap, and subsidized, Iranian gasoline is smuggled in major quantities on pickup trucks into Pakistan, where the perpetrators make a handsome profit. Ironically, one of the major routes used to carry out this illicit trade is the Taftan–Quetta Highway, which runs from the Iranian border deep into Pakistan and was an American-backed project that, decades ago, had been intended to foster legitimate inter-state trade.[10]

Drug smuggling is another major activity in this region. It is known globally as the 'Golden Crescent', where Afghan opium flows via Iran and Pakistan to international markets.[11] Since Afghanistan became the world leader in the production of illicit opium in 1992, smuggling of drugs has consolidated itself in the tri-border region that links Afghanistan, Iran and Pakistan. A long list of recipients depends on this drug income. The United Nations estimated that the Afghan Taliban alone earns around $125 million per year from the trafficking.[12]

It was not, however, the drug trade but Jundollah's deadly anti-government campaign that forced Tehran into action in the mid-2000s.

Millions of dollars were allocated towards better security in the region, particularly along the border. Iran opted to build one of the world's most heavily fortified barriers. It put up a new fence and a 700 km long, 3 m high concrete wall as part of a barrier system that includes trenches and deep ditches, barbed wire and watchtowers. Pakistan did not object to the wall, and said that it was Iran's right to do this, but Pakistani Baluch political voices complained that the community was being divided from its brethren in Iran.[13]

Jundollah's sanctuary in Pakistan

None of Iran's efforts could subdue Jundollah while the group still had a sanctuary on the Pakistani side of the border. The Iranians kept pushing the Pakistanis for more cooperation, but the Jundollah attacks continued. The group even intensified its campaign after hard-line Mahmoud Ahmadinejad became Iran's president in August 2005. In December 2005, in his first visit to Baluchistan, Ahmadinejad was the subject of an assassination attempt by Jundollah that left three of his security entourage dead.[14]

A few months later, in May 2006, Iran appeared helpless when Interior Minister Mostafa Pur-Mohammadi approached Interpol for help in tracking down Abdol Malek Rigi. Iranian intelligence agencies insisted that Rigi was constantly travelling between Iran's Baluchistan, Pakistan and southern Afghanistan. Tehran now began to publicly charge that elements in the Pakistani state were protecting Rigi.

The Iranians had no illusions. Hossein Mousavian, a close confidant of former President Rafsanjani, was in the early 2000s a member of Iran's SNSC. He recalls, 'Our perception at the SNSC was that Jundollah was working under the protection of the Pakistani intelligence services but that not even the Pakistani intelligence services have total operational control' over the group. On the question of Jundollah, the two-dozen minister-level members of the SNSC were in agreement that Islamabad was duping Tehran. Still, no one in Tehran could pinpoint the exact identity of the Pakistani backers of Jundollah, and Tehran never put forward concrete evidence to corroborate the charges leveled against Islamabad.

The small Iranian town of Pishin sits right on the border with Pakistan. The town's roughly 10,000 inhabitants are overwhelmingly ethnic Baluch. That was exactly the reason behind a high-profile morning visit on 18 October 2009. The well-known guest was a sturdy but genial man by the name of Noor-Ali Shushtari, the deputy commander of the ground forces of Iran's Revolutionary Guards. Since the Guards were given full reign to break Jundollah, Shushtari had become the de facto tsar of Iranian Baluchistan.

Shushtari, a war veteran of the Iran–Iraq conflict, came from a peasant background in north-east Iran and he was in his element in the desolate region he had been tasked to tame. He spearheaded Iran's soft-power strategy to reach out to the ethnic Baluch community, and face-to-face engagement was central to his counter-insurgency approach. As he sat in a large white tent to meet and greet local tribal leaders, a lone suicide bomber who was hiding in the crowd detonated his explosives, killing Shushtari among others. Iranian media quoted officials as claiming that the suicide attacker – a man in his 20s by the name of Abdol-Vahed Mohammad-zadeh – had been a member of the Rigi group and had re-entered Iran from Pakistan the day before, following coaching by his mentors.[15] In the days that followed, Iran's state-run media widely publicized pictures of Mohammad-zadeh's decapitated head but this was of little solace.

The fact was that the attack rattled the Iranians enormously. A total of 41 people were killed, including five senior officers from the Revolutionary Guards. Shushtari was not only a top Guard officer, but also someone whom Iran's supreme leader, Ayatollah Khamenei, personally knew well and whose counter-insurgency mission he had encouraged. The head of the Revolutionary Guards, General Mohammad Ali Jaffari, issued a blanket indictment against the United States, Israel and Britain as the culprits. Jaffari charged that Rigi took his orders 'not only from Pakistan but from [the] intelligence services of Britain and the US'.[16]

The Iranians soon zeroed in on the role of Pakistan and its Persian Gulf Sunni Arab allies – more specifically, the Saudis and the United Arab Emirates. The Pakistanis – at least in public – took the charges on the chin. Pakistani Foreign Minister Mehmood Qureshi said: 'Pakistan will help [Iran] and support them in unearthing the people responsible.'[17] The Iranians, however, were far from convinced. In the eyes of Tehran, statements made by Pakistani politicians did not amount to much. It was the Pakistani intelligence services that were most probably handling Jundollah, and they did not answer to politicians such as Foreign Minister Qureshi and his ilk.

The truth was that Pakistan's intelligence services and its powerful military had for some time been incensed by Tehran's growing ties with India. This reality led to an Iranian perception that Jundollah was Pakistan's 'payback'. Among Islamabad's list of grievances against Iran was the charge that Tehran was giving India a free hand to stage anti-Pakistan operations from Iranian Baluchistan. While Iran had been wrestling with the Jundollah attacks, the Pakistani authorities had had to tackle anti-government violence at the hands of groups such as the Baluchistan Liberation Army, which Islamabad judged to be an Indian pawn.

As argued by a paper from the Institute of Strategic Studies in Islamabad – the country's premier think tank – Pakistan has 'long been complaining about the goings-on at the string of consulates established by New Delhi close to Pakistan's borders'. The paper quoted a US analyst who had visited the Indian Consulate in the Iranian city of Zahedan and assessed that the Indians were not 'issuing visas as the main activity'.[18] The implication of such analyses out of Islamabad was that Tehran and New Delhi were somehow hand-in-hand in destabilizing Pakistan, even though this was rarely said so bluntly.

Iran, the CIA, al-Qaeda and Mossad

After the attack in Pishin, Tehran ratcheted up the pressure on Pakistan. Senior Revolutionary Guards commanders lead the campaign. 'Jundullah [sic] relies on the support and facilitation of provincial Pakistani authorities to be able to manage its cross-border logistical operations,' one senior commander alleged. On 16 December 2009, the Iranian press reported that Tehran had presented evidence to Islamabad that showed 'links between Pakistani intelligence services' and Jundollah.[19] A few days later, Mohammad Pakpour, the commander of the Islamic Revolution Guards Corps (IRGC) Ground Forces and Shushtari's superior, came out fighting. 'It is intolerable for Iran,' he said, 'that terrorists are able to use a neighboring state

[Pakistan] as a sanctuary.' He then made a public pledge that 'the Revolutionary Guards will definitely take revenge'.[20] The stakes had never been this high.

The bruised Guards leadership at times seemed to warn not only the Pakistanis but Iran's own diplomatic corps as well. 'The Foreign Ministry of Iran has to pressure Islamabad to disband Jundullah [sic] or accept Iran to enter that country to do the job,' the IRGC subsequently threatened. As part of this posturing, the Guards made threats to unilaterally cross the border and hit Jundollah bases inside Pakistan with missiles regardless of Islamabad's feelings on the matter. The notion that Iranian armed forces would overrun a nuclear-armed Pakistan uninvited was less outlandish than it might first appear. At the time there had been at least one example of such an armed incursion, in 2006, and more such surprise incursions have occurred since.[21]

Officials in Islamabad repeatedly denied the charges of complicity. However, given the Byzantine character of the Pakistani state, collusion with Jundollah – at least, by certain elements in Pakistan – could never be entirely ruled out. Such suspicions about Pakistani complicity were heightened by the way in which the long-time fugitive leader of Jundollah, Abdol Malek Rigi, was suddenly arrested by the Iranians in February 2010, only a few months after the Pishin attack and the pledge of the Revolutionary Guards to avenge the death of Shushtari.

Rigi was on board a flight from Dubai to Bishkek, the capital of Kyrgyzstan, when the commercial aircraft he was travelling in was forced to land once it entered Iranian airspace. According to the official version of events, two Iranian F-14 fighter aircraft were dispatched to force the passenger airliner to land, and it did so only after they repeatedly fired warning shots.[22] After some seven years on the run, Iran's most-wanted man was unceremoniously arrested. One news outlet linked to Iran's Revolutionary Guards said: 'Rigi who was protected by [Pakistan's] ISI lobbies and supported politically and financially by America and Saudi Arabia never for a second thought he would be captured by Iran's intelligence service.'[23]

While Tehran hailed the arrest as a major victory for its intelligence services, many accused Pakistan of having handed Rigi over to reduce tensions with Tehran following the growing threats by the Iranians.[24] As one prominent Pakistani scholar on militant groups put it: 'Rigi could not have been captured without Pakistani cooperation.'[25]

This theory that Rigi's arrest had been made possible due to some kind of arrangement between the Iranian and Pakistani intelligence services gained more momentum soon afterwards. The circumstances were made even more intriguing when al-Qaeda was suddenly thrown in the mix. A couple of weeks after Rigi had been apprehended, Iran managed to secure the release of one its diplomats who had been kidnapped in November 2008 in Pakistan as he was commuting to his workplace. Heshmatollah Attarzadeh, a diplomat at the consulate in Peshawar, had been in the successive hands of different, unknown abductors for 17 months before he was freed.

The Iranians had, throughout his captivity, claimed that Islamabad had not been forthcoming in cooperating to free Attarzadeh. Reports in the Arab media, however, made the case that the Iranian diplomat had not been rescued but exchanged in a deal with al-Qaeda. These Arab reports suggested that Sulaiman Abu Ghaith – an al-Qaeda spokesperson, and once a right-hand man of Osama Bin Laden, who had been in Iranian custody since 2002 – was reportedly released by Tehran in the deal.[26] There is otherwise no information available about the role that Pakistani services played in the affair or in the exchange that ended the Attarzadeh affair, but the episode was tantalizing to observers.

Meanwhile, the arrest and subsequent execution of Rigi in June 2010 did not spell the end of Jundollah's attacks, which have since continued. The Iranians also sought to link Jundollah with an alleged broader Western plot to tap into Baluchistan as the volatile underbelly of Iran, and thereby destabilize the government in Tehran. The scale of any possible US collusion with Jundollah is still unknown. Nonetheless, the George W. Bush Administration had, in late 2007, asked the US Congress for a $400 million budget for covert operations against Tehran that included support for various Iranian opposition groups.[27]

Other sources claim that the Israeli intelligence service, Mossad, was the Western service most dedicated to Jundollah's cause.[28] Anonymous senior US intelligence officials leaked to the press that Israeli agents were passing themselves off as CIA when trying to appeal to Jundollah fighters. In any case, widespread speculation and uncertainty about the identity of Jundollah's foreign benefactors helped Islamabad's plea of innocence. After all, Tehran had never been able to pinpoint the identity of Jundollah's Pakistani backers. More importantly, Tehran never looked to burn any bridges as far as Pakistan was concerned. Iran

had enough adversaries to contend with, and had no need to open up a
new front to its east.

§

With the coming of Barack Obama's administration in 2009, Washington
soon took concrete steps. In November 2010, the US Department of State
designated Jundollah a foreign terrorist organization.[29] President Obama
even went public with this US policy and in denouncing Jundullah's
'cowardly acts'.

A fact little mentioned in Tehran was that the Americans were not
indifferent to lawlessness in this south-eastern corner of Iran. Jundollah
militants and Baluch smugglers were known to take recruits and weapons
to the Taliban and al-Qaeda only a couple of hundred kilometres further
north in Afghanistan, where the US military was bogged down in counter-
insurgency operations. Rigi was a known associate and ideological
soulmate of Baitullah Mehsud, the leader of the Pakistani Taliban, who
was killed in a US drone attack in August 2009.[30] To Washington,
Jundollah was an offshoot of the same violent Sunni jihadist ideology that
US troops were battling from the Horn of Africa to Iraq to Afghanistan.
Still, no one could tell for sure if Washington saw Jundollah's jihadist
associations as preventing it from becoming an instrument against the
government in Tehran.

§

Jundollah never justified its killing of Iranian Government troops on
sectarian grounds. Nor has the group ever indiscriminately attacked
non-state targets such as civilians. However, Jundollah's Pakistani
kindred souls – groups such as the Pakistani Taliban and Lashkar-e
Jhangvi – were indiscriminate in their attacks against the Shi'a
minority in Pakistan. Hatred for Shi'as and for Iran was, in the eyes
of Pakistan's Sunni extremists, interchangeable – two sides of the
same coin.

As militant sectarianism in Pakistan grew as a phenomenon, a
corridor of sectarian bloodshed cut across from Pakistan to Iran.
Symbolically, Pakistani Shi'a travelling to Iran on religious pilgrimage
have become easy targets, leaving hundreds dead in recent years.
In 2012, a total of some 400 Shi'as were killed in sectarian attacks in
Pakistan. Of those, 152 were killed in the country's sparsely populated

Baluchistan Province.[31] Most of the killings were at the hands of the Lashkar-e Jhangvi, Jundollah's Pakistani counterpart.[32]

One of the hardest-hit towns was Quetta, the provincial capital of Pakistani Baluchistan and home to a sizeable Shi'a and ethnic Hazara community. In Quetta, Iran's religious and cultural influence are perhaps more visible than anywhere else in Pakistan. Here, in this distant corner of the country, the Iranians have always suspected that local Pakistani security forces deliberately refuse to confront extremist Sunni groups.[33]

The Iranians were not alone in this assessment. In September 2012, Human Rights Watch concluded, 'Sunni militant groups such as the ostensibly banned Lashkar-e Jhangvi (LeJ)' had operated with 'widespread impunity across Pakistan while law enforcement officials looked the other way'.[34] 'Some Sunni extremist groups are known to be "allies" of the Pakistani military, its intelligence agencies, and affiliated paramilitaries, such as the [Pakistani] Frontier Corps,' the rights organization concluded.[35] The behaviour of the Pakistani security forces only deepened suspicions. On 30 August 2012, the police in Lahore arrested the leader of Lashkar-e Jhangvi – Malik Ishaq – as he was returning from Saudi Arabia, but only to release him again.[36] Within only few months, LeJ would carry out another deadly bombing against the Shi'a of Quetta, which left some 90 people dead.[37]

A common view in Tehran is that the attacks on the Pakistani Shi'a in Quetta and elsewhere in Pakistan are sanctioned as a way of containing Iran's influence. Nonetheless, within the borders of Pakistan, Iran's influence is not limited to single pockets. What complicates the nation's role is Tehran's propensity to focus on spreading and defending Shi'a Islam in order to gain authority among Pakistan's large Shi'a minority. This approach was always going to be a double-edged sword, given rising sectarian tensions in Pakistan.

Iran and the Pakistani Shi'a

Since the 9/11 attacks and Pakistan's participation in the US-led war on terrorism, Islamabad has periodically banned militant Islamist and sectarian groups. President Musharraf himself has said that 'the greatest danger to [the Pakistani] nation is not external, it is internal'.[38] During his nine-year rule, the frequency of attacks by extremist groups inside Pakistan grew noticeably. Much of the violence was sectarian. What began under Zia ul-Haq as a trend had mushroomed into a full-fledged national demon. Between 2003 and 2013, some 3,500 Pakistanis were killed in sectarian attacks across the country.[39]

The menace of Shi'a–Sunni violence is not only a catastrophe for the Pakistani nation, it is also a yardstick to measure the readiness and abilities of Tehran to act as a protector of the Pakistani Shi'a. The Iranian authorities go out of their way to bear the mantle of the global champion of Shi'a Muslims. However, while the plight of Pakistani Shi'as has become a rallying cry for certain elements of the Iranian regime, Tehran's actual actions rarely match its most fervent rhetoric about the suffering of Pakistan's Shi'a.

§

As early as 2007, parts of Iran's state-run media began to describe Parachinar – the Pakistani tribal city, which has experienced great sectarian turmoil – as a 'Second Gaza'. They lamented the situation of the '500,000 inhabitants under siege'. The siege in Parachinar began in 2007, and was attributed to provocative remarks against Shi'as by a local Wahhabi cleric.[40] Iran's Grand Ayatollah Lotfollah S. Golpayegani, a prominent cleric in Qom, became an early advocate of Parachinar's Shi'a. In late 2007, Golpayegani famously told his congregation that in Parachinar they 'cut heads and limbs off the Shia and no one [in Iran] utters a word'.[41]

Without mentioning the Iranian regime explicitly, the ayatollah criticized Tehran's official inaction. Iranians, Golpayegani said, 'do not do as we should [in helping the Pakistani Shi'a] and we will have to answer to God'. Tehran's official silence about Shi'a killings in Pakistan was at times so deafening that figures from elsewhere saw fit to intervene. Grand Ayatollah Ali Sistani, the Iranian-born top Shi'a religious authority in Iraq, encouraged all his brethren to do everything they could to help the Shi'a in Parachinar and elsewhere in Pakistan. In March 2009, the leading Pakistani Shi'a religious figure Ayatollah Basheer Najafi also spoke out. Najafi, who is based in Najaf in Iraq, the epicentre of Shi'a Islam, told a visiting former Iranian president, Ali Akbar Hashemi Rafsanjani, that Tehran ought to back the Pakistani Shi'a out of religious sympathy and not only when political expediency called for it. Najafi is said to have reminded his Iranian visitor that the 'mantle of Shia leadership does not necessarily sit in Iranian hands'.[42] Such apprehensions were not limited to anxious Shi'a clergy.

Nonetheless, Tehran's strategic stance vis-à-vis Islamabad remained intact. Both Iran's supreme leader, Ayatollah Khamenei, and President Ahmadinejad were preoccupied with preventing a complete rupture in relations with Pakistan – particularly over the row about Jundollah. Turning the conditions of Pakistani Shi'a into a bone of contention would undoubtedly have further agitated Tehran–Islamabad relations. This was not a scenario that Iran welcomed, given that it faced regional and international isolation due to its controversial nuclear programme.

§

This reality did not mean that Iran's leaders chose to shun the broader Shi'a political scene in Pakistan. In fact, the Pakistani Shi'a constitute one of the key foreign target audiences for Ayatollah Khamenei's political messages. Today, one of the most important Pakistani Shi'a outfits in this regard is the Imamia Students Organization Pakistan (ISO). The group, founded in 1972, advertises itself as the 'largest student organization in Pakistan', with a nationwide network of some 800 branches. ISO is very public and emphatic about the fact that it considers Khamenei as its spiritual guide. It sees itself as a regional outpost for Iran, and its mission and role in Pakistan as no different from that of the Lebanese Shi'a Hezbollah political–military organization or Iran's Islamist Basij paramilitary force.

In an interview in 2009, the then-ISO leader, Syed Hassan Zaidi, claimed that the organization had a 'supervisory council with 19 members' at the top of its hierarchy, and that this council is directly linked to the office of Ayatollah Khamenei in Tehran. Zaidi said that the ISO had a combined student membership of 18,000–20,000 male and 6,000 female members. Khamenei's ties with the ISO do, in fact, run deep. In the autumn of 1989, shortly after he became supreme leader, Khamenei met a group of ISO activists in Tehran. In his speech to them, he revealed a great deal about the agenda that still lies at the core of his worldview.[43] He spoke of the need for unity in the ranks of the world's Muslims. In particular, he blamed the 'imperialists' (the West) for undermining Muslim unity. Back in 1989, Khamenei said, 'Imperialism and corrupt rulers, in the old and new ages, divided the Muslims and separated the houses [sects of Islam] and made them [Muslims] suspicious of each other.' Fast-forward a quarter of century, and the crux of Khamenei's message to the Shi'a of Pakistan has effectively remained the same.

While Khamenei clearly desires to claim religious leadership over Pakistani Shi'a, he remains reluctant to make his ambitions obvious as he surely anticipates an angry official Pakistani response. In a sense, this kind of discretion has been evident in Khamenei's relationship with the Pakistani Shi'a going back to his first trip to the country in 1986 as Iran's then-president, when he upstaged his host, Zia ul-Haq.

Since Khamenei became supreme leader in 1989, the Shi'a religious linkages between Iran and Pakistan have noticeably shifted away from the *marjas* (the Shi'a clerical 'sources of emulation') of Qom. Now, the bonds appear to be focused on fostering an acceptance among Pakistan's Shi'a Muslims of the Khomeinist concept of the *velayat-e faqih* (rule of the Supreme Jurisprudent). This idea — formulated in the 1960s and 1970s by the late Ayatollah Khomeini, and the bedrock of theocratic rule in Iran today — is still highly controversial, even among pious Shi'as. Iranian state-run religious agencies, which are invariably answerable to the Supreme Leader, are tasked with lionizing the idea of a *velayat-e faqih*, and rendering Ayatollah Khamenei as the unequalled spiritual leader.

The reason for this is basically twofold. First, at the end of the Iran – Iraq war in 1988, Tehran's hands were financially freed to propagate its ideals more vigorously around the world. Khamenei was selected as supreme leader soon afterwards, in June 1989. Second, the relatively young (49-year-old) Khamenei's religious qualifications were still lacking at the time. He opted to first look beyond Iran's borders to establish his name as a *marja*, or source of religious emulation. Because of the considerable size of the Shi'a population in Pakistan (some 20 per cent of the country's 190 million, or about 39 million), and because there are relatively few leading Shi'a religious figures in the country, Khamenei evidently decided that Pakistan was fertile ground for his religious outreach.

In addition to providing funds for Shi'a religious causes in Pakistan, Tehran also sponsors Shi'a religious students from that country to pursue studies in Iran. There are no precise figures for how many Shi'a Pakistanis attend Iranian seminaries, but their presence is prominent. This is also in contrast to the past, when Pakistani Shi'a religious students tended to go for training to Najaf and Karbala in Iraq rather than to Iran. The balance has now tilted towards Iran, thanks largely to the patronage system it has established in Qom, including the availability of stipends.[44] It is therefore unsurprising that many of Pakistan's Shi'a religious figures have become highly vocal and partisan supporters of Khamenei.

Clearly, Khamenei has both the desire and the financial resources at his disposal to cultivate his religious leadership and political influence among Pakistan's Shi'a population. Nonetheless, the Supreme Leader's appeal in Pakistan, and the appeal of Iran more generally, fundamentally depends on the political and security circumstances of Pakistan's Shi'as and the evolving needs of the country's Shi'a population. At the moment, Islamist Shi'a activists in Pakistan can in large numbers turn to Iran for support and patronage. They appear especially inclined to do so now, as violence at the hands of radical Sunni anti-Shi'a (*takfiri*) groups continues unabated.

As a result, while Tehran is careful not to act overtly as an agitator of the Shi'a in Pakistan, or take unilateral action – as in the case of the besieged Shi'a of Parachinar – it does seek to capitalize on the grievances of the Pakistani Shi'a. For example, Khamenei's public comments about Pakistani affairs are routinely peppered with condolences about Shi'a deaths at the hands of extremist Sunni groups such as Lashkar-e Jhangvi.

Invariably, Khamenei pushes two central themes: that Islamic sectarianism is essentially a foreign plot to divide the worldwide Muslim nation, and that local authorities in Pakistan are either collaborators in such schemes or simply do not do enough to bring an end to the violence. Seen in a regional context, Tehran's outreach towards Pakistani Shi'a Muslims is heavily based on its desire to confront what it deems to be Saudi encroachment and the further spread of anti-Shi'a activities by extremist Sunni groups inspired by Saudi-style strict Sunni Islam. This Iranian–Saudi rivalry on Pakistani soil is particularly palpable when Iranian information campaigns explicitly lay the blame on Saudi ideology and policies for violence against Shi'as in Pakistan. This Iranian narrative, however, has many critics, who argue that Tehran is hardly blameless in fuelling sectarian tensions.

Khalid Masood, the former chairman of Pakistan's Islamic Ideology Council, is one such voice. He says that sectarian differences have always existed in Pakistan, but without today's bloodshed: 'As a child I remember Shia and Sunnis quizzing each other's religious practices. But it never ended with violence. We [Sunnis] venerated Imam Ali [the first Shi'a imam] as much as the Shia did.' Those days are long gone. While Masood would not only blame Tehran, he says that the Iranians are not innocent. He recalled the visit of Ayatollah Ahmad Jannati, a top hard-line Iranian regime figure, to Faisal Mosque in Islamabad, a $120 million, Saudi-funded architectural marvel. During the tour of the mosque, Jannati asked, 'Can a Shia imam lead the prayer here some day?'

Masood, a moderate man and by no means a Sunni diehard had to be truthful. 'Yes,' he replied to Jannati, 'When a Sunni Imam can lead the prayer in Tehran.'[45] To this day, the Iranian authorities have refused permission for a large Sunni mosque to be built in the capital Tehran, despite the fact that Iran has itself some 8 million citizens who belong to the Sunni sect. In this sectarian tussle on Pakistan's soil, the Saudis are the other principal guilty party and most Pakistanis readily admit to this fact. General Asad Durrani, the former head of the ISI and himself a former ambassador to Riyadh, calls the anti-Shi'a policies of the Saudis and its funding of extremist groups a 'dangerous game', for which Pakistani society is paying dearly.[46]

§

For the foreseeable future, Tehran will very likely stick with the same policies towards Pakistan's Shi'a that have effectively been in place for the past decade. The Islamic Republic will continue to present itself as the ultimate champion of the global Shi'a, including those living in Pakistan, but it will do so carefully and in a targeted fashion aimed at maximizing ideological influence over ISO and other Pakistani Shi'a Islamist groups who subscribe to the principles of *velayat-e faqih*.

Tehran will attempt to disguise the pursuit of its political objectives as religious outreach, but Iran's influence among Pakistan's Shi'a Muslims should still not be exaggerated. Iran's clerical-led government, and its religious interpretations, are by no means acceptable or appealing to all the Shi'a of Pakistan. Because Tehran's concrete actions often do not match its official rhetoric, even Pakistan's Islamist-minded Shi'as cannot be blamed for quietly questioning the reliability of Tehran as a guardian or benefactor.

Tehran's reticent reaction to the siege of Parachinar is a good example of the kind of caution that so often guides Iranian conduct vis-à-vis Pakistan. In fact, Tehran's support for the Shi'a in Pakistan has become as much, if not more, a product of geopolitical calculation as it is based on religious sympathies or even on promoting a particular Islamist ideology associated with Ayatollah Khamenei himself. This restraint is especially noticeable when compared with Tehran's open-door policy of hosting Shiʻa Islamist activists from the Arab world, who have very often found in Iran not only an ideological sanctuary but also an operational base from which to lash out against political enemies in their home countries. In the case of the Pakistani Shiʻa, Iran has never been this adventurous.

Ongoing rivalry in Afghanistan

On 6 December 2011, a series of devastating attacks brought mayhem to the Afghan cities of Kabul, Mazar-e Sharif and Kandahar, killing 80 people in total. The targets of these attacks were the country's Shiʻa minority. Even by Afghanistan's bloody standards, the incidents were particularly gruesome. The Pakistani sectarian group Lashkar-e Jhangvi quickly claimed responsibility.[47] About six months after the attack, the Afghan Government claimed that it had evidence that Lashkar-e Jhangiv had acted on behalf of 'regional spy agencies' − a clear hint at Pakistan's ISI. The Afghan attorney general, Eshaq Aloko, said that the attack had been planned across the border in Peshawar.[48]

At first, Iran's official state media sought to downplay the sectarian nature of the attacks. Tehran painted the Western media's reaction to the killings as part of a broader agenda of fostering division among Muslims and justifying a Western military presence in Afghanistan by pointing to the continuation of lawlessness in the country.

Behind such headlines, however, Iranian assessments are generally far less conspiratorial. They focus on Pakistan's record as a supporter of militant organizations such as Lashkar-e Jhangvi and Lashkar-e Taiba (another extremist Sunni group), and various smaller offshoot cells.[49] Even before the December 2011 attacks, speculation in Tehran had been rife about whether Iran would again find itself in a violent proxy conflict with Pakistan in Afghanistan, as had been the case in the 1990s. By the late 2000s, as the Western military presence in Afghanistan began to wind down, another power vacuum appeared highly feasible. Intense Iran−Pakistan rivalry is, however, hardly something that Tehran needs right now. Iran is still under unprecedented international isolation thanks to its controversial nuclear programme. It would have to be hard-pressed before it chooses to confront the Pakistani state, either in Afghanistan or by inciting Pakistan's Shi'a population against the Islamabad government.

Playing the sectarian card in Afghanistan is not such a straightforward proposition for Iran as it might appear at first. Zalmay Khalilzad, the former US ambassador to Kabul and someone who has worked closely with various Iranian officials over the years, put it this way: 'Afghan national identity is very strong but sectarianism is undoubtedly gaining ground. But it is not an upfront opportunity for Iran. Playing only to the Shias in Afghanistan means Tehran will cut itself from the Farsi-speaking but Sunni Tajiks.'[50] This is exactly the dilemma that Tehran had back in the 1990s, when it strove to merge a 'rainbow' coalition against the Taliban.

The hope in Tehran is that Islamabad could instead look more favourably towards Iran, as US–Pakistani relations also remain tormented and Islamabad seeks to augment its list of partners. Then again, the Iranians have not forgotten how, back in 1989 and again in 2001, agreements were reached for Iran and Pakistan to refrain from cut-throat competition in Afghanistan only to see the deal scrapped by Islamabad at the 11th hour. The perennial lack of trust continues to shackle relations.

§

Throughout the 2000s, even with hundreds of thousands of US and other Western troops on the ground in Afghanistan, the Iranian–Pakistani rivalry in that country continued unabated. For Iranians on the ground in Afghanistan, Pakistan's ire was closely felt. One such individual was Hossein Sheikh-Zeineddin, a diplomat at the Iranian Consulate in Kandahar, which has over the years been repeatedly attacked by unknown assailants. He says: 'We assumed at first it was the [Afghan] Taliban that was behind the attacks given the past acrimony but we would then get letters from the Taliban saying they were not responsible.' The Taliban would more than once tell the Iranians that the Pakistanis were behind the attacks on Iranian interests in southern Afghanistan, according to Sheikh-Zeineddin: 'When we would send cables back to Tehran and tell the foreign ministry that the Taliban and Mullah Omar were not the same anti-Shia and anti-Iran voices of the 1990s, the reactions were dismissive.' Sheikh-Zeineddin pointed out that Kandahar has always had a Shiʻa minority community, but 'there was no sectarian violence here' previously.[51]

At least to this Iranian diplomat, the idea of Pakistani elements actively targeting Iran was entirely believable: 'Look, Iranian policies [in Afghanistan] were far from perfect. We had serious management issues. Iran failed to reach out to the [ethnic Afghan] Pashtun despite opportunities and common ground that could have been utilized. But even the small successes we had were bad enough in Pakistani eyes.'[52]

To the Pakistanis, Iran had committed the mortal sin of working with India to establish a road linking the Iranian port of Chabahar on the Arabian Sea to the Afghan road network. The Indians financed the 218 km road project, which was completed in 2009 and was heavily motivated to break Pakistan's control over transit routes linking southern Afghanistan to the outside world.[53] This, and other encouragements by Tehran, resulted in Iranian–Afghan trade volumes increasing substantially, from about $500 million in the mid-2000s to $2 billion in 2011.

Afghan exporters now received a 90 per cent discount on port fees in Iran and a 50 per cent discount on warehouse charges, while for the first time Afghan vehicles were issued full transit rights on Iranian roads. As the Shah had sought to achieve in the 1960s and 1970s, Iran strenuously sought to lessen Afghan reliance on Pakistani ports and roads. President Ahmadinejad went as far as telling President Karzai that if the Americans were looking for ways to cooperate with Iran, then a good start could be to stop opposing Iranian infrastructure projects in Afghanistan, and asked Karzai to ask Washington to stop blocking the Iranians from bidding for US-funded projects.[54]

Ahmadinejad's foolhardy call was brushed off, and the United States continued to instead invest more in Pakistani infrastructure efforts to link Afghanistan to the world. Between 2009 and 2012, American funding helped to build over 650 km of roads in Pakistan's tribal areas adjacent to Afghanistan, including a $70 million project to reconstruct a 46 km road between Peshawar and the border town of Torkham.[55] Washington still preferred Islamabad over Tehran.

Instead, the Indian–Iranian partnership to break Pakistan's grip on Afghanistan continued. As part of such efforts, New Delhi continues to be committed to the development of Iran's Chabahar as a strategic alternative to the joint China–Pakistan port of Gwadar about 150 km away in Pakistan.[56] India is anxious about the port in Gwadar because it gives Pakistan and China the option to threaten Indian naval activity and maritime interests in the Persian Gulf and Arabian Sea. The Pakistanis see Chabahar emerging as a road and rail transit hub to serve the landlocked Central Asian states, and this obviously threatens the commercial prospects of Pakistan's Gwadar. The attitudes in Tehran and Islamabad – at least on the quest for prominence in Afghanistan – are still very much one of a zero-sum game mentality.

Musharraf and steering clear of Iran

Despite the efforts of its diplomats to keep close to Iran, the trajectory of Islamabad's regional policy is set by the Pakistani military and intelligence agencies. The latter are not particularly interested in closer ties with Tehran. A good illustration of this was the attitude of Pervez Musharraf, Pakistan's military leader, who ruled from 1999 to 2008.

Despite choosing Tehran for his maiden trip as Pakistan's president, Musharraf made a point of keeping a good distance from the Iranians. Unlike most of the Pakistani leaders before him, he did not see an increasingly isolated Iran able to bring much to the table. Close ties with Iran were also a liability given that Musharraf's enthusiasm was geared towards the United States, Iran's foremost adversary, and the Persian Gulf Arab countries. Musharraf opted to steer clear of Tehran.

In his memoir, *In the Line of Fire*, Musharraf curiously had very little to say about Iran. He devotes no more than a single paragraph to this western neighbour, which only three decades earlier had been promoted by his predecessors as a partner for a political confederation. Musharraf – born into a Muslim family in New Delhi in 1943 but with much of his childhood spent in Turkey, where his diplomat father had been posted – did not have any close emotional attachment to an Iran that had been in the hands of the ayatollahs for most of his professional life. He did not have strong memories of Iranian support for Pakistan in its 1965 and 1971 wars with India, and this was reflected when he wrote about the topic in a cautious and aloof fashion:

Iran is our important neighbor. Our effort has always been to have close, cordial relations, but in reality we continue to have our ups and downs. The nuclear standoff between the US and Iran, our separate relations with India, and our stands on Afghanistan do create complications in our bilateral relationship. Quite clearly we have to understand each other's sensitivities in order to forge the strong friendship that our geography and our history dictate.[57]

He was far warmer towards the Arab countries of the Persian Gulf:

In the Gulf, besides maintaining cordial relations with all states, Pakistan has always been very close to Saudi Arabia and the United Arab Emirates. These very special relationships continue. I have strengthened them through my personal contacts with the leaders of both countries.[58]

It was not just practical factors – such as vast Pakistani expatriate remittances from the Gulf States – that pushed Musharraf away from Tehran. He called himself a 'moderate Muslim' and advocated a soul-searching renewal at home and in the Islamic world. In speaking to Western audiences he sought to tantalize with the question of Israel, that forbidden fruit in the Islamic world. 'I have always wondered what we [Pakistan] stand to gain by this policy of anti-Israeli stance,' he wrote in his memoir, published in 2006, 'It is a given that Israel, besides being the staunchest ally of the US, has [a] very potent Jewish lobby there that could wield influence against Pakistan's interests.'[59] He took concrete steps to back up such sentiments.

On 17 September 2005, Musharraf had in fact become the first head of state from Pakistan to speak to a US Jewish audience. He told members of the American Jewish Congress: 'Pakistan has no direct conflict or dispute with Israel. We pose no threat to Israel's security. We trust that Israel poses no threat to Pakistan's national security.' The only other time a Pakistani leader had publicly been so warm and sympathetic toward the Jewish state was back in 1992, when Prime Minister Nawaz Sharif – after India recognized Israel – was believed to have contemplated establishing relations with the country.

In New York in the autumn of 2005, Musharraf received half a dozen standing ovations from his Jewish–American audience. He responded: 'What better signal for peace could there be than the opening of embassies in Israel by Islamic countries like Pakistan?' Musharraf's attempt to build up the image of Pakistan as a progressive Muslim country and responsible international actor was a stretch to say the least, but his timing was nonetheless very fortunate. Only a few hours earlier, Iran's then brand-new President Ahmadinejad not only lambasted Israel but went on to even doubt the historical truth of the Holocaust. That evening, Musharraf's speech must have been like a fresh breath of air in New York. However, this was not an attempt by the Pakistanis to capitalize on the blundering Ahmadinejad. Jack Rosen, the chairman of the American Jewish Congress, later revealed that his organization had for three years been working towards reestablishing ties between Israel and Pakistan.[60]

These very different speeches by Musharraf and Ahmadinejad that day showed Islamabad as searching for international respectability while a new Islamist–populist breed in Tehran looked for ways to break down the global order that they claimed to be unjust. How the tables had turned. In 1960s and 1970s, it had been the Shah of Iran who resisted Islamabad's attempts to make the state of Israel into the *bête noire* of the region. It did not much matter whether Musharraf's gambit was opportunistic or not. What counted was that Tehran and Islamabad were failing to agree even on one of the most basic common denominators in the Islamic world.

Zardari, another Shi'a, comes to power

President Musharraf's rule came to an abrupt end in August 2008. The man who succeeded him was Asif Ali Zardari, the ostentatious and controversial husband of the assassinated Benazir Bhutto. Zardari would become the first democratically elected president in the history of Pakistan to complete his five years in office, but his arrival at the Aiwan-e-Sadr, the enormous white marble presidential palace in Islamabad, unsettled ties with the Gulf Arabs. In the larger picture of Iranian–Arab and Shi'a–Sunni rivalry unfolding across the region in the 2000s, Zardari was viewed by the Gulf Arabs as a plausible instrument in the hands of Tehran. He was, after all, a Shi'a Muslim.

Among the Gulf Arabs, the Saudis early on made it known that they did not like or trust President Zardari. In him, they saw a Shi'a and feared that he was in bed with the Iranians. As the foreign minister of the United Arab Emirates, Sheikh Abdullah bin Zayed, told US Secretary of State Hillary Clinton in April 2009, the Saudis feared 'a triangle in the region between Iran, the [Shi'a] Maliki government in Iraq, and Pakistan under Zardari'.[61] The Saudis had been petrified since the fall of Saddam Hussein in 2003 – a professedly 'Sunni' leader – and sensed an Iranian hand everywhere they looked. This latest Saudi hint of a Shi'a 'triangle' followed the 2004 warning by King Abdullah of Jordan about the forging of a Shi'a 'crescent' from Lebanon to Iraq to Iran. Sunni Arab leaders now saw the region's Shi'a Muslims on the political rise, and they openly opposed it. Pakistan was a key battleground, with its nearly 190 million people divided between a Sunni majority and a Shi'a minority.

The Saudi King Abdullah told a visiting General Jim Jones – President Obama's national security advisor – that Zardari was a 'rotten head' that infected the entire Pakistani body. Riyadh would let it be known that they preferred another strong military man to take over in Islamabad.[62] Riyadh's dislike of Zardari quickly created financial consequences for Pakistan. Saudi aid in 2008, the year Zardari took the presidency, dropped to $300 million – considerably less than in previous years.[63] Officials in Islamabad were convinced that the Saudis deliberately curtailed the aid to hasten Zardari's fall.

In Washington, Saudi Arabia's ambassador, Adel Al-Jubeir, put the Americans on notice: Riyadh will not let Pakistan fall into Tehran's lap in the way that President George W. Bush's unseating of Saddam had turned Iraq into an Iranian vassal. The Saudis had been very close to successive Pakistani leaders – from Ayub Khan in the 1960s onwards – and Al-Jubeir boldly reminded the Americans: 'We in Saudi Arabia are not observers in Pakistan, we are participants.'[64] Riyadh's line stayed constant: 'stability in Pakistan', they argued, 'is an essential strategic matter' for Riyadh. By stability, the Saudis meant the status quo – and they certainly had no desire to see Iran's wings spreading any further.

The words of Al-Jubeir, a confidant of King Abdullah, were a glimpse into the calculations made by the Saudi monarch and the country's intelligence service, which together set the course on relations toward Pakistan and also Afghanistan. Based on leaked US diplomatic cables, Al-Jubeir did not openly mention the Iran or sectarian angles in deciding Saudi support for Islamabad. But he did not have to do this. The intention was clear as day, and the fires of sectarian violence that had engulfed the entire region were now burning intensely in the battleground country of Pakistan.

In the end, Riyadh's aversion to Zardari only helped to push his government in Tehran's direction. In March 2009, Presidents Zardari and Ahmadinejad signed a new $7.5 billion draft agreement for the supply of Iranian natural gas. This was just another attempt to resuscitate a deal that had by now been under planning for over a decade, but the step was still symbolically significant. The agreement was finalized in February 2010. Interestingly, this came only days after the high-profile arrest of Abdol Malek Rigi, the leader of Jundollah who had often hidden on the Pakistani side of the border. Had Tehran and Islamabad cut a deal? Needless to say, speculation along these lines was rife at the time.

Zardari's dealings with the Iranians might have enraged the Saudis and other anti-Iran Arabs, but there was no popular blowback at home.[65] General Pakistani opinion of Iran remained overwhelmingly positive – globally the most positive view of Iran, with a 76 per cent approval rating according to a survey from 2012.[66] As had occurred before in 1979 and again in the late 1980s, for the Pakistanis the question of Iran morphed into leverage, if not a bargaining chip, against not only the Gulf Arabs but also the United States.

Zardari, too, plays the 'Iran card' for Washington

Very soon afterwards, US–Pakistani relations were in tatters following the May 2011 killing of Osama Bin Laden in Abbottabad. Zardari paid two quick successive visits to Tehran in June and July of that year. The Pakistani press reported that the visits came 'despite serious reservations by Saudi Arabia'. It seemed Zardari was not afraid to ruffle some Saudi feathers; he felt that geopolitical circumstances demanded it. There were more to these visits than met the eye. A senior Pakistani official told the press that the main focus of Zardari's talks with Ahmadinejad would rest on the situation in Afghanistan and 'Washington's ambitions to establish six military bases in Afghanistan.'[67] The timing of Zardari's visits, and the press leak by the Pakistanis about their purported purpose, seemed to be an orchestrated effort to generate some anguish in Washington about Islamabad's intention vis-à-vis Iran, a country the United States was desperately seeking to quarantine.

There was otherwise no sign whatsoever that Tehran and Islamabad were in any way engaging to reach a common understanding about

Afghanistan once the US military presence came to an end in that country.[68] The Iranians were acutely aware that the Pakistani military–intelligence apparatus – which they deemed the policy maker on the Afghan question – was playing them as a card to keep the United States from abandoning Islamabad following the outbreak of fury in Washington around Bin Laden's long-time sanctuary in Pakistan.[69] Nonetheless, the Iranians played along. They, too, wanted to give the impression of a blossoming partnership with Islamabad in an attempt to demonstrate that Tehran was not isolated despite Washington's best efforts.

In the midst of this political theatre, there were moments when official statements made about this purported new-born Iranian–Pakistani friendship came across as excessive. In one instance in February 2012, when Iranian–Israeli hostilities linked to Tehran's nuclear programme were at a peak, Pakistan's High Commissioner in London told the British newspaper the *Sun* that: 'Pakistan would be left with no option but to support Iran if Israel attacks it.' The senior diplomat warned, 'We have a Shia population in Pakistan who will not take it lying down.'[70] The state-run media in Iran naturally treasured such pledges in Tehran's defence, and splashed the announcement as big news.

Behind the scenes, however, the greater part of the Pakistani view on Tehran was quite different. Iran's nuclear programme was a case in point. In public, officials in Islamabad steered clear of the international controversy. In private, US diplomats in Islamabad heard about suspicions and fears that the Pakistanis harboured, and that Pakistan 'does not want an additional nuclear-armed state in the region'.[71] By claiming to have its back to the wall, Pakistan subsequently abstained from voting to sanction Iran in 2009.

The American–Iranian–Pakistani triangle

On 4 August 2013, Hassan Rouhani became the Islamic Republic of Iran's seventh president. The election of this mid-ranking Shi'a clergyman – who had been a long-time regime insider, and yet showed reformist tendencies – generated ample excitement inside Iran and beyond. On foreign policy, Rouhani pledged to overhaul Tehran's relations with the world. In that spirit, he promised to make improvements in relations with Pakistan a top foreign-policy priority in his administration.

Many in Tehran and Islamabad see such pledges as commendable, but are nonetheless unconvinced. As the history of Iran–Pakistan relations since 1947 undoubtedly demonstrates, the sceptics have a point. These two giants of south-west Asia – with a combined population of some 270 million people – have a chequered history, which includes, as in the 1990s, violent rivalry for influence in Afghanistan.[72] This conflict could be repeated, given that most international forces were set to withdraw from that country by the end of 2014 and a likely power vacuum would prove irresistible for Afghanistan's neighbours, Iran and Pakistan. In the meantime, Rouhani will have to square off with Pakistan's re-elected Prime Minister Nawaz Sharif, a man whose past political track record shows little sign of enthusiasm for Iran.[73]

In the midst of the complexities of Iranian–Pakistani relations, the attitude of the United States is an added complicating factor. Washington is vehemently opposed to the one key strategic project – the planned multi-billion-dollar natural-gas pipeline – that could perhaps bring Iran and Pakistan closer together. However, to suggest that Washington is the only drag on Iranian–Pakistani relations is to ignore the history of suspicion and competition between the two countries.

On the question of closer ties with Iran, Pakistan is still on the fence. Much will depend on other foreign policy priorities, and particularly the state of its relations with Washington and the Persian Gulf Arab countries. During US Secretary of State John Kerry's visit to Islamabad on 1-2 August 2013, an agreement was reached between Islamabad and Washington to resume partnership negotiations. This was suspended in 2011, after relations hit a new nadir following the unilateral US military raid to capture Osama Bin Laden outside Islamabad. From Iran's vantage point, the resumption of US–Pakistan talks is significant in several ways. One important aspect is linked to Pakistan's ongoing need for US financial and military assistance.

However, the Pakistanis have made it clear that the present scale of US aid is not sufficient to rescue them from the energy crisis that they face, and which is projected only to worsen with time. They reportedly told Kerry point-blank that the planned $7.5 billion gas pipeline from Iran is critical for Pakistan.

This Pakistani bluster stood out largely due to its timing. The Peace Pipeline, as the project had initially been dubbed, has had many false starts since it was first seriously mooted in 1994. Acute power shortages in Pakistan have been a reality throughout this time, which raised questions about Islamabad's sudden dogged stance in the face of breaching international and US sanctions against Iran. The enormous economic scale of the pipeline enables it to outweigh the trend of recent years, when Tehran's foreign partners have abandoned projects in droves due to US pressure. This is exactly why Tehran enthusiastically showcases the project as an example of American failure to isolate it. This Iranian line, however, is mostly public-relations bluster.

The many sceptics in Tehran see Pakistan playing a shifty game, aimed at turning the pipeline into further leverage in its own transactional relationship with Washington. The fear is that if and once the United States sweetens its counter-offers, Islamabad will rethink its commitment to the pipeline. In the meantime, the Pakistanis are seen to be maximizing on Tehran's isolation.[74]

This decidedly Machiavellian picture has some elements of truth to it. Islamabad very quickly resumed asking for adjustments to the contract, including a new request to President Rouhani that Iran finance the entire project. Sensing that Islamabad was in many ways asking for a handout, Rouhani's government in December of 2013 let the Pakistanis know that the project was off unless Pakistan could find the $500 million to finance its section of the pipeline.[75]

The bottom line, however, is that should Washington become serious about stopping the pipeline, the Pakistani government and the country's powerful military–intelligence apparatus will not downgrade the strategic relationship with the United States – even with its many contradictions and its ups and downs – for closer relations with Iran. This profound preference for Washington leaves a bad taste in the mouths of Iranian officials, but it has been a constant factor in relations with Pakistan for decades and is hardly a new development.

It is not just the United States that is against the pipeline. Saudi Arabia – Tehran's chief regional rival, and a close ally of Pakistan – also opposes it. Riyadh has its own 'carrots' to dangle in front of the Pakistanis. In May 2013, only days after Nawaz Sharif returned to power, Riyadh agreed to provide its favorite Pakistani politician with $12–15 billion in oil supplies over three years with deferred payment. This sort of bailout is bound to make any Pakistani government at least reconsider the logic of pushing ahead with the Iran pipeline if it stands in the way of greater benefits.

The close personal ties that Sharif has with Saudi Arabia – where he lived in exile for eight years – will surely also be one of President Rouhani's challenges as he sets out to cajole the Pakistanis.[76] However, it would be a mistake to exaggerate the role of individuals in this relationship. If the political storm around the pipeline project has shown anything, it is that Iranian–Pakistani ties are inherently of secondary importance both for Tehran but also Islamabad. After all, the scope and intensity of Iran's interest in the project was dictated by a lack of alternatives, while Islamabad has dragged its feet in the hope that a better counter-offer is just around the corner.

In the big picture of relations, their ties have lacked depth for some time. Since Iran's revolution of 1979, Islamabad has without doubt prioritized its ties to the US and the oil-rich Arab countries of the Persian Gulf region over Tehran. From Islamabad's perspective, an isolated and often cash-strapped Iran could not provide much in terms of diplomatic and material support as Pakistan pursued its regional ambitions. In its overarching rivalry with India, generous financial assistance from the Persian Gulf Arab countries and US diplomatic muscle and supplies of arms and other military assistance have been of much more use to Islamabad than anything Iran has been able to offer.

It had been quite different before 1979 during the era of the Shah of Iran, when Pakistan and Iran, as allies in the anti-communist camp led by the United States, experienced genuine collaboration on different levels. In hindsight, there is no doubt that the 1960s and the first half of the 1970s were the heyday of Iranian–Pakistani partnership. Throughout the 1980s, the two countries had, at best, cordial ties, but never too intimate. The geopolitical break in relations came over the issue of Afghanistan. It happened precisely when Sharif had his second stint as prime minister from 1997 to 1999. In May 1997, at a time when Tehran was on a war footing against the Taliban, it was the Sharif Government that extended diplomatic recognition to the band of Afghan diehard Sunni extremists around Mullah Mohammad Omar.

To the deep dismay of Tehran, Islamabad's support for the Taliban in Afghanistan peaked during the Sharif Government. As a former Pakistani Ambassador to Tehran put it in Islamabad, 'this was the bottom in Iran-Pakistan relations'. This point is not lost on the Rouhani Administration as it looks to gauge this third Sharif Government. If the natural-gas pipeline has the potential to bring Iran and Pakistan closer, the anticipated jockeying for influence in post-2014 Afghanistan could easily pull them apart – as it did in the second half of the 1990s.

The 'elephant in the room' is the lack of trust that exists in relations. Both Iranian and Pakistani officials admit to this, albeit quietly. On paper, Iran and Pakistan are engaged in a number of efforts designed to further political and economic integration – from membership in the regional Economic Cooperation Organization, to a host of bilateral agreements on trade, to security cooperation. There is, however, relatively very little to show for all of this – and depth in the relationship is still missing. For example, bilateral trade levels have always been dismal – standing at about $1 billion per year. By comparison, Iran's trade volume with the considerably smaller and more impoverished Afghanistan is greater, at about $2 billion per year. These are the kind of hard facts that will continue to stare the Rouhani and Sharif governments in the face.

US opposition to the Iran–Pakistan pipeline is, in the short term, the most visible test for Tehran and Islamabad. Officials in both countries will paint Washington as the spoiler that stands in the way of closer ties. However, to blame the United States for the distance that exists in relations is disingenuous. It also ignores the other underlying conflicts of interest that continue to impede Iranian–Pakistani ties and which are not the making of the United States – or of anyone else for that matter.

EPILOGUE

By October 2014, Iran's nightmare on its border with Pakistan was continuing unabated. After a brief lull over the course of the summer months, violence in the volatile border region was once again on the rise.

Tehran again accused Pakistan of turning a blind eye to cross-border raids by militants operating from its soil – which Islamabad, predictably, strongly rebutted. Despite this latest public falling out, neither Iranian nor Pakistani officials appeared any closer to admitting that this recurrent violence is a symptom of broader underlying problems that continue to mar relations. At its core, as this survey of the last four decades of interaction between Iran and Pakistan illustrates, is the reality of a combination of state-to-state disengagement, conflicting foreign-policy priorities and regional competition that persists in undermining relations between the two largest countries of south-west Asia.

This particular round of hostilities began in the first week of October 2014, after attacks by anti-government militants resulted in the death of four Iranian security personnel. The group that took responsibility – Jaish al-Adl (Army of Justice) – is an ethnic Baluch and Sunni faction that claims to fight for the rights of the people of Baluchistan, which still suffers as Iran's most impoverished province.

Tehran's reaction was to point the finger at outside players. As it had frequently done over the previous decade, Iran maintained that elements in Pakistan, with financial support from Arab states in the Persian Gulf region, sponsor the group as leverage against Iran. The Iranians claimed that they had detected foreign culprits engaged in augmenting subversion in this troubled corner of Iran, in an attempt to make Tehran bleed.

This charge against foreign rivals mirrored exactly the stance that the late Shah had adopted throughout the 1960s and 1970s in dealing with instability in Baluchistan. Back then, the foreign culprits that Iran spotted were the Soviet Union and Iraq – and the Baluch militants of the Shah's days were communist-leaning rather than Islamists, but the same dynamic was otherwise in play. Nor were the Iranians always simply imagining plots hatched between anti-Tehran militants and foreign conspirators. As the *New York Times* put it following an investigation, US intelligence services had at least on one occasion, in 2007, known about an imminent attack inside Iran by Baluch militants. The newspaper claimed, 'the unusual origins and the long-running nature of the United States' relationship with Jundullah are emblematic of the vast expansion of [US] intelligence operations since the terrorist attacks of September 11, 2001'.[1]

Tehran's blunder has been to be overly consumed with the violence arising from Baluch grievances and not interested enough in addressing its underlying causes. Jaish al-Adl is the successor to Jundollah, the militant group led by Abdol Malek Rigi, which the United States designated as a terrorist organization in November 2010.

Jaish al-Adl achieved its big breakthrough with an audacious operation that it carried out in February 2014, when it kidnapped five Iranian border guards. After months of acrimonious negotiations, said to have involved Iranian and Pakistani diplomats and tribal leaders from the border regions, four of the guards were released, but the fate of the fifth is still unknown. However, as this latest attack only eight months later showed, Jaish al-Adel – and Iranian Baluch militancy in general – was not a phenomenon that could be subdued with any quick remedies. Meanwhile, the roots of the failure to tackle cross-border militancy lay in the dysfunctional and wary relationship between the Iranian and Pakistani states.

Following the attack in early October, Brigadier General Hossein Salami, the deputy head of Iran's elite Islamic Revolution Guards Corps (IRGC), warned that if 'any neighboring country fails to fulfill their obligations to protect the border' then Iran would 'have no choice but to act on its own'. This pledge to act unilaterally was carried out on 18 October when some 30 Iranian security forces unilaterally crossed the international border, resulting in the death of a Pakistani Frontier Corps soldier.

Islamabad lodged a 'strong protest' and summoned the Iranian Ambassador, but its overall reaction was predictably restrained. After all, the same Iranian warnings and actions, including a few hot pursuits of militants by Iranian forces on Pakistani soil, had repeatedly taken place over the last decade. This time around, as in earlier such episodes, things went like clockwork.

Pakistan's foreign ministry asked for 'evidence' from Iran that Jaish al-Adl had found sanctuary in Pakistan, and urged Tehran to stop 'externalizing' its problems and focus on fighting militancy at home. In reply, Abdollah Araghi, a senior IRGC commander, told Iran's state television that his forces have documentation demonstrating that militants cross the border to stage attacks. Brigadier General Mohammad Pakpour, the commander of the IRGC ground forces, slammed Islamabad for 'allowing terrorists to use its soil as a platform' to attack Iran. He warned that Pakistan could expect further Iranian unilateral action unless it stopped infiltration by militants. 'Unfortunately,' reported an Iranian news service, 'the Pakistanis have no control over the border {with Iran}, and warned that Iran might "bear terrorist acts to [a] certain threshold" but there is a tipping point.'[2] The unofficial Iranian line, however, was far more incriminating about Pakistan's role.

Despite the rancour, and very predictably, officials from both countries then met on 22 October in Tehran and agreed to increase intelligence cooperation. The dust from this latest round of border skirmishes soon settled, but the underlying factors that feed Iranian–Pakistani tensions will surely continue to keep the two countries considerably apart.

Recrimination by pattern

The cyclical aspect of this state of affairs is by now undeniable. What is surprising is how little attention Iran and Pakistan continue to give to the poor state of relations between them. Security-related incidents are the ones that grab headlines, but it is the underlying political suspicions, geopolitical rivalry and a glaring economic disconnect that are at the heart of troubled Iranian–Pakistani relations.

The combined population of Iran (80 million) and Pakistan (190 million) is about 270 million people, representing a significant economic market, and yet the volume of bilateral trade is dismal. Even before international sanctions took serious effect on Iran in 2011-12, Tehran's trade with Pakistan amounted to $300-400 million per year out of Tehran's $100 billion international trade. In comparison, Tehran claimed trade with China, its biggest commercial partner, of $40 billion in 2013.[3] Iran's immediate neighbours have also found ways to bolster trade ties. Turkey and Iraq have, over the last decade, emerged as key trading partners, with annual trade volumes of $22 billion and $12 billion respectively. Even impoverished Afghanistan does more business with Iran (about $1.5 billion per year) than does Pakistan. In fact, Pakistan's trade volumes with Iran mirrors those of Armenia – by far Iran's smallest neighbour, with a population of only 3 million people. The significance of economic interdependence and trade lies in the fact that it acts as a stabilizing factor in relations, and it is conspicuously absent in Tehran–Islamabad ties.

In the case of Iranian–Pakistani relations, not only is such a stabilizing economic factor missing but the reverse trend is arguably in motion. Instead of facilitating more trade and finding areas of cooperation for mutual benefit, the Iranian side has opted instead to build its first physical frontier wall on the 909 km border with Pakistan. Following the October 2014 skirmishes, Iran's police chief, Ismail Ahmadi Moqqadam, went out of his way to assure the Iranian public that sealing the Pakistan border is nearly complete. The border is even 'closed to the passage of [trespassing] animals', Moqqadam was quoted as saying. The statement was a strong example of Tehran's security-oriented approach to all things Pakistan-related. But hard security-centric prescriptions have by now been proven to fail in reversing the spiral of instability that has beset this rugged border.

The Pakistani side is also guilty of neglect. Despite its massive energy shortage, and after years of negotiations and many false starts, Islamabad is still yet to begin physically constructing its part of a $7.5 billion pipeline deal that is meant to deliver Iranian natural gas. This is a project that would have turned the question of border security into a joint interest, and made both countries stakeholders.

The Iranians claim that they are still committed to the deal but quietly will express strong doubt that Islamabad will ever go through with it, given opposition from Saudi Arabia and the United States. A deadline to have the pipeline operational by the end of 2014 proved all but impossible to achieve thanks largely to a lack of a political commitment. Meanwhile, the project's symbolism cannot be under-estimated. This was meant to be a strategic marvel, with a potential to reverse the drift in relations that has over the years proven so destructive.

The enduring rot

An October 2014 article in Pakistan's *Times* newspaper placed the deterioration of relations in a historical context. It suggested that, 'since the advent of the Pakistan Muslim League (PML-N) government [of Nawaz Sharif] in June 2013, perceived to be pro-Saudi Arabia, the [gas pipeline] project appeared to be in jeopardy because of Iranian-Saudi rivalry'. The paper asked for Islamabad to 'stem the rot' and 'retain old friends with sincerity rather than turn them into foes'.

The fact, however, is that the 'rot' in relations is nothing new – nor is it the making of the likes of the United States, Saudi Arabia or any other single country. The truth is that Iranian–Pakistani relations took a decisive turn for the worse after the Indian–Pakistani war of 1971. It was not the Islamic Republic of Iran, but the pro-American Shah of Iran who then determined that Tehran should not prioritize Pakistan over India. It was the Shah who set that fundamental trajectory in motion – a policy that Tehran has followed ever since, to Islamabad's deep resentment.

Any Pakistani bid to overturn this basic reality is bound to fail, be it though coercion or by enticing the Iranians away from India. Instead, as the Shah back in the 1970s sought to encourage, pan-regional economic and political projects should be inclusive of all three countries – Pakistan, Iran and India – if not also Afghanistan, which is likely to remain a major source for instability in years to come. The Shah used to tell Zulfikar Bhutto that keeping India out was a futile exercise in bluster, a perspective that still resonates strongly in Tehran nearly half a century later.

For now, however, it is evident that both Tehran and Islamabad are more or less resigned to accept the ongoing reality of 'managed tensions' in relations, not to mention considerable economic underutilization. Both sides have other overriding foreign-policy priorities. Pakistan's national security apparatus is still India-obsessed. Meanwhile, Iran continues its quest for regional influence but it is primarily preoccupied with its interests in the West and in the Arab world, and considerably less focused on its east as a gateway to regional influence and enhanced security. The one common threat that decades ago brought Iran and Pakistan together, the Soviets to the north, is long gone, and no substitute has since emerged.

§

From the perspective of the West – and particularly the United States, which has invested enormous human and financial capital to secure and promote its national-security interests in this region since the terrorist attacks of 11 September 2001 and the removal of the Taliban in Afghanistan – south-west Asia continues to be a key global battleground. And in this highly volatile region, the relationship between Iran and Pakistan is without doubt the most significant, and yet largely unmapped, affair – one that is overlooked by international observers more often than not.

This is not necessarily out of apathy but a reflection of the complexity of Iranian–Pakistani relations, which not cannot be readily captured or pigeonholed. When observers look at the interactions between these two neighbouring countries, they are confronted by a multilayered relationship that defies the typical typecasting prevalent in international relations. It is not one of outright hostility or one of constructive partnership. Instead, it is a relationship that is at times cooperative but which has, since the early 1990s, been increasingly characterized by rivalry.

These two regional powers continue to be intertwined in various cultural, religious and political ways. In Pakistan, people still fondly remember Iran as the first country to recognize the independent state of Pakistan in 1947, and the Shah of Iran as the first head of state to visit the new nation. By the late 1960s and onwards, however, the race for regional leadership had put the Shah on a collision course with Pakistan. The unease in relations only heightened following the Iranian Revolution of 1979 and the emergence of sectarian tensions between Shi'a Iran and Sunni Pakistan.

Over the next two decades, Iran and Pakistan, the once erstwhile allies, engaged in a fierce competition for regional influence. The key battleground was in Afghanistan. But as history shows, Iran–Pakistan relations have throughout remained multifaceted, often contradictory and unpredictable. Today, with much of south-west Asia still in turmoil, the trajectory of Iranian–Pakistani relations is therefore a critically important factor, not to be overlooked.

As of late 2014, nothing perhaps deserves more scrutiny than respective Iranian and Pakistani policies in Afghanistan as the Western military presence in that country comes to a drawdown. Throughout the 1950s, 1960s and 1970s, Tehran and Islamabad shared a common interest in keeping Kabul from falling into Soviet hands. That endeavour, as reactive and as incomplete as it often was, turned out to be a stabilizing factor in this tumultuous region. On the other hand, when Iran and Pakistan jockeyed for maximum influence in Afghanistan – as they did for almost the entire 1990s, at the other's expense – then achieving an Afghan peace seemed a near impossibility. There is no doubt that the future of Afghanistan after Western forces withdraw will depend strongly on whether Iran and Pakistan will seek to engage in a zero-sum game for influence or seek a policy of accommodation that prevents Afghan soil from once again becoming a battlefield for them and their respective Afghan allies and proxies.

Be it on the Afghan question, challenges linked to terrorism or anti-proliferation efforts – or simply in coping with the consequences of their geopolitical rivalry – Western policy makers ought to be far more attentive to the set of dynamics that reinforce and steer Iranian–Pakistani relations. The competing or overlapping interests of these two regional powers can be momentous, as the West – and Washington, in particular – plans and executes its future national-security strategies for south-west Asia.

NOTES

Introduction

1. Unless otherwise stated, all interviews conducted by the author.
2. Interview with Shamshad Ahmad, former Pakistani ambassador, Princeton, NJ, 31 July 2012.

Chapter 1   On the Road to India: Iran's and Pakistan's Intertwined History

1. Shah Alam, 'Iran-Pakistan Relations: Political and Strategic Dimensions', *Strategic Analysis*, Vol. 28, No. 4 (2004), p. 526.
2. Interview with Assad Homayoun, a senior Iranian diplomat stationed in Pakistan between 1964 and 1968, Washington, DC, March 2012.
3. Office of Political and International Studies, Iranian Foreign Ministry, *Selective Documents: Relations between Iran and Pakistan*, Document No. 14. (1996). Available at US Library of Congress, African and Middle Eastern Reading Room.
4. Stanley Wolpert, *Zulfi Bhutto of Pakistan: His Life and Times* (Oxford University Press, New York, 1993), p. 17.
5. Humayun Mirza, *From Plassey to Pakistan* (University Press of America, Lanham, MD, 2002), p. 15.
6. Asadollah Alam, *The Shah and I* (I.B.Tauris, London, 1992), p. 35.
7. Sabir Shah, 'First Ladies Nusrat and Nahid were both Iranian-born', *The News*, 24 October 2011. Available at www.thenews.com.pk/Todays-News-13-9797-First-ladies-Nusrat-and-Nahid-were-both-Iranian-born (accessed 22 October 2014).
8. Nadeem Hasnain and Husain Sheikh Abrar, *Shias and Shia Islam in India* (Harnam Publications, New Delhi, 1988), pp. 41–2.
9. Wolpert, *Bhutto*, p. 33.

10. For extensive background, see Ernest Tucker, '1739: History, Self, and Other in Afsharid Iran and Mughal India', *Iranian Studies*, Vol. 31, No. 2 (Spring 1998), p. 108.

11. See ibid., p. 213.

12. Naimur Rahman Farooqi, *Mughal-Ottoman Relations* (Idarah-i Adabiyat-i, Delhi, 1989), p. 78.

13. Juan Cole, 'Iranian Culture and South Asia – 1500–1900', in Nikkie Keddie (ed.), *Iran and the Surrounding World: Interactions in Culture and Cultural Politics* (University of Washington Press, Seattle, WA, 2002), p. 15.

14. See Fereidoon Zand-Fard, *Iran and a World in Turbulence* (Shiraze, Tehran, 2000), p. 159.

15. Sanjay Subrahmanyam, 'Iranians Abroad: Intra-Asian Elite Migration and Early Modern State Formation', *Journal of Asian Studies*, Vol. 51, No. 2 (1992), pp. 340–63.

16. Cole, 'Iranian Culture', p. 19.

17. Kourosh Hadian, Morteza Dehghannejad and Aliakbar Kajbaf, 'The Explanatory Comparison of Religious Policies in Central Governments of Safavid and Qajar Dynasties (1521/1925-AD)', *Asian Culture and History*, Vol. 4, No. 2 (2002), pp. 182–7.

18. Syed Sharifuddin Pirzada (ed.), *Foundations of Pakistan All-India Muslim League Documents: 1906–1947*, Vol. 1 – 1906–1924 (National Publishing House Limited, Dacca, 1969), pp. 49–50.

19. See Cole, 'Iranian Culture', p. 24.

20. See ibid., p. 28.

21. *Mapping the global Muslim population* (The Pew Forum on Religion and Public Life, Washington, DC, October 2009). According to the Pew study, 'most Shia Muslims (between 68% and 80%) live in just four countries: Iran, Pakistan, India and Iraq', p. 1.

22. Ibid.

23. See Foreign and Commonwealth Office File 1519551, 17 December 1971. Available through the US Library of Congress.

24. White House memorandum of conversation, 27 July 1973.

25. See Hafeez Malik, *Central Asia: Its Strategic Importance and Future Prospects* (St Martin's Press, New York, 1994), p. 259.

Chapter 2   1947–1958: Early Hiccups, as Iran and Pakistan both Look to the US for Protection

1. See Foreign and Commonwealth Office File 7348, 21 May 1949.

2. Ibid., 11647, 6 August 1949.

3. Ibid., 14365, 15 August 1949.

4. See Abbas Milani, *The Shah* (Palgrave Macmillan, New York, 2011), p. 289.

5. See Foreign and Commonwealth Office File 14365, 15 August 1949.

6. Ibid. 12125/10334/85, 17 August 1949.

7. Ibid., 14365/10334/85, 12 October 1949.
8. See Foreign and Commonwealth Office Cable DY10334/01, 20 February 1958.
9. Milani, *The Shah*, pp. 114–17.
10. Lori Lyn Bogle (ed.), *The Cold War: Cold War Culture and Society* (Routledge, New York, 2001), p. 347. For a comprehensive account see Ervand Abrahamian, *Iran Between Two Revolutions* (Princeton University Press, Princeton, NJ, 1982), pp. 220–32.
11. Lawrence E. Grinter, 'The United States and South Asia: New Challenges, New Opportunities', *Asian Affairs*, Vol. 20, No. 2 (Summer 1993), p. 106.
12. Interview with Scott Behoteguy, United States Foreign Assistance Oral History Program, 11 August 1997.
13. See John P. Callahan, 'Turkey and Pakistan Map Broad Mid-East Arms Pact', *New York Times*, 21 February 1955.
14. Ibid.
15. Moyra De Moraes Ruehsen, 'Operation Ajax Revisited: Iran, 1953', *Middle Eastern Studies*, Vol. 29, No. 3 (July 1993), p. 475.
16. Milani, *The Shah*, pp. 171–202.
17. Memorandum of conversation by the Secretary of State (9 March 1956), Eisenhower Presidential Library, 110.11 DU/3–956.
18. Christopher M. Andrew and Vasili Mitrokhin, *The World Was Going Our Way: The KGB and the Battle for the Third World* (Basic Books, New York, 2006), p. 173.
19. Mohammad Reza Pahlavi, *Answer to History* (Stein and Day Publishing, New York, 1980), p. 133.
20. For a discussion about the developments around the 1958 coup, see Juan Romero, *The Iraqi Revolution of 1958: A Revolutionary Quest for Unity and Security* (University Press of America, Lanham, MD, 2011), pp. 155–61.
21. Proposed Action Paper E.O12958, Lyndon Johnson Presidential Library.
22. See Memorandum for the President, The Under Secretary of State, MR87–48 #1, 21 December 1954.
23. Mohammad Ayub Khan, *Friends Not Masters: A Political Autobiography* (Mr. Books, Islamabad, 2006), pp. 179.
24. Memorandum for the President, Department of State, MR79–168 #4, 23 February 1959.
25. Pact of Mutual Cooperation Between the Kingdom of Iraq, the Republic of Turkey, the United Kingdom, the Dominion of Pakistan, and the Kingdom of Iran (Baghdad Pact), 24 February 1955. See http://avalon.law.yale.edu/20th_century/baghdad.asp#art1 (accessed 25 October 2014).
26. Shuja Nawaz, *Crossed Swords* (Oxford University Press, Oxford, 2008), p. 152.
27. Interview with Zahedi, Montreux, Switzerland, 8 September 2012.
28. Mirza's wife, Nahid, is a member of the Qajar royal family of Iran.
29. Mirza, *Plassey*, p. 248.
30. See Aparna Pande, *Explaining Pakistan's Foreign Policy* (Routledge, New York, 2011), p. 105. At independence, Pakistan had received: 'eight infantry regiments, six armored corps units, eight and a half artillery regiments and

34 engineer units. The navy obtained 16 of the 48 vessels including two frigates and two sloops. The air force was given two out of the ten squadrons.'

31. Husain Haqqani, *Pakistan: Between Mosque and Military* (Carnegie Endowment for International Peace, Washington, DC, 2005), pp. 37–8.

32. The Shah often made the point that introducing democracy would harm Iran's economic modernization.

33. *Pakistan chief says he dismissed Mirza* (New York, 30 October 1958). This was a thoroughly disinguous statement. Ayub Khan had been one of the country's key political power brokers since 1951, when he became chief of army staff, the country's top military position. In that period, Pakistan had seven prime ministers, a reflection of the political chaos in the country in the years 1951–8.

34. Mirza, *Plassey*, pp. 249–52.

35. For a thorough discussion of the coup see Wayne Ayres Wilcox, 'The Pakistan Coup d'état of 1958', *Pacific Affairs*, Vol. 38, No. 2 (Summer 1965), pp. 142–63.

36. Ibid., p. 148.

37. Mirza, *Plassey*, p. 237.

Chapter 3   1958–1965: Regional Turbulence and an Unlikely Union

1. Foreign and Commonwealth Office Diplomatic Cable 10321/59, No. 159, 19 November 1959.

2. Ibid.

3. See Nawaz, *Swords*, p. 154.

4. Ibid.

5. Ibid.

6. Interview with Ambassador Ahmad Kamal (8 August 2012, New York City). As part of his 40 years with the Pakistani diplomatic service, Ambassador Kamal was a first-hand witness to the order by Bhutto about the policy papers.

7. Nawaz, *Swords*, p. 152.

8. Larry Goodson, *Afghanistan's Endless War: State Failure, Regional Politics, and the Rise of the Taliban* (University of Washington Press, Seattle, 2001), p. 27.

9. 'Louis Dupree, 63, Anthropologist and Expert on Afghanistan, Dies', *New York Times*, 23 March 1989.

10. Louis Dupree, 'A Suggested Pakistan-Afghanistan-Iran Federation', *Middle East Journal*, Vol. 17, No. 4 (Autumn 1963), pp. 388–91.

11. Quoted in Ibid., p. 385.

12. Quoted in Ibid., p. 392.

13. 'Pakistan, Yemen admitted to UN', *New York Times*, 1 October 1947.

14. Ibid., p. 385.

15. James W. Spain, 'Pakistan's North West Frontier', *Middle East Journal*, Vol. 8, No. 1 (1954), pp. 30–1.

16. George L. Montagno, 'The Pak-Afghan Détente', *Asian Survey*, Vol. 3, No. 12 (December 1963), p. 616.

17. Office of the White House Press Secretary, 17 October 1961.
18. Letter from Zahir Shah to President Kennedy, dated 19 November 1961. Available through the John F. Kennedy Presidential Library and Museum.
19. Shirin Tahir-Kheli, 'Iran and Pakistan: Cooperation in an Area of Conflict', *Asian Survey*, Vol. 17, No. 5 (May 1977), pp. 474–7.
20. Office of Political and International Studies, Iranian Foreign Ministry, *Selective Documents: Relations between Iran and Pakistan*, Document No. 5 (1996). Available at US Library of Congress, African and Middle Eastern Reading Room.
21. Rizwan Hussain, *Pakistan and the Emergence of Islamic Militancy in Afghanistan* (Ashgate Publishing Limited, Hampshire, 2005), p. 73. See also S. M. M. Qureshi, 'Pakhtunistan: The Frontier Dispute between Afghanistan and Pakistan', *Pacific Affairs*, Vol. 39, Nos. 1–2 (Spring/Summer 1966), p. 107.
22. Frank A. Clements, *Conflict in Afghanistan: A Historical Encyclopedia* (ABC-Clio INC., Santa Barbara, CA, 2003), p. 8.
23. Department of State Cable – CERP, Section C, Item 1, 17 December 1960.
24. Afghanistan and the Soviet Union had signed non-aggression and neutrality pacts in 1927 and 1931.
25. Montagno, 'Pak-Afghan', p. 622.
26. Ibid.
27. Ibid.
28. Quoted in ibid., p. 387.
29. Department of State cable from 2 March 1962 (Origin: Kabul, No. 527, Section 2 of 3).
30. Dupree, 'Suggested', p. 398.
31. 'U.S. Policy toward Afghanistan', National Security Council Memorandum MR 76–161 #10, unknown date.
32. Ibid.
33. Interview with Scott Behoteguy, The Foreign Affairs Oral History Collection of the Association for Diplomatic Studies and Training, 11 August 1997.
34. Ibid.
35. Peter Avery, 'Iran 1964–68: The Mood of Growing Confidence', *The World Today*, Vol. 24, No. 11 (November 1968), p. 454.
36. For background information, see Rory MacLean, *Magic Bus: On the Hippie Trail from Istanbul to India* (Ig Publishing, Brooklyn, NY, 2006).
37. Behcet Kemal Yesilbursa, 'The Formation of RCD: Regional Cooperation of Development', *Middle Eastern Studies*, Vol. 45, No. 4 (July 2009), pp. 637–42.
38. Ibid., p. 641.
39. Much of the Pakistani drive behind its push for the creation of RCD was rooted in President Khan and his foreign minister Zulkfikar Bhutto's desire to nurture the idea of closer ties with Muslim countries, as this was very popular with Pakistani public opinion.
40. Yesilbursa, 'RCD', p. 637.
41. Wolpert, *Bhutto*, p. 108.
42. Ibid., p. 265.

43. Department of State Cable A-160 – CERP C-3, 9 September 1963.
44. Ibid. A-86 – CERP C-3, 26 August 1964.
45. W. M. Hale and Julian Bharier, 'CENTO, R.C.D. and the Northern Tier: A Political and Economic Appraisal', *Middle Eastern Studies*, Vol. 8, No. 2 (May 1972), p. 219.
46. Dupree, 'Suggested', p. 397.
47. Successive interviews with Charlie Naas during 2011 and 2012 in Maryland.

Chapter 4 1965–1969: The Northern Tier: A Fluid Fault Line

1. 'Attitude to Indian Aggression', *Pakistan Times*, 7 September 1965.
2. 'Turks and Iranians Due to Meet', *New York Times*, 14 September 1965.
3. 'Pakistan has not Invoked CENTO', *Pakistan Times*, 9 September 1965.
4. 'Tranquility in Tehran', *Washington Post*, 9 April 1965.
5. 'Iran Duty-bound to Help Pakistan', *Pakistan Times*, 8 September 1965.
6. 'Isik in Tehran', *New York Times*, 14 September 1965.
7. 'Turco-Iranian Aid to Pakistan', *Pakistan Times*, 9 September 1965.
8. *Asian Recorder*, Vol. XI, No. 40 (1–7 October 1965), p. 6,695.
9. Interview with Dennis Kux, The Foreign Affairs Oral History Collection of the Association for Diplomatic Studies and Training, 13 January 1995.
10. Interview with Dean Rusk, The Foreign Affairs Oral History Collection of the Association for Diplomatic Studies and Training, 28 July 1969.
11. Dean Rusk Oral History Interview, Lyndon Baines Johnson Library Oral History Collection, 1/2/1970.
12. Conversation between Dean Rusk and UK Foreign Secretary, Department of State, TNA, PREM, 13/692, f. 200, 27 October 1964.
13. W. M. Hale and Julian Bharier, 'Cento, RCD and the Northern Tier', *Middle Eastern Studies*, Vol. 8, No. 2 (May 1972), p. 221.
14. Ibid.
15. Department of State File 8919, 13 September 1965. The Shah told Meyer that he would 'forego sending F-86s but would like to send ammunition and anti-tank rockets' to Pakistan.
16. 'India Says US Shift may Help Pakistan get Arms', *New York Times*, 18 April 1967.
17. Secret cable from US Embassy in Tehran, No. 06363, Department of State, 5 September 1968.
18. 'Correspondence Between President Johnson and Prime Minister Inonu', *Middle East Journal*, Vol. 20, No. 3 (Summer 1966), pp. 386–93.
19. Hale and Bharier, 'Cento', p. 220.
20. Alexander Haig Jr. and Charles McCarry, *How America Changed the World: A Memoir* (Warner Books, New York, 1992), p. 86.
21. See Department of State Memorandum of conversation between Eisenhower and Dulles, Washington, DC, FRUS 1958–60, Vol. XII: 224, 25 January 1958.

22. Memo for the President, Executive Order 12356, SEC 3.4 – 12 April 1962.
23. Department of State Briefing Paper, No. 800136 1324, unknown date.
24. A. G. Noorani, 'Soviet Ambitions in South Asia', *International Security*, Vol. 4, No. 3 (Winter 1979–80), p. 33.
25. Wolpert, *Bhutto*, p. 108.
26. For a broader discussion, see Noorani, 'Ambitions'.
27. Ibid., p. 39.
28. For background, see Stephen M. Walt, 'Testing Theories of Alliance Formation: The Case of South West Asia', *International Organization*, Vol. 42, No. 2 (Spring 1988), pp. 3–41.
29. See 'Shah's Increasing Assurance', CIA, Office of National Estimates, 7 May 1968.
30. 'U.S. Makes the Most of CENTO "Patchwork"', *Christian Science Monitor*, 27 May 1966.
31. Foreign and Commonwealth Office Telegram No. 24931, December 1969.
32. Department of State File 2499, 130800Z, 13 December 1966.
33. Ibid.
34. Nasser's statement that 'Suez is as dear to Egypt as Kashmir is to India' had particularly irritated the Pakistanis. See Moshe Ma'oz, *Muslim Attitudes to Jews and Israel* (Sussex Academic Press, Eastbourne, UK, 2010), p. 194.
35. Telephone interview with Assad Homayoun, 18 March 2013.
36. See Foreign Commonwealth Office Cable 37/199, 6 December 1967.
37. Memorandum of conversation, Department of State, 23 August 1967.
38. '3 Moslem Leaders Meeting Today on the Mideast', *Washington Post*, 28 July 1967.
39. Tahir-Kheli, 'Cooperation'.
40. Foreign and Commonwealth Office Cable 37/199, 6 December 1967.
41. Incidentally, the Iranians also had objections to the character of the Pakistani foreign minister, Syed Sharifuddin Pirzada. One British diplomatic cable quotes an Iranian official describing Pirzada as 'an excessively stupid man', and elsewhere he is referred to as 'remarkably dry'.
42. Foreign and Commonwealth Office Cable 37/199, 6 December 1967.
43. Pahlavi, *Answer*, p. 141.
44. Department of State Archives, Foreign Relations: 1969–1972, Volume E-4, Iran and Iraq.
45. Rouhollah Ramazani, 'Iran's Search for Regional Cooperation', *Middle East Journal*, Vol. 30, No. 2 (Spring 1976), p. 173.
46. Roham Alvandi, 'Nixon, Kissinger, and the Shah: The Origins of Iranian Primacy in the Persian Gulf', *Diplomatic History*, Vol. 36, Issue 2 (April 2012), p. 339.
47. Alam, *Shah and I*, p. 34.
48. Department of State Cable 276775, 22 November 1968.
49. Foreign and Commonwealth Office Cable 37/199, unknown date.
50. Ibid., Telno 231, 6 February 1968.
51. Department of State Note 944, 4 December 1968.
52. Ibid.
53. 'US and Afghans in a Map Project', *New York Times*, 23 August 1970.

54. Walt, 'Testing'.
55. Department of State, E.C. 12365, Sec. 3.4, July 1968.
56. For its part, the United States indicated that it welcomed and was thankful for the Shah's help in assuaging Ayub Khan. See Department of State Cable 0110814, 11 April 1967.
57. 'Map project'.
58. The British interpreted the visit as a 'fence-mending operation', and said nothing had in fact come from Ayub's four day stay in Iran.

Chapter 5   1969–71: Iran's Intervention over the Pakistani Defeat of 1971

1. Noor Mohammad Askari, *Gholle haye ghodrat dar dowrane payanie doodmane Pahlavi* (Arash Publishing, Stockholm, 2004), p. 280.
2. Alam, *Shah and I*, p. 52.
3. Askari, *Gholle haye ghodrat'*, p. 282.
4. Alam, *Shah and I*, p. 40.
5. Wolpert, *Bhutto*, p. 141.
6. Foreign and Commonwealth Office Cable 37/480, 27 November 1969.
7. Henry Kissinger, conversation with US ambassador to India, Kenneth Keating, 3 June 1971. Available via US National Security Archives.
8. Alam, *Shah and I*, p. 99.
9. Ibid.
10. Ibid., p. 100.
11. The Shah had once said: 'All Muslims believe in Allah, His Prophet Muhammad, the same Holy Book, and the same Kaaba in Mecca so are we split into seventy-odd denominations.' See ibid., p. 208.
12. Foreign and Commonwealth Office Cable 1519551, 17 December 1971.
13. Wolpert, *Bhutto*, p. 158.
14. 'Trends in Iranian arms procurement', CIA Memorandum ER IM 72–79, May 1972.
15. Ibid.
16. Wolpert, *Bhutto*, p. 158.
17. Interviews with Ardeshir Zahedi, Assad Homayoun and Akbar Etemad.
18. Recording of Telephone Conversation Between President Johnson and President Eisenhower, 4 November 1967, 10:05 a.m., Tape 67.14, Side B, PNO 40, Lyndon B. Johnson Library, Recordings and Transcripts.
19. Wolpert, *Bhutto*, p. 158.
20. Pahlavi, *Answer*, p. 134.
21. Robert S. Litwak, *Détente and the Nixon Doctrine: American Foreign Policy and the Pursuit of Stability 1969–1976* (Cambridge University Press, Cambridge, 1984), p. 103.
22. Memorandum of telephone conversation, 4 December 1971, Kissinger Telephone Conversations.

23. Ibid.
24. Recording of conversation between Nixon and Kissinger, 6 December 1971, Oval Office, Conversation No. 630–2, US National Archives, Nixon Presidential Materials, White House Tapes.
25. Department of State, 5470, Amman, unknown date.
26. Memorandum of telephone conversation, 4 December 1971, Kissinger Telephone Conversations.
27. Najib E. Saliba, 'Impact of the Indi-Pakistani War on the Middle East', *World Affairs*, Vol. 135, No. 2 (Fall 1972), pp. 129–33.
28. 'West Pakistan: Resupply Problems', CIA memorandum, December 1971.
29. 'Iran Sounds Warning – Don't Rock the Boat in West Pakistan', *Christian Science Monitor*, 17 January 1972.
30. 'Iran's sympathies with Pakistan', *Christian Science Monitor*, 10 December 1971.
31. Kissinger told Indian Ambassador Kaul that the 'State [Department] was on India's side'. Conversation between Kissinger and Indian ambassador to the US, T. N. Kaul, White House memorandum, 15 August 1973.
32. Memorandum of telephone conversation between Kissinger and Pakistani ambassador, N. A. M. Raza, 8 December 1971.
33. Background briefing with Henry Kissinger, NPMP, NSC Files, Indo-Pak War, Box 572 – 7 December 1971.
34. Nawaz, *Swords*, p. 309.
35. Ibid., p. 308.
36. Ross Masood Husain, 'Threat Perceptions and Military Planning in Pakistan', in Eric Arnett (ed.), *Military Capacity and the Risk of War* (Sipri, Oxford University Press, Oxford, 1997), p. 134.
37. Foreign and Commonwealth Office File 1519551, 17 December 1971.
38. 'Iran Supplied US Arms to Pakistan, India Says', *Sun*, 26 December 1971.
39. Conversation between Kissinger and Indian ambassador to the US, T. N. Kaul, White House memorandum, 15 August 1973.
40. Interview with Ardeshir Zahedi.
41. 'US Government gratified by Shah's wholesome influence on Ayub', Department of State Cable 010814, 11 April 1967.
42. *Fereydoon Hoveyda, Interview in New York, 5 May and 20 June 1988* (Foundation of Iranian Studies, Bethesda, MD, 1988), pp. 25–30.
43. Shahid M. Amin, *Pakistan's Foreign Policy: A Reappraisal* (Oxford University Press, New York, 2000), p. 72.

Chapter 6   1971–77: The Shah and Pakistan's Reluctant Dependence

1. Wolpert, *Bhutto*, p. 232.
2. Department of State Executive Order N/A or blank, 18 December 1973.
3. Ibid., 20 October 1973.
4. Interview with Ardeshir Zahedi, the Shah's confidant.

5. P. R. Kumaraswamy, *Beyond the Veil: Israel-Pakistan Relations* (Jaffee Center for Strategic Studies, Tel Aviv University, 2000).
6. 'Upheaval in Kabul', *New York Times*, 20 July 1973.
7. 'Family Feud or Big Power Struggle?', *Financial Times*, 25 July 1973.
8. Alam, *Shah and I*, p. 261.
9. Ibid.
10. 'Nixon and Shah', memorandum of conversation, Saadabad Palace, 30 May 1972.
11. Shaheen F. Dill, 'The Cabal in Kabul: Great-power Interaction in Afghanistan', *American Political Science Review*, Vol. 71, No. 2 (June 1977), p. 469.
12. Department of State Executive Order 11652, 13 July 1973.
13. Ibid.
14. For background, see Askari, *Gholle haye ghodrat*.
15. Alam, *Shah and I*, p. 359.
16. It later emerged that Moscow had not in fact been behind the palace coup in Kabul that eventful summer.
17. 'India Eyes the Persian Gulf', CIA Memorandum No. 1658/73, 6 August 1973.
18. Dilip Mukerjee, 'Afghanistan under Daud: Relations with Neighboring States', *Asian Survey*, Vol. 15, No. 4 (April 1975), p. 302.
19. Ibid.; see also p. 306.
20. 'Baluch Nationalism and Superpower Rivalry' (Selig S. Harrison), *International Security*, Vol. 5, No. 3, 1981, p. 152.
21. Admiral Warton, 'The Perso-Baluch Boundary', *Geographical Journal*, Vol. 9, No. 4 (April 1897), pp. 420–2.
22. 'Echoes of Lord Curzon', *Financial Times*, 28 June 1973.
23. For example, in May 1974, Tehran agreed to pay for three cement and textile factories to be built in Baluchistan at a cost of $35 million.
24. Alam, *Shah and I*, p. 419.
25. Interview with George G. B. Griffin, Association for Diplomatic Studies and Training Foreign Affairs Oral History Project, 30 April 2002.
26. 'Arms in Pakistan for Iran Rebels', *The Times*, 23 February 1973.
27. Department of State Executive Order 11652, 9 March 1973.
28. For speculation about Bhutto's motives, see Nicholas Schmidle, *To Live or To Perish Forever: Two Tumultuous Years in Pakistan* (Holt Paperbacks, New York, 2009), pp. 77–8.
29. Aasim Sajjad Akhtar, 'Balochistan versus Pakistan', *Economic and Political Weekly*, No. 45 (2007), pp. 73–9.
30. Ibid.
31. Imtiaz Ali, 'The Balochistan Problem', *Pakistan Horizon*, No. 2 (2005), pp. 41–62.
32. Jason Heeg, *Insurgency in Balochistan* (Kansas State University). Available at http://fmso.leavenworth.army.mil/Collaboration/universities/Balochistan_final.pdf (accessed 1 November 2014).
33. Department of State Executive Order N/A or blank, 10 August 1973.

34. Selig S. Harrison, 'Baluch Nationalism and Super Power Rivalry', *International Security*, Vol. 5, No. 3 (Winter 1980–1981), pp. 152–63.
35. Department of State Executive Order 11652, 3 September 1973.
36. 'The Shah Mends Fences', *New York Times*, 20 May 1973.
37. US Embassy Islamabad cable, Department of Sate, Executive Order 11652, GDS, 28 March 1973.
38. 'Iran Learns to be Strong', *Guardian*, 14 August 1972.
39. The FSF was later dismissed by General Zia ul-Haq. Scholars often argue that Bhutto established this paramilitary force to balance the country's military. See, for example, Stephen Cohen, 'Pakistan: Army, Society and Security', *Asian Affairs*, No. 2 (1983), pp. 1–26.
40. 'Mr Bhutto's Class C Constitution', *Guardian*, 10 September 1973.
41. Alam, *Shah and I*, p. 320.
42. Ibid., p. 340.
43. Department of State Executive Order 11652, 3 September 1973.
44. 'Shah Mends Fences', *New York Times*.
45. Department of State Executive Order 11652, 12 May 1973.
46. Ibid., 16 May 1973.
47. Department of State Executive Order N/A or blank, 15 May 1973.
48. 'Pakistan and Iran Agree to Strengthen Mutual Defense Link', *Christian Science Monitor*, 31 May 1973.
49. 'India Eyes', CIA Memorandum No. 1658/73.
50. Department of State Executive Order N/A or blank, 31 May 1973.
51. 'Defense Aim to Deter Attack', *Financial Times*, 13 August 1973.
52. 'India Eyes', CIA Memorandum No. 1658/73.
53. 'Pakistan and the Nixon Doctrine', *Washington Post*, 15 July 1973.
54. 'Iran Shares Pakistan's Concerns', *Christian Science Monitor*, 29 July 1974.
55. 'Bhutto's Secret Police Tighten their Grip' *Guardian*, 14 March 1975.
56. Department of State Executive Order N/A or blank, 18 December 1973.
57. 'Shah of Iran: Royal Revolutionary', CIA Memorandum No. 658, 26 January 1973.
58. 'Politics Behind the Scene', *Financial Times*, 11 August 1975.
59. Department of State Executive Order N/A or blank, 26 December 1973.
60. 'Bhutto's Secret Police', *Guardian*.
61. 'Pashtunistan: An historical Survey', CIA Memorandum No. 35 – 2464/73, 6 November 1973.
62. Department of State Executive Order 11652, 2 October 1973.
63. Ibid.
64. Alam, *Shah and I*, p. 310.
65. Department of State, Telegram 2604 – 1302Z, 4 May 1972.
66. Askari, *Gholle haye ghodrat*, p. 291.
67. Alam, *Shah and I*, p. 317.
68. Foreign and Commonwealth Office memorandum, 27 July 1973.
69. Alam, *Shah and I*, p. 316.
70. Ibid., p. 310.

71. For comprehensive background, see Kaveh Farrokh, *Iran at War: 1500–1988* (Osprey Publishing, Oxford, 2011).
72. Alam, *Shah and I*, p. 311.
73. Amin, *Reappraisal*, p. 110.
74. Foreign and Commonwealth Office, Annex A, 29 September 1971.
75. Foreign and Commonwealth Office cable, 3 August 1973.
76. Ibid. Also see Department of State Executive Order N/A or blank, 14 March 1973.
77. Alam, *Shah and I*, p. 41.
78. Department of State, N/A or blank, 8 July 1976.
79. Ibid., AN 0750143 – 1059, 24 April 1975.
80. Department of State Executive Order 11652, 12 December 1973.
81. Ibid., 15 October 1973.
82. Ibid.
83. Ibid.
84. Ibid.
85. Department of State Executive Order N/A or blank, 6 February 1974.
86. Ibid., GS, 8 April 1975.
87. Ibid., N/A or blank, 8 July 1974.
88. Department of State, AN 0750147 – 1024, 27 April 1975.
89. 'Vision in a Persian Market', *Guardian*, 15 October 1974.
90. Department of State Executive Order 11652, 3 April 1973.
91. Staff notes, 84, CIA Memorandum No. 0657/75, 17 April 1975.
92. Department of State Executive Order 11652, 10 January 1974.
93. 'Iran's Arms Buildup Fed Public Unrest', *Los Angeles Times*, 26 March 1980, pp. 689–716.
94. 'Revitalization of CENTO', *Pakistan Forum*, Vol. 3, No. 3 (December 1972).
95. Wolpert, *Bhutto*, p. 211.
96. Hafeez Ur-Rahman Khan, 'Pakistan's Relations with the U.A.R.', *Pakistan Horizon*, Vol. 13, No. 3 (1960), p. 216.
97. Ahmad Shuja Pasha, *Pakistan: A Political Profile* (Sang-e-Meel Publications, Lahore, 1991), p. 285.
98. Department of State Executive Order 11652, 26 November 1973.
99. Wolpert, *Bhutto*, p. 14.
100. Ibid., p. 233.
101. Wolpert, *Bhutto*, p. 234.
102. Alam, *Shah and I*, p. 34.
103. Lewis M. Simons, 'Islamic Summit Taking Shape', *Washington Post*, 19 February 1974.
104. Alam, *Shah and I*, p. 346. In Alam's diaries, there is no reference to any one single reason why the Shah did not go to Lahore as there are no entries between 8 January and 6 March 1974.
105. Department of State Executive Order 11652, 10 December 1973.
106. Alam, *Shah and I*, p. 160.

107. Ibid., p. 345.
108. Department of State Executive Order 11652, 14 December 1973.
109. Proceedings of Second Islamic Summit Conference, Organization of Islamic Cooperation. Available at www.oic-oci.org/english/conf/is/2/2nd-is-sum.htm #Declaration (accessed 2 November 2014).
110. Pasha, *Profile*, p. 286.
111. 'The New Power of Oil: Petroleum Power: The Shah Outlines New World Order', *Washington Post*, 3 February 1974. See also, 'Shah Seeks Dominance in Region for Iran', *New York Times*, 19 May 1974.
112. Alam, *Shah and I*, p. 358.
113. S. R. Ghauri, 'Bhutto Tries to Warm Iran Relationship', *Guardian*, 30 March, 1974.
114. Foreign and Commonwealth Office File FCO 37/1658, FSP 2/2, 1975.
115. Pasha, *Profile*, p. 285.
116. 'Cairo's Military Aid to Libya Curtailed', *Washington Post*, 18 February 1974.
117. 'The Persian Gulf: The End of Pax Britannica', CIA Memorandum 25 X1, 21 September 1972.
118. Department of State Executive Order N/A or blank, 2 April 1974.
119. Foreign and Commonwealth Office File FSP RR 7/1 DS No 2/75, 27 December 1974.
120. Mohammad Aslam Khan Khattak, *A Pathan Odyssey* (Oxford University Press, Oxford, 2004), p. 195.
121. Ibid.
122. 'Centers of Power in Iran', CIA Memorandum No. 2035/72, May 1972.
123. Khattak, *Odyssey*, p. 218.
124. Ibid., p. 200.
125. Ibid.
126. Alam, *Shah and I*, p. 359.
127. Ibid., p. 369.
128. Khattak, *Odyssey*, p. 203.
129. *New York Times*, 8 January 1973.
130. 'Persian Market', *Guardian*.
131. 'The Shah Goes East in Search of Security', *Financial Times*, 16 September 1974.
132. Andrew Scott Cooper, *The Oil Kings* (Simon & Schuster, New York, 2011), pp. 220–3.
133. See Tahir-Kheli, 'Cooperation'.
134. Cooper, *Oil Kings*, pp. 220–3.
135. Department of State Executive Order N/A or blank, 3 December 1973.
136. Ibid., 11652, 7 May 1973.
137. Khattak, *Odyssey*, p. 216.
138. 'India Eyes', CIA Memorandum No. 1658/73.
139. Khattak, *Odyssey*, p. 217.
140. Ibid., p. 221.
141. 'Shah Goes East', *Financial Times*.
142. Wolpert, *Bhutto*, p. 210.

143. Conversation between Kissinger and Indian ambassador to the US, T. N. Kaul, White House memorandum, 15 August 1973.
144. Memo of conversation between Kissinger and the Shah, 1 August 1973.
145. Department of State Executive Order 11652 GDS, 19 December 1973.
146. Ibid., 20 December 1973.
147. Ibid.
148. Department of State Executive Order 11652, 22 December 1973.
149. Ibid.
150. Department of State Executive Order N/A or blank, 17 November 1973.
151. Ibid. Reference 3394, 6 May 1974.
152. See Tahir-Kheli, *Cooperation*.
153. Department of State Executive Order GS, 3 November 1975.
154. Feroz Khan, 'Eating Grass', *Stanford Security Studies* (2012), p. 174.
155. Department of State Executive Order 11652, 23 May 1974.
156. Syed Hossein Mousavian, *The Iranian Nuclear Crisis* (Carnegie Endowment, Washington, DC, 2012), pp. 40–52.
157. Telephone interview with Akbar Ettemad, 23 March 2013.
158. Ibid.
159. Department of State Executive Order N/A or blank, 24 June 1974.
160. Ettemad interview.
161. Ibid., 10 July 1974.
162. Ibid., 16 May 1976.
163. Khan, 'Grass', pp. 117–23.
164. Department of State Executive Order N/A or blank, 16 May 1976.
165. Ibid., 25 September 1975.
166. Ibid., 16 June 1976.
167. Ibid.
168. For a discussion, see Tahir-Kheli, 'Cooperation', pp. 478–83.
169. 'US and Pakistan Try to Avoid Split on Nuclear Plant', *New York Times*, 10 August 1976.
170. David Armstrong and Joseph J. Trento, *America and the Islamic Bomb* (Steerforth Press, Hanover, NH, 2007).
171. Department of State Executive Order N/A or blank, 8 August 1976.
172. See interview with Robert B. Oakley, The Foreign Affairs Oral History Collection of the Association for Diplomatic Studies and Training, 7 July 1992.
173. 'Pakistan Aid Bid: Treat Us Like Iran', *Chicago Tribune*, 9 August 1976.
174. Various interviews with Thomas Lippman.
175. William Burr, 'A Brief History of US-Iranian Nuclear Negotiations', *Bulletin of the Atomic Scientists* (January-February 2009).
176. Department of State Executive Order N/A or blank, 27 December 1976.
177. Khan, 'Grass', pp. 106 and 137.
178. Cyrus Vance, *Hard Choices: Critical Years in America's Foreign Policy* (Simon and Schuster, New York, 1983), p. 318.

179. Itamar Rabinovich and Haim Shaked (eds), *The Middle East between 1967 and 1973* (Transaction Inc., Edison, NJ, 1978), p. 367.
180. Department of State Executive Order N/A or blank, 2 November 1974.
181. Wolpert, *Bhutto*, pp. 265–6.
182. Department of State Executive Order N/A or blank, 16 July 1974.
183. 'Memorandum: Strategy for Your Visit to Pakistan', Department of State Memorandum NEA/PAB, unknown date.
184. Mukerjee, 'Under Daud', p. 303.
185. Daveed Gartenstein-Ross and Tara Vassefi, 'The Forgotten History of Afghanistan-Pakistan Relations', *Yale Journal of International Affairs* (March 2012), p. 43.
186. Department of State Executive Order N/A or blank, 20 April 1976.
187. Ibid., 4 April 1974.
188. Ibid., 3 May 1976.
189. Ibid., 30 October 1974.
190. Cooper, *Oil Kings*, pp. 220–3.
191. Department of State Executive Order N/A or blank, 30 October 1974.
192. 'Beating the Embargo', *Financial Times*, 12 July 1975.
193. 'Shah, President Ford and Kissinger', White House memorandum, 15 May 1975.
194. 'Pakistan Prepares Arms List', *Washington Post*, 10 May 1975.
195. Department of State Executive Order N/A or blank, 4 October 1975.
196. Wolpert, *Bhutto*, p. 210.
197. Department of State Executive Order N/A or blank, 28 March 1973.
198. Ibid., 29 March 1975.
199. 'No rights link to Iran arms sales', *Los Angeles Times*, 14 May 1977.
200. Alam, *Shah and I*, p. 549.
201. Wolpert, *Bhutto*, p. 265.

Chapter 7   1977–1988: Zia, the Shah and the Coming of the Ayatollah

1. Mehrunnisa Ali, 'General Mohammad Zia-ul-Haq Visit to Muslim Countries', *Pakistan Horizon*, Vol. 30 (Third and Fourth Quarter, 1977), pp. 103–7.
2. Miron Rezun, *Iran at the Crossroads: Global Relations in a Turbulent Decade* (Westview Press, Boulder, CO, 1990), p. 73.
3. Malik, *Central Asia*, p. 259.
4. Zand-Fard, *Turbulence*, p. 147.
5. 'Killing Bhutto will not Save Pakistan', *Guardian*, 30 May 1978.
6. Prithvi Ram Mudiam, *India and the Middle East* (British Academic Press, New York, 1994), p. 83.
7. Zand-Fard, *Turbulence*, p. 155.
8. Husain, 'Perceptions', p. 133.
9. Department of State Telegram No. 2182, 10 February 1978.

10. See Panagiotis Dimitrakis, *Failed Alliances of the Cold War: Britain's Strategy and Ambitions in Asia and the Middle East* (I.B.Tauris, London, 2012), p. 77.
11. Ibid., p. 79.
12. Ibid., p. 182.
13. 'Cento: A Tattered Alliance Playing the Great Game in a Geopolitical Disaster Area', *Time*, 18 September 1978.
14. Foreign and Commonwealth Office File 37/2079, FSA 021/1, 15 June 1978.
15. Ibid.
16. Ibid.
17. 'Tehran wary of Red's push to the sea', *Sun*, 27 July 1978.
18. John B. Ritch III, 'Hidden War: The Struggle for Afghanistan', A Staff Report to the US Senate Foreign Relations Committee, unknown date.
19. Vladimir Snegirev and Valery Samunin, *The Dead End: The Road to Afghanistan* (E-book), pp. 375–6.
20. H. Amin speech at the special session of the UN General Assembly on Disarmament, New York, 6 June 1978.
21. See Foreign and Commonwealth Office File FSA/021/1, 6 July 1978.
22. CIA National Intelligence Daily, 8 January 1979.
23. Interview with Haji Mangal Hussain, Kabul, 11 June 2013.
24. See Foreign and Commonwealth Office File FSA 021/11, 17 July 1978.
25. See Foreign and Commonwealth Office, 37/2123, UK delegation to NATO, 14 February 1979.
26. Foreign and Commonwealth Office File FSA 021/1, 1 August 1978.
27. Ibid., 29 June 1978.
28. Ibid., 37/2079, 17 July 1978.
29. Zand-Fard, *Turbulence*, p. 161.
30. Interview with Amir Aslan Afshar (Foundation for Iranian Studies, Bethesda, MD, 1988). Interview conducted as part of Iran Oral History project on 10–12 September 1988.
31. Zand-Fard *Turbulence*, pp. 135–44.
32. Ibid., p. 141.
33. Jack Anderson, 'Kissinger Courts Shah, A Dangerous Megalomaniac', *Kentucky New Era* (3 July 1975).
34. See Gholam Reza Afkhami's profile, *The Life and Times of the Shah* (University of California Press, Oakland, CA, 2009). Interview with Afkhami (Foundation for Iranian Studies, Bethesda, MD, 8 June 2012).
35. Zand-Fard, *Turbulence*, pp. 135–50.
36. Benazir Bhutto, *Daughter of Destiny* (Simon and Schuster, New York, 1989), p. 95.
37. James P. Farwell, *The Pakistan Cauldron* (Potomac Books, Washington, DC, 2011), p. 5.
38. Ibid.
39. Pasha, *Profile*, p. 286.
40. Wolpert, *Bhutto*, pp. 234–5.

41. Telephone interview with Ardeshir Zahedi, former Iranian foreign minister, 13 November 2012.
42. Zand-Fard, *Turbulence*, p. 139.
43. Ibid.
44. Ibid., p. 162.
45. Wolpert, *Bhutto*, p. 265.
46. Ibid., p. 210.
47. Department of State Executive Order N/A or Blank, 8 July 1976.
48. Alam, 'Relations'.
49. Nawaz, *Swords*, p. 364.
50. Tariq Ali, *The Duel: Pakistan on the Flight Path of American Power* (Simon and Schuster, New York, 2009), p. 106.
51. 'Pakistan's Zia Knows How to Stay on Top', *Wall Street Journal*, 30 June 1988.
52. Simon J. Rabinovitch, 'Pakistan's "Jewish" Roots', *Haaretz*, 1 October 2013.
53. Speech by Zia ul-Haq, *Pakistan Times*, 24 April 1979.
54. Telephone interview with Abol Hassan Bani Sadr, Paris, 12 August 2013.
55. Interview with Asad Durrani, Rawalpindi, Pakistan, 16 April 2013.
56. 'US Unperturbed as Iran and Pakistan Quit CENTO', *Sun*, 13 March 1979.
57. Department of State Executive Order 12065, 17 April 1981.
58. CIA National Intelligence Daily, 12 March 1979.
59. Foreign and Commonwealth Office Cable 353/3, 16 October 1980.
60. Foreign and Commonwealth Office File 37/2123, Telegram No. 49, 19 March 1979.
61. 'The CIA's Intervention in Afghanistan', *Nouvel Observateur*, 15–21 January 1998.
62. 'Near East/North Africa Report', Joint Publications Research Service Report 74935, 15 January 1980.
63. Foreign and Commonwealth Office Telegram 1356, British Embassy in Islamabad, 13 November 1980.
64. 'US-PAK Talks: Regional Issues', Department of State Executive Order 12065, 24 October 1979.
65. See Yaroslav Trofimov, *The Siege of Mecca* (Anchor Books, New York, 2007), pp. 88–97.
66. 'Troops rescue 100 in Islamabad', *New York Times*, 22 November 1979.
67. 'A Day of Terror Recalled', *Washington Post*, 27 November 2004.
68. 'Body of 2nd American is Found in Islamabad Embassy', *New York Times*, 23 November 1979.
69. 'US Hails Guards at Two Embassies', *Chicago Tribune*, 25 November 1979.
70. 'Impact of Iranian and Afghan Events on South Asia', National Foreign Assessment Center, PA 80–10007 (January 1980).
71. Department of State Memorandum E2AV, unknown date (declassified on 11 January 2000).
72. Department of State Cable 8004207, 12 January 1980.
73. State Department Executive Order 12065, 26 April 1980.
74. Bani Sadr phone interview.

75. Foreign and Commonwealth Office File Ref 014/1, Kabul Telegram 215, 28 February 1978.
76. 'Implications of Iran for Afghanistan', CIA memorandum, 16 February 1979. Available at the US National Archives, Maryland.
77. 'Kabul Citizens Confirm their Revolutionary Stand', *Kabul Times*, 1 April 1979.
78. 'Amin Addresses Shiite Representatives', *New Kabul Times*, 3 June 1979.
79. 'Great Leader Addresses New Cabinet', *New Kabul Times*, 1 April 1979.
80. Snegirev and Samunin, *Dead End*, p. 361.
81. Barnett R. Rubin, *The Fragmentation of Afghanistan* (Yale University Press, New Haven, CT, 2002), pp. 112–21.
82. Snegirev and Samunin, *Dead End*, p. 387.
83. 'Building of New Society', *Kabul Times*, 2 April 1979.
84. 'Revolution Brings Sectarian Strife to Southeast Iran', *Washington Post*, 26 December 1979.
85. 'Iran Moves on the Baluchis', *Washington Post*, 23 December 1979.
86. 'Baluchistan: Iran's Weakest Link?', CIA Research Paper GC 80–10023, March 1980.
87. Eqbal Ahmed, 'What's Behind the Crisis in Iran and Afghanistan', *Social Text*, No. 3 (Autumn 1980), p. 54.
88. 'Iranian and Afghan Events'.
89. US Diplomatic Cable Islama 00079 – 052009Z, Islamabad Embassy, 5 January 1980.
90. 'Foreign Assistance Legislation for Fiscal Year 1981 (Part 4)', US House of Representatives, Committee on Foreign Affairs, 96th Congress, 2nd Session, 11 February 1980, 21 February 1980, 4 March 1980, 6 March 1980.
91. Department of State Briefing Paper 8001361391, unknown date.
92. Cable from Kabul, Department of State Executive Order 12065, 7 February 1980.
93. 'Everything is Going Zia's Way, But How Firm is Country's Foundation?', *Christian Science Monitor*, 6 December 1982.
94. Department of State Cable 8004203, 2–3 February 1980.
95. Foreign and Commonwealth Office File 1519551, 17 December 1979.
96. 'U.S. Policy Toward Iran', White House Memorandum MSC/ICS 402010, 11 February 1980.
97. 'Russia vs. Iran: US Ponders Unthinkable', *Los Angeles Times*, 18 January 1980.
98. 'Afghanistan Insurgent Status', CIA report, July 1980.
99. 'Afghanistan Seeks to Open Talks to Mend Ties with Iran, Pakistan', *Washington Post*, 18 April 1980.
100. 'Pakistan Asks UN to Appoint Envoy to Start Talks with Afghanistan, Iran', *Washington Post*, 4 January 1981.
101. Department of State Executive Order 12065, 2 June 1980.
102. 'Pakistan: Tough Choices on Afghanistan', CIA Research Paper, July 1982.
103. 'Pakistan's Leader Arrives in Iran for Talks on Conflict', *New York Times*, 28 September 1980.

104. Foreign and Commonwealth Office Cable 353/3, 16 October 1980.
105. Foreign and Commonwealth Office File FSP/021, 17 October 1980.
106. Ibid.
107. 'Iran: Fragmentation in the future', CIA memorandum, 26 September 1980.

Chapter 8   The Arrival of the Shi'a–Sunni Schism in Relations

1. CIA National Intelligence Daily, CO NID 80–214JX, 11 September 1980.
2. 'Soviets Reported Spying on Pakistan in Iran', *Los Angeles Times*, 1 March 1982.
3. Muhammad Qasim Zaman, 'Sectarianism in Pakistan', *Modern Asian Studies*, Vol. 32, No. 3 (July 1998), pp. 70–82.
4. CIA National Intelligence Daily 348, 24 April 1979.
5. Foreign and Commonwealth Office File FSP 014/1, 15 September 1980.
6. See *The Machinery of Takeover*, declassified CIA memorandum, CREST 25-year Program Archive, 1 January 1984.
7. Anatol Lieven, *Pakistan: A Hard Country* (Penguin Books, London, 2011), p. 293.
8. US National Intelligence Council Report NIC 2973–83, 21 April 1983.
9. Hassan Abbas, *Shiism and Sectarian Conflict in Pakistan* (Combating Terrorism Center at West Point, New York, September 2010), p. 34.
10. 'Warning to the US about Plans against Iran'. Available (in Persian) at www.tasnimnews.com/Home/Single/111916 (accessed 7 November 2014).
11. 'In Pakistan, We Want a Khomeini'. Available (in Persian) at www.tasnimnews.com/Home/Single/97118 (accessed 7 November 2014).
12. Fatemeh Aman, 'Iran's Shia Policy keeps Pakistan on Side', *Jane's Islamic Affairs Analyst* (November 2009).
13. See Abbas, *Sectarian Conflict*, pp. 32–5.
14. Maleeha Lodhi, 'Pakistan's Shia Movement: An Interview with Arif Hussaini', *Third World Quarterly*, Vol. 10, No. 2 (April 1988), pp. 806–17.
15. Ibid.
16. 'Iranian President Greeted by Cheering Crowds, Anti-US Slogans', Associated Press report, 13 January 1986.
17. 'Outlook for Revolution in Pakistan', *Crescent International*, 16–28 February 1986.
18. 'Khamenei's Visit: Resurgence of Shia Extremism', cable, US Department of State Executive Order 12356, 23 January 1986.
19. Aman, 'Iran's Shia Policy'.
20. Draft scope paper for foreign ministers visit, Department of State Executive Order 12065, April 1981.
21. 'Soviet Activities Affecting US Interests', CIA, National Foreign Assessment Center (15 February 1989).
22. CIA Director of Intelligence, 'Pakistan: Implications of Military Commitments to Arab States', 14 September 1983.
23. Skype interview with Ali-Akbar Omid-Mehr, 11 August 2011.

24. 'With its Ports Periled by War, Iran Boosts Trade with Pakistan', Reuters report, 8 December 1983.

25. 'China's Arms Trade with Iran', CIA Report GI M 84–10077C, 20 April 1984.

26. 'Iranians Captured Stinger Missiles from Afghan Guerillas, US Says', *New York Times*, 17 October 1987.

27. Mehtab Ali Shah, *The Foreign Policy of Pakistan: Ethnic Impacts on Diplomacy, 1971–1994* (I.B.Tauris, New York, 1997), pp. 29–30.

28. Interview with Shamshad Ahmad, Lahore, 11 April 2013.

29. Adrain Levy and Catherine Scott-Clark, *Deception: Pakistan, the United States, and the Secret Trade in Nuclear Weapons* (Walker Publishing Company, New York, 2007), pp. 133–4.

30. Gordon Corera, *Shopping for Bombs: Nuclear Proliferation, Global Security and the Rise and Fall of the A.Q. Khan Network* (Oxford University Press, New York, 2006), p. 64.

31. John Lancaster and Kamran Khan, 'Pakistanis Say Nuclear Scientists Aided Iran', *Washington Post*, 24 January 2004.

32. 'Pakistan Faces Woes from Within, Without', *Washington Post*, 28 July 1987.

33. 'Iran Signs Secret Atom Deal', *Observer*, 12 June 1988.

34. Kerry Dumbaugh, *Pakistan's Nuclear Program: US Foreign Policy Considerations* (Congressional Research Service, Washington, DC, 19 March 1990).

35. Telegram, Department of State Executive Order 12356, 14 June 1988.

36. 'Implementation of NPT Safeguards Agreement in the Islamic Republic of Iran', IAEA document, 18 November 2005. Available at www.iaea.org/sites/default/files/gov2005-87.pdf (accessed 8 December 2014).

37. CIA Director of Intelligence, 'Near East and Soviet Asia Review', NESA NESAR 85–014, 21 June 1985.

38. 'Tough choices', CIA Research Paper.

39. See CIA Memorandum NESA M 83–10100CX, 28 April 1983. Available at the US National Archives, Maryland.

40. CIA Director of Intelligence, 'Afghanistan: Limits to US Pressure for Resistance Unity', NESA M 85–10189, 17 September 1985.

41. 'High-level Soviet Peace Feeler on Afghanistan', *Christian Science Monitor*, 28 October 1982.

42. Riaz Khan, *Untying the Afghan Knot: Negotiating Soviet Withdrawal* (Duke University Press, Durham, NC), p. 125.

43. Amin, *Reappraisal*, p. 109.

44. CIA Director of National Intelligence, 'Afghanistan: Prospects for the Resistance', NIE 37–83, 4 October 1983.

45. 'The Soviet Presence in Afghanistan: Implications for the Regional Powers and the United States', National Intelligence Estimate NIE 11/37/85, April 1985.

46. Craig Karp, *Afghanistan: Six Years of Soviet Occupation* (US Department of State, Bureau of Public Affairs, Washington, DC, December 1985).

47. A National Security Decision from the White House, MSC/ICS 402010, 11 June 1985.

48. CIA Director of Intelligence, 'Afghanistan Situation Report', NESA M 84–10231CX, 24 July 1984.

49. 'Background Paper: Iranian Support to the Afghan Resistance', National Security Archive: Item number AF01634, 11 July 1985.

50. CIA Director of Intelligence, 'Afghanistan-US: The Alliance at the UN', NESA M 85–10211, 24 October 1985.

51. Geoffrey Kemp, *The Reagan Administration* (The Iran Primer, United States Institute of Peace, Washington, DC, unknown date). Available at http://iranprimer.usip.org/resource/reagan-administration (accessed 7 November 2014).

52. 'When Rouhani Met Ollie North', *Foreign Policy*, 26 September 2013.

53. Secret National Security Council Memorandum of Conversation NSC/ICS 40425, 26 May 1986.

54. Yezid Sayigh, 'Arms Production in Pakistan and Iran: The Limit of Self-reliance', in Eric Arnett (ed.), *Military Capacity and the Risk of War* (Stockholm International Peace Research Institute, Stockholm, 1997), p. 162.

55. 'US Sees Troubling Tilt by Pakistan to Iran', *New York Times*, 1 November 1987.

56. 'Memorandum: The Soviets and the Tribes of Southwest Asia', Southwest Asia Analytic Center, CIA, 23 September 1989.

57. 'Troubling Tilt', *New York Times*.

58. 'Pro-Iran Party Poses Problems in Pakistan', *Washington Post*, 23 July 1987.

59. 'Pakistan President Zia and US Ambassador Killed in Plane Crash' *Wall Street Journal*, 18 August 1988.

Chapter 9   1988–2001: Geopolitical Foes, Sometime Partners

1. Mirza Aslam Beg, 'The Ajam Spring', *Nation*, 2 October 2011.

2. See Sayigh, 'Arms Production'.

3. Steve Coll, *Ghost Wars* (Penguin Books, London, 2004), p. 220.

4. Ibid., pp. 220–1.

5. Interview with Gen. Mirza Aslam Beg, NBC News, 9 February 2004.

6. Ibid.

7. Peter Tomsen, *The Wars of Afghanistan: Messianic Terrorism, Tribal Conflicts, and the Failures of Great Powers* (Public Affairs, New York, 2011), pp. 290–1.

8. Congressional Record, 140, No. 126, 12 September 1994. See also 'Nuclear Army Skips Pakistani Army', *New York Times*, 30 January 2004.

9. Nawaz, *Swords*, p. 449.

10. A. Q. Khan has since said that General Beg explicitly authorized nuclear transfers to Iran. See Henry D. Sokolski (ed.), *Pakistan's Nuclear Future: Worrisome beyond War* (Strategic Studies Institute, Carlisle, PA, January 2008), pp. 17–23.

11. See Alam, 'Relations'.

12. 'Tough Choices', CIA Research Paper.

13. 'Najibullah Refuses to Depart as a Step to Afghan Accord', *New York Times*, 14 June 1989.

14. Sayed Askar Mousavi, *The Hazaras of Afghanistan* (St Martin's Press, New York, 1997), p. 178.

15. Hafizullah Emadi, 'Exporting Iran's Revolution: The Radicalization of the Shiite Movement in Afghanistan', *Middle Eastern Studies*, Vol. 31, No. 1 (1995), pp. 1–12.

16. Vahid Mojdeh, *Political Relations between Iran and Afghanistan in the 20*[th] *Century* (Mivand, Kabul, 2010), pp. 232–41.

17. Ibid., p. 238.

18. For a discussion of the interim Afghan Government, see Zalmay Khalilzad, *Prospects for the Afghan Interim Government* (Rand, Washington, DC, 1991).

19. Mousavi, *Hazaras*, p. 182.

20. Mojdeh, *Relations*, p. 246.

21. Interview with a number of former Pakistani diplomats in Islamabad.

22. Ian Preston (ed.), *A Political Chronology of Central, South and East Asia* (Europa Publications, London, 2001), p. 8. For a description of Najibullah's visit, see Mojdeh, *Relations*, pp. 294–322.

23. Interview with Asad Durrani, Islamabad, 16 April 2013.

24. Tomsen, *Wars of Afghanistan*, pp. 374–5.

25. Shah M. Tarzi, 'Afghanistan in 1991: A Glimmer of Hope', *Asian Survey*, Vol. 32, No. 2 (February 1992).

26. Tomsen, *Wars of Afghanistan*, pp. 15–16.

27. 'Afghan Endgame', *Herald*, 6 February 1989.

28. Nawaz, *Swords*, p. 423.

29. Ahmed Rashid, *Taliban: Militant Islam, Oil, and Fundamentalism in Central Asia* (Yale University Press, New Haven, CT, 2000), pp. 23–35.

30. 'The Unstated Parts of Benazir Bhutto's Trip to Iran', *Mardom Salari*, 1390,09, 19 (Iranian calendar). Available at www.mardomsalari.com/template1/News.aspx?NID=153378 (accessed 9 November 2014).

31. Ibid.

32. From Bhutto's account, given to Steve Coll in 2002.

33. William Maley, *The Afghanistan Wars* (Palgrave Macmillan, Basingstoke, UK, 2002). p. 219.

34. Peter Marsden, *The Taliban: War, Religion and the New Order in Afghanistan* (Oxford University Press, Karachi, 1998), p. 44.

35. Iran blamed the Mujahedeen-e Khalq (MEK).

36. See *The 9/11 Commission Report* (US Government Printing Office, Washington, DC, 2004), p. 73.

37. Interview with Khalid Mahmood, Islamabad, 18 April 2013. For background on anti-Iran attacks in Pakistan, see Dr Syed Minhaj ul-Hassan and Sayyed Abdolhossain Raeisossadat (eds), *Pakistan-Iran Relations in Historical Perspective* (Culture Center of the Islamic Republic of Iran, Peshawar, March 2004), p. 197.

38. 'Pakistan Found to Aid Iran Nuclear Efforts', *New York Times*, 2 September 2004.

39. Interview with Hossein Mousavian, Princeton, NJ, 27 June 2012.

40. 'Afghanistan's Islamist Groups', *Current Trends in Islamist Ideology*, Vol. 5 (23 May 2007), pp. 235–256.

41. Mohsen Milani, 'Iran's Policy Toward Afghanistan', *Middle East Journal*, Vol. 60, No. 2 (Spring 2006), pp. 90–105.

42. Ibid.

43. Khatami's speech at the Islamic Conference summit, 9 December 1997. Available at www.radioislam.org/islam/english/islamwo/khatami.htm (accessed 9 November 2014).

44. 'Iran Applauds Pakistani Nuclear Tests', Associated Press report, 1 June 1998.

45. Interview with Khalid Mahmood, Islamabad, 18 April 2013.

46. Ibid.

47. 'Survivors Describe Taliban', Human Rights Watch report, 2 November 1998.

48. Mojdeh, *Relations*, p. 348.

49. 'An Account of the Martyrdom of Iranian Diplomats in Mazar-e Sharif by the Only Survivor', Fars News report, 10 August 2013.

50. Vali Kouzegar Kaleji, 'Ups and Downs in Iran-Pakistan Ties', *Iranian Review of Foreign Affairs*, Vol. 2, No. 4 (Winter 2012), p. 153.

51. Interview with Abbas Maleki, Cambridge, MA, 10 August 2012.

52. 'Muslims, Yeltsin Denounce Attacks', CNN report, 21 August 1998.

53. Mojdeh, *Relations*, pp. 350–5.

54. Amir M. Haji-Yousefi, Canadian Political Science Association Annual Conference, Waterloo, Ontario, 16 May 2011, p. 6.

55. Rashid, *Taliban*, pp. 239–44.

56. Pervez Musharraf, *In the Line of Fire* (Simon and Schuster, New York, 2006), p. 211.

57. 'Khatami's Visit a Turning Point', *Dawn*, 27 December 2002.

58. 'Interview with a Taliban Insider: Iran's Game in Afghanistan', *Atlantic*, 15 November 2011.

59. See Haji-Yousefi, 'Conference'.

60. 'Afghanistan: One Year Later', CNN report, 10 October 2002.

61. Interview with Jim Dobbins, The Foreign Affairs Oral History Collection of the Association for Diplomatic Studies and Training, 21 July 2003.

62. James Dobbins, *After the Taliban* (Potomac Books, Dulles, VA, 2008), p. 42.

63. 'A Nation Challenged: Transfer of Power; Afghan Leader is Sworn In, Asking for Help to Rebuild', *New York Times*, 23 December 2001.

Chapter 10 2001-Present: Afghanistan, the Arab Challenge and Iran's Soft Power in Pakistan

1. For background, see Sadeq Kharazi's personal notes on his website: www.kharazi.ir/fa/ (accessed 10 November 2014).

2. United Nations Conference and Trade and Development database, *Handbook on Statistics and Date Files* (2003).

3. 'Uneasy Ties with Iran', *Dawn*, 6 December 2006.

4. Interview with Javid Husain, Lahore, 17 April 2013. See also Javid Husain, 'A Window of Opportunity', *Nation*, 25 June 2013.
5. 'Who are Iran's Jundollah Rebels?', *CTC Sentinel*, 23 February 2010.
6. 'When the Mountains were Red', *Dawn*, 1 August 2013.
7. 'Rigi's Arrest a Godsend for Pakistan', *Dawn*, 24 February 2010.
8. 'Iranians Face Terror Threat in Pakistan', *Daily Times*, 9 March 2010.
9. Zahid Ali Khan, 'Balochistan Factor in Pak-Iran Relations: Opportunities and Constraints', *South Asian Studies*, Vol. 27, No. 1 (2012), pp. 121–40.
10. 'Smuggled Petrol is Selling Like Hot Cakes', *Dawn*, 9 June 2009.
11. For background, see Mansoor Akbar Kundi, 'Borderland Interaction: The Case of Pak-Iranian Baloch', *IPRI Journal*, Vol. IX, No. 2 (Summer 2009).
12. *World Drug Report 2010* (United Nations Office on Drugs and Crime, Vienna, 2010).
13. Khan, 'Factor'.
14. 'The Assassination Attempt on Ahmadinejad's Life', Iranian Students News Agency report, 12 May 2012.
15. 'New Details about the Recent Terrorist Incident', Alef news site, 1 Aban 1388 (Iranian calendar). Available at http://alef.ir/vdcc4mqp.2bqp48laa2.html?55788 (accessed 10 November 2014).
16. 'Iran Seeks Permission to Pursue Suicide Bombers into Pakistan', *Jane's Defence Weekly* (21 October 2009).
17. 'Pakistan Says will Help Iran Find Bomb Culprits', Reuters report, 21 October 2009.
18. Ghani Jafar, 'Pakistan-Iran Relations: The Security Scenario', The Institute of Strategic Studies, Islamabad (downloaded on 11 September 2012).
19. 'Iran Presents Evidence of Pakistan's Links with Jundallah', Press TV report, 16 December 2009.
20. Ibid.
21. Alex Vatanka and Fatemeh Aman, 'The Making of an Insurgency in Iran's Baluchistan Province', *Jane's Intelligence Review* (June 2006).
22. 'A Review of Six Big Operations by the Intelligence Ministry in the 10th Government', Tasnim News Agency report, 30 July 2013.
23. Ibid.
24. To this day, there are conflicting official Iranian and Pakistani accounts of how Rigi was captured. Pakistan's Ambassador to Tehran stated that his country's assistance was critical in the arrest of Rigi, while Iran's intelligence minister, Heidar Moslehi, suggested that no other 'regional country' had been involved in the operation. See 'Pakistan Helped Iran Nab Jundullah Chief: Envoy', *Daily Times*, 25 February 2010.
25. Telephone interview with Rahimullah Yusefzai, 19 April 2013.
26. For an overview of such reports, see Thomas Joscelyn, 'Osama bin Laden's Spokesman Freed by Iran', *Long War Journal* (September 2010). See also a debate on this issue in Patrick Clawson's 'Analysis of Iran-al Qaeda "Secret Deal"', *Iran Primer* (July 2011).

27. Seymour M. Hersh, 'Preparing the Battlefield', *New Yorker*, 7 July 2008.
28. Mark Perry, 'False Flag', *Foreign Policy*, 13 January 2012.
29. 'Secretary of State's Designation of Jundallah', 3 November 2010. Available at www.state.gov/r/pa/prs/ps/2010/11/150332.htm (accessed 10 November 2014).
30. 'Jundullah: Profile of a Sunni Extremist Group', Radio Free Europe/Radio Liberty report, 20 October 2009.
31. 'Balochistan Assessment 2013', South Asia Terrorism Portal. Available at www.satp.org/satporgtp/countries/pakistan/Balochistan/index.html (accessed 10 November 2014).
32. 'Violence is on the Rise in Balochistan', *Express Tribune*, 3 January 2013. Available at tribune.com.pk/story/488311/violence-is-on-the-rise-in-balochistan-report (accessed 10 November 2014).
33. 'Massacre of Hazara People: Covert Goals', *Iran Review*, 26 February 2013.
34. 'HRW Pushes Pakistan to "Urgently" Protect the Shiites', AFP report, 6 September 2012.
35. Ibid.
36. 'Pakistan Arrests Leader of Extremist Group', AFP report, 30 August 2012.
37. 'Pakistan Arrests Lashka-e-Jhangvi Leader Malik Ishaq', *Long War Journal*, 22 February 2013.
38. 'Pakistan's Leader Escapes Murder by a Minute', *Guardian*, 15 December 2003.
39. 'Sectarian violence in Pakistan', South Asia Terrorism Portal. Available at www.satp.org/satporgtp/countries/pakistan/database/sect-killing.htm (accessed 10 November 2013).
40. 'Power Rising, Taliban Besiege Pakistani Shia', *New York Times*, 26 July 2008.
41. Alex Vatanka, 'The Guardian of Pakistani Shia', *Current Trends in Islamist Ideology*, 1 June 2012.
42. See Aman, 'Iran's Shia Policy'.
43. The speech is available at www.khamenei.ir at http://farsi.khamenei.ir/speech-content?id=2166 (accessed 8 December 2014).
44. Interview with Khalid Masood, former chairman of Pakistan's Islamic Ideology Council, Islamabad, 16 April 2013.
45. Ibid.
46. Interview with Asad Durrani, Rawalpindi, 16 April 2013.
47. 'Al-Qaida-linked Group Claims Kabul Suicide Attack on Shia Pilgrims', *Guardian*, 6 December 2011.
48. 'Kabul Accuses Pakistan over Shiite Attack', AFP report, 19 June 2012.
49. *Monasebat Rahbordi Iran va Pakestan* (Institute of Strategic Studies, Tehran, 2010), pp. 139–80.
50. Interview with Zalmay Khalilzad, Washington, DC, 12 June 2012.
51. Ibid.
52. Ibid.
53. Telephone interview Hossein Sheikh-Zeineddin, 3 August 2012.
54. Cable, Department of State Executive Order 12958, 2 June 2009. Published by Wikileaks.

55. 'Pakistan Starts Rebuilding Road to Afghan Border', Xinhua report, 19 November 2012.
56. 'India, Iran Talk Chabahar Funding', *Hindustan Times*, 5 May 2013.
57. Musharraf, p. 308.
58. Ibid.
59. Ibid., p. 306.
60. 'Musharraf Links Israel Ties to Palestine State', *Dawn*, 19 September 2005.
61. Department of State Executive Order 12958, 9 April 2009. Source: Wikileaks.
62. Ibid., 12 February 2010.
63. Ibid., 16 October 2008.
64. Ibid., 20 November 2007.
65. 'When Riyadh Provokes Islamabad against Tehran', *Iranian Diplomacy*, 16 April 2012.
66. 'Iran is Popular in Pakistan; Overwhelmingly Disliked Elsewhere Else', *Washington Post*, 11 January 2013.
67. 'Bilateral Talks: Zardari to Meet Ahmadinejad Tomorrow', *Express Tribune*, 15 July 2011.
68. 'Pakistan is not after Peace in Afghanistan', *Iranian Diplomacy* (Persian-language), 26 April 2013.
69. Interview with Iranian diplomat in Islamabad, 20 April 2013.
70. 'Pakistan to Support Iran against Israel', Press TV report, 9 February 2012.
71. Cable, State Department Executive Order 12958, 3 February 2010. Published by Wikileaks.
72. For a contemporary Iranian overview of Iran–Pakistan relations, see 'Rivalry and Friendship between Iran and Pakistan', *Iranian Diplomacy* (Persian-language), 13 September 2011.
73. 'Reactions to Nawaz's Win: The Army's Fear; India's Happiness and America's Doubts', *Iranian Diplomacy* (Persian-language), 19 May 2013. See also, 'Who gave Islamabad the Green Light: An Interview with Iran's Former Ambassador to Pakistan', *Iranian Diplomacy* (Persian-language), 10 May 2013.
74. Pir-Mohammad Mollazehi, 'Pakistan and Necessity for Adopting Correct Policies', Iranreview.org, 21 May 2013.
75. 'Iran Cancels Pakistan Gas Pipeline', AP report, 14 December 2013.
76. 'Saudi Arabia's Voice will be Heard from Iran's East', *Tabnak* (Persian-language), 24 May 2013.

Epilogue

1. 'Getting Close to Terror but Not to Stop It', *New York Times*, 8 November 2014.
2. 'IRGC Ground Force Commander Vows to Dry Up Terrorists Across Border', Fars News report, 20 October 2014. Available at http://english.farsnews.com/newstext.aspx?nn=13930728001316 (accessed 9 December 2014).
3. 'Iran, China Set to Up Trade to $200 Billion: Official', Press TV report, 3 March 2014.

BIBLIOGRAPHY

Abbas, Hassan, *Shiism and Sectarian Conflict in Pakistan* (Combating Terrorism Center at West Point, New York, 2010)

Abrahamian, Ervand, *Iran Between Two Revolutions* (Princeton University Press, Princeton, NJ, 1982)

Ahmed, Eqbal, 'What's Behind the Crisis in Iran and Afghanistan' *Social Text*, No. 3, Autumn 1980

Akhtar, Aasim Sajjad, 'Balochistan versus Pakistan' *Economic and Political Weekly*, No. 45, 2007

Alam, Asadollah, *The Shah and I* (I.B.Tauris, London, 1992)

Alam, Shah, 'Iran–Pakistan Relations: Political and Strategic Dimensions' *Strategic Analysis*, Vol. 28, No. 4, 2004

Ali, Imtiaz, 'The Balochistan Problem' *Pakistan Horizon*, No. 2, 2005

Ali Khan, Zahid, 'Balochistan Factor in Pak-Iran Relations: Opportunities and Constraints' *South Asian Studies*, Vol. 27, No. 1, 2012

Ali, Mehrunnisa, 'General Mohammad Zia-ul-Haq visit to Muslim Countries' *Pakistan Horizon*, Vol. 30, Third and Fourth Quarter, 1977

Ali, Tariq, *The Duel: Pakistan on the Flight Path of American Power* (Simon and Schuster, New York, 2009)

Alvandi, Roham, 'Nixon, Kissinger, and the Shah: The Origins of Iranian Primacy in the Persian Gulf' *Diplomatic History*, Vol. 36, Issue 2, April 2012

Andrew, Christopher M. and Mitrokhin, Vasili, *The World Was Going Our Way: The KGB and the Battle for the Third World* (Basic Books, New York, 2006)

Armstrong, David and Trento, Joseph J., *America and the Islamic Bomb* (Steerforth Press, Hanover, NH, 2007)

Bhutto, Benazir, *Daughter of Destiny* (Simon and Schuster, New York, 1989)

Bogle, Lori Lyn (ed.), The *Cold War: Cold War Culture and Society* (Routledge, New York, 2001)

Burr, William, 'A Brief History of US-Iranian Nuclear Negotiations' *Bulletin of the Atomic Scientists*, January–February 2009

Clements, Frank A., *Conflict in Afghanistan: A Historical Encyclopedia* (ABC-Clio Inc., Santa Barbara, CA, 2003)

Cohen, Stephen, 'Pakistan: Army, Society and Security' *Asian Affairs*, No. 2, 1983

Cole, Juan, 'Iranian Culture and South Asia – 1500–1900', in Nikkie Keddie (ed.), *Iran and the Surrounding World: Interactions in Culture and Cultural Politics* (University of Washington Press, Seattle, WA, 2002)

Coll, Steve, *Ghost Wars* (Penguin Books, London, 2004)

Cooper, Andrew Scott, *The Oil Kings* (Simon & Schuster, New York, 2011)

Corera, Gordon, *Shopping for Bombs: Nuclear Proliferation, Global Security and the Rise and Fall of the A.Q. Khan Network* (Oxford University Press, New York, 2006)

Dill, Shaheen F., 'The Cabal in Kabul: Great-power Interaction in Afghanistan' *American Political Science Review*, Vol. 71, No. 2, June 1977

Dimitrakis, Panagiotis, *Failed Alliances of the Cold War: Britain's Strategy and Ambitions in Asia and the Middle East* (I.B.Tauris, London, 2012)

Dobbins, James, *After the Taliban* (Potomac Books, Dulles, VA, 2008)

Dupree, Louis, 'A Suggested Pakistan–Afghanistan–Iran Federation' *Middle East Journal*, Vol. 17, No. 4, Autumn 1963

Emadi, Hafizullah, 'Exporting Iran's Revolution: The Radicalization of the Shiite Movement in Afghanistan' *Middle Eastern Studies*, Vol. 31, No. 1, 1995

Farooqi, Naimur Rahman, *Mughal-Ottoman Relations* (Idarah-i Adabiyat-i, Delhi, 1989)

Farrokh, Kaveh, *Iran at War: 1500–1988* (Osprey Publishing, Oxford, 2011)

Farwell, James P., *The Pakistan Cauldron* (Potomac Books, Washington, DC, 2011)

Gartenstein-Ross, Daveed and Vassefi, Tara, 'The Forgotten History of Afghanistan-Pakistan Relations' *Yale Journal of International Affairs*, March 2012

Goodson, Larry, *Afghanistan's Endless War: State Failure, Regional Politics, and the Rise of the Taliban* (University of Washington Press, Seattle, 2001)

Hadian, Kourosh, Dehghannejad, Morteza, and Kajbaf, Aliakbar, 'The Explanatory Comparison of Religious Policies in Central Governments of Safavid and Qajar Dynasties (1521/1925-AD)' *Asian Culture and History*, Vol. 4, No. 2, 2002

Hafeez Malik, *Central Asia: Its Strategic Importance and Future Prospects* (St Martin's Press, New York, 1994)

Hale, W.M. and Bharier, Julian, 'CENTO, R.C.D. and the Northern Tier: A Political and Economic Appraisal' *Middle Eastern Studies*, Vol. 8, No. 2, May 1972

Haqqani, Husain, *Pakistan: Between Mosque and Military* (Carnegie Endowment for International Peace, Washington, DC, 2005)

Harrison, Selig S., 'Baluch Nationalism and Super Power Rivalry' *International Security*, Vol. 5, No. 3, Winter 1980–1

Hasnain, Nadeem and Sheikh Abrar, Husain, *Shias and Shia Islam in India* (Harnam Publications, New Delhi, 1988)

Hussain, Rizwan, *Pakistan and the Emergence of Islamic Militancy in Afghanistan* (Ashgate Publishing Limited, Hampshire, 2005)

'Iran 1964–68: The Mood of Growing Confidence' *The World Today*, Vol. 24, No. 11, November 1968

Kaleji, Vali Kouzegar, 'Ups and Downs in Iran-Pakistan Ties' *Iranian Review of Foreign Affairs*, Vol. 2, No. 4, Winter 2012

Khalilzad, Zalmay, *Prospects for the Afghan Interim Government* (Rand, Washington, DC, 1991)

Khan, Feroz, *Eating Grass* (Stanford Security Studies, 2012)

Khan, Hafeez Ur-Rahman, 'Pakistan's Relations with the U.A.R.' *Pakistan Horizon*, Vol. 13, No. 3, 1960

Khan, Mohammad Ayub, *Friends Not Masters: A Political Autobiography* (Mr. Books, Islamabad, 2006)

Khan, Riaz, *Untying the Afghan Knot: Negotiating Soviet Withdrawal* (Duke University Press, Durham, NC, 1991)

Kumaraswamy, P.R., *Beyond the Veil: Israel-Pakistan Relations* (Jaffee Center for Strategic Studies, Tel Aviv University, 2000)

Kundi, Mansoor Akbar, 'Borderland Interaction: The Case of Pak-Iranian Baloch' *IPRI Journal*, Vol. IX, No. 2, Summer 2009

Levy, Adrain and Scott-Clark, Catherine, *Deception: Pakistan, the United States, and the Secret Trade in Nuclear Weapons* (Walker Publishing Company, New York, 2007)

Lieven, Anatol, *Pakistan: A Hard Country* (Penguin Books, London, 2011)

Litwak, Robert S., *Détente and the Nixon Doctrine: American Foreign Policy and the Pursuit of Stability 1969–1976* (Cambridge University Press, Cambridge, 1984)

Ma'oz, Moshe, *Muslim Attitudes to Jews and Israel* (Sussex Academic Press, Eastbourne, UK, 2010)

MacLean, Rory, *Magic Bus: On the Hippie Trail from Istanbul to India* (Ig Publishing, Brooklyn, NY, 2006)

Maley, William, *The Afghanistan Wars* (Palgrave Macmillan, Basingstoke, UK, 2002)

Marsden, Peter, *The Taliban: War, Religion and the New Order in Afghanistan* (Oxford University Press, Karachi, 1998)

Milani, Abbas, *The Shah* (Palgrave Macmillan, New York, 2011)

Milani, Mohsen, 'Iran's Policy Toward Afghanistan' *Middle East Journal*, Vol. 60, No. 2, Spring 2006

Minhaj ul-Hassan, Syed and Raeisossadat, Sayyed Abdolhossain (eds), *Pakistan-Iran Relations in Historical Perspective* (Culture Center of the Islamic Republic of Iran, Peshawar, March 2004)

Mirza, Humayun, *From Plassey to Pakistan* (University Press of America, Lanham, MD, 2002)

Mojdeh, Vahid, *Political Relations between Iran and Afghanistan in the 20th Century* (Mivand, Kabul, 2010)

Montagno, George L., 'The Pak-Afghan Détente' *Asian Survey*, Vol. 3, No. 12, December 1963

Mousavi, Sayed Askar, *The Hazaras of Afghanistan* (St Martin's Press, New York, 1997)

Mousavian, Syed Hossein, *The Iranian Nuclear Crisis* (Carnegie Endowment, Washington, DC, 2012)

Mudiam, Prithvi Ram, *India and the Middle East* (British Academic Press, New York, 1994)

Mukerjee, Dilip, 'Afghanistan under Daud: Relations with Neighboring States' *Asian Survey*, Vol. 15, No. 4, April 1975

Musharraf, Pervez, *In the Line of Fire* (Simon and Schuster, New York, 2006)

Nawaz, Shuja, *Crossed Swords* (Oxford University Press, Oxford, 2008)

Noorani, A.G., 'Soviet Ambitions in South Asia' *International Security*, Vol. 4, No. 3, Winter 1979–80

Office of Political and International Studies, Iranian Foreign Ministry, Selective Documents: Relations between Iran and Pakistan, Document No. 14, 1996

Pahlavi, Mohammad Reza, *Answer to History* (Stein and Day Publishing, New York, 1980)

Pande, Aparna, *Explaining Pakistan's Foreign Policy* (Routledge, New York, 2011)

Pasha, Ahmad Shuja, *Pakistan: A Political Profile* (Sang-e-Meel Publications, Lahore, 1991)

Pirzada, Syed Sharifuddin (ed.), *Foundations of Pakistan All-India Muslim League Documents: 1906–1947* (Vol. 1 – 1906–1924, National Publishing House Limited, Dacca, 1969)

Preston, Ian (ed.), *A Political Chronology of Central, South and East Asia* (Europa Publications, London, 2001)

Qureshi, S.M.M., 'Pakhtunistan: The Frontier Dispute between Afghanistan and Pakistan' *Pacific Affairs*, Vol. 39, No. 1–2, Spring/Summer 1966

Rabinovich, Itamar and Shaked, Haim (eds), *The Middle East between 1967 and 1973* (Transaction Inc., Edison, NJ, 1978)

Ramazani, Rouhollah, 'Iran's Search for Regional Cooperation' *Middle East Journal*, Vol. 30, No. 2, Spring 1976

Rashid, Ahmed, *Taliban: Militant Islam, Oil, and Fundamentalism in Central Asia* (Yale University Press, New Haven, CT, 2000)

'Revitalization of CENTO', *Pakistan Forum*, Vol. 3, No. 3, December 1972

Rezun, Miron, *Iran at the Crossroads: Global Relations in a Turbulent Decade* (Westview Press, Boulder, CO, 1990)

Romero, Juan, *The Iraqi Revolution of 1958: A Revolutionary Quest for Unity and Security* (University Press of America, Lanham, MD, 2011)

Rubin, Barnett R., *The Fragmentation of Afghanistan* (Yale University Press, New Haven, CT, 2002)

Sayigh, Yezid, 'Arms Production in Pakistan and Iran: The Limit of Self-reliance', in Eric Arnett (ed.), *Military Capacity and the Risk of War* (Stockholm International Peace Research Institute, 1997)

Schmidle, Nicholas, *To Live or To Perish Forever: Two Tumultuous Years in Pakistan* (Holt Paperbacks, New York, 2009)

Shah, Mehtab Ali, *The Foreign Policy of Pakistan: Ethnic Impacts on Diplomacy, 1971–1994* (I.B.Tauris, New York, 1997)

Snegirev, Vladimir and Samunin, Valery, *The Dead End: The Road to Afghanistan* (E-book)

Sokolski, Henry D. (ed.), *Pakistan's Nuclear Future: Worrisome beyond war* (Strategic Studies Institute, Carlisle, PA, January 2008)

Subrahmanyam, Sanjay, 'Iranians Abroad: Intra-Asian Elite Migration and Early Modern State Formation' *Journal of Asian Studies*, Vol. 51, No. 2, 1992

Tahir-Kheli, Shirin, 'Iran and Pakistan: Cooperation in an Area of Conflict' *Asian Survey*, Vol. 17, No. 5, May 1977

Tarzi, Shah M., 'Afghanistan in 1991: A Glimmer of Hope' *Asian Survey*, Vol. 32, No. 2, February 1992

Tomsen, Peter, *The Wars of Afghanistan: Messianic Terrorism, Tribal Conflicts, and the Failures of Great Powers* (Public Affairs, New York, 2011)

Trofimov, Yaroslav, *The Siege of Mecca* (Anchor Books, New York, 2007)

Tucker, Ernest, '1739: History, Self, and Other in Afsharid Iran and Mughal India' *Iranian Studies*, Vol. 31, No. 2, Spring 1998

Vance, Cyrus, *Hard Choices: Critical Years in America's Foreign Policy* (Simon and Schuster, New York, 1983)

Vatanka, Alex, 'The Guardian of Pakistani Shia' *Current Trends in Islamist Ideology*, 1 June 2012

———— and Aman, Fatemeh, 'The Making of an Insurgency in Iran's Baluchistan Province' *Jane's Intelligence Review*, June 2006

Walt, Stephen M., 'Testing Theories of Alliance Formation: The Case of South West Asia' *International Organization*, Vol. 42, No. 2, Spring 1988

Warton, Admiral, 'The Perso-Baluch Boundary' *Geographical Journal*, Vol. 9, No. 4, April 1897

Wilcox, Wayne Ayres, 'The Pakistan Coup d'état of 1958' *Pacific Affairs*, Vol. 38, No. 2, Summer 1965

Wolpert, Stanley, *Zulfi Bhutto of Pakistan: His Life and Times* (Oxford University Press, New York, 1993)

Yesilbursa, Behcet Kemal, 'The Formation of RCD: Regional Cooperation of Development' *Middle Eastern Studies*, Vol. 45, No. 4, July 2009

Zaman, Muhammad Qasim, 'Sectarianism in Pakistan' *Modern Asian Studies*, Vol. 32, No. 3, July 1998

Zand-Fard, Fereidoon, *Iran and a World in Turbulence* (Shiraze, Tehran, 2000)

INDEX

A-7 aircraft, 121
Abbottabad
  killing of Osama Bin Laden, 252
Abdullah, King (of Jordan), 251
Abdullah, King (of Saudi Arabia), 251
Abu Dhabi, 75, 87, 107–8
al-Adl, Jaish, 258–61
Al-Qaeda, 218, 221–2, 225, 230
  conflict with Iran, 235–8
  Iranian diplomat kidnapping, 237
Afghanistan, 2–5, 18, 29, 52–3,
    64–5, 67–8, 71, 109, 125, 129,
    157, 176, 218–25, 261–3
  6 + 2 Group, 220
  Bonn Conference, 223–4, 227
  CENTO, 132–4
  civil war, 208
  confederation with Iran and Pakistan,
    29–43, 93
  conflict with Pakistan, 95–100, 124
  coup, 83–6, 135–8
  Democratic Republic of Afghanistan,
    134
  Iranian Baluch, 91
  Iranian-Pakistani rivalry, 245–57
  relations with Iran, 88, 155–69
  riots in Herat, 151–5
  support for Mujahedeen, 185–206
  Taliban, 209–16, 226–9, 231–3, 238

as a target for Soviets, 3, 179–82
  tripartite (peace) talks, 187, 205
Africa, 218
  Horn of Africa, 238
Afshar, Amir Aslan, 75, 139–40, 146
Agnew, Spiro, 65
Ahmad, Shamshad, 4, 182
Ahmadinejad, Mahmoud, 233, 241,
    247, 250, 252
Ahmadis, 173
Ahmed, Khurshid, 148
Al-Ahram, 43
Akhtar, Rahman, 194
Alam, Assadollah, 62, 67, 95–9, 110
  stance on Afghanistan, 88
  trip to Kabul, 67–9
  on Zulfikar Bhutto, 104–5, 128
Albright, Madeleine, 219
Algerians, 214
Aloko, Eshaq, 245
Amer, General, 57
American Jewish Congress, 250
Amin, Hafizullah, 135, 162
Amin, Idi, 106
Amini, Hussein, 231
Andropov, Yuri, 15
Anglo-American leadership, 56
Ankara, 40, 43–5, 47, 49–50,
    54, 59

Arabs (Arab world), 2, 28–9, 43–4, 65, 69, 75, 82–3, 101–10, 172–3, 179, 186, 245, 254, 258
in Afghanistan, 200
Arab-Israeli conflict, 17–8, 58–63, 113–16
Iranian attitude, 101–110, 226, 234, 237
Pakistani overtures, 56–7, 80, 143, 180, 192–3, 249–52
Arafat, Yasser, 83, 106, 149
Araghi, Abdollah, 260
Arif, General Khalid Mahmud, 183
Armenia, 261
arms embargo against Pakistan, 54, 72, 76, 102, 115, 125–6
Al Assad, Hafez, 106
Atoms for Peace, 116
Attarzadeh, Heshmatollah
see Al-Qaeda kidnapping of Iranian diplomat
AWACS (Airborne Warning and Control Systems), 60
Awami League, 70
Azerbaijan (Iranian), 35
Aziz, Sartaj, 2

Baathists, 58, 88, 106
Babar, General Naseerullah, 210
Baghdad Pact, 19, 21, 23–4, see also CENTO
Bagram Air Base, 227
Bahrain, 61–3, 87, 179, 202
Bakhtiar, Shapour, 170
Baluch Liberation Front (BLF), 89
Baluchistan (Iran), 94–6, 160, 169, 189, 230
instability, 157–61, 229
Jaish al-Adl, 258
Jundollah, 231–9
Baluchistan Liberation Army, 235
Baluchistan (Pakistan), 1, 77, 81, 133–7, 161, 259
insurgency, 99–102, 113–4

strategic significance, 87–92
Bay of Bengal, 77
Bayar, Celal, 23
Bazoft, Farzad, 184
Beg, Mirza Aslam, 192, 202–3
on ties with Iran, 195–9
Bhutto, Benazir, 9, 142, 203, 221, 250
nuclear dealings with Iran, 297–200
rise to power, 194
Taliban, 199–200
visit to Tehran as prime minister, 209–15
Bhutto, Nusrat Ispahani, 6–7, 112, 175, 199
Bhutto, Zulfikar, 4, 6–10, 34, 42–7, 151, 162, 173, 175, 194, 230, 262
appeal to Muslims, 80–3, 103–6
campaign in Baluchistan, 88–103
confederation with Iran and Afghanistan, 27–32
defense ties with Iran and the West, 42–7, 53–4
political ambitions, 67–73, 78–83
relations with the Shah, 106–47
secret pact with the Shah, 170
Bombay, 7, 9
Bin Laden, Osama, 237, 252–4
Binori Town seminary, 231
Brahimi, Lakhdar, 220
British Broadcasting Corporation (BBC), 91
British Foreign Office, 14, 16
British India, 7, 16, 33
Brzezinski, Zbigniew, 152, 165–6
Bush, George H., 206–7
Bush, George W., 222–5, 237, 251
Bushehr (nuclear reactor), 183
Byroade, Henry, 108

C-130 aircraft, 194
C-141 aircraft, 65
Canada, 49, 116
Caribbean
Shah's exile in, 21

Caroe, Olaf, 88
Carter, Jimmy, 122, 127, 151–2, 155–6, 159, 162–7
Casey, William J., 163
Caspian Sea, 69
Cave, George, 191
CENTO (Central Treaty Organization), 18–9, 23–4, 28–9, 36, 38, 41, 41–58, 62–4, 78, 82–3, 91, 93, 103, 105, 124, 127, 130, 132, 133, 137–8, 150–2, 162, 198
Central Asia, 32, 161, 213–4
    energy riches, 219–21
    transit routes to and from, 247–9
Central Intelligence Agency (CIA), 18, 31, 55, 72, 76–7, 93, 114, 141, 148, 151, 161, 163, 170, 175, 181–2, 186, 188
Chabahar, 102, 161, 247–8
Chagla, Mahommedali Currim, 66–7
Chechens, 214
China, 45, 53–5, 74, 95, 101, 104, 115, 142, 159, 163, 181, 208, 220, 247–8, 261
Christopher, Warren, 166
Clinton, Bill (William J.), 218
Clinton, Hillary, 250
Commonwealth, 13–14
Commonwealth Relations Office, 14
Communism
    see Soviet Union and USSR
Concorde (flights to Iran), 110
confederation between Iran, Afghanistan and Pakistan, 28–32, 36–7, 40, 43, 196, 248
crusade, 104
Cyprus, 44, 49–50

Dar es Salaam, 218
Dari, 214
Dayan, Moshe, 149
Delhi
    see New Delhi

Dobbins, Jim, 223–4
drugs (see also opium), 41, 232
Dubai, 87, 170, 236
Dubs, Adolph, 151
Dulles, Allen, 18
Dulles, John Foster, 73
    against Soviets, 18–21, 51–2
Dupree, Louise, 31, 38
Durrand Line, 33, 86
Durrand, Sir Mortimer, 33–4
Durrani, Asad, 150, 205, 244

East Pakistan, 10, 70–81
Economic Cooperation Organization, 182, 212, 257
Egypt, 17, 29, 32, 43–4, 51, 56–60, 84, 103, 108, 134, 146–7
Eisenhower, Dwight
    encouraging Iran-Pakistan common defense against Soviets, 17, 22, 24, 51–2, 72
Empty Triangle (region of), 37–40
Esfahan, 27, 215
Ethiopia, 52, 134
Ettelaat, 57–8
Ettemad, Akbar, 116, 184
Europe-Asia Trade, 38
expatriates
    Pakistani, 107–8, 249
    Persian, 8–10

F-4 jets, 76, 113
F-14 jets, 60
F-16 jets, 166
F-86 Sabre jets, 49, 72
Faisal, King (Iraqi), 22–3, 29
Faisal, King (Saudi), 104–6, 143
Faisal Mosque (Islamabad), 244
Faisal, Prince Turki bin, 206, 209
Federal Security Force (FSF), 91
Ford, Gerald, 122, 125–6
France, 87, 116, 121, 142, 148
    nuclear talks with Iran, 118
Frontier Corps (Pakistani), 239, 259

Gailani family, 136, 186
Gandhi, Indira, 66, 73–7, 115, 117–18
Gates, Robert, 163
Gaza, 240
Geneva
    Accords, 188
    peace talks on Afghanistan, 187–8,
        204–5
George VI, King, 14
Germany, 49, 116
Ghaith, Sulaiman Abu, 237
Ghazi, Mohammad, 98
Ghotbzadeh, Sadeq, 164, 168
Golden Crescent, 232
Golpayegani, Ayatollah Mohammad, 249
Gorbachev, Mikhail, 192, 201
Great Game, 33, 208
Greater Afghanistan, 33
Greater Baluchistan, 88, 91
Greece, 44, 50
Griffin, George G.B., 88–9
Gromyko, Andrei, 168
Gwadar, 102, 247–8

Hafizullah, Amin, 135, 162
ul-Haq, Zia, 6, 15, 107, 127, 175–79,
    195–6, 199, 212, 240, 242
    Afghan anti-Soviet efforts,
        187–192
    attitude towards the Shah, 138–44
    balancing Iran and Arabs, 192–4
    Iran-Iraq war, 179–185
    mediation between US and Iran, 169
    relations with Ayatollah Khomeini,
        129–134, 148–56, 171–6
    Soviet invasion of Afghanistan,
        162–67
Harrison, Selig S., 88
Harvard University, 31, 210
Hashemite, 29, 32
Hazara, 185, 188, 201, 203, 206–7,
    217, 222, 239
Hekmatyar, Gulbuddin, 124, 186, 188,
    201, 203, 206–9

Helmand River, 98–100, 219
Helms, Richard, 95, 114, 118, 120
Herat, 40, 96–7, 151, 222, 224
    fall to the Taliban, 209, 217
    Iranian role in 1979 riots, 158–9,
        188–9
Hezb-e Eslami-Khalis, 210
Hezb-e Islami, 186
Hezb-e Wahdat, 202–3, 207–8
Hong Kong, 66
Hoveida, Amir Abbas, 47
Human Rights Watch, 217, 239
Hummel, Arthur, 132, 155, 164–5
Husain, Javid, 229
Hussein, King (of Jordan), 29, 43, 75
Hussein, Saddam, 88, 169, 180,
    183–4, 206, 230, 251
Hussaini, Syed Arif Hussain, 193

Imamia Students Organization Pakistan
    (ISO), 241, 244
India, 2–5, 7–10, 13, 16, 20, 25, 29,
    33, 35, 41–54, 56–7, 59,
    66–9, 71, 88, 94, 109, 121–2,
    124–7, 135, 140, 142–4, 151,
    153, 163, 173, 179–80, 185,
    193, 198–200, 208, 213, 224,
    235, 256
    Iran's warning to, 21
    nuclear tests, 116, 216
    Pakistani concerns about ties to Iran,
        235, 247–9
    position on Afghanistan, 138
    Shah's view on, 110–9, 123, 131,
        134
    against Taliban, 214
    views on Iran-Pakistan ties, 37
    war of 1971, 73–81, 90, 101
Indian Ocean, 8, 37, 123, 131, 150,
    162
Indian Ocean Economic Community,
    123, 131
India-USSR Friendship Treaty, 54, 93
    Treaty of Peace, 73

Indonesia, 184
Institute of Strategic Studies
  (Islamabad), 235
Inter-Services Intelligence Agency (ISI),
  169, 175
International Atomic Energy Authority
  (IAEA), 118, 183
Iran
  Axis of Evil, 224–5
  border treaty with Pakistan, 16
  common interests with Pakistan,
    10–2
  confederation with Pakistan, 28–32
  contemporary relations with
    Pakistan, 2–6
  early years of relations with Pakistan,
    6–10, 12–16
  loyalty to Mirza Iskander, 24–6
  security pact with Pakistan, 16–22
Iranian-American Defense Agreement,
  150
Iranian oil
  Afghan need for, 205
  Iran-Pakistan Friendship Treaty, 5,
    12–6, 41
  Pakistani attitude toward, 30, 58,
    76, 81, 88, 97, 105, 110–11, 116,
    125, 138, 141, 143, 147, 152,
    157, 181, 197, 228
  protecting facilities, 61
Iran's supreme leader
  see Ayatollah Ali Khamenei
Iran Zamin (the Land of Iran), 172
Iraq, 32–3, 60, 69, 84, 88–90, 93,
    103, 109, 148, 160, 176, 180–4,
    195, 205, 212, 214, 229, 238, 259
  Centre of Shia Islam, 240
  home of Ayatollah Khomeini, 177–9
  invasion of Kuwait, 206
  original member of CENTO, 18, 22,
    23, 28–9
  Osirak nuclear reactor, 183
  plot to destabilize Iran's Baluchistan,
    95–6, 89

relations with India, 123
relations with Iran in post-Saddam
  era, 251, 261
war with Iran, 168–9, 188–92, 230,
  234, 242
IRGC
  see Islamic Revolution Guards Corps
IRNA (Islamic Republic News
  Agency), 217
Isik, Hasan, 47
Islam, 6, 24, 205, 210
  'American Islam', 177, 215
  official religion of Pakistan, 9
Islamabad
  attack on US embassy, 153–7
  early contacts with Ayatollah
    Khomeini, 148
  Iraqi embassy affair, 89–92
  ties to China, 55
  US embassy, 114, 128
  war of 1965, 48–52
Islamic bomb, 142
Islamic conference in Lahore, 104–6,
  143
Islamic Ideology Council (Pakistan), 243
Islamic Revolution Guards Corps
  (IRGC), 160, 235–6
Islamic world (also Islamic alliance), 42,
  104, 106, 116, 165, 184, 249–50
Ismaili (Muslims), 9
Israel, 17, 83, 103–6, 113, 116, 119,
  142, 149, 152, 154, 155, 184
  attack on Iraq's Osirak nuclear
    reactor, 183
  attitude toward Iran's nuclear pro-
    gram, 253
  Iran's attitude to Arab-Israeli wars,
    58–9
  Islamic attitudes toward, 249–50
  support for Baluch militants, 234,
    237
Ittehad-e-Islami, 207
Izmir
  RCD summit, 123

Jaffari, Mohammad Ali, 234
Jaish al-Adl (Army of Justice), 258–60
Jamaat-e-Islami, 171, 189, 203, 207–8
Jannati, Ayatollah Ahmad, 244
Japan, 66
Jeddah, 216, 221
Jerusalem, 104
Jews, 59, 83, 103
    lobby, 249–50
Jinnah, Mohammad Ali, 6, 67, 70, 82
Johnson, Lyndon, 47, 51, 54–5,
    72, 94
Jones, James (Jim), 250
Jordan, 29, 32, 43, 58, 75, 77, 107,
    129, 148–9, 251
Jubeir, Adel Al, 251
Jundollah, 229–39, 241, 252, 259

Kabul Times, 158, 165
Kahuta (nuclear plant), 184
Kalili, Amir Teymour, 6
Kandahar, 245–7
Karachi, 6–7, 13–14, 18, 24, 40
    Indian blockade, 75–6
    Iranian Baluch immigrants, 87
    port of, 33, 39, 181, 193, 231
    sectarian conflict, 176
    Shah and Dulles meeting, 19–21
Karbala, 242
Karmal, Babrak, 162, 167–8, 175
Karzai, Hamed, 136, 224, 247
Kashmir, 9, 16, 46, 48, 57, 59, 74,
    77, 131, 198
Kasuri, Khurshid, 228
Kaul, T.N., 78, 113
Kazakhstan, 208
Kennedy, John F., 21, 33–4, 48, 51–2,
    79, 90
Kerry, John, 254
Keyhan, 93
KGB, 21, 137
Khalatbari, Amir-Abbas, 109, 141
Khalilzad, Zalmay, 246
Khalis, Younis, 211

Khamenei, Ayatollah Ali, 201, 204,
    210, 234, 241
    post-Taliban, 227
    religious guidance for Pakistani Shia,
    242–5
    on the Taliban, 218
    trip to Pakistan, 178, 183
Khan, Aga, 9
Khan, A.Q.
    nuclear network, 197–8
Khan, Ayub, 23, 25–9
    relations with the Shah, 31,
    34–7, 43, 46–8, 53, 56–9,
    61, 63–7, 69, 72, 79, 83,
    212, 251
*Khaney-e Farhang (House of Iranian
    Culture)*, 70
Khan, Ismail, 188–9, 207, 224
Khan, Khan Abdul Ghaffar, 135
Khan, Mohammad Daoud, 83–8, 91,
    94, 134–5, 137–9, 210
    conflict with Pakistan, 94–100
    death of, 132
Khan, Munir Ahmad, 118, 120, 184
Khan, Naim, 97–8
Khan, Shahnawaz, 145
Khan, Tikka, 93
Khan, Wali, 95, 135
Khan, Yahya, 3, 82, 66–75
Kharazi, Kamal, 216, 219–20, 224,
    226–8
Kharazi, Sadeq, 227–8
Khatami, Mohammad, 215–6, 219,
    222, 225, 228
Khattak, Mohammad Aslam Khan,
    109–10, 112
Khomeini, Ayatollah Ruhollah,
    147–57, 159–74, 176, 177–83,
    186, 188–90, 192, 201
Khorasan, 189
Khrushchev, Nikita, 21, 35
    message to Shia of Pakistan, 252
Khuzestan, 160
Khyber Pass, 36

Kish Island, 110
   summit, 106–7
Kissinger, Henry, 68, 90, 102, 113–14, 120–3
   efforts during 1971 war, 74–9
   meeting with Shah, 10–11
Kosygin, Alexei, 53, 159
Kurdistan (Iranian), 16, 35, 160
Kurram Agency, 176
Kuwait, 77, 108, 138, 129, 205–6, 211
Kyrgyzstan, 208, 236

Lahore, 68, 104–6, 108, 121, 143, 193, 239
Larkana, 147
Lashkar-e Jhangvi, 231, 238–9, 243, 245
Lashkar-e Taiba, 245
Lebanon, 180, 191, 200, 251
Libya, 84, 104, 106–7, 110, 121, 129, 143, 180, 214
Lippman, Thomas, 122
London, 26, 33, 41, 48, 106, 253
   as a former colonial power in Pakistan, 12–14
   in relation to CENTO, 47, 54–6, 78, 91, 105, 132–3
   in relation to Persian Gulf Arab states, 60–3, 108

M-1 tanks, 114
M-47 tanks, 194
Mahmood, Khalid, 211, 216
Malaysia, 184, 202
Maleki, Abbas, 218
Maliki Government (in Iraq), 251
Mangal Hussain, Haji, 136
Mao, Zedong, 47, 55, 104
Marxism, 135
   in Afghanistan, 159–200
Mashhad, 27, 40, 69–70, 204–5
   bombing, 211
Mashkal, 230

Masood, Khalid, 243–4
Massoud, Ahmad Shah, 124, 217
Maududi, Abu Ala, 171–2
Mauritius, 123
Mazar-e Sharif, 245
   killing of Iranian diplomats by Taliban, 217–9
Mecca, 104, 172, 180
   custodian of the Two Holy Mosques, 104
   Grand Mosque siege, 154–5
Medina, 104
Mehr Abad Airport, 145, 209
Merchant, Livingstone T., 33
Meyer, Armin, H., 49–50
Milani, Abbas, 25
Mirza, Homayun, 25–6
Mirza, Iskander Ali, 6, 19, 21
   Iranian wife, 24–6
   membership in Cento, 22–6
Mirza, Nahid, 6, 25–6
Mohammad, Khalid Sheikh, 211
Mohammad-zadeh, Abdol-Vahed, 234
Mojaddedi, Sibghatullah, 136, 186
Montazeri, Hossein-Ali, 190
Moqqadam, Ismail Ahmadi, 261
Moscow, 3, 16, 29, 35, 46–7, 50, 56, 58, 65, 73, 91, 96, 98, 100, 161–3, 175, 179, 199, 201–2, 230
   aid to Afghanistan, 84–87
   Asian Security, 53–4
   clash with Khomeini, 152
   close ties to India, 75
   intervention in Afghanistan, 132–138, 158–9, 165, 168–9, 187–90
   split from China, 53–4
Mossadeq, Mohammad, 19
Mousavi, Mir Hossein, 204
Mousavi, Mir Mahmoud, 204–5
Mousavian, Hossein, 212, 233
Mowlavi, Abdolaziz, 160
Moynihan, Patrick, 114

Mujahedeen (Afghan), 124, 163,
    199–211
  mobilization, 167–9, 182–94
Mujahedeen Khalq (MEK), 193
Multan, 8
Musharraf, Pervez, 221–3, 228, 239,
    248–50
Mutawakel, Wakil Ahmad, 219

Naas, Charlie, 44
Nairobi, 228
Najaf, 243
  home of Ayatollah Khomeini, 177
Najafi, Ayatollah Basheer, 240
Najibullah, Mohammad, 200
  overtures to Tehran, 201–7
Nasiri, Nematollah, 112, 139
Nasser, Gamal Abdel, 32, 43, 51,
    56–9, 64, 69, 103, 147
National Awami Party (NAP), 89–90,
    95
National Security Council (US), 191
NATO (North Atlantic Treaty
    Organization), 17–18, 23,
    29, 44, 49–50, 64, 132,
    137, 225
Nawaz, Asif, 198
Neauphle-le Chateau, 148
Nehru, Jawaharlal, 20, 51
New Delhi, 20, 37, 49, 68, 73, 77–8,
    80, 111, 113, 138–40, 144, 235,
    248
  American pressure on, 213
  battle of Karnal, 7
  nuclear policy, 118
  Persian Gulf, 122–4
  Shah state visit, 131
  suspicions about Iranian arms
    supplies, 114
  ties to Russia, 75
New York, 18, 80, 135, 190, 211, 219,
    227, 249–50
New York Times, 46, 83, 92, 193, 259
Nixon Doctrine, 60

Nixon, Richard, 20, 60, 62, 67–8, 84,
    94, 97, 101–2, 113
  asking for Iran's help in
    Indo-Pakistani war of 1971,
    73–7, 79
Niyavaran Palace, 100
Non-Aligned Movement, 80, 150
Non-NATO Major Ally, 225
Non-Proliferation Treaty, 120
North Africa, 179
North Korea, 158, 181
North, Oliver, 191
North Western Frontier Province
    (NWFP), 77
Northern Alliance, 214, 217, 220–8
Northern Tier, 35–6, 45–61, 63, 65
Nuclear Free Trade Zone
  Middle East, 119
  South Asia, 119

Oakley, Robert, 196–7
Obama, Barack, 238, 251
Observer, The, 184
Oman, 87, 107–8, 115–16
Omar, Mullah Mohammad, 210, 214,
    219, 222, 246, 256
Omid-Mehr, Ali-Akbar, 283
OPEC (Organization of Petroleum
    Exporting Countries), 111, 125
Operation Ajax, 18
Operation Eagle Claw, 156
Operation Enduring Freedom, 223
Operation Infinite Reach, 218
Operation Staunch, 182
opium (see also drugs), 38, 232
Organization of Islamic Conference
    (OIC), 165, 169, 215
Osirak nuclear reactor
  see Iraq
Oveisi, Gholam Ali, 170
Oxford University, 210

Pahlavi, Princess Ashraf, 9, 105, 110,
    145–6

Pahlavi, Mohammad Reza
 Afghanistan, 97–8
 arms to Pakistan, 48–51, 72–5
 confederation with Afghanistan and
  Pakistan, 27–32
 defense ties with Pakistan, 42–7,
  53–4
 earliest views on Pakistan, 3–11,
  16–30
 exile, 21
 mediation between Afghanistan and
  Pakistan, 85–8
 paternalist toward Pakistan, 78–9,
  111
 relations with Bhutto, 101–47
 secret pact with Bhutto, 170
 suspicion of the West, 48–56
 unease about Pakistan's Arab policy,
  56–66
 visit to Pakistan in 1950, 5
Pahlavi, Queen Farah, 131, 147, 170
Pakistan Muslims League (PML-N),
 262
Pakistani Ocean Industries, 42
Pakistan People's Party (PPP), 71,
 175, 199
Pakpour, Mohammad, 235, 260
Pakravan, Hassan, 57
Palestine, 82–83
Palestinian Liberation Organization
 (PLO), 106, 149
Parachinar
 as a battleground between Shia and
  Sunnis, 176, 240, 243, 254
Paraguay, 146
Paris, 148, 170
Partition of British India, 2, 8, 25, 67, 85
Pashtun, 78, 91, 110, 124, 152, 157,
 162, 165, 176, 201–3, 205–7,
 209, 214, 217, 224, 247
 attitude towards Tehran, 31, 85–6
Pashtunistan, 32–6, 67, 88, 95, 97,
 134–7, 210
Pax Britannica, 60

Peacock Throne, 7, 114, 141, 146, 169
Pentagon, 223
Persia, 4–5, 7–9, 16, 73, 96, 98–9,
 104–5, 114, 126, 171–2, 203,
 230
 Friendship Treaty with Pakistan, 13
 Yahya Khan as a descendant of
  Persians, 68
Persian Gulf, 39, 69, 87, 100, 103,
 107–8, 110, 115, 143, 150–1,
 162, 167, 173, 179, 181–2, 189,
 192–3, 213, 234, 248–9, 254,
 255, 259
 fishing, 42–3
 islands dispute, 60–5
 name dispute, 59–65, 105
 security of, 116, 122
Persianization, 160
Peshawar, 64–5, 86, 124, 136, 170,
 185, 187, 200–2, 204, 207, 211,
 237, 245, 247
pipelines
 Central Asia-Pakistan, 220–1
 Iran-Pakistan, 213, 226, 254–7,
  261–2
Pishin, 234–6
Podgorny, Nikolai, 73
Politburo (Soviet), 159, 162
proliferation (nuclear), 119–20, 142,
 164, 212, 264
Prophet Mohammad, 176
Punjab, 9, 131
Punjabi, 78
Pur-Mohammadi, Mostafa, 233

Qaddafi, Muammar, 104, 106, 143, 147
Qajar, 9
Qasim, Abd Al-Karim, 23
Qatar, 62, 107, 213
Qom, 172, 177, 190, 240, 242–3
Quaid-i-Awam, 82
Quaid-i-Azam, 6, 82
Quetta, 37, 91, 193, 209, 232, 239
Qureshi, Mehmood, 234–5

Rabbani, Burhanuddin, 186–8, 207–8, 214
Rafsanjani, Ali-Akbar Hashemi, 201, 228, 234, 240
  attitude on the Afghan civil war, 204
  meeting with Benazir Bhutto, 209–210
  meeting with General Beg, 197–8
  Reconstruction Era, 211–12
Rajasthan, 131
Ramazani, Rouhollah, 61
Raphel, Arnold, 194
Raphel, Robin, 214
Ras Al Khaimah, 61
Rastakhiz, 95
Rawalpindi, 74, 140, 155, 195, 211
Raza, N.A.M., 76
RCD
  see Regional Cooperation for Development
Reagan, Ronald, 166, 183, 187, 190–1
Refugees
  Afghan, 136, 168, 175, 189, 199
  Iranian, 193
Regional Cooperation for Development, 42–4, 123, 125, 153, 182, 212
Rigi, Abdol Malek, 230–1, 233–4, 236, 237, 238, 252
Riyadh, 166, 179, 207, 216, 244, 251–2, 255
Rome (Italy), 85
Rouhani, Hassan, 191, 228, 253, 254–7
Rusk, Dean, 47–8, 54, 57–8, 62, 72

Saadabad Agreement, 18
Saadabad Palace, 84
Safavid Dynasty, 9
Salami, General Hossein, 259
Sandhurst, 24
Sanjabi, Karim, 148
Sattar, Abdul, 226–7
Saudi Arabia, 17, 62, 64, 106, 125, 129, 134, 150–1, 154, 162, 166, 169, 175, 179–80, 185, 188, 190, 201–2, 206, 236, 239, 244, 249, 250–2, 256, 261–2
  as an anti-Shia power, 186, 205, 207, 209, 214–16, 220–2, 227, 234, 243
  support for Pakistan, 75, 77, 104, 107, 130, 143, 173
SAVAK, 57, 96, 112, 133, 139
Sayyaf, Abdul Rasul, 186, 201–2, 206–7, 209
Scowcroft, Brent, 122
sectarianism
  see Shia-Sunni conflict
Shah
  see Pahlavi, Mohammad Reza
Shahanshah (King of Kings), 130
Shahi, Agha, 145, 148, 153, 156, 164, 168, 172, 179
Shah, Nader, 7–8, 68
Shahsoon, Allahmadad, 217
Shah, Sultan Muhammad, 9
Shariatmadari, Ayatollah Mohammad, 177
Sharif, Nawaz, 2, 215–6, 221, 249, 254, 255, 262
Shatt Al Arab (Alvand Rud), 69
Sheikh-Zeineddin, Hossein, 246
Shia Muslims
  Iran, 24–5
  Iranian stance on Pakistani Shia, 240–253
  leverage with Pakistan, 171–8
Shia-Sunni conflict, 1, 25, 31, 153, 160, 169, 171–81, 183, 185–7, 198
Shiraz, 27
shrine of Imam Reza (in Mashhad), 27, 69, 211
Shushtari, Noor-Ali, 234–6
silkworm anti-ship missiles, 181
Sindhi, 78
  separatists, 162
Singh, Swaran, 111
Sipah-e Sahaba, 217

Sistani, Ayatollah Ali, 240
Soraya, Queen, 26
Sources of Emulation, 242
South Africa, 116, 119
South East Asia Treaty Organization
    (SEATO), 17–19, 22, 48
Soviet Union (USSR), 3, 39–40, 43–4,
    46–7, 55, 73, 93, 114–15,
    123–4, 152, 156, 160–2, 167,
    193, 227, 259, 263–4
    Afghanistan, 35–40
    anti-Soviet, 15–23, 28–30, 132–41
    Cold War, 10
    Friendship Treaty with Afghanistan,
        133
    Friendship Treaty with Iraq, 169
    impact of collapse, 207–225,
        229–30
    occupation of Afghanistan,
        151–205
    relations with Iran and Pakistan,
        50–102
Special Coordination Committee (US
    Department of State), 150
Spin Baldak, 209
Stalin, Joseph, 16
Stewart, Michael, 61
Stinger missiles, 181–2
Strait of Hormuz, 61, 87, 115
Sudan, 202
Suez Canal, 58, 60
Sun, The, 253
Sunay, Cevdet, 59
Sunday Observer, 125
Sunni Muslims, 6, 9, 24, 153, 200–3,
    230–1, 234, 238–40, 243–6,
    250–1
    Afghan hardline, 206–11, 214–5,
        224, 256
    Iranian Baluch, 229
Supreme National Security Council
    (SNSC), 218, 228–9, 233
Symington Amendment, 130, 166
Syria, 29, 32, 103, 106

Tajikistan, 208, 220
Tajiks (in Afghanistan), 203, 207–8,
    221, 246
Takfiri
    see Shia-Sunni conflict
Taliban, 124, 210, 229, 231–2, 238,
    246, 256, 263
    killing of Iranian diplomats,
        217–28
    relations with Iran, 211–12
    takeover of Afghanistan, 209,
        214–5
Tanai, Shahnawaz, 203
Taraki, Nur Mohammad, 135, 137–9,
    158–9, 162
Tayyib, Hussain, 59, 63, 69
Tehran
    annual CENTO meeting in 1965, 46
    Asia Games, 113
    Ayub Khan's visit, 65
    Bhutto's visit in 1973, 92–5
    British Embassy, 78
    Indira Gandhi visit, 117–19
    Islamist takeover, 4
    university, 27
    US Embassy, 35, 153–7
    Yahya Khan's visit, 68–70
    Zia's visit to, 129
Tehrik-i-Nifaz-Fiqah-i-Jafria (TNFJ), 178
Teicher, Howard, 191
Third World, 141
Times (Pakistan), 262
Tomsen, Peter, 206
Torkham, 247
Tripartite Talks
    see Afghanistan
Tunisians, 214
Turkey, 130, 148, 182, 184, 192, 196,
    199, 248
    Iran's trading partner, 261
    regional CENTO partner of Iran,
        17–18, 20, 23–4, 29, 41–2,
        46–52, 55, 58–9, 63, 71, 95,
        108, 124

Turkmenistan, 208–9, 220
  pipeline from, 213

Uganda, 106
United Arab Emirates (UAE), 62,
  107–8, 139, 173, 214, 234,
  249, 251
United Arab Republic, 29, 32
United Kingdom, 18, 41–2, 48, 116
United Nations (UN), 220, 227, 232
  Development Program (UNDP), 226
UnoCal, 220–1
US Air Force, 65
US Department of State, 24, 31, 39, 52,
  75–6, 92, 98, 151, 165, 179, 184,
  206, 238
USS *Enterprise*, 77
USSR *see* Soviet Union
Uzbekistan, 208, 220

Vahdati Air Base, 69
Vance, Cyrus, 122, 155
Velayat-e faqih (rule of supreme
  Jurisprudent), 202, 242, 244
Victoria, Queen, 32
Vietnam War, 52, 74

Wailes, Edward Thomson, 22
Walker, Patrick Gordon, 48
war of 1973, 103
Washington, 10, 33, 36, 58, 60, 62,
  64–5, 67, 84, 101, 105–6, 113,
  146, 150, 161, 172, 177, 213–15,
  247, 264
  aid to Mujahedeen, 185–7,
    189–90, 192–3
  attitude towards Soviets, 3, 17–24,
    163–8
  attitude on Iran-Pakistan ties,
    46–56, 96–99, 132–133, 151–7
  Courted by Iran and Pakistan, 4,
    108–10

nuclear proliferation, 118–22,
  125–28, 141–44, 196
regional integration efforts, 36–41,
  251–7
Taliban, 218, 221, 223–5, 238
war of 1971, 74–9, 90, 93–4
Zia ul-Haq, 178–80, 183
Washington Post, 122
Western Bloc, 17, 55
White House, 51, 62, 108, 113, 130,
  165–7
  Jimmy Carter, 151
  George H. Bush, 206
  John F. Kennedy, 48
  Richard Nixon, 68, 76–7, 101
  Ronald Reagan, 187, 191
Wilcox, Wayne A., 26
Wilson, Harold, 61
Wolpert, Stanley, 72
World War II, 16–17, 31, 51, 156
Wright, Denis, 62

Yazdi, Ebrahim, 160
Yemen, 84, 214
  south Yemen, 52
Yousef, Ramsi, 211
Yugoslavia, 80

Zahedan, 75, 160, 235
Zahedi, Ardeshir, 25–6, 59, 66–8, 143
Zahir Shah, Mohammad (Afghan
  king), 31, 33–4, 83–5, 91, 97,
  190, 223
Zaidi, Seyd Hassan, 241
Zakat, 174
Zand-Fard, Fereidoon, 141–6
Zardari, Asif Ali, 9
  Shia heritage, 250–2
Zayed, Sheikh (bin Sultan Al Nahyan),
  107–8
Zayed, Sheikh Abdullah bin, 250
Zionists, 95, 103